TOWARD AN
Evangelical
PUBLIC POLICY

Political Strategies
for the Health
of the Nation

Ronald J. Sider
and Diane Knippers

BakerBooks

Grand Rapids, Michigan

Published by Baker Books
a division of Baker Publishing Group
P.O. Box 6287, Grand Rapids, MI 49516-6287
www.bakerbooks.com

Printed in the United States of America

Library of Congress Cataloging-in-Publication Data
Toward an evangelical public policy : political strategies for the health of the nation /
[edited by] Ronald J. Sider and Diane Knippers.
        p.   cm.
    Includes bibliographical references.
    ISBN 0-8010-6538-0 (pbk.)
        1. Christianity and politics—United States. 2. Public policy. 3. Church and social problems—United States. 4. United States—Foreign relations—2001– 5. Christianity and international affairs. 6. Church and state—United States. I. Sider, Ronald J. II. Knippers, Diane.
    BR526.T69 2005
    261.7′0973—dc22   2004021405

Contents

Foreword—*Ted Haggard* 5

Introduction—*Ronald J. Sider and Diane Knippers* 9

Part I Learning from the Past

1. Seeking a Place—*John C. Green* 15

2. A History of the Public Policy Resolutions of the National Association of Evangelicals—*Richard Cizik* 35

3. Evangelical Denominations at the Foundations of Modern American and British Social-Political Structures and Policies—*Paul de Vries* 64

4. The Mainline Protestant Tradition in the Twentieth Century—*Max L. Stackhouse and Raymond R. Roberts* 77

5. Insights from Catholic Social Ethics and Political Participation—*Kristin E. Heyer* 101

Part II Toward an Evangelical Methodology

6. Toward an Evangelical Ethical Methodology—*David P. Gushee and Dennis P. Hollinger* 117

7. Theological Foundations for an Evangelical Political Philosophy—*Nicholas Wolterstorff* 140

8. Justice, Human Rights, and Government—*Ronald J. Sider* 163

9. Citizenship, Civil Society, and the Church—*Joseph Loconte* 194

Part III Central Themes for an Evangelical Framework

10. The Sanctity of Life in the Twenty-first Century—*Nigel M. de S. Cameron* 213

11. Caring for the Vulnerable—*Clive Calver and Galen Carey*   227

12. Family Integrity—*Tom Minnery and Glenn T. Stanton*   245

13. Stewardship—*R. Scott Rodin*   265

14. The Ethics of War and Peacemaking—*Glen H. Stassen*   284

15. Human Rights—*Paul Marshall*   307

Part IV   Implementation

16. In the Arena—*Stephen Monsma and Mark Rodgers*   325

Notes   343

For the Health of the Nation: An Evangelical Call to Civic Responsibility   363

Contributors   376

Foreword

THE COMPLEX AND EVOLVING ISSUE of the church's role in public policy is among the most challenging for twenty-first century American evangelical leaders. This issue is framed by two phenomena that occurred almost simultaneously over the last fifty years. Through the second half of the twenty-first century, we experienced (1) the steady emergence of the evangelical movement as the dominant voice of American Christianity and (2) the steady decline in American culture's adherence to the mooring of its traditional Judeo-Christian ethic. As we begin to piece together the geo-political and cultural landscape of twenty-first-century America, it is becoming evident that the result of these two trends is a church that is both increasingly united in its understanding and expression of Christian faith and increasingly detached from the formation of our ever-evolving national culture.

Against this backdrop, we face the imminent challenge of deciding the appropriate extent and most effective methods of American evangelical organizations' and individuals' involvement in the process of governance. In the last two years alone, several prominent legislative actions and Supreme Court cases have heightened evangelicals' attention to this issue. The publicity surrounding the proposed Federal Marriage Amendment (FMA), the case against Alabama Supreme Court Chief Justice Roy Moore, and the Lawrence anti-sodomy challenge, for example, have demanded an evangelical response and have instead garnered scarcely a mark on the public policy radar screen.

Why has united evangelical response proven so challenging? Perhaps it is because the spectrum of opinion as to the nature and extent of Christians' public engagement is as diverse as the church itself. Many in the body of Christ are nervous about the erosion of the influence of biblical values on American law, and consequently hold a strong view of our responsibility in the political process. The recent string of high-profile court cases has exacerbated this growing tension. The Supreme Court's Lawrence decision of June 26, 2003, made illegal the anti-sodomy laws that have been used to restrict private homosexual behavior. The Court ruled that the state cannot dictate the sexual practices of two consenting adults within the privacy of their own home. Sodomy is unquestionably a violation of God's law, but Christians are divided as to whether it is the role of civil government to govern private sexual behavior between two consenting adults. Pointing to the biblical foundation of so much of the uncontested body of civil law—for example, murder and theft—many are confounded at the seemingly arbitrary attack on particular tenets of scripturally based civil law that have become politically incorrect, inexpedient, and unpopular. After all, why shouldn't we protest when the government says, in effect, "It's wrong to steal, but it's now okay to commit sodomy . . ."?

By contrast, other evangelical leaders highlight that, though it is common among Christians to believe that national health will result from the restored use of legislation to enforce morality, too often the use of the state to enforce our moral code has gotten negative results. Criminalizing consensual immorality, these might argue, puts us squarely on the path of the witch trials of the seventeenth century and the Taliban in Afghanistan. Are we to outlaw whatever the Bible forbids? Then logically we must conclude that adulterers, fornicators, even gossips should be apprehended and punished according to their offense to God. Our aim as Christian leaders might then be to produce people who choose virtue not because it is *required*, but because it is *good*.

We as religious leaders have a long history of struggle with this idea. With the recent landslide defeat of the FMA in Congress amid slouching, inconsistent support even from religious conservatives, it is apparent that the discussion over the extent of Christians' involvement in public affairs is no more decisive now than it was at the time of the American Civil Rights movement. The stakes are higher now than they have ever been. The increasingly concerted cultural assault on the institution of marriage, according to Dr. James Dobson, threatens to trigger the holistic extrication of the Judeo-Christian value system from American public policy. The biblical foundations of our good and just society are shaking under the gaining force of secular postmodernism. Right now in Sweden, it is a criminal offense to read publicly certain politically incorrect portions of the Bible, and without intervention, that is the trajectory of America. Astounding as it is to think that the same civil law could defend as the right to free expression and privacy a pedophile's "man-boy love" and condemn as hate speech the public reading of Scripture, that is the apparent future.

Legislators and judges make daily decisions regarding the liberties allowed our citizens. In order to stand for the cause of Christ in the face of the strong wind of cultural secularization, we evangelicals are compelled to revisit and come to some resolution over an age-old dilemma: At what point is it appropriate to impose our moral convictions upon the unwilling through the power of the state?

On the one hand, who wants to remember the days of horrific segregation, brutality, and genocide at the hands of the totally secular Stalinist regime? Apart from a clear and present expression of a society's moral foundation in the laws which govern its people, there is no reason to suppose a powerful government will not ultimately express its preferences among people in atrocious ways. Amorality in governance is an impossibility and a lie. On the other hand, who can forget the images CNN beamed around the world of oppressed Afghani women, shrouded in bhurkas, compelled to obey strict Muslim modesty codes. Most of these women didn't follow fundamentalist law because they were persuaded of its value; they did it because they feared the consequences of *not doing it*. Compulsory morality is no morality at all.

For a decent, civil, and orderly society, the role of the state and the role of the church must be complimentary; each must do its job well for people to thrive. We must have a combination of internal constraint (the stuff that is birthed in people most authentically and most lastingly out of genuine religious conviction) and external restraint (the thing that good government produces). Our message as evangelical leaders deals primarily with internal strength that enables people to be godly. But as citizens, we are responsible to participate in the American provision of government by and for the people. It is the purpose of the document that follows to offer a common approach to this most difficult and most imminent challenge facing the twenty-first-century American church.

Ted Haggard

Introduction

WARNING: THIS BOOK may frustrate or irritate you. It will no doubt challenge and perhaps convict you. Hopefully, it will also inspire and encourage you. Reading and editing this book have prompted those responses in us.

But more about that later. First, why was this book published?

Evangelical Christians in the United States enjoy a historic opportunity to use their political influence to shape a better world. We represent one quarter of all voters in the most powerful nation in history.

All around the world, the rapidly growing evangelical community has joined the political debate in unprecedented numbers in the last couple of decades.[1] There have been evangelical presidents on several continents and scores of evangelical elected officials in dozens of countries.

That is the good news. The bad news is that too often our new political engagement has not been grounded in adequate, careful thought. Too often, as Ed Dobson has ruefully noted, the process has been "ready, fire, aim."

Evangelicals do not have the kind of sustained, theologically grounded reflection on social and political issues that shapes some other Christian traditions. As Kristin Heyer's chapter in this volume suggests, Catholics, for example, look to more than one hundred years of numerous papal encyclicals that shape, guide, and give depth to their current political activity. The chapter by Max L. Stackhouse and Raymond R. Roberts points to a body of scholarly thought within the historic Protestant tradition. Partly because we lack this kind of extended, careful reflection on politics, recent evangelical political engagement has too often been unbalanced, inconsistent, and ineffective.

If evangelicals are to seize this historic opportunity to use our vast political potential to shape better societies around the world, three things are essential. First, our politics must be grounded in our faith in Christ. Second, we must do far more sophisticated study. Third, we need to discover how to listen to and cooperate with each other and other Christians.

Evangelicals must endeavor consistently to submit our political activity to the lordship of Christ and the authority of the Bible. If evangelical political

9

engagement merely reflects secular political agendas of left or right or even center, our efforts will be largely irrelevant. Only if we allow a biblical worldview and a biblically balanced agenda to guide our concrete political work can we significantly improve the political order.

We must seek to develop a responsible political philosophy—informed first by Scripture, but also taking advantage of godly resources found in church tradition and sanctified reason. We also need sophisticated socioeconomic analysis. The Bible doesn't mention nuclear energy, the Internal Revenue Service, or global warming. Careful study of the contemporary world is essential.

Listening carefully to other Christians is also important. Deeply committed evangelical Christians who love and worship our Lord Jesus and submit wholeheartedly to the Bible nonetheless come to honest disagreements on specific political issues. This side of heaven, we will never overcome all disagreements. But we could resolve many differences if we regularly, openly listened to each other carefully, spelling out what we consider to be the biblical principles and detailed social analyses that lead us to our (differing) conclusions. This is the first step toward more productive cooperation. This book represents an example of such listening.

This book is part of a process, launched several years ago by the National Association of Evangelicals (NAE), to articulate an evangelical framework for public engagement. A steering committee (Rich Cizik, Murray Dempster, David Gushee, Diane Knippers, JoAnne Lyon, George McKinney, Tom Minnery, Jesse Miranda, Stephen Monsma, Richard Mouw, David Neff, Vinay Samuel, Ron Sider, Jim Skillen, Dean Trulear, Gary Walsh, and Tim Ziemer) eventually cochaired by the two of us decided that a group of evangelical scholars should be asked to write chapters on important topics where evangelicals needed deeper reflection to nurture a widely embraced evangelical framework for public engagement. Hence this volume.

Part 1 seeks to gather important reflections on what evangelicals today should learn from both our own evangelical past and that of other Christians engaged in politics. Part 2 discusses a number of key methodological and theological issues. Part 3 focuses on six central areas of contemporary political engagement. And part 4 has a chapter by two practitioners reflecting on the doing of politics.

We recognize that evangelicals have exhibited no small measure of ambivalence about political engagement. At various times throughout the twentieth century, the evangelical movement has moved from ambitious reform campaigns to periods of passivity and withdrawal. We believe that as evangelicalism has matured it is increasingly committed to the regular, steady task of participating in our nation's democratic political community.

At the same time, we recognize that while politics matters, politics isn't everything. We wholeheartedly concur with the point made in the concluding chapter by Stephen Monsma and Mark Rodgers—that the direction of our culture is determined by institutions "upstream" from the political arena and that it is essential for evangelicals to become much more involved in academia, journalism, and the entertainment media.

Each author in this book speaks for himself or herself. This volume does not represent "the official position" of the NAE. Some of the evangelical disagreement mentioned earlier appears in this volume and thus points to the continuing need for ongoing listening and dialogue.

At the same time, we believe that this volume also represents a great deal of consensus among a broad group of evangelicals about the central components of an evangelical framework for public engagement. In particular, we note a great deal of agreement on the ends we seek—from protecting human life to fighting oppression and poverty to caring for creation. Often our disagreements are over the means of achieving those ends, particularly regarding the role of government.

The consensus that has emerged is spelled out in "For the Health of the Nation: An Evangelical Call to Civic Responsibility." This declaration was prepared by a drafting committee[2] that worked from earlier drafts of the essays in this volume. A very broad range of evangelical leaders has signed this declaration. This underlines the fact that the reality of evangelical disagreement on specific political issues dares not conceal widespread agreement on foundational principles.

The process that has led to this book and the related declaration offers hope for the future. The various members of the steering committee and drafting committee—indeed, we cochairs—continue to disagree on specific issues. But we all long to submit our thought and action unconditionally to Christ our Lord and the Bible, God's revealed truth. As a result, we have discovered much common ground. We believe an ongoing process of listening and dialogue, both in the evangelical community and also with other Christians, can expand that common ground in political engagement in a way that will bless the nations.

Ronald J. Sider
Diane Knippers
Cochairs, National Association of Evangelicals' Project
"Toward an Evangelical Framework for Public Engagement"

Part I

Learning
from the Past

1

Seeking a Place

Evangelical Protestants and Public Engagement in the Twentieth Century

John C. Green

EVANGELICAL PROTESTANTS HAVE spent most of the twentieth century seeking an appropriate place in American public life. This search was precipitated by their displacement from public affairs in the 1920s, and by century's end had returned them to prominence. But in the early years of the twenty-first century, the exact place of evangelicals in public affairs is still under debate.

During this long search, evangelicals experimented with three major avenues of public engagement: *movement politics* (challenges to political institutions), *quiescent politics* (detachment from political institutions), and *regularized politics* (adaptation to political institutions). Between 1920 and 1940, movement politics (in the form of opposition to teaching evolution) and quiescent politics (a withdrawal from public affairs) were predominant. After 1940, the founding of the National Association of Evangelicals brought regularized politics alongside the two other approaches (an anti-Communist movement and an uneasy passivity). And after 1970, movement politics (the Christian Right) and regularized politics (a plurality of political groups) largely replaced quiescence.

Each of these approaches has its own strengths and limitations, and taken together they provide an inventory of lessons and cautions relevant to evangelical public engagement in the future. Movement politics can mobilize new people into public life, but it can also be contentious and unproductive. Quiescent politics can influence the broader culture that underlies public life, but it can also leave critical problems unaddressed. Regularized politics can apply persistent pressure on behalf of desirable public policies, but it can also lead to accommodation with the existing alignment of power.

After a brief review of some conceptual matters, I will describe the major features of evangelical public engagement throughout the twentieth century in rough chronological order and then turn to the lessons and cautions this experience suggests.

Evangelicals and Three Approaches to Public Engagement

The term "evangelical Protestant" is used in a variety of ways, so it is worth defining it for the present purposes. By evangelicals, I mean a set of historically white Protestant denominations, congregations, and related institutions that share a common set of traditional Protestant beliefs.[1] Thus defined, evangelicals are largely a product of the twentieth century. By 1901, modern intellectual and social developments were fragmenting the major Protestant churches in the United States (Marsden 1990, 168–79). The largest fragment came to be known as "mainline" Protestantism, the culturally dominant churches whose leadership steadily adapted many traditional Protestant beliefs to modern ideas. Many members of these large denominations continued to hold traditional beliefs, and although their numbers diminished during the twentieth century, a significant traditional constituency remains to this day. Toward the end of the century, this constituency sparked a series of renewal movements among mainline Protestants that often use the term "evangelical" and are influenced by the other fragments of American Protestantism (Wuthnow 1988).

Three other fragments made strenuous efforts to maintain traditional Protestant beliefs by one means or another, slowly coalescing into what is known as "evangelical" Protestantism in the present day. The first of these fragments was a set of religious movements created in conscious reaction to the modernist drift of mainline Protestant leaders. The best known is fundamentalism, whose influence was so extensive that it still dominates discussions of religion in America and around the world. But other examples include the Holiness, Pentecostal, Neo-evangelical, and Charismatic movements. (The "evangelical" renewal movements within the Protestant mainline were often influenced by these movements.) A second fragment was made up of ethnic churches with traditional Protestant beliefs, such as the Lutheran Church Missouri Synod and the Christian Reformed Church. The third and largest fragment was southern Protestant churches, such as the Southern Baptist Convention, which maintained traditional beliefs as part of their regional identity.

A debate over the place of churches in public life was a major reason for the initial fragmentation of Protestantism and also the eventual coalescing of the evangelical tradition. In this regard, three major approaches to public engagement have been especially important. It is worth reviewing these concepts in turn.

Movement Politics. The most controversial form of evangelical public engagement is movement politics (Wilcox 1992). In its simplest form, a "movement" is the mobilizing of an inactive constituency to challenge existing political institutions on behalf of a grievance. Often thought of as "disorganized politics," a movement brings new people and resources into confrontation with organized politics. Religious communities have often led and supported movements. While movements sometimes succeed in resolving their grievances, they can also change political institutions by expanding the participants in the political process.

Quiescent Politics. For most of the twentieth century, evangelicals were better known for quiescent politics than for political movements (Carpenter 1997). In its purest form, quiescent politics is a deliberate detachment from political institutions as a matter of principle. Such disengagement may arise from the perception that politics is sinful, disorderly, and uncivil, and thus not a fit activity for religious people. Quiescence may also arise when spiritual matters are given priority over public affairs. Some religious groups choose such an emphasis on private life as a means of influencing the broader culture, and by such indirect means, influencing public affairs. And quiescence politics may arise for practical reasons as well, such as a sense of futility or a lack of opportunity in public life.

Regularized Politics. Like most Americans, evangelicals have often engaged in public affairs by adapting to the regular political processes and political organizations (Smidt 2001). One major form of regular politics is the activities of interest groups formed to advance religious values. Another form of regular politics is participation in political parties and elections. Religious communities have often aligned themselves with one or both of the major parties and sometimes support minor party revolts. Clergy and lay leaders participate in party politics, sometimes even running or holding party or public office. Religious publics have been a staple of electoral coalitions for most of American history.

A People Displaced, 1901–1940

From the point of view of evangelical public engagement, the beginning of the twentieth century was unremarkable: The first two decades of the new century looked much like the last several decades of the previous one. However, the closely related social and theological crises that were fragmenting American Protestantism accelerated during this period, coming to a head in the aftermath of the First World War. Thus, 1920 is in many respects a better dividing line than 1901.

In the early 1920s, fierce contention erupted among Protestants between a more traditional faction, known as the "fundamentalists," and a less traditional one, often referred to as "modernists" or "liberals." The root of this fundamentalist-modernist controversy was religious, with the fundamentalists aggressively defending what they held to be the "fundamentals" of the Protestant tradition (including some relatively new doctrines, such as dispensational premillennialism). In contrast, the modernists sought to adapt Protestantism to the modern world. However, an equally important disagreement was over the role of the churches in public life: The fundamentalists argued for an "individual gospel" of personal transformation and government moral regulation, while the modernists advocated a new "Social Gospel" of public welfare programs and reform of private economic institutions. Both sides waged a bitter battle for control of the major Protestant denominations, and by the late 1920s the fundamentalists had been defeated (Marsden 1980, part 3). After a movement against the teaching of evolution failed, the fundamentalists largely withdrew from both denominational battles and public affairs, participating only modestly in the regular politics of the era.

The Anti-Evolution Movement. The fundamentalists believed they were fighting to preserve the "Christian civilization" of the nineteenth century, and thus their efforts included a political program from the beginning. An initial target was the theory of biological evolution, which contradicted the fundamentalist view of God, biblical authority, and science. From this perspective, evolution threatened to support the spread of atheism, tyrannical government (including Communism), and personal immorality. These fears were reinforced by an association of evolution with German culture and the horrors of World War I (Marsden 1991, chap. 6).

In response, the fundamentalists launched a movement to mobilize their followers for the purpose of prohibiting the teaching of evolution in public schools (Furniss 1963, chap. 5). Their primary goal was passing legislation to that effect in state legislatures. In many respects, this movement was modeled on the Prohibition movement, which had just achieved its goal of amending the U.S. Constitution to prohibit the sale of alcoholic beverages (1919). The prospects looked bright in 1920 when the movement gained a prominent secular advocate: William Jennings Bryan, a former Democratic presidential candidate and U.S. secretary of state. Thanks in part to the "Great Commoner," the debate over evolution became a national sensation extensively covered by the press.

A series of movement organizations quickly came into existence, including the Research Science Bureau (1920), the Anti-Evolution League of America (1923), and the Defenders of the Christian Faith (1925), all aided by the main fundamentalist organization, the World Christian Fundamentalist Association (1919), and its founder, William Bell Riley (Cole 1963, chap. 12). Bryan and movement leaders traveled across the country to lobby public officials and mobilize local church leaders to do the same. Although bills were introduced in eleven northern and western states, they met with no success. In contrast, all but one southern state debated the issue, often with determined opposition (Bailey 1964, chap. 4). Local clergy and lay leaders participated on both sides of these debates, as did a host of other social and political elites. Eventually five southern states passed legislation between 1923 and 1928, with the strongest law enacted in Tennessee in 1925.

It was the Tennessee law that occasioned one of the most famous trials in American history, when a public school teacher, John Scopes, deliberately violated the law (Marsden 1980, 184–95). Both sides of the controversy saw an opportunity to gain valuable publicity. Bryan was allowed to prosecute Scopes, while the defense was provided by the ACLU and the famous trial lawyer Clarence Darrow. Although Scopes was convicted, the trial was a public relations disaster for the movement. Bryan, fundamentalists, and by implication all who agreed with them were portrayed as ignorant and backward. The debacle was compounded by Bryan's death several days after the trial. A spate of new organizations arose to carry on Bryan's legacy, but the movement quickly dissipated.

One reason for the dramatic failure of the anti-evolution movement was the lack of cohesion in the broader evangelical community, itself in the throes of the fundamentalist-modernist controversy. In addition, the movement itself was poorly organized and failed to marshal popular support. In fact, very little grassroots mobilization was undertaken. In this regard, it is likely that most evangelicals rejected evolution in 1925: Seventy-five years later, two-thirds of evangelicals did not agree with evolution—and science curricula in public schools remains a live controversy.[2] But overall, the movement did little to change the political institutions it challenged.

Withdrawal and Detachment. By 1930, fundamentalists and many other evangelicals had withdrawn into their own religious circles and largely detached themselves from public affairs (Carpenter 1997). Practicality played an important role in this withdrawal: The defeats of the 1920s had alienated and embittered many evangelicals, leaving a widespread sense of frustration and despair about the course of American civilization. These feelings were reinforced by religious principles. Common interpretations of biblical prophecy helped explain the current crises, including the "apostasy" of the major Christian churches. This perspective suggested the futility of social reform and political action, a position reinforced by an intense focus on individual redemption. Indeed, most evangelicals gave evangelism and building religious institutions top priority, and to some, revival was a potent indirect strategy for influencing American culture.

Led by the fundamentalists, evangelicals directed prodigious energy toward religious matters. One result was the creation of an extensive set of new religious institutions, including denominations, missionary organizations, parachurch groups, Bible schools, publishing houses, and religious broadcasting. The American tradition of "evangelism" at home and abroad passed largely into the hands of evangelicals. These gains were especially impressive because they occurred during the Great Depression, a time when mainline Protestantism faced organizational troubles. Taken together, these efforts helped forge a common identity among evangelicals and gave them some purchase in modern society. Survey evidence from 1944 suggests that evangelicals made up about 20 percent of the adult population, or some 18 million adults (about one-half the size of mainline Protestants).[3] These numbers offered considerable potential for political influence in the future, but at the time, the dominant approach to public affairs was quiescence and detachment.

Tribal Politics. Evangelical detachment from public affairs was by no means sudden or complete (Marsden 1980, 206–11). For one thing, many evangelicals continued to be engaged on moral issues at the local level.[4] But to the extent evangelicals remained politically active, it was as a continuation of the "tribal politics" of the 1920s—a politics based on ethnic, religious, and regional differences. During this period, fundamentalist leaders regularly commented on domestic policy and international affairs. This commentary was overwhelmingly negative in tone, offering an often bitter critique with little in the way of positive proposals. It was especially hostile to the Social Gospel in the 1920s, and after 1932, to the welfare and economic policies of President Roosevelt's New Deal (both often compared to Communism). Another focus was the decay of personal morality, symbolized by the repeal of Prohibition (1935). Much of this commentary wove in ethnic and religious prejudices of the era and indulged in conspiratorial thinking. Many of these arguments can only be described as bizarre and intolerant, even by the standards of the day.

On rare occasions, political groups actively promoted these perspectives in regular politics. A good example is Gerald Winrod's Defenders of the Christian Faith, one of the few anti-evolution groups to survive the 1920s (Ribuffo 1983, chap. 3). Winrod's publications, first *The Defender* and *The Revealer*, interpreted public events in light of biblical prophecy and religious individualism, and became controversial for promoting anti-Semitic conspiracy theories. By the late 1930s, *The Defenders* had a membership of more than one hundred thousand, and Winrod was able to deploy these resources for political purposes, such as an effective letter-writing campaign against President Roosevelt's proposal to expand the Supreme Court in 1937 and an unsuccessful senatorial nomination in 1938. Winrod's ideas and political resources were taken seriously enough that he was indicted for Fascist subversion during the "Brown Scare" of the early 1940s (for which he was later acquitted).

Evangelicals were also modestly involved in party politics. A few fundamentalists flirted with minor party opposition to President Roosevelt in 1936,

1940, and 1944. A prominent figure here was Gerald L. K. Smith, an eclectic and charismatic leader whose virulent anti-Semitism eventually discredited his "America First" and "Christian Nationalist Crusade" parties (Ribuffo 1983, chap. 4). Like Winrod, Gerald Smith offered a largely negative vision of politics. These efforts probably found little support in the evangelical public, a conclusion supported by the limited polling data from the late 1930s.[5] But in the absence of a more positive approach to public affairs, these efforts were often taken as the public face of the evangelical community.

A similarly negative but more impressive effort was the opposition in 1928 to Democrat Al Smith, the first Catholic to win a major party presidential nomination (Marsden 1991,187–91). Fundamentalists were especially critical of Smith on religious grounds, but also because he favored the repeal of Prohibition and represented northern, urban culture. In the North, they made common cause with many mainline Protestants on behalf of the Republican nominee Herbert Hoover. A much fiercer battle was waged in the South, where the anti-Smith forces were part of an ongoing factional dispute within the Democratic Party that had been evident in 1924. These efforts probably cost Smith votes, but most southern states stayed in the Democratic column. Although Hoover did carry some border states in the Democratic South, he also won Smith's home state of New York.

Despite the conservatism of fundamentalist leaders, the evangelical public was often more liberal in its voting habits. For example, fragmentary survey data suggests that evangelicals joined the rest of the country in reelecting President Roosevelt in 1936. Overall, 62 percent of evangelicals voted Democratic that year, but there was a strong regional pattern: 52 percent of northern evangelicals backed FDR compared to 74 percent of their southern counterparts.[6]

A People in Flux, 1941–1970

Like World War I, the Second World War is a convenient marker for new developments among evangelicals, although it did not have the same cataclysmic effects. In the early 1940s, the broader evangelical community was in flux, borne forward by several ecumenical efforts. The prime motivation was more effective evangelism, but the question of public engagement was important as well. A subsidiary issue was the practical need to have advocates before the federal government, whose expanded activities touched on evangelical interests ranging from religious broadcasting to chaplains in the military (Carpenter 1997, chap. 8).

This development took two directions. First, the core of the fundamentalist movement, now larger, reinvigorated, and better organized, sought a more vigorous opposition to modern society (Jorstad 1970, 40–50). Led by Carl McIntire, the American Council of Christian Churches (ACCC) was founded in 1941, followed by the International Council of Christian Churches (ICCC) in 1948. Strongly traditional and aggressively separatist, these groups saw themselves as the counterparts to mainline Protestant and broader ecumenical organizations such as the Federal (now National) Council of Churches and eventually the World Council of Churches.

Second, "moderate" or "positive fundamentalists" launched a religious movement to reform fundamentalism and were quickly labeled the "new" or "neo" evangelicals (Stone 1997). In 1942, these reformers founded the National Association of Evangelicals (NAE). Based on the New England Evangelical Fellowship, the NAE sought to unite the broader evangelical community for evangelism and other religious goals. This inclusiveness set the NAE apart from the ACCC, but at the same time, the NAE understood itself as an alternative to mainline Protestantism.

Led by Carl Henry and a new generation of theologians, the neo-evangelicals argued that traditional beliefs required a greater social engagement on the part of believers. In their view, classic fundamentalism ignored the relevance of the church to social problems. An appropriate mix of evangelism and "sociopolitical action" would allow for a "Christian culture" to be reestablished in modern society (Stone 1997, 140–45). The neo-evangelicals were aided by the successful evangelism of Billy Graham, who was inclusive and willing to work with non-evangelicals. These characteristics eventually brought the disagreement between the neo-evangelicals and fundamentalists to a head in 1957. Insisting on strict separatism, the ACCC and allied fundamentalists severed ties with the broader evangelical community (Gasper 1963, 141–43).

During this period, the fundamentalists led a movement against Communism, most evangelicals maintained an uneasy passivity, and the neo-evangelicals participated modestly in the regularized politics of the era.

The Anti-Communist Movement. Fundamentalists had become vocal opponents of Communism by the end of World War I. However, it was not until the beginning of the Cold War that anti-Communism emerged as the subject of movement politics. It became a master frame that brought together many of the things fundamentalists opposed, including opposition to modernism, religious and ethnic prejudice, government social programs, and social reform (Gasper 1963, 46–49).

Between 1945 and 1969, fundamentalists sought to mobilize evangelicals against individuals, organizations, and policies they regarded as aiding Communism or being Communist inspired (Jorstad 1970). The movement was largely the creation of Carl McIntire, who helped create or revitalize a host of special organizations. Besides McIntire's own empire (the ACCC, ICCC, and the Twentieth Century Reformation), these groups included the American Council of Christian Layman (1950), the Christian Crusade (founded in 1947 and expanded in 1958 by Billy James Hargis), Church League of America (founded in 1937 but revitalized in 1956), and the Christian Anti-Communist Crusade (founded in 1958 by Fred Schwartz). Hargis's group was the most overtly political and best known, while Schwartz's crusade was the most influential in secular circles.

Like the anti-evolution movement, this effort had prominent secular allies. Between 1950 and 1954, Senator Joseph McCarthy worked with the movement leaders during the "Red Scare." After McCarthy's fall from grace in 1957, the movement cooperated with the newly founded John Birch Society. The high point of the movement was the turmoil of the 1960s.

But unlike its predecessor, the anti-Communist movement did not have a clearly defined target in politics or public policy (Gasper 1963). This lack of specificity made the movement less effective but also gave it a wider scope of operation. A sampling of the major issues covered include foreign policy, civil rights, school prayer, education, social welfare, sex education, water fluoridation, the Revised Standard Version of the Bible, and rock and roll music. The movement was especially hostile to mainline Protestants but also singled out Catholics, Jews, African-Americans, Billy Graham, and the NAE for criticism. The movement's tactic of choice was accusations of disloyalty, and at one time or another, it attacked the full range of political leaders, Republicans and Democrats alike. Although the movement conducted rallies and distributed literature, it did little grassroots mobilization. The extraordinary contentiousness of Carl McIntire undermined its efforts on a regular basis. It was in decline by 1969.

Although the anti-Communist movement caused a great deal of trouble for its opponents, it is hard to point to any concrete achievements. Its impact was largely negative even within the evangelical community. Survey evidence from 1964 suggests that only about one-eighth of the evangelicals had a positive view of the Christian Anti-Communist Crusade.[7] The movement's ability to attract attention and its lack of lasting achievements appear to arise from the same source: The Cold War and the rapid social change of the era made many Americans, and not just evangelicals, deeply anxious. The movement spoke to these concerns, but so did a wide variety of other groups and leaders. Like the anti-evolution movement, the anti-Communist movement did not change the political institutions it challenged in any significant way.

Uneasy Passivity. Despite the invective of the anti-Communist movement and the new arguments put forward by the neo-evangelicals, the level of evangelical detachment remained high. Some remained resolutely opposed to public engagement. A good example is this statement in 1965 by Jerry Falwell (who would later launch a movement of his own): "I would find it impossible to stop preaching the gospel of Jesus Christ, and begin to do anything else—including fighting Communism, or participating in civil rights reforms" (FitzGerald 1981, 63). Other evangelicals found this posture inadequate, especially during the tumultuous 1960s, and opted for more limited forms of engagement at the local level. A sense of unease about American public life became common in the evangelical community between 1945 and 1970. Meanwhile, the evangelical community continued to grow. In 1976, evangelicals numbered approximately

37 million adults or 23 percent of the adult population (roughly on par with mainline Protestants).[8]

The Politics of Transition. Beginning in the early 1940s, the neo-evangelicals provided a new voice in the public square. The NAE established an office in Washington, DC, in 1943, and although the effort was modest at first, its presence and influence slowly increased (Marty 1996, 434–48). The NAE provided a forum for evangelicals to address the pressing public questions of the time by means of resolutions on a wide range of topics and conferences on controversial matters. This voice was amplified in the mid-1950s by *Christianity Today* and editor Carl Henry, and also by the public pronouncements of Billy Graham. Organizations that helped further this engagement included the Christian Embassy, which brought neo-evangelical leaders into contact with political leaders in Washington, and the Christian Freedom Foundation, which promoted active citizenship and free market economics (Martin 1996, chap. 1). Many of these efforts continued into the tumultuous 1960s.

The perspective advanced by the neo-evangelicals was reformist. On the one hand, it supported modest social welfare reforms that were consistent with the Protestant ethic and not "anti-redemptive" in focus. Such an approach might fairly have been called "Christianized Republicanism," being similar to the "modern Republicanism" of President Eisenhower (Marsden 1991, 62–82). Such policies accepted the basic thrust of the New Deal programs, but with more moderation and caution. During this period, neo-evangelicals took positions on pressing public issues, including opposition to *de jure* racial segregation. On the other hand, the neo-evangelicals were sharply critical of modern society and comprehensive government solutions to its ills, especially those proposed by mainline Protestants. They also tended to be nationalistic, supportive of religious expression in public life, and conservative on economic matters. In this regard, they were quite critical of the counterculture of the 1960s. Although the neo-evangelicals could not point to a large number of concrete political or policy achievements during this period of transition, their approach presented a sharp contrast to the anti-Communist movement.

Overall, evangelicals also became more active in party politics during this period. A major political trend of the period was defection of the "solid South" from the Democratic Party (Jorstad 1970, 1981). Some southern evangelicals backed Strom Thurmond's State Rights Party in 1948, and others supported George Wallace's American Independent Party in 1968. In between, the anti-Communist movement opposed John F. Kennedy in 1960 because of his Catholicism. In something of a reprise of 1928, Kennedy nonetheless carried the South in a close election. The movement also rallied behind the 1964 Republican presidential nominee Barry Goldwater, despite his lack of religious orthodoxy and his Catholic running mate. Goldwater carried five states in the Deep South but lost in a landslide to Lyndon Johnson.

The neo-evangelicals engaged in a more moderate approach to party politics, finding the Republican Party of Eisenhower and Nixon attractive. Here

Billy Graham's personal relationship with these leaders was important (Pierard 1980). While concerned with Kennedy's faith in 1960, neo-evangelicals offered restrained criticism, and they clearly preferred Lyndon Johnson over Barry Goldwater in 1964 (Graham also had a personal friendship with President Johnson).

During this period, northern evangelicals moved in the Democratic direction at the ballot box, joining their southern counterparts in the Democratic fold. For example, in 1944, 56 percent of the evangelical public voted for President Roosevelt; northern evangelicals voted 41 percent Democratic, compared to 70 percent of southern evangelicals. In 1964, 61 percent of evangelicals backed President Johnson; northern evangelicals voted 56 percent Democratic and southern evangelicals 67 percent.[9]

A People Prominent, 1971–2000

The 1960s were a period of great social turmoil, but it was primarily in the 1970s that the effects appeared among evangelicals (Jorstad 1981). The civil rights, women's, environmental, and anti-war movements contributed to the appearance of liberal voices in the evangelical community (Quebedeaux 1974). Arising largely from colleges and seminaries, a new group of "progressive" evangelicals advocated a further expansion of the public engagement advocated by the neo-evangelicals. A critical event was the "Chicago Declaration" published in 1973, which connected traditional evangelical beliefs to a social justice agenda. The signers proclaimed:

> As evangelical Christians committed to the Lord Jesus Christ and the full authority of the word of God, we affirm that God lays total claim upon the lives of his people. We cannot, therefore, separate our lives in Christ from the situation in which God has placed us in the United States and the world (Jorstad 1981, 153).

The Chicago Declaration was an extraordinary innovation in how evangelicals thought about public engagement (Carpenter 2003).

However, the dominant response of the evangelical community was in a conservative direction (Wilcox 1992). Many evangelicals were uncomfortable with the results of the 1960s. Of particular importance was the U.S. Supreme Court decision *Roe v. Wade*, which legalized abortion in 1973, and the Equal Rights Amendment to the Constitution, formerly proposed in 1972.

This period also saw serious theological divisions among evangelicals (Stone 1997, chap. 6). Symbolized by Harold Lindsell's book *The Battle for the Bible* (1976), evangelical leaders debated the inerrancy of Scripture and the broader question of traditional beliefs. These disputes made their way into denominational battles as well. In the 1970s, the Lutheran Church Missouri Synod, and in the 1980s, the Southern Baptist Convention, experienced struggles between more and less traditional factions. The resulting victories for the traditionalists brought these large bodies into closer alignment with conservative elements in the larger evangelical community. In the same vein, evangelical renewal movements among mainline Protestants came to prominence during this period (Wuthnow 1988).

This ideological division reflected a growing diversity among evangelicals, including a moderation of the separatist impulse among fundamentalists, the development of the "electronic church" of televangelists, and the rise of suburban "megachurches." Evangelicals continued to grow in numbers, reaching some 54 million adults in 2000, or about 25 percent of the adult population (a bit more than mainline Protestants).[10]

The election of Jimmy Carter to the White House in 1976 brought evangelicals to political prominence. As a "born-again" Christian and a moderate southern Democrat, Carter and his administration held the prospect of bringing some unity to the evangelical community and perhaps the nation. Instead, fundamentalists launched a movement to restore traditional moral values (an effort that eventually provoked dismay among some key participants), while other evangelicals joined the pluralism of the public square.

The Christian Right. The decline of personal morality had been a theme of evangelical discourse since the "Jazz Age" of the 1920s but did not become the focus of movement politics until the 1970s, when conservative evangelicals launched a movement dedicated to restoring "traditional values" to public policy (Wilcox 1996), commonly known as the "Christian Right."

There were a number of factors behind the rise of this movement. The advent of legalized abortion, sexual permissiveness, no-fault divorce, pornography, and homosexuality was critical. These changes were understood primarily as a threat to the traditional nuclear family. Related threats to the family were trends in public education, limitations on the public expression of religion, the state of popular culture (especially television), and the changing role of women. There was also a religious dimension to these complaints: Evangelicals began to see the secular population as a strong opponent, a point popularized by Francis Shaeffer's *A Christian Manifesto* (1981) and its description of "secular humanism." Other important factors were the disillusionment of many conservative evangelicals with President Carter, and a series of government rulings against religious broadcasting and Christian schools (Guth 1996). While hardly a model of tolerance, the Christian Right was less given to conspiratorial thinking and religious prejudice than its predecessors.

The Christian Right originated in a host of separate reactions to cultural liberalism in the 1970s (Wald 1987, 186–87), including the battle to prevent state ratification of the ERA (1972–1978); a bitter controversy over school textbooks in Kanawha County, West Virginia (1975); a gay rights referendum in Dade County, Florida (1977); and a series of "I Love America" rallies conducted on statehouse steps by Jerry Falwell, newly politicized (1975–1978). In fact, such local "culture wars" became commonplace in the 1980s and 1990s, including fights over schools, abortion, public expression of religion, and gay rights, and show no signs of abating in the early twenty-first century.

These initial revolts were forged into a movement with the assistance of secular conservatives (Bruce 1988). A set of young "New Right" operatives, led by Paul Weyrich, approached Falwell with the idea of a broader effort, and in 1979 the Moral Majority was born. Falwell was something of a reformer among fundamentalists. Strongly committed to fundamentalist beliefs, including religious separatism, he had nonetheless accepted the need for public engagement on moral issues. If this change was not unusual enough, Falwell had an inclusive vision: He believed that a majority of Americans from many religious backgrounds shared a common morality that was under assault. And in order to mobilize this "moral majority," he was willing to work with all manner of evangelicals, mainline Protestants, Catholics, and Jews. Although the Moral Majority never came close to mobilizing such a coalition, the idea of a broad "religious Right" was quite influential.

The Moral Majority was just one of several movement organizations created around 1980, including the National Christian Action Council (1977), Christian Voice (1979), and the Religious Roundtable (1980) (Moen 1989). Many of these groups had a dimension lacking in previous movement organizations: Relying largely on pastors in state and local chapters, they had the potential to reach down to the grass roots. In 1984, many of the movement groups worked together to register voters under the umbrella of the American Coalition for Traditional Values, led by Tim LaHaye. Falwell and his associates had a clear set of political and policy targets, but the high point of this phase of the movement was Pat Robertson's unsuccessful bid for the Republican presidential nomination in 1988.

By the end of the decade, the Christian Right appeared to be spent despite some political success. Falwell disbanded the Moral Majority in 1989, and most of the other movement organizations were defunct or in decline. But in a fashion reminiscent of the anti-Communist movement, the Christian Right developed a second wind in the 1990s (Moen 1992; Rozell and Wilcox 1996). And just as opposition to President Carter motivated the initial movement, dislike of President Bill Clinton provided a strong impetus for the second phase of the Christian Right. Clinton's peripheral attachment to the evangelical community (having been raised among Baptists in the South) and his extensive use of evangelical language (his platform in 1992 was called "the new covenant") (Walz 2001) appear to have intensified the hostility among Christian Rightists.

In 1991, Pat Robertson organized the Christian Coalition from the remnants of his presidential campaign and hired Ralph Reed, a talented organizer, to manage the organization (Watson 1999). As its name implies, this organization took the inclusiveness of the Moral Majority a step further. The Coalition had a more sophisticated and extensive set of state and local chapters and relied more on secular activists. One of Reed's mottos reveals the pragmatic (and partisan) orientation of the group: "Think like Jesus. Lead like Moses. Fight like David. Run like Lincoln." Reed left the Coalition in 1997, and the organization's fortunes have waxed and waned since. A spin-off of the Coalition, the American Center for Law and Justice (1995), specialized in litigation.

Other Christian Right groups came to prominence at this time. One important cluster of groups was fostered by Focus on the Family, a parachurch group concerned with family life and founded by James Dobson in 1977 (Green, Rozell, and Wilcox 2003). Most of Focus's efforts were nonpolitical, but it supported three developments that were political. First, it encouraged the formation of "community impact committees" in local churches, thus creating a separate grassroots structure. Second, it helped form the Family Research Council in Washington, DC, and similar organizations in many state capitals. This second era also ended with another movement leader seeking the Republican presidential nomination in 2000, Gary Bauer, a former head of the Family Research Council. Bauer formed a new group, the Campaign for Working Families, which had an explicit electoral focus. Third, Dobson and other movement leaders founded the Alliance Defense Fund (1993) to carry out litigation, and Focus on the Family Action (2004) to engage in nonpartisan electoral work.

Still other important groups were Concerned Women for America, an evangelical women's organization founded in 1979; the Traditional Values Coalition (1983), a group focused on opposition to gay rights; the American Family Association (1977), which specialized in criticism of network television; and Operation Rescue (1987), an antiabortion group known for civil disobedience at abortion clinics.

In both of its stages, the Christian Right engaged in a wide variety of political activities, including public relations and protests, voter registration and mobilization, campaigning and party activities, lobbying and issue development, and litigating (Green, Rozell, and Wilcox 2003). In contrast to previous movements, the Christian Right had an impact on the political institutions it challenged. Perhaps the most lasting impact of the Christian Right was to solidify conservative evangelicals as a constituency of the Republican Party, especially but not exclusively in the South. The movement organizations were certainly more popular with evangelicals than the previous movements. In 1984, for example, 40 percent of evangelicals had a positive view of the Moral Majority, and in 2000, 65 percent had a similarly positive view of the Christian Coalition.[11]

Despite these political gains, the Christian Right achieved very few of its policy goals in the 1980s or 1990s, and has had just a few victories in the new century (Green and Bigelow 2004). Examples of successes include the $500 child tax credit in 1997 and the ban on later term abortions enacted in 2003. Although more successful than its predecessor movements, most of the Christian Right's agenda remains largely unfulfilled. It may well be that sustained effort over many years will be needed to achieve its policy goals, if they can be achieved at all. This reality and the continued debates over personal morality may generate a permanent set of interest groups to pursue traditional morality through regularized politics. If so, the Christian Right may soon decay as a movement. Since the late 1990s, there has been some evidence of the weakening of prominent movement organizations. However, a new hot-button issue, such as the prospect of same-sex marriage or a liberal Democrat in the White House, may give the Christian Right a third lease on life.

The Politics of Dismay. One impact of the Christian Right was to largely replace quiescence as an approach to public engagement among evangelicals. But in the 1990s, arguments for a more limited engagement reappeared from an unlikely source: former movement operatives. Former Moral Majority officials Cal Thomas and Ed Dobson (1999) argued strongly that the Christian Right had been "blinded by might" and that evangelicals needed to refocus their efforts on evangelism as a way to address social ills. Similarly, New Right operative Paul Weyrich, who helped organize the Moral Majority, argued that the failure to remove President Clinton from office revealed that politics could not "reform the culture" and that evangelicals should turn to religious pursuits as a better strategy to change society (Weyrich 1999). These leaders worried that the Christian Right had become captive of the GOP, trading its principles for access to power. While stopping short of a complete withdrawal from public life, this perspective represents a version of quiescent politics.

The Politics of Pluralism. After 1970, evangelicals were represented by many voices in public life, reflecting in part the broader pluralism of American politics. In 1990, one observer found seven different perspectives among conservative Christians, with evangelicals found in most of them (Skillen 1990). Toward the end of this period, there were organizations representing the center, left, and right of evangelical politics (Hofrenning 1995).

After 1978, the NAE developed a more robust operation in Washington, DC, and has since maintained a small staff of lobbyists, attorneys, and policy analysts (Hertzke 1988). These resources have given the NAE a significant presence among the other religious lobbies in the nation's capital. Between 1980 and 1992, the NAE was perceived as enjoying "insider status" with the Reagan and the first Bush administrations. After 1992, it charted a more independent course, including innovations in foreign policy and human rights. In a similar vein, the NAE supported the second President Bush's faith-based initiative, ban on late-term abortions, limits on stem cell research, and a constitutional amendment to preserve traditional marriage, but the NAE also broadened its agenda to include issues such as the environment and social welfare traditionally associated with the Democratic Party.

Widely respected among lawmakers, the NAE speaks for the "center" of the evangelical community in a pragmatic fashion. Substantially reflecting the perspective of the original neo-evangelicals, it combines a cautious support for social welfare programs and social reform, with conservative positions on social issues, national defense, and economic policy. The NAE also works closely with the Washington representatives of evangelical denominations, which became more numerous during this period, and is often part of broader coalitions with other religious groups.

Progressive evangelicals are also active in the public square.[12] Perhaps the best-known group is Evangelicals for Social Action (ESA). Founded in 1973 by the signers of the Chicago Declaration, ESA is committed to social justice, holding liberal views on poverty, foreign policy, and the environment, as well as pro-life and pro-family positions—a perspective that can be described as "completely pro-life." Part lobby and coordinating body, ESA has played a special role in training students in policy analysis with the Crossroads program. The longtime leader of ESA, Ron Sider, has been an important voice not only in public policy debates, but in the quest to integrate evangelism and social action. A similar voice is provided by the Center for Public Justice (CPJ) and its president, James Skillen (active since 1981). A combination of lobby and think tank, CPJ has developed expertise on a variety of policy matters, such as welfare reform and charitable choice. It also runs a leadership development program, Civitas, and a Christian civic education program, Saints & Citizens.

Yet another important figure is Jim Wallis, one of the founders of the Sojourners community in Washington, DC, and for many years the editor of *Sojourners* magazine. In 1995, Wallis helped organize the Call to Renewal (CTR), an ecumenical coalition dedicated to a renewed political vision that transcends "the old political language of the right and left." Its principal goals are overcoming poverty, dismantling racism, affirming life, and rebuilding family and community. CTR specializes in mobilizing church and parachurch groups and bringing them in contact with public officials. Liberal evangelicals frequently participate in coalitions with other faith-based lobbies, such as Bread for the World, the anti-hunger lobby, and denominational agencies with a social justice agenda.

The Christian Right also has had a presence in Washington, DC, but instability has hurt its effectiveness (Green and Bigelow 2004). Indeed, the first generation of movement organizations, including the Moral Majority, lobbied and litigated extensively, but these efforts declined with the sponsoring groups. The Christian Coalition maintained a large operation initially, but its size and sophistication have varied with its fortunes. More stability was evident with Concerned Women for America and the Traditional Values Coalition. The largest of these "pro-family" groups is the Family Research Council (FRC). The FRC has become a prominent voice in the policy debates on social issues. Other evangelical organizations with a presence in Washington are the American Family Association, the Prison Fellowship, and the Christian Legal Society.

During this period, evangelicals also became more involved in party politics. Some liberal evangelicals were associated with the Democratic Party. For example, in the 1972 campaign, some progressive evangelicals formed "Evangelicals for McGovern," and others worked actively for Jimmy Carter in 1976 (Jorstad 1981). Some progressive evangelicals enthusiastically backed Jesse Jackson's presidential bids in 1984 and 1988, and others supported Bill Clinton in the 1990s. However, evangelicals are not especially influential in the Democratic Party structure (Hertzke 1993).

The Christian Right led conservative evangelicals to participate more fully in the Republican Party (Green, Rozell, and Wilcox 2003; Hertzke 1993). It strongly supported Ronald Reagan in 1980 and 1984. Movement activists also worked for Pat Robertson and Jack Kemp in the 1988 primaries, supported Pat Buchanan's insurgencies in 1992 and 1996, and backed Gary Bauer and Alan Keyes in the 2000 primaries. Conservative evangelicals went on to support the Republican nominees in these general elections. The Christian Right was also quite active in down-ticket races, especially campaigns for Congress. The results of these efforts were mixed, but the high point of these activities was the small but significant contribution the movement made in 1994 when the Republicans took control of Congress for the first time in forty years (Green and Bigelow 2004). Partly as the result of electoral activity, conservative evangelicals wield considerable influence with the Republican Party structure at the state and national levels.

The evangelical public became a reliable Republican constituency during this period, ending the north-south division. The period began in 1976 with evangelicals voting 52 percent Republican (but 48 percent Republican in the South). But by 1984, they voted 74 percent for the GOP nationally (and 71 percent in the South). And in 2000, one of the closest presidential elections in American history, evangelicals voted 71 percent Republican (and 74 percent in the South).[13]

Lessons and Cautions

At the beginning of the twenty-first century, evangelical Protestants have returned to prominence in American public life, recovering from their displacement near the beginning of the twentieth century. However, their exact place in public life is still under debate, with numerous perspectives advanced from the right, center, and left. What lessons and cautions can be gleaned from evangelical public engagement in the twentieth century?

First, each of the major approaches to public engagement has its strengths and limitations. Movement politics has been attractive to evangelicals who felt alienated from modern society. Certainly, a vigorous opposition to the dominant social trends can be of value. And if movement politics brings ordinary people of faith into the political process and builds alternative organizations, it serves the broader cause of democracy as well. In this sense, the Christian Right was a valuable form of public engagement.

However, not all movements produce positive results. The Christian Right has thus far achieved few of its policy goals—an experience common to the anti-evolution and anti-Communist movements. The latter movements failed in part because they did not mobilize very many people and in part because of their relentless negativity. Here the anti-Communist movement is notable: It was largely an exercise in destruction. Evangelicals, like other religious communities, must be careful not to turn a defense of cherished values into opposition for opposition's sake. Indeed, movement politics may oppose social changes that are just rather than those that are wrong.

Given these difficulties with movement politics, the attractiveness of quiescent politics is clear. And there are certainly good reasons why evangelicals, like other religious communities, would choose to deemphasize public life. Evangelism and spiritual matters are special activities of the church and it is a mistake to neglect them. To the extent that religious communities can change the nation's culture, then quiescence can be an effective strategy for public engagement. But the other side of quiescence is the potential to neglect serious social problems. The "apathy of the church" is problematic and might even be thought of as a form of apostasy. And as the record of the 1930s reveals, in the absence of a serious commitment to public engagement, truly pernicious ideas can arise among religious people.

One thing movement and quiescent politics can have in common is impatience with the slow pace of regularized politics. It is indeed tempting to crusade against evil or give up on an imperfect world. But none of the movements reviewed achieved very much in policy terms—and neither did the periods of quiescence. In a large, complex, and diverse polity such as the United States, it takes a great deal of sustained effort to make even modest changes. And for all their limitations, interest groups and political parties are the most effective instruments of long-term political change. This is why religious people typically turn, perhaps reluctantly, to regularized politics.

Of course, there are dangers here as well: It is quite possible to be caught up in power seeking for its own sake. If it is problematic to be "conformed to this world," it is surely worse to be "conformed to politics as usual." Compromise, pragmatism, and strategic decision making are the stuff of regularized politics, and they can easily undermine principle. For example, the close association of the Christian Right with the Republican Party may rob the movement of its special values.

However, at the beginning of the twenty-first century, evangelicals may have the skills and resources with which to navigate the shoals of mainstream politics. The maturation of the NAE, the rise of progressive evangelicals, and the development of the pro-family interest groups are all cause for great optimism. These diverse voices suggest that many evangelicals can offer a distinctive voice and also be effective in regularized politics. Indeed, a "principled pluralism" may be the best response to the reality revealed by the record of evangelical public engagement in the twentieth century: There are no easy answers, only tough choices with real consequences.

Bibliography

Bailey, Kenneth K. *Southern White Protestantism in the Twentieth Century.* New York: Harper & Row, 1964.

Bruce, Steve. *The Rise and Fall of the New Christian Right.* Oxford: Clarendon Press, 1988.

Carpenter, Joel. *Revive Us Again: The Reawakening of American Fundamentalism.* New York: Oxford, 1997.

————. "Compassionate Evangelicalism." *Christianity Today* 47 (2003): 40–43.

Cole, Steward G. *The History of Fundamentalism.* Hamden, CT: Archon Books, 1963.

FitzGerald, Francis. "A Disciplined, Charging Army." *The New Yorker,* May 18, 1981.

Furniss, Norman E. *The Fundamentalist Controversy, 1918–1931.* Hamden, CT: Archon Books, 1963.

Gasper, Louis. *The Fundamentalist Movement.* The Hague: Mouton & Co., 1963.

Green, John C., and Nathan Bigelow. "The Christian Right Goes to Washington: Social Movement Resources and the Legislative Process." In *The Interest Group Connection,* edited by Paul S. Herrnson, Ronald G. Shaiko, and Clyde Wilcox. Washington, DC: CQ Press, 2004.

Green, John C., James L. Guth, Corwin E. Smidt, and Lyman A. Kellstedt. *Religion and the Culture Wars.* Lanham, MD: Rowman & Littlefield, 1996.

Green, John C., Mark J. Rozell, and Clyde Wilcox. *The Christian Right in America.* Washington, DC: Georgetown University Press, 2003.

Guth, James L. "The Politics of the Christian Right." In *Religion and the Culture Wars,* edited by John C. Green, James L. Guth, Corwin E. Smidt, and Lyman A. Kellstedt, 7–29. Lanham, MD: Rowman & Littlefield, 1996.

Hertzke, Allen D. *Representing God in Washington.* Knoxville: University of Tennessee Press, 1988.

————. *Echoes of Discontent.* Washington, DC: CQ Press, 1993.

Hofrenning, Daniel J. B. *In Washington But Not Of It.* Philadelphia: Temple University Press, 1995.

Jorstad, Erling. *The Politics of Doomsday.* Nashville: Abingdon, 1970.

————. *Evangelicals in the White House.* New York: Edwin Mellen Press, 1981.

Marsden, George M. *Fundamentalism and American Culture.* New York: Oxford, 1980.

————. *Religion and American Culture.* San Diego: Harcourt Bracc Jovanovich, 1990.

————. *Understanding Fundamentalism and Evangelicalism.* Grand Rapids: Eerdmans, 1991.

Martin, William. *With God on Our Side: The Rise of the Religious Right in America.* New York: Broadway Books, 1996.

Marty, Martin E. *Modern American Religion: Under God, Indivisible, 1941–1960.* Chicago: University of Chicago Press, 1996.

Moen, Matthew C. *The Christian Right and Congress.* Tuscaloosa, AL: University of Alabama Press, 1989.

————. *The Transformation of the Christian Right.* Tuscaloosa, AL: University of Alabama Press, 1992.

Pierard, Richard P. "Billy Graham and the U.S. Presidency." *Journal of Church and State* 22 (1990):107–27.

Quebedeaux, Richard. *The Young Evangelicals.* New York: Harper & Row, 1974.

Ribuffo, Leo P. *The Old Christian Right.* Philadelphia: Temple University Press, 1983.

Rozell, Mark J., and Clyde Wilcox. *Second Coming.* Baltimore: Johns Hopkins University Press, 1996.

Shaeffer, Francis A. *A Christian Manifesto*. Westchester, IL: Crossway Books, 1981.

Skillen, James W. *The Scattered Voice: Christians at Odds in the Public Square*. Grand Rapids: Zondervan, 1990.

Smidt, Corwin E., ed. *In God We Trust? Religion and American Political Life*. Grand Rapids: Baker, 2001.

Stone, Jon. R. *On the Boundaries of American Evangelicalism: The Postwar Evangelical Coalition*. New York: St. Martin's Press, 1997.

Thomas, Cal, and Ed Dobson. *Blinded by Might*. Grand Rapids: Zondervan, 1999.

Wald, Kenneth D. *Religion and Politics in the United States*. New York: St. Martin's Press, 1987.

Walz, Jeff. "Religion and the American Presidency." In *In God We Trust? Religion and American Political Life*, edited by Corwin E. Smidt, 191–212. Grand Rapids: Baker, 2001.

Watson, Justin. *The Christian Coalition*. New York: St Martin's Griffin, 1999.

Weisskopf, Michael. "Energized by Pulpit or Passion, The Public Is Calling." *Washington Post*, February 1, 1993.

Weyrich, Paul. "The Moral Minority." *Christianity Today*, September 6, 1999.

Wilcox, Clyde. *God's Warriors*. Baltimore: Johns Hopkins University Press, 1992.

———. *Onward Christian Soldiers*. Boulder, CO: Westview Press, 1996.

Wuthnow, Robert. *The Restructuring of American Religion*. Princeton, NJ: Princeton University Press, 1988.

2

A History of the Public Policy Resolutions of the National Association of Evangelicals

Richard Cizik

Spirit of St. Louis, 1942–1943

It was the summer of 1943 and midway through World War II. J. Elwin Wright, as executive director, visited the nation's capital to open an office of public affairs for a newly formed association. He signed a lease on an office in the Kellogg Building, 1422 F Street, N.W., a half block from the Willard Hotel and the Treasury Department building, located next to the White House. The quarters were small, befitting a year-old organization. In such modest circumstances began the public witness for evangelicals in the nation's capital.

A year earlier, on April 7, 1942, in St. Louis, Missouri, Harold John Ockenga, pastor of historic Park Street Church, Boston, Massachusetts, had delivered a keynote address called "The Unvoiced Multitudes." His speech had been a ringing challenge to the 150 gathered leaders "to abandon their rugged independency which had been responsible for failures, divisions, and controversies."[1]

Four months before Ockenga's speech, the Japanese had attacked Pearl Harbor. Ockenga warned his war-conscious audience that evangelicals were in a position similar to that of small nations in the path of the rampaging German and Japanese military machines: "One by one, various forces have discredited or attacked them, or even forced them out of positions of leadership, until today many of them are on the defensive or even the decline. The hour calls for a united front for evangelical action."[2]

It was, by all accounts, a brilliant call to arms that led to the creation of the "National Association of Evangelicals United for Action," which later became simply the National Association of Evangelicals (NAE). As the visionary leader elected to the presidency of the organization, Ockenga declared that "secularism was the greatest danger facing America and that unbelief and infidelity were the greatest obstacles to spiritual and political advance." Under his leadership the new organization would combat modernism without resorting to "dog-in-the-manger, reactionary, negative, or destructive type" tactics. Mindful of the absolutist tendencies associated with fundamentalism, evangelicalism's new leaders promised to "shun all forms of bigotry, intolerance, misrepresentation, hate, jealousy, false judgment, and hypocrisy."[3] They adopted a seven-point "Statement of Faith" that would counter fragmentation and yet provide hope and power through spiritual unity.

At least a dozen church-related organizations—ranging from the Anti-Saloon League to the Catholic Church—had been active for years in the nation's capital. The possibility of war and the preparation for war had brought church leaders to oppose military training, to protect conscientious objectors, and to try to prevent the entrance of the United States in the war. But many groups had already moved beyond mere opposition to "liquor, war, and sin." The trend was to form agencies or offices to represent their respective constituencies.

According to one account of the period, the NAE opened "a foreign missions office," so lobbying efforts "were minimal" and chiefly connected with displaced persons legislation and the separation of church and state.[4] This was "not inconsistent with the Eisenhower years when such offices operated at relatively low levels of activity, each concentrating on its own special preoccupation."[5] Other than the American Council of Christian Churches, a fundamentalist group of churches led by Carl McIntire, the NAE was the only organization that viewed itself to be a competitor and challenger to the Federal Council of Churches.

The Federal Council of Churches, founded in 1908, had thirty-two denominations but was increasingly dominated by theological liberals. When *Newsweek* described it as having a "virtual monopoly" in American Protestantism, it was describing how evangelicals felt about how the Council operated by exerting political pressure.[6]

The Federal Council of Churches, renamed the National Council of Churches in 1950, emphasized the "worth and dignity of man" as the basic principle for social reasoning and action. Many evangelicals believed that in its social programs it had substituted humanistic political action for the ameliorating influence of the gospel. When Council president G. Bromley Oxnam, boasting of a Council accomplishment, said, "Washington politicians knew they were not dealing with a paper organization," he was seen by evangelicals as tacitly admitting that the Council was a "political pressure group." Evangelicals critically wrote that the Council had a "staff of politico-religious lobbyists in Washington," aiming to increase its pressure tactics upon Congress and the president.[7]

The irony is that evangelicals were also keenly aware of the need for friends in Washington. In the fall of 1941, Charles E. Fuller, founder of *The Old Fashioned Revival Hour*, was the target of a union organizing effort by the American Federation of Musicians. The president of the union, James Caesar Petrillo, told the radio preacher that all of his singers and instrumentalists had to join the union. If they didn't, the program would be put off the air. "I cannot do it," Fuller maintained. "Conscientiously, these are all volunteers. Nobody is paid any salary, and they don't believe in the union, and can't afford to join the union just to sing in my choir on Sunday morning."

Elwin Wright went to Washington to meet with a senior senator, who said that Petrillo had "gotten too big, and we've been waiting for a chance to put him down in his place." "You tell him," the senator said, "that if he doesn't do differently, why we'll have a Senate investigation." Petrillo backed off when Wright got word to him that he was in danger of being quizzed under oath.

Wright had been successful and thought that there were at least eight million evangelicals who needed representation in the corridors of power. According to Elizabeth Evans, his longtime assistant, "it was a strong point in favor of starting a National Association of Evangelicals."[8] Just how many evangelicals there were before World War II is not known, maybe as many as twenty million, but Fuller knew that there were about eight million people listening to him.

Although having "relations with government" was a high priority, it was the issue of access to the airwaves that would unite evangelicals. NBC and CBS had "almost entirely excluded" from their network programs "doctrinally conservative groups," and if their example was followed industry-wide, the result would be an absence of evangelicals from the airwaves.

Wright and his cohorts believed that they should be able to "buy time" since broadcasting companies were not likely to contribute the amount of time "which the presentation of religion deserves." There was also a proposed prohibition of on-air solicitation due to unscrupulous profiteers. Wright declared his opposition to that idea by recommending that "broadcasts for which payment is made be confined to established churches or incorporated organizations approved by the NAE or one of the other three major faiths."[9] This idea never gained traction, but already there was a perception that "charlatans" were damaging the image of Bible-believing Christians.

Nevertheless, evangelical leaders perceived that religious freedom was at risk. The future of evangelical radio broadcasting was in jeopardy. And it was this public issue more than any other—that some time should be available for purchase and that they had a right to voice their convictions on the air without dilution—that galvanized evangelicals into forming the association. Scholars of the period would later write that "supporting radio revivalists would be one of the most important jobs the NAE would perform." It put the organization on the map as a "second major Protestant voice."[10]

How did the leaders of the Federal Council of Churches view the founding of this new association of evangelicals? They immediately attacked it "as giving sectarianism a new lease on life and as encouraging the reactionary and dissident wings of the great Protestant denominations" in the Federal Council.[11] The leaders of the NAE were unfazed by the criticism. They had declared their freedom "from the shackles which liberal leadership had forged."

Crusader Decades, 1943–1956

Chosen to head the new office in Washington was the Reverend Clyde D. Taylor, who had been a pastor, faculty member at Gordon College of Theology and Missions, and three-term missionary to Peru. His experiences in Peru, where Protestants frequently clashed with Catholics, would impact the organization's statements.

An evangelical philosophy toward "citizenship in heaven and earth" began to emerge that would be taught at summer Bible conferences and then broadcast over evangelical radio stations. "What is almost wholly unintelligible to the naturalistic and idealistic groups, burdened as they are for a new world order," wrote Carl F. H. Henry in *The Uneasy Conscience of Modern Fundamentalism*, published in 1947,

> is the apparent lack of any social passion in Protestant Fundamentalism. On this evaluation, Fundamentalism is the modern priest and Levite, by-passing suffering humanity. The picture is clear when one brings into focus such admitted evils as aggressive warfare, racial hatred and intolerance, the liquor traffic, and exploitation of labor or management, whichever it may be.[12]

Henry would recount how he had asked in the company of more than one hundred representative evangelical pastors the following question: "How many of you, during the past six months, have preached a sermon devoted in large part to a condemnation of such evils [cited above] or the like—a sermon containing not merely an incidental or illustrative reference, but directed mainly against such evils and proposing the framework in which you think the solution is possible?" He wrote that "not a single hand was raised in response."[13]

The founders of the NAE believed their role to be "watchmen" to prevent violations of separation of church and state and to be a "witness" for the moral conscience of the nation. On the other hand, they clearly stated that "evangelicals do not want the Church in politics." Only its members are citizens, and when the church enters politics, it degenerates into another political lobby.

But unlike the fundamentalists, whom Henry described as people debating "whether it is right to play 'rook' while the nations of the world are playing with fire," these "neo-evangelicals," as they would come to be called, would "move beyond the issues of ecclesiastical purity and personal morality, lest the gospel would be dismissed as irrelevant."[14] They listened to Henry's direct plea to respond to the needs of the postwar world and seized the moment.

Henry served as the editor of NAE's publication *United Evangelical Action* and no doubt had some influence, at least indirectly, in the creation in 1948 of the Committee of Christian Liberty set up to be the official liaison between the Board of Administration and the Washington office in matters pertaining to public affairs. The association, according to its records, "soon came to be recognized by the Congress and other government agencies as having a right to express the views of a considerable sector of Protestantism on conferences, investigations, or opinionnaires affecting legislation or government policy in areas of morals or religion."[15]

By the next year, 1949, a historic National Conference on Human Rights, sponsored by the State Department, became an occasion for objections to the proposed Universal Declaration of Human Rights for the United Nations. Dr. Stephen W. Paine, speaking immediately after Eleanor Roosevelt, wife of President Franklin D. Roosevelt, objected to that part of the document which dealt with the social and economic rights of man: "Our objection would strike at the underlying assumptions of this entire Declaration of Human Rights. It begins with the assertion that man has certain 'inherent dignity and inalienable rights.' We believe this is an erroneous point of beginning. The founders of the nation started, not with certain rights inherent in man, but described man's rights as given by God, saying that man is endowed by the Creator with certain inalienable rights."[16]

Government was ordained by God to guarantee the rights and freedoms that are God's gifts, and governments fail when they conceive of these rights as granted by human beings. Paine said, "I feel that I can rightly report the constituency of the NAE as feeling that this sort of thing is socialistic, that it leads in the direction of statism, and that our members would be opposed to having our country adopt any covenant which would attempt to enforce these principles." James DeForest Murch, reporting from the State Department in Foggy Bottom, wrote that "the voice of religious and political liberalism was supreme throughout the conference" and that "without the NAE there would have been no open stand for the orthodox Christian viewpoint."[17] Ironically, fifty years later evangelical activists would use the UN Declaration of Human Rights, particularly Article 18 on religious freedom, in campaigns not just against anti-Christian persecution but against persecution of believers of all faiths.

In these early years, the "separation of church and state" seemed threatened from three sides. First, evangelicals felt that the Roman Catholic Church wanted "to promote Church-State union with the Church dominant, which included an effort by the Roman lobby in Washington to secure federal aid for parochial schools, federal funding for Catholic hospital buildings, and to participate in USA politics." A second challenge was posed by "agnostics, atheists, and misguided zealots who sought to take all religion out of government or who were aiming at promoting government ownership of resources, industry and property," which would make "citizens wards of the state, placing them economically on the dole." Finally, a third set of violations was attributed to "minorities who abused their right to restrict the majority, such as Hebrew faith members opposing the distribution of bibles as a sectarian book," and by the activity of religious lobbies [i.e., the Roman Catholic Church] that "seek special and generally illegal appropriations of funds for schools, hospitals and other basically religious activities."[18]

As a response to these violations, annual resolutions opposing "federal aid to education" were adopted nearly every year between 1947 and 1958. Periodic statements opposed the persecution of Protestants in Columbia, Italy, Mexico, Quebec, and Spain.[19]

Did the Washington office take any specific action on these resolutions? There was occasional testimony before congressional committees and advocacy to the State Department on overseas concerns. For example, during the first session of the Eightieth Congress, the Reverend Frederick Curtis Fowler, the fifth president of the NAE, delivered testimony opposing federal aid to nonpublic schools. Speaking before a Senate Labor and Public Works Subcommittee, Fowler suggestively charged that "the Church of Rome continually denounces the public-school system of the United States" and that "to Roman policy makers, state support of their schools is only one step toward Roman Church control of all Government functions, and of the Government itself."[20]

In response to incidents in Italy, in which missionaries from the Church of Christ Evangelists were stoned, NAE officials joined by other Protestant leaders met in 1950 to draft a letter of complaint to the prime minister of Italy, Aleide de Gasperi, which was then released to the press. An appointment also was made with the undersecretary of state for Western European affairs, citing evidence of murders, stonings, and other religious liberty infractions. He was told that if their demands for compliance with the peace treaty signed with the United States after the war were ignored, the NAE would lobby Congress to have the treaty annulled and any financial aid to the country halted. (It was not the last instance in which the NAE would threaten the denial of foreign aid to countries that persecute their own people; the strategy would be employed fifty years later in a 1996 "Statement of Conscience on Worldwide Religious Persecution.")

The association also conducted a decades-long campaign against the United States government establishing diplomatic ties with the Vatican. Franklin D. Roosevelt, as a war emergency measure on December 23, 1939, appointed Myron C. Taylor as a "personal envoy" to the Vatican. When Harry S. Truman appointed Mark Clark as ambassador to the Vatican, Clyde Taylor played a key role in getting the decision reversed. The move was regarded as an "unholy relationship between our government and the Papacy," a preference of one religion over others, and unwarranted entangling between church and state. The NAE adopted resolutions opposing the idea at annual conventions nearly every year between 1943 and 1953. There were no further protests after President Ronald Reagan, in 1983, established full diplomatic relations with the Vatican.

Was such advocacy at the time born of an anti-Catholic bias? The leaders at the time maintained that they were just standing on the principle of the "separation of church and state," code words for many that meant "stop the Catholic Church." The official record of NAE history states that their efforts were intended "to counterbalance the influence of the Roman hierarchy and other forces that constantly exerted their influence for their own interests." But to Ebersole and other scholars of the period, "Whatever lofty ideas the leaders may hold, in the minds of many the abstractions might be reduced to anti-Catholicism."[21]

Ironically, by the 1970s, the phrase "separation of church and state" would become a secular slogan and come to mean "Keep (all) the churches in their place," and that "place" was thought to be the sanctuary, the cloister, and the sacristy. By the end of the twentieth century, many evangelicals would work together with Catholics to oppose secularism.

Among the other issues the Washington office expressed opinion on during the 1940s were the following: Indian affairs (pleas for religious liberty for non-Catholic Indians); public schools (opposition to federal aid and control; preservation of rights for Bible reading and distribution; released time for religious instruction); immigration (preservation of reasonable limitations on the type and number of immigrants to be admitted to American citizenship); liquor (legislation restricting the advertisement, sale, and manufacture of intoxicating liquors for beverage purposes); salacious literature (advocacy to outlaw the sale and distribution of obscene and pornographic books and magazines); Communism (encouragement of investigations of subversive activities, anti-Communist propaganda, and the enactment of legislation protecting the nation and its citizens from the menace of Communism); and statism/Fascism (opposition to governmental regimentation and bureaucratic controls).[22]

In 1951, with Dr. Carl F. H. Henry as chairman, a Forum on Social Action was included in the program of the NAE national convention. Historically, this was the first time that a deliberative interchurch body of evangelicals had realistically faced modern social problems in the light of Holy Scriptures. Topics for discussion featured reflection on evangelical thinking in three areas—the politico-economic problem (capitalism vs. socialism), labor relations (labor-management disputes), and race relations (segregation issues).

How did evangelicals view this period of time? Looking toward the 1952 political conventions, an NAE resolution submitted by Dr. Henry noted that "lawlessness and intrigue in international relations has stunned the American people" and that "incontrovertible evidence continues to disclose a sustained lack of moral and spiritual integrity in influential segments of American politics and public life."[23]

Henry's recommendation, adopted by the Resolutions Committee, called for evangelicals to be "vigilant in prayer, vigilant also in the untiring proclamation of the sole ability of the Gospel to cope with the depth-dimension of human sin," and for sponsorship of a "national call to Christian citizenship" on February 11 and 22, the birthdates of Lincoln and Washington, as a means of "stimulating widespread interest in the safeguarding of those rights and freedoms characteristic of the American way of life and rooted in the historic Christian faith."[24]

That was also the year that the NAE endorsed a "Christian Amendment" to the Constitution. The official resolution of 1951 endorsed S. J. Resolution 29 and H. J. Resolution 156, joint Christian Amendment Resolutions, which proposed that "our nation devoutly recognize the authority and law of Jesus Christ, Savior and ruler of the nations, through whom are bestowed the blessings of Almighty God." To apparently address concerns that the idea was a violation of the Establishment Clause of the First Amendment, the NAE resolution added that it "agreed with sections 2 and 3 of the proposed amendment which held that no 'ecclesiastical organization was to be established in our nation, that present freedoms are to be safeguarded, and that the religious scruples of all citizens are to be protected.'"

Critics of this idea, then and now, saw the effort as a violation of the ideals of both Jefferson and Madison. But the National Reform Association, begun by evangelicals in 1864, worked until 1945 to insert an amendment to the Constitution's preamble to "indicate that this is a Christian nation, and will place all the Christian laws, institutions and usages of our government on an undeniable legal basis in the fundamental laws of the land." Other sources record that "the National Association of Evangelicals campaigned in 1947 and 1954 for another wording that would add, 'This nation divinely recognizes the authority and law of Jesus Christ, Savior and Ruler of Nations, through whom are bestowed the blessings of Almighty God.'"[25]

Representative John Anderson, a Republican from Illinois, introduced into Congress in 1961, 1963, and 1965 a constitutional amendment to make Christianity the official faith of the nation. He received the NAE's "Layman of the Year" award in 1964, presumably for his leadership on this issue.

One of the problems of claiming the United States to be a Christian nation, of course, was how that ideal could exist alongside the hypocrisy of racism. The first official statement on "race relations" was adopted in 1956 and cited the Christian message as the answer to difficult interracial relations: "We believe that the teachings of Christ are violated by discriminatory practices against racial minorities in many, if not all, sections of our country; that the propagation of the Gospel is hindered in many foreign countries by these practices; and that many from these minority groups in our own country are alienated from the Gospel by these actions."

The leaders of the NAE went on to "urge all of our constituency to use every legitimate means to eliminate unfair discriminatory practices, and that, therefore, we deplore extremist tactics by any individual or organized groups. We believe that those in authority, political, social, and particularly evangelistic Christian groups have a moral responsibility to work effectively and openly for the creation of that cultus of life which will provide equal rights and opportunities for every individual."

Relations with the federal government were said to have "reached an all-time high in cordiality" when a delegation from the association was received by President Dwight D. Eisenhower at the White House on July 2, 1953. The president reportedly discussed with NAE leaders "the need for a moral and religious base for the guarantee and perpetuity of our American freedoms and affixed his signature to a document which called for a national reaffirmation of faith in God, the Author of man's freedom, repentance from sin and a new dedication to the task of bringing freedom to the world."[26]

At the 1954 annual convention, there was no public record of any mention of the Supreme Court's decision in *Brown v. Board of Education* requiring racial desegregation of the public schools. The decision had led many fundamentalist churches, mostly in the South, to start so-called "Christian academies." The minutes from the event, held in Cleveland, Ohio, were commendation and prayer for President Eisenhower ("the nation being blessed by his Christian testimony") and top government officials, opposition to restrictions on religious liberty in Colombia, support for outlawing "morally contaminating magazines and books," and legislation "to prohibit all liquor advertising in interstate commerce."

Later in the 1950s, NAE resolutions reflect some of the foreign policy debates that took place at the time, including support for the so-called Bricker Amendment, which was designed to prevent any treaty or executive agreement from taking precedence over the U.S. Constitution. Other statements, for example, opposed a proposed treaty with Haiti (1957) that omitted "religious liberty clauses," which would in turn have had detrimental effects on treaty negotiations with Spain and Colombia (where evangelicals were denied religious freedom), and opposed recognition of the government of Red China (1957, 1959, 1960, 1964) and its seating in the United Nations for having "betrayed humanity by the murder of more than 20 million of their own people and . . . liquidated other millions in slave labor camps."

Surprisingly, there was no specific mention of the Korean War, but separate statements on Communism were adopted in 1950, 1952, 1958, 1960, and 1961–1964 pledging the NAE to "commit itself wholeheartedly to an aggressive and unrelenting campaign against this enemy of righteousness" and to "proclaim the Christian Gospel as the only and final answer to the Communist and secularist philosophy which threatens to subvert our youth and to destroy our American freedoms."

In an apparent reference to the Army-McCarthy hearings in 1957, NAE's 1961 statement recommended a "positive approach to the problem of communism with a dynamic presentation of the Gospel rather than [to] engage in the investigation and exposure of individual communists." Senator Joseph McCarthy, in the 1950s, had waged a years-long battle against subversive conduct and against Communists who he believed were hiding in various walks of life, particularly in Hollywood, academia, and government.

On the domestic front, a 1958 resolution on "Christian Education" took note of increasing government intrusion into private school education by measures intended to compel "certain minimum standards which tend to rob private schools of private local control" and the Labor Department's attempts to "construe the wage and hour law of the Fair Labor Standards Act to churches and relief organizations in the same way as it applies to commercial profit organizations."

Nevertheless, during these years the National Association of Evangelicals largely steered clear of domestic political action. In 1958, *Life* magazine called attention to an emerging "Third Force" in Christianity alongside Protestantism and Catholicism that was "the most extraordinary religious phenomenon of our time."[27] Although the article did not mention the NAE, it identified among the new force five denominations that comprised nearly two-thirds of its membership: Assemblies of God, Church of God (Cleveland), International Church of the Foursquare Gospel, the Pentecostal Holiness Church, and the Pentecostal Church of God.

From the 1940s, conservative politicians recognized that evangelicals battling modernism offered a potential source of electoral support. But the affinity of many fundamentalists for anti-Catholicism, anti-Semitism, and racism caused most mainstream conservatives to play the evangelical card with caution. President Eisenhower, for example, like Robert Taft and Barry Goldwater, wanted to attract supporters outside the northern Protestant base but kept their distance from "right-wing preachers who could be depended upon to insult major groups from which recruits for the conservative coalition might be drawn."[28] Eisenhower's willingness to meet with the NAE, on the other hand, was a positive sign of the organization's growing reputation.

Moving into the Mainstream, 1957–1967

In 1957, meeting in Buffalo, New York, leaders of the NAE took the unusual action of commending an upcoming Billy Graham Crusade to be held in New York City. A statement adopted unanimously declared their "profoundest regard for our beloved brother and wholeheartedly assure[d] him of our united prayerful support in the coming campaign for the greatest city of our nation."

Billy Graham's greatest achievement—apart from his more directly religious role—was to bring evangelicals back into the mainstream of American life.

"Building on the platform established by the NAE, he shaped evangelicalism as a positive force" and "skirted the anti-Catholicism that galvanized most evangelicals against John Kennedy."[29]

The leaders of both the Billy Graham Evangelistic Association and the NAE understood that a new "rebirth of faith in God" would be required to stem the escalating trends toward secularism within the culture. Without a Christian philosophy of life, our freedoms would be lost. Daily reading of the Bible in public schools was encouraged as well as the praying of the Lord's Prayer and the granting of released-time instruction.

Kennedy's campaign for the presidency prompted a 1960 resolution entitled "Roman Catholicism and the President of the United States." All of the candidates for president, regardless of their religious affiliation, were urged to be committed to the principle of the separation of church and state. While his name was never mentioned, the commitment of a Roman Catholic candidate (i.e., JFK) to the principle was "particularly necessary because the Roman Catholic Church, both as a political and religious organization, had for many centuries fostered the policy of church establishment in various degrees, and exerted pressures on public officials to that end." NAE's leaders were not optimistic about the matter: "We doubt that a Roman Catholic president could or would resist fully the pressures of the ecclesiastical hierarchy."

In 1962, the NAE issued a "Call to Action" to meet with leaders of other Bible-believing groups to discuss methods of strengthening evangelical witness and to find ways to initiate more comprehensive united action. One issue of concern was "secularism in education" and the Supreme Court's upcoming consideration of state-sponsored Bible reading and prayer in the public schools.

Given its presuppositions, the NAE had every reason to be concerned. Later that year, in *Engel v. Vitale*, the Supreme Court struck down as unconstitutional the New York Board of Regents nondenominational school prayer, and the next year in *Abington School District v. Schemp* ruled as unconstitutional the practice of reading ten verses from the Bible and reciting in unison the Lord's Prayer at the beginning of each day. There was outrage at these decisions, which were described in a 1963 resolution as "practical atheism" that excluded all references to God in the public schools and produced a "religious vacuum" in the land.

Did the justices of the Supreme Court intend that the government of the United States should not recognize God? Did they have in mind a completely secular government? The NAE met that fall in a special meeting and endorsed six courses of action, including support for an amendment to the Constitution, intended to "allow reference to, belief in, reliance upon, or invoking the aid of God, in any governmental or public document, proceeding, activity, ceremony, school, or institution," and "active resistance to any hostility to a religiously based view of life in the public schools, which may require the establishment of Christian day schools to safeguard the American Christian heritage."

On race relations, the most important moral issue of the day, the NAE spoke out in 1956 and again in 1963, three months before the House Judiciary Committee opened hearings on the Civil Rights Act. Another resolution on race relations was adopted the following year (1964), pointing "with thanksgiving to Billy Graham's integrated Easter Service rally in Birmingham, Alabama," and calling upon churches "to accelerate the desegregation of their own institutions both in spirit and practice and the opening of all sanctuaries of worship to every person, regardless of race or national origin."

Nowhere in NAE resolutions or public statements is there any mention of actually supporting the Civil Rights Act of 1963 or the Voting Rights Act of 1964, but a 1965 statement declared, "We are deeply concerned about the anguish suffered by those minority groups who have been denied their civil rights." It was in 1991 that the NAE adopted an official statement entitled "Racism" in which its numbers agreed to "commit ourselves to take with utmost seriousness the current [NAE] dialogue with leaders of the National Black Evangelical Association and improve race relations through appointments, programs, publications and employment practices." Practical expressions of the organization's commitment would be "to encourage local churches to reject de facto segregation; partnerships to plant churches in urban America; affirming biblical norms on race relations in churches and communities; and challenging schools, colleges, universities and seminaries to provide caring and loving environments for students of various races or economic classes."

On the Vietnam War, the other crisis issue of the period, the NAE in 1966 stated, "We decry any action by our government that would favor communism under the leadership of Red China; we object to any action by our government that would weaken the security of the non-communist nations of the world; and we declare our loyalty to the established constitutional government of our country and the accompanying requirement of civil obedience." A second resolution called "The New Treason" stated, "Believing that the authority of the state is sanctioned by God, the NAE deplores the burning of draft cards, subversive movements and seditious utterances, and prevalent disloyalty to the United States of America."

A "25th Anniversary Manifesto" in 1967 included a resolution on the "Communist Threat" that warned:

> As evangelical Christians we greatly deplore the evidences of accommodation to the ideology supportive of Communism observable in America today. In the church it appears in the insistence one increasingly hears that revolution, even violent revolution is inevitable in the process of social change. There's a growing disregard for the rights of the private sector and a growing acceptance of the doctrine "from each according to his ability, to each according to his need." When godless materialism promises to dominate a society which once was described as Christian, we urge the strengthening of those things that remain before the darkness comes. On this account we reaffirm our unalterable opposition to every form of atheistic Communism.

(It also affirmed the U.S. government's allowance of conscientious objector status to war based only on "religious training and belief" and opposed relaxation of Selective Service laws to include those opposed to "any particular act of war" or a "particular war at the time of their induction," without reference to religious conviction.)

A Changing Mind-Set, 1968–1980

A 1968 resolution entitled "A Witnessing Church in a Secular World" stated that the "first and foremost" duty of evangelicals was to "seek and save the lost." To remain aloof from concrete decisions affecting social developments, according to the resolution, would be to suggest that evangelicals do not believe that God is sovereign in all the affairs of men. The Christian witness, then, is that of "the whole Gospel for the whole man to the whole world, by the whole people of God."

However, that same call to engage the world warned that social involvement carries with it a "double risk" that the Christian "who devotes his energies to justice, equality and peace may fail to keep uppermost in his testimony that Christ came to seek and to save those who were lost. And, in his desire to be relevant in his testimony, he may lend support to objectives that seem to advance the cause of justice, equality and peace by secular standards, but which do not accord with the will of God."

This was a cautious statement toward public engagement. During the 1960s, studies indicated that "without exception evangelicals were less inclined toward political participation than were their less-evangelical counterparts." Neither Billy Graham nor even high-profile fundamentalist preachers of the day sought to change that stance of noninvolvement. In 1965, Falwell said that "we have few ties to this earth . . . and our only purpose on this earth is to know Christ and to make him known."[30] But surprisingly, by the late 1970s and early 1980s, surveys showed evangelicals to be the religious group most favorable to political action by churches.[31]

What changed the evangelical mind-set? The moral decline of the nation revealed a nation adrift, and evangelicals came to realize they had a responsibility to help restore traditional morality. The theme of the 1968 NAE Convention was "Crisis in the Nation," and the theme the following year was "Saving the Seventies." The country was divided by a major war in Asia, and at home "a social revolution with economic overtones has made arson, looting, mayhem and murder commonplace in some metropolitan areas." It was a crisis of "unparalleled proportions."

A 1971 convention theme of "Jesus Christ, Lord of All" lamented the "spiritual chaos" in the land. The "hippie" revolt, the student revolt, the morality revolt, and the "new religion" were all described as mere symptoms of a deeper disease said to be that "men of every color, class and condition are alienated" from God and in need of the message of the church, Jesus Christ. There was a sense in these statements that the "noble experiment" of America was under assault from both governmental action and the crumbling of the moral foundations. The leaders of the NAE stated, "We can make our influence felt as citizens where concrete social action is justified in areas of domestic relations, education, law enforcement, employment, housing and equal opportunity."

Due to encroaching federal controls over public schools, and to provide a way for private schools to receive the support they needed, a "possible solution" was suggested in tax credits. Thus began the reversal of a long-standing opposition to any form of aid benefiting "parochial" schooling. The following year, a resolution entitled "Christian Day Schools" lauded the establishment of private schools as an alternative to schools that extol the "secular philosophies of the day." Within a decade, evangelicals were united behind "parental choice" and the enactment of tuition tax credits as a matter of economic justice.

The growing visibility of environmental concerns led to the first-ever NAE statements in 1970 and 1971 on the environment: "Beyond the scientific, biological and political ramifications of our environment problem is a basically theological and religious issue. Those who thoughtlessly destroy a God-ordained balance of nature are guilty of sin against God's creation." It would be the summer of 2004 before the NAE would join others such as *Christianity Today* and the Evangelical Environmental Network in cosponsoring a major event to mobilize their movement behind a biblical rationale for environmental activism. Nonetheless, these early statements were an indicator of an evolving mind-set on evangelical public responsibility.

Again in 1970, a full three years before the infamous *Roe v. Wade* decision legalizing abortion, the NAE affirmed its conviction that abortion is "a question of those circumstances under which a human being may be permitted to take the life of another. Abortion on demand for reasons of personal convenience, social adjustment or economic advantage is morally wrong, and we express our firm opposition to any legislation designed to make abortion possible." Given that other evangelical groups such as the Southern Baptist Convention adopted a "pro-choice" position on abortion, this was a forward-thinking statement of what would eventually become the evangelical norm.

An official position on homosexuality was adopted saying that evangelicals should "stand firm" in asserting that the Scripture condemns practicing homosexuality, extending the healing ministry to those in need of God's love, and calling on physicians, psychologists, and sociologists to "expand research on the cause and cure of homosexuality."

The Watergate scandals, 1973–1974, prompted a resolution lamenting that "waves of political scandals from the White House to the City Hall have engulfed America." There was a "Prayer in National Life" statement that called for "suitable legislation" to strengthen the free exercise of religion in our national life. Annual resolutions during this period called for the following: Sunday observance; enforcement of motion picture ratings; curtailing of indecency on television; local action against pornography; opposition to tax-deductibility of liquor advertising; opposition to smoking and alcohol on airlines; and enforcement of laws against marijuana and drug trafficking.

The aforementioned resolutions reflected an emphasis on personal sin and morality, but there was also an increasing emphasis on corporate social responsibility. In 1975, for example, a statement called "Let the Earth Hear His Voice" lamented that "more than two-thirds of the world's population have yet to be evangelized" and that "all of us are shocked at the poverty of millions." A statement that year on "Human Hunger and Compassion" stated that one-fifth of the human race in thirty-two countries faced death by starvation and that "the evangelistic task is executed within a sociological context." It was acknowledged that "Christians may disagree about appropriate government roles, and they should debate political prescriptions for addressing human needs," but "we call on the Christian community to commit to renewed efforts to remove racism, prejudice, and other barriers to employment in the community and society." (Similar kinds of resolutions on the responsibility of evangelicals to assist the poor and marginalized in America were adopted in 1971, 1977, 1986, 1990, 1994, 1995, 1996, and 1999.)

A change at the Federal Communications Commission (FCC) would have a major impact on the evangelical movement. Previously the FCC had always required television stations to devote a fixed amount of time to religious programming. This was met by free time, but in the seventies many stations began charging for the time they had set aside for religion. Evangelical and fundamentalist preachers, willing to make fund-raising appeals on the air, took advantage of the option. The audience for television preachers soon grew to an estimated 24 percent of all Protestants.[32]

The cover story of *Newsweek* proclaimed 1976 the "Year of the Evangelical." The NAE held a bicentennial joint convention with its affiliate the National Religious Broadcasters in the nation's capital. The annual theme statement "Let Freedom Ring" recited the call to repentance in 2 Chronicles 7:14 and a challenge to "commit ourselves to participate in every lawful and morally right function of human government and oppose with all our determination whatever is unlawful and morally wrong." President Gerald Ford spoke at the event, as did Ronald Reagan in 1981, the only two times the organizations held combined conventions.

Jimmy Carter, a self-described "born-again" believer, ran a campaign that attracted widespread support from evangelicals. Television broadcasters such as Pat Robertson outright endorsed his candidacy, and he won against President Ford (56 percent to 43 percent).[33] It wouldn't be long, though, before Carter would disappoint evangelicals by supporting the Equal Rights Amendment, failing to act to stop federally funded abortions, and advocating homosexual rights. His explanation that his sincerely held view of separation of church and state did not allow his spiritual convictions to shape his policy positions did not sit well with evangelicals. Without mentioning President Carter, all three issues were the subject of a 1979 resolution called "Man and Woman" that couldn't help but be interpreted as a rejection of Carter's presidency.

A decision by the Internal Revenue Service in 1978 would have enormous political significance. It decided to tighten the standards for church-operated schools so that the percentage of their student bodies drawn from racial minorities must be at least one-fifth of the percentage of the local community.[34] A massive protest led to an IRS decision to postpone the implementation of its proposal, and in 1980, Congress passed the Ashbrook-Dornan amendments that prohibited the IRS from yanking the tax-exempt status from religious schools.

On an international level, during these years of 1974 to 1978, resolutions warned against any precipitous end to our involvement in Vietnam; protested against persecution of Christians overseas; affirmed United Nations resolutions 242 and 338 regarding Israel; and supported the Mutual Defense Treaty of Taiwan. While most of the members of the association opposed Carter's Panama Canal Treaty, missionaries and other Latin American ministry heads successfully persuaded NAE leaders against taking a stand.

Political Insiders, 1980–1992

If the association wanted to defend evangelical values—especially against government intrusion into the affairs of the church—it would have to expand its Washington presence. Clyde Taylor, director of the NAE office, had retired in 1974, and Floyd Robertson, a retired naval officer who had ably served as head of the Chaplain's Commission, served as interim director of the public affairs office until 1978.

The Board of Administration made a commitment to find a new director of the Washington work and to expand its presence. They hired Robert P. Dugan Jr., a Conservative Baptist pastor and former Republican congressional candidate from Lakewood, Colorado, who had been the president of the Conservative Baptist Association of America. Within a few short years, a legislative researcher (this writer) and Forest Montgomery, who for a decade had been the chief of the legal opinion section of the Treasury, as well as Curran Tiffany, a former top lobbyist for American Telephone and Telegraph (AT&T), were added to make good on the promise to beef up the NAE image and presence in the nation's capital.

A 1979 resolution on "Religious Freedom" decried actions by the IRS a year earlier that had become a rallying cry for the creation of a number of so-called "religious Right" organizations, including the Moral Majority. The resolution condemned the IRS commissioner's decision to (1) assume the prerogative of determining the mission of the church by defining an "integrated auxiliary"; (2) adopt a ruling that would severely restrict the publication of voting records of political candidates by church groups; and (3) publish a procedure that would allow the IRS to revoke the tax-exempt status of private schools for failure to maintain a racial balance.

In 1980, a resolution entitled "The Christian and His Government" called on evangelicals to pray for those in authority, to become involved in the political process, to register, and to vote. A Gallup poll that year discovered that evangelicals were more likely to be registered to vote than non-evangelicals, despite being overrepresented in demographic groups that were historically low in political participation.[35]

Ronald Reagan's election that fall, aided by the votes of 61 percent of "born-again" white Protestants, raised expectations for action on constitutional amendments on abortion and prayer in schools that were not fulfilled. The new administration proposed a School Prayer Amendment to the Constitution that would have overturned the 1962 and 1963 Supreme Court decision outlawing Bible reading and state-sponsored prayer. Ironically, it was the NAE that testified before Congress that the government shouldn't be in the business of writing prayers. In other words, government, even through its appointed officials, should not have any "influence over the form or content of prayers." At first, it was viewed as a "killer amendment" by White House officials, but within a year they had adopted the language as their own.

Although controversial and opposed by some within NAE circles, it was a historic change on school prayer and the role of government. A more successful approach, passed by the Congress and signed by the president in 1984, was "equal access" legislation to prevent discrimination against public high school students on the basis of the content of their speech.

Francis Schaeffer's 1981 book *A Christian Manifesto* argued that secular humanism was itself a religion "which the government and courts in the United States favor over all others."[36] That same year, and in 1982, the annual meetings of the association adopted statements called "A Response to Secular Humanism" and "The Fruit of Secular Humanism." Both warned against "secular humanism," which was defined as that "form of atheistic humanism which denies any need for God and places man or woman in his or her so-called goodness on center stage." The consequences of this philosophy were described in NAE resolutions as "unrestricted abortion, free love and homosexual practices, permissiveness in divorce, genetic engineering or cloning to help mankind evolve into brave new men."

But what if government is part of the problem? That was a question addressed to at least one hundred denominational officials who attended a 1981 "Government Intervention in Religious Affairs" conference in Washington, sponsored by a dozen groups including the National Association of Evangelicals, U.S. Catholic Conference, National Council of Churches, Synagogue Council of America, and others. "The danger of the moment," wrote Dean M. Kelly, "is not the dominance by a Church or all the churches but the increasing dominance of government and its propensity to press the churches back into ever smaller sanctums of time and space and subject."

One case in particular, *Bob Jones University v. United States*, pitted the association's desire to stand for racial equality against its concern for protecting the free-exercise rights of its member churches, schools, and institutions. While the case turned on a technicality—whether the IRS had exceeded its authority to act without specific guidelines from Congress—it raised more fundamental questions of whether the denial of the university's tax exemption because of policies based on religious beliefs (i.e., a school policy of prohibiting interracial marriage) infringed upon the university's right to the free exercise of religion.

After much deliberation and prayer, and with reluctance, the association filed a Friend of the Court brief on behalf of the university, fearful that future "public policy" on sex discrimination, for example, could result in the denial of tax exemption to any church that believes God has ordained different roles for men and women. (Three years later, the NAE officially opposed the Equal Rights Amendment for this very reason.) Nevertheless, the Fourth Circuit Court of Appeals, on December 30, 1980, upheld the revocation but avoided deciding whether a religious organization is subject to the public-policy limitation imposed on other tax-exempt organizations. However, it seemed to imply as much, namely that a religious organization per se would be subject to the public-policy limitation.

One other solution to the encroachment of government upon the private sector was to get evangelicals registered to vote and actually voting. The non-partisan "NAE Citizenship Campaign" of 1984 was one of many such efforts. On election day, 81 percent of white evangelicals voted for Reagan, up almost one-third from 1980. More significantly, 77 percent of white evangelicals voting in congressional elections supported Republican candidates for the House. A survey also revealed that religion was an "extremely important" factor in evangelical voting behavior, up from 18 percent in 1982 to 30 percent in 1984. The groups of evangelicals who were the most likely to take religion into account in casting their ballots were those who were the "most religious, who regularly attend religious services and say it is extremely important to them."[37] The "religion factor" would rise in significance for most congressional and presidential elections.

President Ronald Reagan addressed the NAE in Orlando, Florida, on March 6, 1983, and delivered his famous "Evil Empire" speech. The staff of the Washington office met with White House officials, including speechwriters, in advance of the event, which marked the first time any president traveled outside of Washington to speak to evangelicals. Reagan stated that the Soviet Communists were "the focus of evil in the modern world" and that military strength was necessary "to restrain the aggressive impulses of an evil empire." The speech received more than a dozen standing ovations, but it was panned by liberals such as columnist Anthony Lewis who described the language in the speech referring to the "reality of sin in the world" as simplistic theology.

Reagan addressed the NAE the following year in Columbus, Ohio, and White House staff disagreed again over what message to deliver to the audience. Chief of Staff James A. Baker wanted to deliver a noncontroversial speech on school prayer, but the president's speechwriters wanted "Reagan to be Reagan" and speak on the sanctity of human life (which two NAE Washington staff members had suggested in meetings with White House officials). The president resolved the dispute—he defended the sanctity of human life.[38]

The NAE staff members were increasingly consulted about administration appointments and policy, and they seized the opportunity to influence government. The organization was also gaining influence on Capitol Hill and was given credit for helping to pass legislation, including bills on drunk driving, church audit procedures, and equal access facilities for religious organizations.[39]

In order to give leadership to the debate over foreign and defense policy, in 1984 the NAE launched the highly praised "Peace, Freedom and Security Studies" (PFSS) program, which advanced the idea that work for peace must be linked to advances in international human rights. Nations that do not respect the rights of their own people will not respect the rights of other nations. That same year the NAE cohosted with the U.S. State Department and other groups an "International Conference on Religious Liberty" with speeches by the secretary of state, George Schulz, and the president of the United States, Ronald Reagan.

A 1987 resolution entitled "Peace, Freedom and Human Rights" called upon all Christians "to fulfill their biblical responsibility to be peacemakers, and in so doing to avoid the most common errors of the political left—opposition only to American military power; and of the political right—support of all defense programs." The link between peace and human rights would foreshadow major initiatives of the 1990s on religious persecution, sexual trafficking, and peace in the Sudan.

Through the PFSS program, directed by staffer Brian O'Connell, the NAE was saying that there was a single standard for judgments about human rights—a standard that applied to both right-wing regimes and totalitarian ones. During the tension, unrest, and bloodshed in the Republic of South Africa, for example, the NAE (1986) condemned apartheid "as an affront to a just God and contrary to Biblical teaching" and urged prayer for a "speedy and peaceful end to this injustice." In 1987, a resolution urging prayer for churches in Nicaragua called for "freedom for all churches [to] be restored, that radio stations with religious programming be permitted to reopen and . . . church publications, now forbidden, to be published and mailed." The intent behind these and other such statements ("Go Liberate," 1986)—directed at regimes of both the right and left practicing religious, racial, and economic oppression—was to express a nonideological consensus of biblical concern.

Religious broadcaster Pat Robertson sought the Republican presidential nomination in 1988, but he was unable to capture the evangelical community, let alone find support elsewhere among the electorate. In polls of NAE leaders, Robertson was only the fourth choice among the Republican contenders.

George H. W. Bush won the presidency in 1988 with a 426–112 Electoral College victory, which was attributed by evangelical leaders to the political power associated with the "third rail" of politics, traditional values. In a May 2004 PBS *Frontline* special called "Bush's Faith," Doug Wead, an advisor to Bush, enthused about the 82 percent of evangelicals who cast their ballots for Bush over Michael Dukakis. "We lost the Jewish vote, Hispanics, and even Catholics. We were the first modern presidency to lose the Catholic vote, just barely. We were frightened by those losses, but the message came home. My God, you can win the White House with just the support of evangelicals, if you can get enough of them to vote."[40]

Evangelicals, with their newfound political strength, would narrowly prevail in 1990 congressional votes over religious liberty. The NAE hosted press conferences and organized a coalition of groups that successfully defended the "Armstrong Amendment," named after its author, Senator William Armstrong, which protected the rights of a Catholic institution, Georgetown University, not to have to grant space and funds to a gay-rights group. The issue at stake was whether religious schools could be forced to subsidize groups promoting beliefs and practices contrary to their religious tenets. A similar issue arose over whether the District of Columbia government could require organizations like Big Brothers and Girl Scouts to admit homosexuals into their ranks as counselors, coaches, and leaders. Both votes were won, but by small margins. One-third of the House and Senate had preferred gay rights over religious freedom.

In the spring of 1990, there was a perception that governmental resolve was weakening. The Bush administration's invitations to several gay-rights activists to attend White House bill-signing ceremonies and its failure to circumvent the funding of pornographic art at the National Endowment of the Arts alerted religious groups with offices in Washington that their support was being taken for granted. The NAE and the Southern Baptist Convention asked for and received a high-profile meeting with President Bush in the Roosevelt Room of the White House. Bush offered no apology and pointed to his protection of churches and other religious providers in legislation on child care and disability legislation. But the perception of insensitivity, added to an agreement with Democrats on taxes, violating his "Read my lips: No new taxes" pledge, undercut his evangelical support.

In the months leading up to the Gulf War, officials of the NAE expressed their support for President Bush's leadership in assembling a coalition of nations to forcibly remove Saddam Hussein from Kuwait. Afterward, the association would commend him for his "principled leadership and also commend him and other national leaders for calling the American people to prayer during this crisis." (The statement also lamented that in his March 6, 1991, address before a Joint Session of Congress, "the President thanked everyone but God. We reject the temptation to pride and humbly ask God to continue to intervene in human affairs.")

On its fiftieth birthday, in 1992, the NAE could take credit for being a "voice and forum" for evangelicalism. President George H. W. Bush and Billy Graham addressed the convention, which adopted a document entitled "Forward in Faith." While Graham called for a renewed commitment to spreading the gospel, Bush reiterated his support for traditional family values—a reminder that over the past dozen years it had been electoral politics, not evangelism, that had become the movement's calling card.

In the fall election, with the economy in the doldrums, George Bush would be defeated by William Jefferson Clinton. A reappraisal of the association's connection to Republicans and the "religious Right" would begin.

Evaluating Partisan Politics, 1992–2000

Bill Clinton's election was celebrated in the offices of mainline Protestant and Jewish headquarters and bemoaned by most white evangelical leaders. However, it had always been a mantra in the NAE Washington office that a religious group should "never forget that the doors to the White House swing both ways." The election of a Democrat would mean putting that admonition into practice.

President Clinton's capacity for outmaneuvering Republicans on Capitol Hill, referred to as "triangulation," or the winning of votes from conservatives to pass innovative legislative efforts such as welfare reform that liberals opposed, meant that he would assiduously court certain religious conservatives. The end result was that there was always an open door for the NAE staff members at the White House.

Clinton's staff put on briefings for the association's board of directors, often with the president himself speaking. The administration courted NAE officials with invitations to White House events, such as the first World AIDS Day event, White House State Dinners, annual "Religious Leaders Breakfasts" in the East Room, and many other such events.

In 1993, at the annual convention, NAE President Don Argue called for evangelicals to distance themselves from (GOP) partisan politics without sacrificing efforts to influence the nation's morals: "We are in danger of becoming, if not already identified as, the political arm of one party, a very dangerous position to be in."[41]

But the annual resolutions usually criticized Clinton administration policies. A 1993 resolution on "Homosexuals in the Military" urged President Clinton to "withdraw his initiative or for Congress to confirm by the law the current ban." It went on to state, "We believe that such presidential action would defy the moral law of God and the standard of natural law, subvert military law, and also undermine the integrity of the armed forces of the United States of America."

And in 1994, a resolution on "Health Care Reform" said the need for change was evident: Health care inflation rates were double that of general inflationary rates, and millions were without any health insurance or uninsurable. The principles that should guide the debate included the following: Abortion is not health care; euthanasia should never be endorsed by government or surrogates, including mandatory health alliances; any health care plan should reinforce, not undermine, personal responsibility; tort reform is necessary without compromising the ability of injured persons to receive just compensation. The statement was a response to the report of the Health Care Commission that Hillary Clinton, the First Lady, had chaired.

Clinton, a Southern Baptist by background who attended Foundry United Methodist Church in downtown Washington, took great interest in religious liberty questions. On at least one issue there was complete agreement. Clinton and the Office of Legal Policy strenuously opposed the Supreme Court's ruling in *Employment Division v. Smith* (1990) that the government need no longer demonstrate a "compelling governmental interest" for the public good before restricting religious practice. Justice Scalia, a conservative appointee, had argued, "We have never held that an individual's religious beliefs excuse him from compliance with an otherwise valid law prohibiting conduct that the State is free to regulate."[42]

The NAE warned that "the right to the free exercise of religion is in jeopardy. Religious liberty will likely be eroded unless decisive action is taken." Staff attorneys worked with church-state specialists to come up with acceptable legislative language, the Religious Freedom Restoration Act, to restore the standard of "strict scrutiny" that protected the free exercise of religion against state incursions except in cases of "compelling state interests."

The bill passed in 1993 by overwhelming majorities in both houses of Congress and was signed by President Clinton at a signing ceremony on the South Lawn of the White House. The Supreme Court responded by striking it down as unconstitutional for its "sweeping coverage," saying that it "threatened intrusion at every level of government."[43] In a partial response, religious groups endorsed and successfully lobbied for passage of the Religious Liberty and Institutionalized Persons Act, remedial legislation to protect zoning rights of churches and the religious freedom of prisoners.

In the midterm elections of 1994, the Republicans took over both houses of Congress for the first time in forty years. An exchange of insults between the still rising religious Right and the mainline Protestant denominations, meanwhile, proceeded with unchecked venom. All of this controversy worried some of the leaders in the association.

Thus, a resolution was drafted and passed at the following convention cautioning about excessive entanglement in politics. The resolution said in part: "Partisan political activity is properly an individual matter, and Christian citizens are free to be as partisan as they may choose to be. For the church, however, political partisanship is not proper and poses great problems. A church should not endorse or oppose political parties or candidates, but should remain faithful to its spiritual mission."

Clinton's friendship with NAE president Argue led to participation in a high-profile delegation of clergymen to China in 1998 to meet with President Jiang Zemin and provincial officials about religious persecution. Mainline Protestant leaders such as Joan Brown Campbell lobbied President Clinton to include a representative from the National Council of Churches on the delegation. Instead, Argue (along with the acting director of the Washington office, Richard Cizik) joined Rabbi Arthur Schneier and Archbishop Theodore McCarrick, the future Cardinal of Washington, in the effort to release religious prisoners and press for legal and political reform within China. The month-long trip, objected to by some human rights activists, foreshadowed debates on Capitol Hill over most-favored-nation status for China that would divide the evangelical community. NAE testimony made the claim that permanent normal-trade-relations (PNTR) would over time best serve the cause of religious freedom.

In 1998, just before the House of Representatives vote on articles of impeachment, the association released a statement entitled *A Defining Moment: Biblical Considerations Regarding Leadership* that outlined the moral considerations for impeachment. It stated, "Not all Christians, including evangelicals, will agree on whether President Clinton ought to be impeached. The value systems we employ to make decisions are not all the same. Nor is our understanding of the Constitution's 'high crimes and misdemeanors.' But the following can be said: the prospect for a prudent decision is at least possible when we acknowledge an obligation to a Higher Law and its standards." The NAE registered its opinion of the moral scandal and constitutional crisis by declining an invitation to a September prayer breakfast with President Clinton at the White House on the basis that it "could be misconstrued" as support.[44] The impeachment trial was the top religion story of the year, with an NAE leader suggesting that the scandal was also an opportunity "for the church to examine itself, particularly in the way it trains men and women for civil society. This crisis could be a viewed as God's wake up call to the church, as much as to Bill Clinton or the Congress."[45]

By 1999, religious Right groups were in a state of decline, and some evangelicals urged a retreat from politics. Most evangelical leaders, however, were not about to give up. John Green, Ph.D., director of the University of Akron's Bliss Institute for Applied Politics, had been commissioned back in 1990 to survey NAE leaders and was able to compare their views a decade later. In 1990, 75 percent believed "changing individuals" one by one through evangelistic means was the best way to change society; by the year 2000, a nearly identical number of leaders (64 percent) had concluded that "changing both individuals *and* the institutions of society" was the preferable and most effective way to translate biblical values into a secular society. On political involvement, 50 percent of the leaders said that evangelicals should "stay focused" on politics, and only 9 percent said that they should "withdraw" from politics.

The retirement of Robert P. Dugan Jr. as director of the office in 1997 closed out an important chapter in the history of the office. Named to replace him was the Reverend Richard Cizik, a seventeen-year veteran of the organization, who came with foreign-policy expertise and a desire to employ new strategies for public engagement.

New Internationalism and Faith-Based Initiatives, 1996–2004

When Nicholas D. Kristof's column entitled "The New Internationalists," acknowledging evangelical activism on foreign policy, ran in the *New York Times* in May 2002, the NAE and other groups had already been influential in changing government policy for at least five years. This oversight would lead the scribe of the movement, Allen D. Hertzke, a professor of political science at the University of Oklahoma, to charge that it was time to "end the blindness that causes a great human rights movement to be tainted by the fact that it is led by believing Christians."

Kristof's "new internationalists," as he called this new cadre of activists, were "saving lives and reshaping American policy." They had replaced the "destructive religious right of Jerry Falwell and Pat Robertson, which sought to battle Satan with school prayers and right to life amendments."[46] Edith Blumhofer, director of the Institute for the Study of American Evangelicals, responded on the weblog of *Christianity Today* (May 29, 2002) that "this interest is characteristic of evangelicalism at least since American foreign policy went international, and probably even before."

Indeed, evangelical advocacy on behalf of human rights—even inside the beltway and within governmental circles—had been occurring for decades. In 1985, a "Conference on International Religious Liberty" to discuss human rights and religious freedom was held at the U.S. State Department. (It was cosponsored by the NAE, the Synagogue Council of America, the Institute of Religion and Democracy, and the Jacques Maritain Institute.) President Ronald Reagan addressed the gathering and said, "I believe that the most essential element of our defense of freedom is our insistence on speaking out for the cause of religious liberty. I would like to see this country rededicate itself wholeheartedly to this cause."[47]

Speaking at the event, Arthur E. Gay Jr., NAE's president, asked a poignant question: "What will it take for men and women of goodwill to sit down, to talk, if it is not religious liberty? I don't know, but I call for conversation. Not for the changing of our organization's limits, distinctive, or ties. Not some ecumenical malaise, but rather a conversation of people who know what they are about in their own areas, who come together and build a new network for a grand purpose."[48]

It would take the fall of the Soviet Union and the end of the Cold War, combined with stalemate on Capitol Hill over hot-button social issues, to bring onto the agenda the cause of the persecuted church and religious freedom abroad. The effort would also prompt a reevaluation of political strategies and methodologies.

Despite Gay's challenge for a "new network" to collaborate together, evangelicalism was still hamstrung by some of the dynamics of its own tradition. In particular, it was a public philosophy that prevented the construction of meaningful coalitions with non-Christians. A secular Jew who had taken into his home a persecuted Christian from Ethiopia, tortured for his faith, would change the status quo.

Michael Horowitz, a senior fellow at the Hudson Institute, wrote in July of 1995 an essay for the *Wall Street Journal* entitled "New Intolerance between Crescent and Cross." He wrote that "the evidence of growing and large scale persecution of evangelicals and Christian converts is overwhelming. Yet the State Department and the INS have largely reached the opposite conclusion, and many American officials fail to seriously consider the asylum applications of victims of anti-Christian terror." Horowitz argued forcefully: "This issue tests us all. For American Jews who owe our very lives to the open door of 'the blessed land,' silence should not be an option in the face of persecutions eerily parallel to those committed by Adolf Hitler. America's Christian community is most directly challenged. Its moral authority will be gravely tarnished if it fails to exercise its growing political influence on behalf of people now risking everything to engage in the 'simple' act of Christian worship and witness."[49]

The article caught the notice of the NAE, and with the help of Diane Knippers at the Institute for Religion and Democracy and Nina Shea at Freedom House, an event described as "A Conference on the Global Persecution of Christians" was planned for January 23, 1996. Evangelical executives of mission agencies and advocacy groups invited by the NAE who declined were called by Horowitz, who is Jewish, urging their attendance. Over a hundred Christian leaders assembled at the Mayflower Hotel in the nation's capital for what would become a historic event.

Released that day was a document entitled *The National Association of Evangelicals' Statement of Conscience on Worldwide Religious Persecution.* It became the first draft on legislation to curb religious persecution and helped launch a movement that would rattle diplomats in foreign capitals. After a two-year battle that included opposition by the Clinton administration, the State Department, the business lobby, and the National Council of Churches, the International Religious Freedom Act was passed unanimously by both houses of Congress in 1998 and signed by President Clinton. According to the *New*

York Times, the victory was "a new sign of the growing influence of conservative religious groups."[50]

It was but one example of coalition building across religious lines and with groups who would normally oppose evangelicals on hot-button domestic concerns. Allen D. Hertzke, a professor of political science at the University of Oklahoma and the scribe of the movement, wrote, "Leaders like Charles Colson of Prison Fellowship, Richard Land of the Southern Baptist Convention, and Richard Cizik of the National Association of Evangelicals worked closely with liberal Jews and Tibetan Buddhists to press landmark religious freedom legislation in 1998. They joined with Gloria Steinem and all the major feminist organizations to pass the *Victims of Trafficking and Protection Act of 2000* and with the Congressional Black Caucus for passage of the *Sudan Peace Act of 2002*. In 2003 they worked with Ted Kennedy and civil-liberties groups such as the NAACP, La Raza and Human Rights Watch to pass legislation targeting prison rape."[51]

In May of 2000, the NAE cohosted with Freedom House the "Second Summit of Christian Leaders on World-Wide Religious Persecution: An Examination of Sudan and North Korea." After passing legislation aimed at preventing genocide in Sudan, evangelicals turned their attention toward leading similar coalitions on behalf of North Korean refugees, which represented the main bulwark against granting further license to the Pyongyang regime to perpetuate its internal human-rights atrocities in return for "concessions" on the international front.

That same fall, in October, the NAE cohosted with the Religious Action Center of Reform Judaism a "Conference on Sexual Trafficking." Speakers included William Bennett, a spokeswoman for Gloria Steinem, liberal Senator Paul Wellstone, and conservative Senator Sam Brownback. A third successful legislative initiative, the Trafficking Victims Protection Act, led the *New York Times* op-ed page writer, Nicholas D. Kristof, to write: "In the battle against sexual trafficking, it is conservative Christians who have taken the lead in the fight on behalf of third-world women."[52] The group later lobbied successfully for the appointment of John Miller, a former Republican member of Congress from Seattle, to be given ambassadorial status as the head of the State Department's newly created Trafficking in Persons Office. A Domestic Trafficking Initiative will soon attack the massive abuses of the domestic commercial sex "industry."

The *New York Times* profiled the movement for a morally based foreign policy in a front-page story entitled "Evangelicals Sway White House on Human Rights Issues Abroad," subtitled "Liberals Join Effort on AIDS and Sex Trafficking." Reporter Edith Bumiller's surprising acknowledgment of evangelical influence caught everyone but the evangelical leaders themselves by surprise: "Administration officials and members of Congress say the religious coalition has had an unusual influence on one of the most religious White Houses in American history. The groups have driven aspects of foreign policy and won major appointments, and they were instrumental in making sure that the president included extensive remarks on sex trafficking in his speech to the United Nations General Assembly in September."[53]

What accounted for this influence? It took a former British member of Parliament, Jonathan Aitken, to remind observers of the spiritual element to this modern-day campaign against slavery. He wrote, "Whether that power comes from the Holy Spirit or from good vote-counting politics, we should see it as a good use of power and rejoice about it."[54]

The election of George W. Bush that October over Vice President Al Gore was credited to moral disgust over the Clinton scandals involving Monica Lewinsky and subsequent cover-up, or his perjury, according to many analysts. President Bush's language and programs resonated with the NAE and evangelicals generally. One of his first actions was to announce a "Faith-Based and Community Initiatives" program to bring equality of treatment by the government toward faith-based providers.

At the 2001 convention meeting in Dallas, President Bush sent a message to the delegates thanking them for their support of the initiative, saying, "Your decision to endorse the concept of Charitable Choice is noteworthy and lends an important voice to the public discussion of the role of faith-based organizations in society." On church-state issues, the NAE had done a 180-degree turn over the past forty years. Once opposed to state aid to religious schools, it was a supporter of private school vouchers and now had come out in support of "charitable choice" provisions of the 1996 welfare bill promoting government aid to faith-based charities.[55]

The first director of Bush's faith-based office, John DiIulio, a Catholic believer and a Democrat, was well received by the evangelical audience when he spoke at the 2001 convention in Dallas, a small indication of how evangelicals and Catholics were united in a new culture war against secularists. Controversy over how to protect the "hiring rights" of charities would plague the faith-based initiative, and legislation to implement Bush's program failed to get enough votes from the opposition party to be enacted.

Undeterred, President Bush issued Executive Order 13279 on December 12, 2002, which was designed to ensure equal protection for faith-based and community organizations that administer social service programs. The executive order stated, among other things, that "no organization is to be discriminated against on the basis of religion or religious belief in the administration or distribution of federal financial assistance under social service programs." As a result of the action, religious organizations will no longer be required to give up their right under Title VII to give preference to members of their religion when hiring employees in order to receive federal funds.

White House director of the Office of Faith-Based and Community Initiatives, Jim Towey, spoke to the 2003 convention held in Eden Prairie, Minnesota, and a "Faith-based Training Day on Government Grants" drew hundreds of participants. A resolution entitled "Staffing Rights of Ministries" indicated that the NAE "opposes all legislative, regulatory, and judicial efforts on behalf of the faith-based initiative, federal and state, where guarantees of religious autonomy, including staffing rights, are not an expressed part of the effort." The so-called "hiring rights" of ministries, opposed by the leadership of the Democrat Party, had already become a new battleground in the culture wars.

The convention delegates also discussed the 9/11 attack, the war under-way against terrorists in Afghanistan, and impending war against Iraq. The organization's board of directors declined to take a position on the Iraq conflict, citing concern for missionaries and indigenous Christians overseas. One board member reasoned that "the comments by some evangelists had poisoned the well" and anything the NAE per se would say could be misinterpreted in the Islamic world. It was a historic decision and an indication that the leaders of the association were sensitive to the image created by the perceived "anti-Muslim" comments of others within the broader evangelical movement.

But this decision wasn't a sign that evangelicals were morally neutral or engaging in some new kind of "moral equivalence" over the morality of war against terrorism or the wisdom of taking military action against Saddam Hussein. Everyone understood that the Iraqi conflict was part of a larger war of ideas and that evangelicals had to be wisely engaged. As to President Bush's use of religious rhetoric, the vice president for governmental affairs (this writer) said, "He hasn't been narrowly sectarian about it. Even in today's pluralistic America, I don't find that Buddhists, Hindus, Muslims, or for that matter, Christians, complain about his reverence for God in public life. I believe that Americans expect and respect it."[56]

Christian-Muslim relations suffered after the terrorist attack on September 11, 2001, and NAE leaders recognized that this was in no small measure because of the comments of some evangelical leaders. "A particular danger is oversimplification about Islam and Muslims—either positive or negative—that thwarts true dialogue, true education, and genuine Christian mission," wrote Alan F. H. Wisdom, the author of *Guidelines for Christian-Muslim Dialogue*.[57] The guidelines were released at a one-day "Consultation on Islam" held on May 7, 2003, by the National Association of Evangelicals and the Institute on Religion and Democracy. Two recommended courses of action were to initiate dialogue with Muslims, in the United States and abroad, on the topics of religious freedom, democracy, and human rights, and to initiate compassionate ministries overseas that would "communicate the love of Christ."

To respond to these recommendations, a March 1–7, 2004, "Evangelical Delegation to Morocco" reported on an agreement with the kingdom to allow for the first time openly identified evangelical relief and development projects and other Christian cultural events in that Islamic country.[58] A second initia-tive was to assemble a delegation of Christian representatives to the "Congress of Rabbis and Imams for Peace" in Ifrane, Morocco, in late November 2004. Both efforts were an attempt to provide guidance and direction on an issue with long-term significance—the negative perception of evangelicals in Islamic regions.

President George W. Bush, speaking via teleconference on three giant screens at the NAE's 2004 annual meeting held at New Life Church in Colorado Springs, Colorado, didn't bring up the war with Iraq or any international issues. He told the delegates, "We're working to build a culture of life," adding that his administration was committed to "defending the most basic institutions and values of this country. I will defend the sanctity of marriage against activist courts and local officials who want to redefine marriage."[59] The president received the heartiest applause for signing the Partial Abortion Ban Act and for his recent backing of a federal marriage amendment, endorsed earlier by the association.

No one can predict the future of the NAE, but the organization serves a critical need, providing stability and order for a diverse and competitive movement while projecting a respected voice for otherwise silent multitudes from coast to coast. The NAE's weakness over the past six decades has been that the market-driven character of evangelicalism has nurtured spiritual individualism and a plurality of leaders and ministers with little cohesion. The task of pulling the movement together into a united voice will be a task for the next century.

The influence of the broad evangelical movement is undeniable. It has become the center and anchor of American Protestantism. Evangelicals are being described by major print and electronic media in 2004 in the same way *Life* magazine did in 1958—a phenomenon. Boston College sociologist Alan Wolfe in *U.S. News & World Report* described these "new evangelicals" accordingly: "From the halls of Congress to the developing world, the growing influence of evangelicalism is everywhere."[60]

Evangelicals have made significant progress in converting that influence into changes in law and public policy. The identity of evangelicals is no longer always narrowly religious or bound up with a narrow set of political issues. Evangelicals are beginning to offer political solutions on national and international problems that are acknowledged by even their most critical opponents. And they have done so by constructing meaningful coalitions with non-evangelicals, including leaders of other faith traditions.

Will this positive direction continue? To ensure that it happens, the leaders of the NAE intend to release a statement in March 2005 (see appendix) entitled *For the Health of the Nation: An Evangelical Call to Civic Responsibility*. And the purpose of this book is to begin to address what has been called the "scandal of evangelical thinking," part of which has been the failure to provide a public philosophy for the movement. The future of a vibrant evangelical witness to all of society may just depend upon it.

3

Evangelical Denominations at the Foundations of Modern American and British Social-Political Structures and Policies

A Philosopher's Perspective

Paul de Vries

OUR PURPOSE IS to develop a working comprehension of the key eighteenth- and nineteenth-century American and British Protestant evangelical denominations and their perspectives and influences on modern social-political thought, structures, and issues.

In an important sense this task is intensely easy, since in both of these countries there was a sizable Protestant majority throughout the eighteenth and nineteenth centuries, and during this period most Protestants were evangelical, trusting the Bible as the final authority for behavior and belief. The "liberal" attacks on Scripture had not distracted seminaries, their professors, and mission boards in the way that they did in the twentieth century. Moreover, most of these citizens made decisions, in part, based upon their professed Protestant perspectives. What is astounding is the profound impact of evangelical Protestant perspectives on the political policies and structures of America and the United Kingdom of the time, and the marked successes and failures that ensued.

Evangelical Denominations' Social-Political Teachings

People of different Protestant perspectives have tended to give different emphases in their approaches to social and political issues. While there is no rigid unity among all Lutherans or among all Methodists, each major evangelical denomination has had its characteristic perspectives nevertheless. We will look through the perspectives of Lutheranism, Calvinism (especially the perspectives of the Presbyterian and Reformed denominations), Anabaptist and Baptist denominations, and Methodism.

Each of these evangelical perspectives has to resist three marked tendencies in the Christian community. First, they have to resist the temptation to separate from society and develop a social-political ethic just for themselves. Too often evangelicals have replaced the world-changing message of the gospel with an unbiblical world-resisting or world-escaping message. Second, they have to resist the temptation to oversimplify the gospel by concentrating only on "saving souls." Such revivalist religion is really a denial of biblical wholeness and social-political responsibility. Third, they have to resist the temptation simply to repeat earlier formulations of Christian ethics that were formed for another time and place. In short, all have to resist the hazards of separation, oversimplification, and formalism.[1]

Lutherans

The "two kingdoms" perspective has shaped Lutheran social-political thought and action. Jesus said that his kingdom is not of this world, and so Lutheran church leaders have thought that they should not try to dominate the government and that political leaders should not try to manipulate the churches. The power of government should never be used to either dissuade or punish those with wrong beliefs. As a result, in this world all are subject to the political authorities, including the ministers, priests, and the pope. The Lutheran approach has often resulted in quiet acceptance and peaceful coexistence even with unfair and unjust political realities, being grateful if the state does not interfere with the churches' work. Peaceful means of resolving any problem should be pursued completely. Traditionally the churches' quiet acceptance has often been further guaranteed by the Lutheran churches becoming state churches in some continental European countries, dependent on political institutions for financial support and policy direction.[2]

Of course, in Britain and America, Lutheranism was never a state church. Still, the "two kingdoms" approach led Lutherans to be less separatist, less critical, and also less transformative of social, economic, and political structures and policies. The "two kingdoms" framework allowed for some bracketing or compartmentalizing of life issues.

While good works do not contribute to salvation, it is essential for Christians to do good works to please God and to fulfill responsibilities as citizens—in "both kingdoms." In church the Christian is perfectly free, subject to none; in society the Christian is subject to all, servant of all. This is a paradox: Insofar as he is free, the Christian does no "good works," but insofar as he is servant, he does all kinds of "good works."[3]

The general tendency of Lutheran approaches is to privatize one's faith and to mainly acquiesce to the social-political "realities" around one. There is a strong propensity to pietism, developing robust personal faith within the church and in the privacy of one's heart and mind, regardless of the social-political environment. Martin Luther's own dependence on the protection of German princes for his personal safety and for the success of his part of the great Reformation could have dramatically shaped the perspectives of his followers even centuries after his dramatic life. His dependence on the princes may have made even Luther's powerful mind and masterful pen acquiesce when political power was abused.

Lutheran immigrants to America have often been quite comfortable with this detachment from political action—because of Lutheran theology and also partly because they were not personally or culturally prepared for democracy. Especially first- and second-generation Lutheran immigrants often remained politically isolated.

Calvinists

Calvinists have generally considered the Lutheran approach to be too politically conservative and too accepting and acquiescing of the political structures, policies, and leadership, even in seriously unfair and unjust settings. Calvinists tend to be less institutionalized, less tied to a state church role, less acquiescing to social-political "realities," and less remote from the surrounding political and economic problems. Calvinists are more politically active and more committed to reform the political and economic structures and policies—out of personal gratitude to God for salvation by grace, and also as a vivid expression of the biblical belief that God is the sovereign Lord of his entire universe.[4]

Calvinists have often been active reformers; their belief in divine predestination does not limit their political activity by leading them to merely trust God's will, but rather gives them all the more confidence in the successes of fair and loving causes because these are obedient to the Lord. They focus generally on what is possible and practical, including the tasks of making government more representative of citizens and making the economic markets freer and more fair. Calvinists see that even social structures are the result of human decision, and being made by us they can be altered by us. In fact, the social structures and policies must be altered by us because they are infected with sin and limited by finitude, and the changing historical circumstances require them to be changed anyway.[5] Calvinism contains "a passionate desire to re-shape the social world so that it would no longer be alienated from God." The Calvinist's explicit goal is a reformed society and social structure that is also no longer alienated from people, the very images of God. Once this Calvinist "passion to reshape the social world" entered British and American thinking, it remained a continuing factor.[6]

While Lutherans tend to think of the whole structure of society as God-ordained, Calvinists see both the social structures and the constant process of social reform as God-ordained. While Lutherans believe that we should obey the Lord *in* our daily occupations, Calvinists believe that we should seek to obey God *through* our daily occupations, because we cannot blindly assume that our occupations actually serve the common good.[7] While Lutherans es-pecially value social stability, Calvinists will more likely exploit even unstable times to work toward benevolent and just reforms. The tools of negotiation and compromise were simply necessary evils in the achievement of more fair and caring social-political structures and policies. They are also content *not* to have a state-sanctioned church, in order to keep the churches' leadership and moral judgments truly independent and biblical.[8]

Presbyterians have had tremendous influence in America, especially in the formative decades just before and after the Revolutionary War, including in our concept of property and property rights, and in the functional values structure of the free market. Presbyterians handled some key issues in the vivid context of God's sovereignty and under the authority of his Word over every aspect of life—including the key aspects of free market and property rights.

The Calvinist doctrine of "sphere sovereignty" teaches that God is sovereign over each and every "sphere" of life, such as church, state, economic system, and education. No sphere is superior to any other—church should not con-trol state, nor vice versa—but each sphere has an assigned place in the whole kingdom of God. Also, in every sphere those chosen by God for salvation can express their gratitude to God, appropriate to each individual sphere. Instead of Lutherans' "two kingdoms," there is one kingdom with numerous spheres all under the authority of the one sovereign God.

Consider this question: What makes a free market work? Adam Smith (1723–1790), with a Presbyterian perspective, saw the truly free market of the future based upon the evident handiwork of God as the Impartial Spectator and the Invisible Hand that makes the miracle of a mutually beneficial, win-win, growing economy possible. Smith also saw as necessary fundamentals of a free market the core biblical values of justice, benevolence, and prudence. In fact, for Smith the main ones were justice and benevolence, because prudence is a parasite: One cannot simply be prudent, but rather "prudent at" something else, such as justice, benevolence, or self-interest. Justice is necessary, as he states dozens of times in his classic *Wealth of Nations*, because employees, customers, business partners, and fellow citizens fulfill their roles better if they have a high level of trust. Benevolence or goodwill is required because neither individual businesses nor an economy can grow without a community.

The roles of land and property rights are also very significant in modern life. From the earliest colonial settlements in North America, the question "Who owns the property?" was prominent. What claims did the Native Americans have on the land? How should those claims be treated? What about the nationalistic and royal claims to certain lands? Among the European-American settlers, how should the land be divided? Should land claims be based upon wealth, labor, common humanity, or what?

Among the original thirteen colonies, the answers to these questions varied tremendously. However, the issue was thrown before the whole nation when in 1783 the armistice with England deeded the sparsely settled land between the Appalachian Mountains and the Mississippi River to the newborn United States of America. The new country was suddenly more than three times as big as the total land area of the thirteen former colonies.

Immediately there were competing claims to portions of this land. Many leaders wanted the government to sell portions of the land at high prices to those who could afford to buy them, thereby contributing handsomely to the national treasury. As a consequence, taxes could be kept low, and the land would be developed by those with substantial material resources to do it. This sensible approach nearly became our active national policy.

However, guided by the Bible as well as by the writings of seventeenth-century Presbyterian philosopher John Locke, our founding fathers designed a massive "give-away" program called the Northwest Ordinance. This is perhaps the biggest give-away program since the Lord gave the earth and all the plants and animals to Adam and Eve to dominate, based on their human accountability to the Lord for the uses of those precious resources.

The Bible provided many insights for this extraordinary policy. First of all, the earth and all the plants and the animals were given to Adam and Eve and their descendants to bring under control and master, ultimately accountable only to the Sovereign God.[9] As a result, each human being, as a blood descendant of Adam and Eve, has some inherited claim to a portion of land and is to be an accountable steward of the property before God.

Second, the Levitical law provided for a frequent redistribution of land among citizens, so that every family would have a portion.[10] These land regulations given by the Lord through Moses were so *formative* that the verse inscribed on the Liberty Bell was taken from the very same text: *"Proclaim liberty throughout the land to all its inhabitants."*[11] Scriptural "liberty" includes the access of property given to everyone, a liberating biblical and Presbyterian perspective that endures in our sustaining the Small Business Administration, the Federal Housing Administration, Section 8 programs, and the like, which put economic resources within every person's reach.

Anabaptists and Baptists

Anabaptists and Baptists are even further away from the Lutheran perspective than are Calvinists. They have tended to think that both Lutheranism and Calvinism have failed to accomplish the moral improvement in the social-political structures and policies that should be achieved. They rejected the self-righteous piety of Puritan Calvinism in England and America and pushed for a more consistent scriptural purity and moral earnestness. This third group of evangelicals believed that the acquiescence of Lutherans and the engaged political negotiation of Calvinists missed the clear standards of scriptural purity. Moreover, these two Reformation groups were too identified with earthly civil government, both Anabaptists and Baptists thought.[12]

Anabaptists and Baptists have sought instead to develop holy communities—through local churches separated from any government control, and sometimes even through establishing separate whole communities where only true believers can live and work. Church discipline can be used to keep the special communities pure, and Jesus' Sermon on the Mount is the uncompromising standard for community policies and behavior. This sincere commitment to social-political purity leads Anabaptists and Baptists generally to tolerate earthly sufferings in secular settings, create safe havens of pure living, sometimes ignore injustices in regular society, treat Jesus' earthly example as normative, and endure until Christ returns.[13]

Anabaptists today include especially Mennonites and Amish people. The diverse groups of Baptists—including Southern Baptists, American Baptists, and Conservative Baptists—have also drawn from the Anabaptist traditions, although often in less secluded or separatist ways and generally with less commitment to nonviolence and Christian pacifism. Partly because Anabaptists and Baptists themselves have often chosen to be more biblically radical than Lutheran and Calvinist evangelicals in their behavioral expressions of biblical faith commitment, both Anabaptists and Baptists have exemplified dramatic and effectual leadership for religious liberty. They have consistently asserted that all denominations be treated equally by the government. Moreover, they believe the state should be concerned mainly with the second half of the Decalogue but not take a position on theological and doctrinal issues. In history these beliefs were practiced with both great sacrifice and effect, and often in the face of the fierce resistance of Calvinist and Lutheran evangelical brothers and sisters.

One heroic Baptist in early America was Roger Williams (1604–1684). As a twenty-one-year-old Baptist thinker in Massachusetts, he was banished from the colony because he taught that the government leaders have no power of conscience, that property should not be taken but purchased from Native Americans, and that oaths cannot be required of unregenerate people because oaths are a form of worship. Similarly, Anne Huchinson (1591–1643) was banished from the Massachusetts colony because she as a white woman taught the Bible to men and to Native Americans, and in the process she also taught that people can know God apart from the approval of local church leadership. The banished Roger Williams went on to launch the first Baptist church in America and to establish Rhode Island, the first colony with complete religious liberty. Anne Huchinson brought her Bible teaching to New York, where she was martyred by Native Americans and where now a well-known river and a highway are named after her.

In another dramatic example, the sincere biblical faithfulness and persistence of Baptists in Virginia in the face of severe punishments for preaching caught the attention of Thomas Jefferson. In that Episcopalian-controlled colony, the Baptists were put into prison for simply preaching or teaching the Bible, because they had not been approved by the established church. Each time after these Baptist ministers had served their prison sentence and were released, they quickly resumed their calling as Bible preachers and teachers, only to be arrested again, and then again. Jefferson so respected their consistent faith commitment that he wrote the Virginia Statute on Religious Liberty—and worked assiduously for its approval. This Baptist-inspired, Jefferson-composed document became also the explicit model for America's national Bill of Rights, including the celebrated First Amendment. Thomas Jefferson received the credit, but such radical religious liberty was in fact a Baptist-Anabaptist idea that he wisely borrowed.

Lutheranism and Calvinism were rooted in the Reformation, and their basic perspectives were shaped from that context. Baptist and Anabaptist leaders wanted to learn from what they saw as failures of the reformers, and they sought to follow the basic principles of the Scriptures with even more purity and consistency.

Among African-Americans there were many very effective Baptist social-political leaders, including Maria Stewart (1803–1879), a member of Boston's African Baptist Church, who was the very first black female political writer. Guided by the Old Testament record of a just and avenging God, she called for the abolition of slavery even by violence, if necessary. This Baptist lady's cogent appeals for biblical justice brought together people from many other denominational perspectives also—both to oppose slavery and to recognize the human rights of women.

Also in the critical decades preceding the American Civil War, many Baptists such as journalist William Lloyd Garrison (1803–1879) were devotedly non-violent leaders in the abolitionist movement, seeking to eradicate the American practice of human bondage by moral and spiritual persuasion *alone*. A somewhat unconventional Baptist, Garrison was one of the most effective leaders to transform the American nation, utilizing his role as the president of the American Anti-Slavery Society for twenty years, from 1843 until emancipation. The effective political campaigning that made the abolition of slavery both feasible and necessary was largely due to this politically astute Baptist's *inflexible spirit, invincible courage, and inflammatory leadership.*

It is noteworthy that the 1960s debates that took place within the black community concerning nonviolence were a direct extension of the same deep-seated conflict that had taken place in the nineteenth-century antebellum era. William Lloyd Garrison's most notable biographer thus draws a straight line from Mr. Garrison to Dr. Martin Luther King Jr., both of whom "willingly understood themselves as radicals and used the *integrity of their spiritual vision* as an independent political force."[14] While there was some influence from the nonviolent militant Mohandas Gandhi, the deeper American precedent to the nonviolent social action of the civil rights era was the *fervent pacifist militance* of Anabaptists and Baptists such as Garrison and his followers.

Methodists

The Methodist movement began two hundred years after the Reformation, especially through the extraordinary ministries of John Wesley (1703–1791) and his brother Charles in both the British Isles and the American colonies. Methodism includes the very large United Methodist Church denomination as well as the African Methodist Episcopal denomination, Wesleyans, Nazarenes, and Free Methodists—and later, to a large extent, Pentecostal denominations. However, at first Methodism was an evangelical subgroup within the Episcopal Church, developing vibrant small fellowship groups of devout Christians. In God's timing, and through unabashed, holistic biblical ministry, the tremendous need for special social-political ministry in the face of the ravages of the Industrial Revolution gave even the Wesleys and the earliest Methodists an immediate social-political relevancy.

The Wesleys and their followers consciously rejected the economic-political-social tendencies of most of the Episcopalians and Calvinists who were deathly silent about the social injustices and brutalities of the Industrial Revolution. Such unprophetic silence was apparently largely brought about by the main evangelical leaders' personal economic stake in the "establishment" and by their churches' financial dependence on the robber barons and the captains of industry. In stark contrast, the initial Methodist appeal was especially to the miners, industry workers, and their families.[15] In fact, it is well argued that the Wesleyan movement's impact measurably fortified the British culture, social order, and politics from ungodly influences and consequences of the French Revolution.

Methodism emphasizes markedly the sacred value of every person—woman or man, rich or poor, weak or strong, educated or ignorant. All humans are precious by virtue of being God's image and a recipient of God's love and care. Nevertheless, unswerving self-discipline was also required of every person. Biblical ethical perfection was to be the goal for all individuals as they sought to master their own lives. In fact, very often primary attention was given to the achievement of perfection in each person's temporal life—so much so that every member of a "Methodist Society" was graded every three months. If they passed the quarterly evaluation, they were given "tickets" allowing them to sustain their Methodist affiliation for another three months. Every member's sanctification that was achieved through the consistent practices of personal holiness and self-discipline was the very lifeblood of early Methodism.

The impact of Methodism on America was tremendous from its very inception. In fact, the first popular American religious leader with a truly national recognition was George Whitefield (1714–1770), an Anglican itinerant revival preacher who was known in nearly every community and who helped found the Methodist denomination. The First Great Awakening that he had helped lead brought many people to Christ—and at the same time galvanized the colonies into a national consciousness, based upon shared and mutual reference points of gospel values. This gospel unity was achieved in spite of the fact that official church membership made up only 10 percent of the American population. Still, the church was the most powerful cohesive factor in the country prior to the Revolutionary War, and also in the first decades after it.[16] Even when he studied American culture in 1831, Alexis de Tocqueville was surprised that diversity of denominations did not divide Americans because the "Christian morality is everywhere the same," thanks in large measure to the consistent teachings of national evangelical leaders, especially gifted Methodist preachers like George Whitefield.

Both Baptists and Methodists enjoyed great successes in winning black converts in the frontier revivals associated with the Second Great Awakening of the late eighteenth and early nineteenth centuries. Frontier evangelical outreach was less formal and did not stress the need for an academic clergy, and so appealed widely to less-educated whites and blacks. Methodism especially presented a powerful alternative to traditional Calvinistic religion, not only with its Wesleyan doctrines but also with its personally devoted circuit-riding preachers, fiery camp meetings, and emphasis on sincere spiritual informality in ministry. Like the later Pentecostal movements, openness to unceremonious ministry not only allowed for racially integrated worship, but also encouraged many more blacks to participate directly in ministry.

For the first time many converts were won among the enslaved. Perhaps the most notable illustration of this new dynamic is found in the ministry partnership of Bishop Francis Asbury (1745–1816), a vibrant leader of Methodism in the United States, and Harry Hoosier ("Black Harry"), a dynamic black minister who often preached—with great acclaim—as a substitute for the sickly bishop. Methodism had the added advantage of being heavily influenced by the antislavery teachings of John Wesley, who with his brother Charles had largely failed in establishing ministry in colonial Georgia because they had "denounced slavery in the harshest terms."[17]

The Methodist antislavery perspective was especially strong among African-Americans. The story of Methodist blacks in ministry—as well as black ministers in other denominations—is inseparable from the narrative of the black struggle for liberation and justice. Unlike the white evangelical, who has always had the luxury of debating over the extent to which ministry should touch upon politics, African-American pastors saw the urgent necessity to address the sin of racial injustice with apostolic precision.

An early example is Daniel Coker's *A Dialogue between a Virginian and an African Minister* (1810), in which a black clergyman discusses slavery with a southern slaveholder, eventually winning him over to the righteous claims of abolitionism. Coker was an African Methodist Episcopal minister in Baltimore, Maryland, and fashioned his *Dialogue* as a brilliant overview of historical and biblical themes—even quoting the old Puritan divine Richard Baxter, who himself had declared that slavery was "enough to make the heathen hate Christianity."[18] What is amazing, in fact, is that it was not until the twentieth century that organized opposition to Christianity blossomed among African-Americans in reaction to continued white injustice and escalating secularism. Indeed, Coker was at the vanguard of the myriads of Christian black men and women who would repeatedly denounce slavery, social injustice, and the rampant racism in the white community without ever renouncing Christianity.

Other antebellum African-American Methodist leaders included Frederick Douglass, Harriet Tubman, Sojourner Truth, and Richard Allen, to name just a few. For example, African Methodist Episcopal founder Richard Allen (1760–1831) actively hid escaped slaves in the basement of the first African Methodist Episcopal church, and other black Methodists risked their freedom and even their lives in their resolute resistance to the policies supporting human bondage. Black Methodist Harriet Tubman (1820–1913) was the chief "conductor" of the Underground Railroad, personally saving more than three hundred slaves before the Civil War. During the war this indomitable Christian lady served the Union military as a spy, scout, nurse, and the only woman to strategize and lead a military operation behind enemy lines.

Across the pond, Methodist-influenced statesman William Wilberforce (1759–1833) led the arduous nonviolent fight against slavery in the British Empire. The abolition cause was fought successfully through decades of debate, moral persuasion, and political pressure in the halls of Parliament, and without catastrophic violence such as the American Civil War. Wilberforce in his childhood had been deeply influenced by his uncle and aunt's passionately evangelical Methodism. They had also introduced him to John Newton, the former slave ship captain whose evangelical conversion had led him not only to become an outspoken antislavery advocate, but also to compose one of the most influential and familiar Christian hymns, "Amazing Grace." Although Wilberforce had "lost his faith" in school and university studies, his faith was later restored as an adult, and his ardent evangelical commitment formed and fueled his unbending Parliamentary campaign against human bondage.

As an outspoken citizen and as a member of Parliament, Wilberforce persistently worked the political processes for forty-six years, until he was near his death, to see his legislation finally passed to abolish both slavery and the slave trade throughout the British Empire. However, this often discouraging legislative leadership for Empire-wide abolition stigmatized Wilberforce in English society, occasioned even vicious physical assaults and death threats against him, and also cost him dearly in terms of potential political advancement and power. Nevertheless, he was sustained in this moral and spiritual struggle by his extraordinary oratorical skills and his personal commitment to the Lord Jesus Christ. As the founding father of abolition, he has been called the "Washington of humanity," a title first given to him by Italian statesman Count Pecchio. For his consistent and effective devotion to Jesus Christ and biblical values, Methodist William Wilberforce has deservedly become an eminent evangelical hero.[19]

Some Conclusions

These four classic evangelical perspectives—Lutheran, Calvinist, Anabaptist-Baptist, and Methodist—are all overtly based upon the Bible; were all developed in different times and places by finite, fallible, and flawed men and women; and all contributed heavily to the development of American and British thought, culture, and social, political, and economic institutions and policies. In spite of the occasional rivalries between these denominations, each evangelical Protestant perspective is committed to evangelism and church ministry—and to helping make our life on earth more congruent with biblical teachings.

As members of one body, and as citizens of one kingdom, contemporary evangelicals can richly benefit from all four of these perspectives—transcending their limits, incarnating their godly insights, and traversing more clearly the "Word-enlightened" paths before us.[20]

Bibliography

Ahlstrom, Sydney. *A Religious History of the American People.* New Haven: Yale University Press, 1972.

Bell, Howard, ed. *Minutes of the Proceedings of the National Negro Conventions.* New York: Arno Press, 1969.

Bellah, Robert, and Phillip Hammond. *Varieties of Civil Religion.* New York: Harper & Row, 1980.

Belmonte, Kevin. *Hero for Humanity: A Biography of William Wilberforce.* Colorado Springs: NavPress, 2002.

Britannica Encyclopedia. New York: Britannica, 1911. (This was the last of the encyclopedias that was made up of comprehensive, classic essay articles.)

Britannica Encyclopedia. New York: Britannica, 2003.

Campbell, I. R., and A. S. Skinner. *Adam Smith.* New York: St. Martin's Press, 1982.

Campbell, T. D. *Adam Smith's Science of Morals.* London: Allen and Unwin, 1971.

de Vries, Paul. "Adam Smith's Theory of Justice." *Business and Professional Ethics Journal* 8, no. 1 (Summer 1990): 37–56.

———. "Resource X: Sirkin and Smith on a Neglected Economic Staple." *Business and Professional Ethics Journal* (Fall 1989).

———. *The Taming of the Shrewd*. Nashville: Thomas Nelson, 1992.

de Vries, Paul, et al. *Ethics Applied*. New York: Simon & Schuster, 2000.

DeCaro, Louis. *Fire from the Midst of You: A Religious Life of John Brown*. New York: New York University Press, 2002.

Douglass, Frederick. *Life and Times of Frederick Douglass*. Hartford, CT: Park Publishing, 1881.

Filler, Louis. *The Crusade against Slavery, 1830–1860*. New York: Harper Torchbooks, 1960.

Fiske, John. *The Critical Period of American History, 1783–1789*. New York: Houghton, Mifflin and Company, 1897.

Foner, Philip, ed. *The Life and Writings of Frederick Douglass*. New York: International Publishers, 1975.

Goen, C. C. *Broken Churches, Broken Nation: Denominational Schisms and the Coming of the American Civil War*. Macon, GA: Mercer University Press, 1985.

Jackson, Thomas. *Memoirs of Stonewall Jackson*. Louisville: Prentice Press, 1895.

Jellema, Dirk. "Ethics." In *Contemporary Evangelical Thought*, edited by Carl F. H. Henry. Great Neck, NY: Channel Press, 1957.

Latourette, Kenneth Scott. *Christianity in a Revolutionary Age: The 19th Century Outside Europe*. Grand Rapids: Zondervan, 1961.

———. *A History of Christianity*. New York: Harper & Row, 1953.

Lincoln, C. Eric, and Lawrence Mamiya. *The Black Church in the African American Experience*. Durham, NC: Duke University Press, 1990.

Locke, Marty. *Anti-Slavery in America*. Gloucester, MA: Peter Smith, 1965.

Mayer, Henry. *All on Fire: William Lloyd Garrison and the Abolition of Slavery*. New York: St. Martin's Press, 1998.

Niebuhr, Reinhold. *Children of Light and Children of Darkness*. New York: Charles Scribner's Sons, 1944.

———. *The Nature and Destiny of Man*. Gifford Lectures. New York: Charles Scribner's Sons, 1964.

Noll, Mark. *A History of Christianity in the United States and Canada*. Grand Rapids: Eerdmans, 1992.

———. *Turning Points: Decisive Moments in the History of Christianity*. Grand Rapids: Baker, 1997.

Novak, Michael. *The Spirit of Democratic Capitalism*. New York: Simon & Schuster, 1982.

Painter, Nell. *Sojourner Truth: A Life, a Symbol*. New York: W. W. Norton, 1996.

Porter, Dorothy, ed. *Negro Protest Pamphlets*. New York: Arno Press and *New York Times*, 1969.

Porter, J. M., ed. *Luther: Selected Political Writings*. Philadelphia: Fortress Press, 1957.

Samuels, Warren. "The Political Economy of Adam Smith." *Ethics* 87 (April 1977): 189–207.

Sider, Ronald. "An Anabaptist Perspective," a chapter in a forthcoming book to be published by InterVarsity.

Sirkin, Gerald. "Resource X and the Theory of Retro-Development." In *Economics of Resources*, edited by R. Leiter and S. Friedlander. New York: City University of New York, 1976.

Smith, Adam. *An Inquiry into the Nature and Causes of the Wealth of Nations*. Indianapolis: Liberty Classics, 1981.

————. *The Theory of Moral Sentiments*. Indianapolis: Liberty Classics, 1976.

Stout, Henry. *The Divine Dramatist: George Whitefield and the Rise of Modern Evangelicalism.* Grand Rapids: Eerdmans, 1991.

Taylor, E. L. Hebden. *The Christian Philosophy of Law, Politics, and the State.* Nutley, NJ: The Craig Press, 1966.

Tinder, Glenn. *The Political Meaning of Christianity: An Interpretation.* Eugene, OR: Wipf and Stock Publishers, 2000.

Troeltsch, Ernst. *The Social Teachings of the Christian Churches.* New York: Harper Torchbooks, first published 1911, translated 1931, printed by Harper Torchbooks 1960.

Walker, David. *Appeal to the Colored Citizens of the World, but in particular, and very expressly, to those of the United States of America.* Boston: D. Walker, 1829.

Warfield, Benjamin. *Perfectionism.* Philadelphia: Presbyterian and Reformed Publishing Company, 1980.

West, E. G. *Adam Smith.* Indianapolis: Liberty Press, 1976.

Westbrook, Robert. "Nullifiers and Insurrectionists: America's Antigovernment Tradition." *The Christian Century*, March 8, 2000, 275–78.

Wolterstorff, Nicholas. *Until Justice and Peace Embrace.* Grand Rapids: Eerdmans, 1983.

Wyatt-Brown, Bertram. *Lewis Tappan and the Evangelical War against Slavery.* New York: Athenaeum, 1971.

4

The Mainline Protestant Tradition in the Twentieth Century

Positive Lessons and Cautionary Tales

Max L. Stackhouse and Raymond R. Roberts

THE FIRES OF the Second Great Awakening gave birth to a kind of ecclesiastical "united front" whose distinctive union of revivalism and social reform left an indelible mark on what some have called the "Protestant Century" in American life.[1] It would be too much to say that Protestants were united in ecumenical bliss at the time of the American Centennial in 1876. Fractures within denominations created by the Civil War persisted, and newly freed slaves were striking out on their own, developing their own Methodist and Baptist traditions out of evangelicalism, African traditions, and a dedication to prophetic social justice. Yet despite these divisions, Protestants largely stood united in upholding the political, economic, and social order. They defended the constitutional democracy of the Union that had been so recently tested in the Civil War. They supported a free economy that was booming in the industrial cities of the East and expanding across the free soil of the Western frontier. They also supported a Victorian morality that had evolved out of an older Puritanism and that selectively enforced a new prudery and stereotyped roles for men and women. There were dissenting voices to be sure—socialists, anarchists, free love advocates, proto-feminists, communitarian utopians, prophets of new revelations or revolutions—some militantly violent, some thoughtfully reformist;[2] but the U.S. defeat of Spain in the Spanish-American War a quarter century later seemed to confirm Protestantism's hold on the future. It was to be a "Christian Century."

As the new century dawned, however, new problems were apparent. On the social front, the frontier was closing in the West. Immigrants flooded American cities, creating problems that were becoming increasingly hard to ignore. Tensions between labor and management were exploding in a series of violent, and violently suppressed, strikes, while poverty and crime haunted the growing slums. Disagreements over how the church should respond to these developments split the united front. The splintering led to two new broad movements, each claiming rootage in the great traditions of the past: one that we loosely call evangelicalism and another that we loosely call mainline Protestantism.[3]

Both movements sought to address the alienation and dislocation of their times. Evangelicals such as Dwight L. Moody and Billy Sunday mobilized crusades to save the cities by converting individual souls. Their imitators took tent revivals to every growing town, offering hot gospel messages of salvation from eternal damnation, and offering entertainment as well, to those burdened by the lonely drudgery of farm life or the temptations and alienations of urban life. They introduced a new, pious aesthetic with their hymnody and advanced a strict moralism to constrain the temptations offered by gamblers, barkeepers, and dance-hall ladies.

Although many mainline Protestants joined these crusades, they increasingly doubted whether revivalism's focus on individual salvation was able to address the social crises associated with industrialization and urbanization. As crop failures, recessions, lockouts, and violent strikes rocked the nation, and as anarchist and socialist ideas captured the loyalties of the more radical workers, pioneering thinkers such as Washington Gladden, Richard T. Ely, Walter Rauschenbusch, and Shailer Matthews searched the Scriptures and the new disciplines of sociology and economics for better ways to understand the emerging conditions. They developed a practical theology to support a "Social Gospel," one that could guide their efforts to "Christianize the social order."[4] And they developed new para-ecclesial institutions to incarnate their ideas: from the YMCA and YWCA to settlement houses; from mission societies to workers' or farmers' associations; from Sunday schools to colleges.

Many leaders of the American denominations that evolved into what we now call "mainline" joined this movement: the American Baptist Churches, the Disciples of Christ, the Episcopal Church (USA), the Evangelical Lutheran Church in America, the Presbyterian Church (USA), the Reformed Church in America, the Congregational Christian Churches who joined with the Evangelical and Reformed Church to become the United Church of Christ, and the United Methodist Church, plus several African-American denominations.

Most of them began working together in the first decade of the century in the newly formed Federal Council of the Churches, the precursor of the National Council of Churches. One of its first actions was the unanimous adoption in 1908 of a resolution on "The Church and Modern Industry," later expanded and called the "Social Creed." It called for respect for the workers, a fraternal spirit between labor and capital, arbitration in disputes, protection from dangerous machinery or occupational hazards, the abolition of child labor, a living wage for all employees, and provisions for people in their old age. During the first half of the twentieth century, church-related publishing houses, mission boards, and "social responsibility" departments developed a large repertoire of materials and programs that extended these themes to many areas of American society, and through mission board policies, around the world.

The optimism that they could bring this world closer to the New Jerusalem was soon challenged intellectually by the growing impact of Darwin, Freud, Marx, and Nietzsche, who saw more destructive and purely material forces driving human affairs than the social gospelers acknowledged. Some mainline Protestants heard a kind of secular prophecy in these voices and took it as a crisis in the Social Gospel message, one that demanded a more radical theology with a deepened sense of social sin. Nevertheless, for the most part, the optimism continued. It was challenged repeatedly but not shattered; not even by the bitter fighting and great losses of World War I, the violence of the Russian Revolution soon thereafter, the Depression, the rise of Fascism in Europe, or World War II and the Cold War that followed. The optimistic spirit of the Social Gospel and the Federal Council of Churches prepared the way for the New Deal;[5] and it, modified by more realistic assessments of power relationships, contributed to the mobilization of the American population against the threats from the neo-pagan ideology of the Nazis and the secularist ideology of Marxism-Leninism. Moreover, this optimism continued over decades for most of the mainline Protestantism into the struggle for civil rights under the leadership of Martin Luther King Jr.

This movement had its triumphs, but many in the leadership of mainline Protestantism, those in the seminaries and those in the church bureaucracies, became more and more alienated from American society and sometimes even contemptuous of the piety and patriotism of most church members. The "New Left" movements against the Vietnam War, with which many mainline clergy identified, alienated many politically; the common view of these same clergy that capitalism was the source of selfishness and poverty while socialism had the message of community and sharing alienated many economically; and the development of "situation ethics" and "contextualism" in morality alienated many culturally. The churches of mainline Protestantism began losing members rapidly, declining by roughly one-third in the last third of the century. Meanwhile, the evangelical churches were growing. More dismaying to the leaders, the actual social impact of the mainline seemed to decline, while evangelical influence, plus that of certain Pentecostal, fundamentalist, and neo-Anabaptist movements, seemed to increase. It may be too soon to do so fully, but we may be able assess the mainline's engagement with various spheres of life and their theological bases for it over the last century and identify some positive lessons and cautionary tales in ways that offer insight to both mainline Protestants and evangelicals as we face a new century, which we surely must do together.

A Century of Engagement

Social engagement by the mainline Protestant churches, of course, did not begin with the Social Gospel; it had its roots in the Puritan belief that God called the church to form society according to the Divine Law and Purpose. The Pilgrims at Plymouth and the Puritans at Boston, like their earlier Reformation forebearers, held a "world-formative" view. They believed that the gospel required them to establish a new righteousness in society and politics as well as in the church. Later, preachers of many stripes joined the agitators for independence from England and supported the framers of the Constitution and the Bill of Rights. Movements for social reform pervaded the antebellum revivals. This heritage, of course, shaped the social gospelers' new engagement with society. What was new was the way the social gospelers read the Bible. Focusing on the prophets and on Jesus' message of the kingdom of God, they understood that, despite the many rebellious, even demonic, social forces in the world, God's law and God's purpose are, in principle, the decisive governing, ordering, and redeeming power in the world. They did not believe that God actualized that law and purpose by fiat, but that God called humans to be the agents of love and good order in the world, and that a primary mark of fidelity is participation in the struggle to build up communities of justice that allow life to flourish.

Those who held this view disputed the understanding of the gospel held by those evangelicals who, from their perspective, identified the kingdom too narrowly with the church of obedient saints, distinct from the world, or individualized it as a personal relationship with Jesus. They accused many evangelicals of spiritualizing the moral implications out of the kingdom and of postponing the sociohistorical implications of the gospel to the next world. They argued, instead, that God rules the world through the power of the kingdom, the dynamic of a loving and just spirit of renewal that is now imminent in the world and discernable in various movements for justice and peace. They believed that God calls the churches and all people of faith to bear witness to this spiritual presence, to exemplify the dynamic by energetic action for the good, and to bring it to full flower in every sphere of life. A number of variations on these views of the kingdom shaped a more or less unified posture toward the world that has characterized mainline Protestantism in America for most of the twentieth century.

Although some Social Gospel pioneers had been deeply involved in ecumenical exchange over the century, especially since the World Missionary Conference of 1910, the mainline way of defining Protestantism was belatedly modified by international ecumenical interactions. These pioneers were familiar with the Evangelical Social Congress that had taken place in Amsterdam led by Abraham Kuyper, with the new work among the poor in England by William Booth (which became the Salvation Army), with the ethical theologies of the Germans Albrecht Ritschl and Ernst Troeltsch, and with the growing missionary cooperation around the world—all near the turn of the century. Large numbers of the Social Gospel leaders went to Europe to study. This was, of course, sharply curtailed during World War II, but a new Euro-American cooperation, with a new openness to the churches of the emerging nations thereafter (notably established in the Madras Conference), was celebrated in Amsterdam in 1948—with pronounced accents on a developing ecumenical spirit.

In the last third of the twentieth century, however, these contacts were modified further by new developments, especially the growing influence of Karl Barth in Europe, of Eastern Orthodoxy through the World Council of Churches, of a renewed Roman Catholicism after Vatican II (1962–65), and of new movements of "liberation" in Latin America and at home. These interactions influenced the ways in which mainline Protestants and their ecumenically active partner Christians modified their inherited approach to social issues. In the pages that follow, we offer an interpretation of these developments by identifying three major areas of mainline Protestant social engagement—economics, politics, and family life—and then surveying another set of deeper theological themes that lie just below the surface of all these issues: the ways that mainline Protestants and evangelicals have approached Scripture and interpreted it by the use of tradition, reason, and experience.

I. Economy

Mainline Protestants made a lasting impact upon the economic institutions of American society during the twentieth century.[6] In the deeper background, most of the American churches had, without explicitly intending capitalism in its modern forms, encouraged those attitudes and habits of hard work, disciplined consumption, and rational calculation of the costs and gains associated with every stage of production and distribution that we associate with Max Weber's hypothesis about the Protestant ethic and its relationship to modern capitalism.[7] This hypothesis was first developed in a series of essays published in Germany when the Social Gospel was in its infancy. It attempted to explain why, if economics works entirely by natural laws, as was conventionally accepted in intellectual and business circles, it develops among some parts of the population in an area in one way and among other parts in other ways; and why whole cultures seem to develop in one direction while others develop quite differently. Weber argued that the Reformation had, in a fundamental way, shaped the industrializing economy of modernity. The social gospelers thought that if it had done so unintentionally, a new, intentional reformation could also tame and humanize the capitalism that had become ethically unguided.

The kingdom of God, as the social gospelers understood it, was not a fixed or natural order, where some were born as lords of the manor and others born to be peasants, or some to be owners of factories and others to be sellers of their labor only; but was a revolutionary dynamic that called for social change. But there were several competing theories of social change at the time. The social gospelers' understanding of the gospel led them to resist the social-Darwinist notion that economic life necessarily consisted of a dog-eat-dog world of unfettered competition governed by the law of tooth and claw. Instead, they argued that poverty was the result of either a badly formed religion or an individual's sloth or disordered life that needed religious discipline, or both.[8]

These social gospelers shared with the socialists the view that there is no way to a better world than through industrialization, but they wanted to humanize the process, modulate its raw edges, and sweeten its bitter fruits by reform rather than by trying to overthrow it by revolution. They sometimes spoke of socialism, and some were more radical than others; but it was most often a pre-Marxist, even romantic, "spirit of brotherhood," a communitarian-cooperative spirit that they sought. We see this most clearly in their mission efforts. The mainline Protestant mission boards founded schools and colleges both at home and abroad that emphasized science and technology, commerce and "mechanics" (engineering), accounting and economics at the same time as they were agitating against the dislocations of industrialization and urbanization and founding model villages for workers to get them out of the slums. They viewed the exodus from feudal economies, the domestication of capitalist excess, a living wage so each worker could support his family, and the recovery of lost community as progressive manifestations of the kingdom.

Over the course of the century, mainline Protestants continued their engagement with economic issues but modified the Social Gospel approach. During the Depression and World War II, a school of thinkers and activists criticized the romanticism, pacifism, and optimism of the Social Gospel, even as the New Deal turned many of its positions into public policy. The newer voices, often following Reinhold Niebuhr, took the name "Christian Realism" for themselves. Niebuhr and the other realists wrestled less with the communitarian forms of socialism than with the blood and steel of national socialism and Marxist-Leninist socialism. Niebuhr, Paul Tillich, James Luther Adams, John Bennett, and Walter Muelder in America, and Karl Barth, Joseph Hromadka, and Arthur Rich in Europe, all influential teachers in the middle years of the twentieth century, differed in many things; but they all were convinced that Marxist analysis could lay bare some key aspects of the viciousness of capitalist practice, although they were suspicious of Lenin and even more of Stalin. Thus, they selectively adopted Marxian tools for the interpretation of history, and in that sense they were all socialists. Yet they were also acutely aware of the fact that socialism in either its nationalist or proletarian forms was driven by utopian illusions, a false anthropology, and a militant contempt for profound religion and its social meanings. Indeed, followers of those forms of socialism tended to become idolatrous worshipers of their own social group—their race or their class—and committed all sorts of atrocities.

These leading Protestant teachers also sought a more accurate reading of history and a more realistic anthropology, and their convictions led them to believe that democracy was both possible and necessary. Thus, they called for the democratization of economic life, although they were often more preoccupied with defending political democracy against the threats posed by Fascism and Communism than with economic theory itself. Still, they conveyed a suspicion of capitalism to their students, even if it was a capitalism constrained by growing bodies of law and by democratic policies that gave unions and government power to check the abuses of a free market, and that provided a safety net for widows, orphans, the ill, the elderly, and handicapped citizenry. Subsequent developments reinforced this suspicion.

During the 1960s and 1970s, civil rights leaders refocused mainline Protestant thinking by pointing out not only the discrimination institutionalized in the Jim Crow laws of the South, but also economic discrimination in the industrialized centers of the North. People commonly remember that civil rights leaders led the struggle for the right to vote and for legislation that ended legal segregation and racial discrimination in places of public accommodation. Less often remembered is that these civil rights leaders also led the "Poor People's March," a rather large demonstration in Washington, DC, that, with much other agitation, brought about a national policy called the "War on Poverty."

During this same period, many "third world" leaders adopted liberation theology. Using a more overt Marxist form of social analysis, they saw the world as being increasingly divided into the rich and poor nations due to the exploitation by the ever-expanding corporations from the rich nations that plunged the rest of the world into "dependency"—this in spite of the fact that those nations sought capital from abroad.

These views captured the moral imagination of a number of leaders in the mainline Protestant leadership in the last third of the twentieth century, although others had doubts and reservations about them.[9] Some in the seminaries and bureaucracies of mainline Protestantism saw the overcoming of poverty through liberation movements as the key mark of God's redemptive kingdom. In fact, liberation theology as it developed in the anticolonial movements spawned by the crumbling of empires following World War II seemed to become the unofficial orthodoxy in the activist wings in many mainline Protestant circles. Ecumenical church bodies gave these voices a hearing and sometimes scuttled other programs of ministry to support these developments. Literally thousands of pastors went to Latin America or Cuba or Eastern Europe as if on a pilgrimage to the New Jerusalem, often returning to preach fiery sermons against the multinational corporations and the political parties that backed them—although wings of the major communions carried out other ministries and supported other theological agendas.

However, the liberationist ideas were not widely accepted by the laity. Many simply tuned out—some developing alternative groups outside the churches to connect their faith with the realities of contemporary business life through programs in the "ministry of the laity," and others turning to the renewal of missions, liturgy, Christian education, and advocacy of community development. As enthusiasts for liberation theology gravitated to the denominational centers of power, they became further removed from the congregations. A growing number of scholars began to question the socialist and liberationist assumptions that guided the increasingly frequent statements on the economy passed by mainline bodies. They too opposed the economic exploitation of the poor peasants and workers, but they believed in democratic capitalism as the corollary of the faith they knew and were pilloried by professional colleagues and leaders of the mainline for that view.[10]

Looking for other alternatives, some ecumenical leaders turned to the study of "secular theology." The German martyr Dietrich Bonhoeffer had advocated a "religionless Christianity" for a "humanity come of age" in a scientific era, and this was interpreted to be a critique of the pietism of many churches; the neglect of the religiously alienated youth, workers, intellectuals, and artists; and the failure of the faithful to address continuing issues of racism, poverty, urban distress, and existential angst. These leaders were fueled by "secularization theory" among sociologists and social theorists—the idea that "modernization," "urbanization," and "technological development" inevitably bring with them "secularization"—a theory now widely disputed by social scientists. Still, the critiques of the church and its ways on these bases by Peter Berger, Gibson Winter, and Harvey Cox, and the "Death of God theologians," in spite of reservations by such leaders as Charles West, Robert Spike, Roger Shinn, and Gabriel Fackre, became the standard fare of mainline pastors, seminarians, and "progressive" lay leaders for a time. This too fed the developing split between the activist elements in the denominations and many of the parishioners—almost as much as liberation theologies. Some pastors, college chaplains, and community organizers began to think that "church work" was irrelevant to what God was doing in the world.

In a rather sad way, these developments meant that the intellectual and ecclesiastical leadership of the mainline churches were utterly unprepared for, and some were quite angry about, developments that displaced their heartfelt commitments to socialism, liberation theology, and secular programs to do good. The Thatcher-Reagan elections and policies reversed the trends to extend welfare provisions at home that had been the hallmark of most Western powers since the Depression. It no longer appeared to be an international fact that socialism was the wave of the future, and movements for "faith-based social services" were renewed. The Soviet Union collapsed, and China turned capitalist under financial pressures and the loss of moral and spiritual legitimacy. Many abandoned support for Liberation movements, while the United States funded counterinsurgency actions against militant pro-socialist movements.

Today, most third world countries are trying to become democratic and to dismantle their statist economies. They seek to get multinational corporations to locate in their countries and call for more economic cooperation with the United States and the European Union. Meanwhile, at the grass roots, the people in Latin America and around the world have opted for evangelicalism and, particularly, Pentecostalism, while even the Catholic Church and mainline Protestants have become more charismatic or are in decline. Globalization continues at an ever-increasing pace and is including higher percentages of the world's population in newly created middle classes, even though the distance between the very rich and the very poor also increases. Today mainline churches are working hard, often against the mental habits of a century, to find new, more responsible ways of shaping capitalism and reforming the global economy into a global civil society that provides more equitable opportunities for those still left behind. It is, in a way, a quest for a new Social Gospel now on a world scale, but without the utopian hope or real prospects of a socialist future.

II. Politics

Mainline Protestants also made lasting contributions to the political realm during the twentieth century. The deep history of these contributions is rooted in the fact that those who had been deeply formed in the Reformation traditions as modified by the political liberalism of the Enlightenment drafted the American Constitution. Many heirs of this tradition had supported the abolition movement that led to a bloody Civil War. Proponents of the Social Gospel lived in the shadow of Abraham Lincoln. They accepted the view that constitutional democracy was the structural, political form of the faith and that human rights, with which all are "endowed by their Creator," had to be extended to those previously treated as chattel. In contrast to those who turned only to personal evangelism after the end of the Civil War, the Social Gospel leaders reengaged political power domestically in order to address the economic and social crises of the day.

At the turn of the century, the Spanish-American War brought the United States out of its relative isolation to become something of a world power. The victory confirmed in the mind of many that Protestant democracy was superseding the hierarchical and statist patterns of authority of European Catholicism. The fact that the United States would play a role internationally in the twentieth century became even clearer during World War I. Politics would henceforth have an international dimension. However, some heirs of the Social Gospel movement resisted this idea. Kirby Page, editor of the largely pacifist and soft socialist *World Tomorrow*, and Charles Clayton Morrison, editor of the mainline Protestant journal *The Christian Century*, were disgusted by the mindless slaughter in the trenches of World War I. They resisted efforts to involve America in the disturbing developments in Europe and Asia that would eventually lead to World War II. They did not resist because they were pacifists, in the peace-church sense of eschewing all violence, or because they were complete isolationists. To be sure, they had a very high threshold of doubt about any use of coercive force, but they also supported America's entrance into the League of Nations. They articulated a more peace-oriented stance mainly because they believed God had given America a special role to manifest the kingdom as a light to the world. In one sense, they were merely following George Washington's warning in his Farewell Address: "Beware of entangling foreign alliances."

They feared that intervening in world affairs would corrupt America, that its politics would decay into propaganda, that foreign international bankers and munitions manufacturers would invade its economy, and that national interests played out on a world stage would distort America's internal moral mission. They counseled Americans not to risk our "goodness and moralism," but to stay home.[11]

Reinhold Niebuhr, John C. Bennett, and other Christian realists engaged in a bitter debate with this wing of mainline Protestantism. They challenged the Social Gospel establishment on this point by retrieving the Augustinian doctrine of human nature. Human sinfulness, they said, made it impossible to achieve the kingdom of God in history. The kingdom of God existed on the far side of history as an "impossible possibility." As a possibility, it revealed the fallen character of all human social structures, summoned humility in moral agents, and created moral tension that could energize efforts for social change. As an impossibility, it authorized a political realism and ratified the tragic necessity of just uses of coercion and even war when failure to join the fight would bring greater tyranny or injustice.[12]

Guided by this more pessimistic view of human nature, Christian realists defended democracy and called the nation to face the challenges of Fascism and, later, Communism. Their ideas about the political realm and the need for balancing power in the world permeated deeply into both the church and society. In 1942, the Federal Council of Churches adopted the "Six Pillars of Peace" statement that outlined a way to secure a "just and durable peace" following the war. John Foster Dulles, who chaired the commission that produced this document, went on to become secretary of state. George Kennan, former ambassador to the Soviet Union and architect of America's post–World War II foreign policy, spoke for many when he credited Reinhold Niebuhr for giving him the insights into human nature that guided him throughout his career.[13]

Moreover, in fresh research, the British scholar-pastor Canon John Nurser has documented in extended detail the ways in which, from 1939 until 1947, leading ecumenical Protestant figures worked with key figures in developing the Bretton Woods agreements. Anticipating a postwar need for economic stability and development, they formed the Commission for a Just and Durable Peace, the Church's Commission on International Affairs, and later the Joint Committee on Religious Liberty. All of this was done under the auspices of the Federal Council of Churches, with close connections to the emerging World Council of Churches and the International Missionary Conference. These organizations, notably led by Lutheran O. Frederick Nolde, Congregationalist Richard Fagley, Baptist M. Searle Bates, and Presbyterian John A. Mackay, among others, were dedicated to shaping what they then called a "new world order" that would honor human rights. They worked closely with Jacob Blaustein and Joseph Proskauer of the American Jewish Committee and with twelve bishops of the Roman Catholic Church to encourage the formation of the drafting committees of the United Nations Charter Committee and the committee that composed the Universal Declaration on Human Rights and deeply shaped their results. Further, they worked through their church and synagogue contacts at the local level to build the popular support for what they were doing. In fact, the more of this history that is dug out, the clearer it becomes that they supplied much of the intellectual and ethical substance that formed these so-called "secular" developments.[14]

The advent of nuclear weapons at the end of World War II, however, signaled a new chapter in mainline Protestants' reflection on war and power. The indiscriminate and terrible power of nuclear weapons caused many to question Christian realism's prudential calculation of consequences. Paul Ramsey led many mainline leaders to rediscover the just war doctrine, which had been a part of the Christian tradition since Augustine and had been refined in several respects by Thomas Aquinas and most of the Reformers.[15]

This doctrine teaches that the use of force by legitimate political authorities, at least in police actions but also in some wars, was not outside the domain of God's rule or the magistrate's calling to seek justice as a way of loving those neighbors who needed defense from victimization or needed punishment for doing harm to others. It teaches that political authorities that deploy lethal force must follow ethical principles in deciding when to go to war and in conducting war. Ramsey did not object to using nuclear weapons against legitimate military targets but made a persuasive case that nuclear deterrence that targeted noncombatants was morally unacceptable. His influential writings led many mainline denominations, such as the Methodist Church, to issue papers calling for unilateral nuclear disarmament. Other mainline leaders, extending Ramsey's argument about target discrimination, declared that modern warfare could never adequately discriminate between combatants and noncombatants. This fact of modern war, coupled with the possibility that conventional wars could escalate into a nuclear conflagration, led many mainline church leaders to adopt a de facto pacifistic position that opposed any use of military force.

During the 1960s, mainline Protestant attitudes toward war and peace underwent yet another shift. The national offices of all the mainline Protestant denominations were deeply engaged in the civil rights movements of this time. Their activism and moral passion helped bring about new civil rights legislation that is one of the great triumphs of this heritage. Many saw the "freedom movement" in the United States as the sister movement to the struggles of the Vietnamese against reactionary forces, and of the liberation forces in Central America against authoritarian governments in the region. The arguments that the latter two movements were driven by Marxist ideologies quite different from King's theology were overlooked. Many who had demonstrated with Martin Luther King and used his "active nonviolence" to bring about progressive social change with regard to race, followed his famous "Sermon at Riverside Church" against the war in Vietnam and developed a deep and lasting suspicion of government leaders and American purpose. Many defined political engagement less as building coalitions to advance policies called for by clear theological principles, and more as using the techniques of the protest demonstration to oppose policies or practices in operation.

Traditional "peace churches" such as the Anabaptist and Quaker wings of Protestantism had always opposed just war theory, believing that it merely provided moral window dressing for killing. They believed that the message and life of Jesus taught that all forms of violence are incompatible with the faith. They urged believers not to take the destiny of the world into their own hands but to trust it to God. The Quaker Roland Bainton, the Mennonite John Howard Yoder, and the Methodist Stanley Hauerwas articulated this position and inspired many mainline Protestants to take a more pacifistic stance.[16] Other mainline Protestant leaders opposed them, believing that this pacifism undercut the legitimacy of Christian participation in not only police and military matters, but also all government, since every effective regime must accumulate, sometimes threaten, and occasionally use force for the establishment and defense of justice. The influence of the new pacifism is revealed by the fact that during the last decades of the century, many denominations, including the United Church of Christ, the Presbyterian Church (USA), and the United Methodist Church, have declared themselves "just-peace churches." Most mainline church leaders and the National Council of Churches opposed the Gulf War of 1991[17] and the war in Iraq. An exception to this trend toward isolation and pacifism was when several denominations supported the use of military force under United Nations auspices in Kosovo, citing as justification the overwhelming humanitarian need and the importance of "just-peacemaking."[18]

Early in the century, Social Gospel proponents viewed America as a Christian nation and believed that God called them to Christianize society. They hoped that the twentieth century would be the Christian Century. This attitude underwent considerable revision over the course of the century. When the pacifist wing of the Social Gospel movement failed to keep America out of World War II, some declared that they could no longer call America a Christian nation. During the 1950s and 1960s, however, most mainline Protestants viewed the Cold War as a conflict between Christian America and global atheistic Communism. In the disillusionment that followed Vietnam, however, many church leaders resisted any identification of God's will or way with Americanism. By the time of the counterinsurgency policies against Latin liberation movements, some were comparing the trends in the United States to those in Germany in the 1930s. Many were heavily influenced by Karl Barth's "Barmen Declaration," which refused to subordinate church teachings to state policies. Toward the end of the century, theologians of various liberationist stripes began deconstructing America's political history and its claims to any serious Christian influence itself. They charged that the idea of a Christian America had been a tool for oppressing the Native Americans, African-Americans, other people of color, and women. They accused Christian realists and their heirs of ignoring the malevolent side of the American experiment and for articulating a theology that justified political triumphalism in the world and too easily accommodated the evils of racism and sexism at home. These charges do not go undisputed.

By century's end, however, most mainline church leaders no longer hold that America is a Christian nation, as evidenced by the criticism many of them leveled at Franklin Graham's inaugural prayer for George W. Bush and their widespread contempt for the piety and politics that are apparently driving the "Christian Right" and the current administration. Many have given up efforts at Christianizing society by means of overtly advocating biblically and theologically based principles in public life, in favor of an intentional "inclusivity" and "diversity" couched in liberal political terms. This has left many mainline Protestants searching for new ways to faithfully engage a pluralistic and fallen society. Some now are exploring, with ecumenically open evangelicals and Roman Catholics, the prospects of a reconstructive "public theology" that also takes wider global developments into account.[19]

III. Family and Cultural Institutions

The mainline's impact upon the family has been more ambiguous than its impact on the economic and political spheres. Historically, of course, we know that Christianity came to promote patterns of monogamy with a higher level of equality between husband and wife than the surrounding cultures in which it developed, although patriarchy was never fully erased. This was formalized in the Roman Catholic and Eastern Orthodox theories of marriage as a sacrament, and later in the Lutheran idea that family is an "order of creation" and the Calvinist idea that marriage is a covenantal relationship. Each understanding recognized that marriage fulfilled a basic natural drive, involved a mutual and voluntary contract as well as the gracious gift of love, and led to the formation of a household for sustaining companionship and the nurturing of children. These classic ideas underwent various adaptations over time, as can be seen in the various liturgies of the marriage ceremony that came to dominate the West.

At the dawn of the twentieth century, the proponents of the Social Gospel generally assumed and reinforced Victorian views of the family, although they more frequently advocated greater equality for women and more often supported the suffrage movements than did other Christians. They saw the "Christian home" as a haven of morality, propriety, and affection, a locus for the cultivation of the tender virtues and moral character in contrast to the harsh worlds of business competition and new industrial factories. The image of the ideal family also reinforced stereotyped roles for men and women and was propagated by church, school, the medical profession, and moralistic politicians—such as those trying to outlaw prostitution, child labor, and pornography. For example, the social gospelers argued for prohibition and Sabbath observance because they would have a salutary effect on the family. Yet the family was not the central focus of either the Social Gospel leaders or the subsequent Christian realists.

The Depression put a terrific strain on the American family, but the pressures on the family during the second half of the twentieth century were even greater. Women who worked in the factories during World War II sometimes relinquished their positions to the ex-GIs when they came home; but many found that buying that dream house in the suburbs took two incomes. That second income, however, also conferred a new possible independence if the guy who marched off to fight evil was less than heroic when he came home. Technology in many forms invited changed patterns of life—new appliances made housework less time consuming, birth control devices made intimacy less consequential, new medical procedures made abortion less risky, a wider availability of cars offered a new mobility and privacy, and industrial machinery meant that women could perform the workplace tasks as well as men, blurring traditional role definitions. These and other sociological developments challenged traditional conceptions of the family.

The churches grew in the 1950s, and during this time mainline Protestant pastors increasingly turned to psychological understandings of the faith and morality that treated persons rather than forming institutions. Many mainline church leaders were reluctant to "impose their values" on anyone else, and many declared old standards obsolete. They offered pastoral ministry that tended to be strong on "therapeutic" care and weak on normative guidance about the conduct of life.

A domestic "cultural revolution" of the 1960s radicalized this "tolerant or permissive" religious ethos. Popular culture fostered "sex, drugs, and rock and roll" and reflected disenchantment with traditional institutions of many kinds, the family included. Whatever the social causes, between the 1960s and the start of the new century, there was a momentous increase in divorce, so that nearly half of all marriages today do not last. Of this same period, as Don Browning has recently observed:

- nonmarital births increased from 5 percent to 33 percent in the U.S.
- out-of-wedlock births increased tenfold to 25 percent among Anglo Americans and 70 percent among African Americans

- the marriage rate declined by 30 percent
- the number of people cohabiting increased eightfold
- evidence grows that children from single-parent, cohabiting, blended families have more problems with crime, more health and substance abuse problems, and lower earning capacity[20]

Especially worrisome to some religious leaders is the way in which a secular view of marriage as a private, temporary contract, entered into for the advantage of the parties, eroded classic sacramental and covenantal views of marriage. While in economic and political life, mainline Protestants criticized individualistic autonomy and arbitrary contracts as a morally insufficient way of organizing human relationships, that is precisely the view of the family that triumphed in the popular mind. No longer was sex viewed as a gift of God designed for procreation and the celebration of love within a publicly approved, sacred, bonded relationship: it was seen as a recreational option, a natural happening, or an entirely private choice.[21]

Although many mainline Protestants faced these changes with a great deal of anxiety, a considerable number of leaders adopted the attitudes of the social science of the 1970s and '80s. Many believed that these changes were benign for children and adults and generally welcomed the greater adult freedoms these changes afforded those caught in unhappy or violent marriages. Sensibilities inherited from the civil rights movement led many to attribute the exclusions of women in many areas of public authority to a sexism comparable to racism, and the decline of marriage among persons of color to previous victimization or unimportant cultural differences. The influence of feminist theologies led many to criticize traditional forms of marriage as patriarchal and to advocate greater mutuality in marriage and easier exit from it by "no-fault" divorce.[22] Concerns for the rights of gays led some mainline church leaders to mute their support for traditional heterosexual marriage.[23] Indeed, debates about the ordination of homosexual persons and the possible recognition of same-sex marriages by the churches have been a rancorous and divisive issue in the mainline Protestant churches for a quarter of a century. At stake are not only questions of church polity and the discernment of what is genuine and what is false prophecy, but the fundamental question of the authority of the Bible and of classic theological doctrines on matters of "personal" morality.[24] All but one of the major denominations (United Church of Christ) have sought to preserve something of the classical traditions in official teachings or pronouncements; but they also have strong minority voices who are persistent advocates of the full acceptance of gay and lesbian persons and behaviors as coequal in moral standing to heterosexual ones.

Mainline Protestants have yet to make a concerted, institutionalized effort to address the dissolution of the American family. Evidence that families around the world are undergoing similar changes to those experienced in America has not received much response either.[25] Many denominational leaders have viewed evangelically oriented organizations attempting to address "family values," such as Promise Keepers, with deep suspicion. They often sharply oppose both evangelical and Roman Catholic attempts to limit abortion, prevent the ordination of gay candidates for ministry, stop legislative approval of "civil unions" for same-sex marriages, alter sex education in the public schools, which treats all sexual orientations and family forms as equal in value, or gain support for homeschooling or private and parochial schools that could teach other values.

These issues regarding sex and marriage are closely related to issues of the media and of higher education, for they have to do with the moral formation of the next generation. Over the course of the twentieth century, mainline Protestants have gradually disengaged from the media. At the early part of the century, they welcomed radio as a way to bring the Christian message to the masses. Federal regulations required the national radio (and later television) networks to offer free public service programming. Networks offered this programming to mainline Protestants in recognition of their place in society. To coordinate these efforts, the Federal Council of Churches created a Radio Commission. During the 1960s, the Federal Communications Commission reduced these public service requirements, and mainline Protestants declined to make up the difference by paying for airtime. By the end of the century, most voices on radio and television were evangelical, funded by voluntary contributions.[26]

The mainline Protestant engagement with the visual media also dissolved over the course of the century. Early in the century, the Federal Council of Churches and other mainline denominations protested and boycotted movies with offensive language, violence, and nudity. During the 1940s, the Federal Council of Churches established a Film Commission that produced educational films for use in churches and encouraged commercial film producers to accurately portray religion in their films. By midcentury they joined their voices with Catholic and Jewish organizations and forced the Motion Picture Producers and Distributors of America to give up self-regulation and create the Production Code Administration (PCA). During the middle of the century, the PCA was powerful enough that most producers thought it was better to consult the PCA before filming rather than make cuts later. In 1950, when the Federal Council of Churches became the National Council of Churches, they merged the Film Commission with its Radio Commission, creating the Broadcast and Film Commission. This commission produced film reviews and study guides for church members but ceased operation in 1978, a victim of budget cuts.

When competition from television eroded studio profits, the Motion Picture Association of America (formerly the Motion Picture Producers and Distributors of America) responded by creating a ratings system for films. This enabled Hollywood to produce racier films than audiences could see on television. In

1985, the National Council of Churches issued a report deploring the impact that depictions of sex and violence have on children. At the dawn of a new millennium, American media corporations dominate the global media markets. The thought that the mainline Protestant churches would seriously engage the media and provide a moral check on the industry, much less protest and boycott films the way they did in the early part of the century, seems far-fetched.[27]

The ways in which Christian colleges have modified their sense of mission reveal another dimension of the abandonment of responsibility for teaching public morality and for clarifying the relationship of Christian scholarship in relation to the arts and the sciences. Indeed, one cannot understand mainline Protestant social engagement during the twentieth century apart from its surprising disengagement from higher education. The ancestors of mainline Protestants founded most existing colleges and universities to train future leaders for church and society. They spread this alliance of faith and learning, of *pietas et veritas*, around the world in the colleges and universities founded by the missionary movement. Early in the twentieth century, these colleges and universities were the chief institutions through which mainline Protestants engaged the world. Nearly all institutions of higher learning manifested an ethos of liberal Protestant nonsectarianism and sought to uphold the universal Christian ideals of freedom, democracy, benevolence, justice, reform, and service. Ironically, reformers would later call upon these same ideals to erode the Christian distinctiveness of these schools.[28]

The fundamentalist controversies of the 1920s were followed by a neo-orthodox renaissance in the 1930s. It held that one could not address the depths of human existence apart from the classical insights of Christian doctrine—restated for our times, of course. Led by Paul Tillich, the Niebuhr brothers, and other "neo-orthodox" leaders, the mainline Protestant establishment mounted a new attempt to engage the university. In 1953, the National Council of Churches published *The Christian Scholar* under the enthusiastic editorship of J. Edward Dirks. During the 1950s, every denomination launched aggressive new campus ministry programs. By the 1970s, however, the mainline denominations abandoned most of these efforts. Neo-orthodoxy generally did not penetrate the university ethos. The academic community, not yet having experienced the deconstruction of knowledge that was yet to come, remained in the thrall of the Enlightenment, often denying its roots in wings of the Reformation. As a result, it continued to sharply divide faith from science and privilege scientific knowledge. The National Council of Churches eventually ceased publishing *The Christian Scholar*. Death of God theology, honest to God debates, and a "shattered spectrum" of theologies that spoke on behalf of the dispossessed, women, and people of color soon replaced neo-orthodoxy.[29] In the name of tolerance, openness, and sensitivity, colleges and universities ceased requiring chapel services, and mandatory classes on religion and the Bible gave way to electives in religious studies. Mainline Protestants had exercised cultural dominance not by directly wielding power, but by shaping the ideals of the public. By the 1980s, they lost the central institution through which they shaped these ideals for most of American history. This capitulation accompanied massive membership losses.[30]

In terms of influence upon the institutions of society, the mainline's engagements with the economic and political realms were more successful than its engagements with the family, the media, and higher education. This reflects the lasting impact of the Social Gospel tradition as modified by Christian realism and the later civil rights movement, which tended to view political engagement as the primary testimony of the power of faith in public life. Unfortunately, during this same period, many gradually lost sight of the importance of the institutions of civil society in which people lived most of their lives, including the growing influence of the corporation.

IV. Sources of Authority

The differing approaches that evangelical and mainline wings of Protestantism developed to engage society reflected differences in a complex cluster of theological commitments as well. In every one of the debates and developments mentioned above, basic views of how we can best come to decisive convictions lie just below the surface. Perhaps none was more important than the weighting of the touchstones of authority that each side referred to when discerning God's will and way for humanity. All recognized the primal authority of Scripture, but each side came to approach and utilize Scripture differently in their theological and ethical arguments.

Traditions that grew out of the Reformation viewed Scripture as sovereign over the other points of reference, and indeed, in some circles the slogan of Luther, "*sola scriptura, sola gratia, sola fidei*," was reduced to the first of the three, the primary evidence of grace and the only sure aid to faith. That view, however, was never able to sustain itself entirely alone. Most Protestants felt compelled to write confessions that, in addition to their polemical purpose, served as summaries and guides to interpreting the Bible. People brought up in the traditions established by these confessions believed that these confessions were, in principle, subordinate to Scripture. At the same time, they saw them as continued elaborations of the implicit meanings of the ancient creeds, and they accorded them a place of honor, regularly deferred to them when interpreting difficult passages in the Bible, and sometimes persecuted those who read the contested passages differently. Moreover, less overtly authoritative traditions also developed, such as hymnbooks and distinctive styles of worship.

In addition to Scripture and tradition, Protestants inherited from their Roman Catholic forebearers an accent that incorporated influences of Aristotelian and Stoic conceptions of reason and natural law in theological and ethical writings. Many Puritan divines also believed that one could use reason to read the book of nature and discern the glorious order of God's logical creation and the moral order of God's laws. The belief that scientific discoveries brought glory to God and could serve one's neighbor spurred the development of modern science. The Protestant belief that government and politics were a *res public* in the sense that they were a matter of the people's business, rather than a matter entrusted by God to royalty, spurred the democratic development of public reason of the ordinary person. Science and populism were key influences in the development of the Enlightenment. As the Enlightenment came to full flower, it became ever more confident of the power of human reason to grasp the fundamental structure of the world and human nature. Some Protestants, such as John Toland, responded to the Enlightenment's exaltation of human reason by defending the reasonableness of Christianity. Others, such as Immanuel Kant, talked about "religion within the limits of reason alone." When scientific discoveries called some things in the Bible into question, still others, in an attempt to defend the Bible, developed the sort of deductive rationalism that we associate with fundamentalist apologetics. Thus, ironically, those most interested in defending Scripture and tradition, like those who attacked them, appealed to reason.

In addition to tradition and the light of reason, many held that one could not fully grasp the meaning of the text unless one experienced the inspiration of the Holy Spirit in the reading or hearing of the Word, as Calvin and the later Puritans claimed, or experienced a "warmed heart," as Wesley and the later Pietists claimed. During the Great Awakenings that swept the new American republic, many claimed that the Spirit of Christ entered their hearts, and others argued that the Holy Spirit was needed to give one an immediate impression of God's holiness to effect true conversion. These subjective experiences could then confirm the truths of Scripture and the larger tradition and make them existentially real.

Thus, far from operating in a scripturally confined fortress of faith, Protestants have always interpreted the Bible in conjunction with other touchstones of authority. These points of reference have been identified in the twentieth century by the term "quadrilateral," which refers to the authority of Scripture, tradition, reason, and experience. Although the term is most frequently used in the Methodist circles, it is widely acknowledged to have captured something not only present in John Wesley's modification of an earlier Anglo-Catholic tradition, but present, in different measures and combinations, in all major Christian traditions.[31] From the continental Reformation through the English Reformation, from the Puritan foundations of the United States to the middle of the nineteenth century, proliferating Protestant movements combined these touchstones of authority in a variety of distinctive ways, all under the mantle of the primacy of Scripture. Seen this way, it is as if Christianity is a giant playing field, with many teams playing roughly the same game. Each team has its own preferred formations, strategies, and tactics for thinking and living that define how to simultaneously stay inbounds and configure the key reference points of the quadrilateral. Each can recognize that the others are playing the same game while also believing that some teams play better than others.

When evangelicals and mainline Protestants began to part ways in the late nineteenth century, divergent understandings of reason and experience that guided the interpretation of Scripture began to surface. The evangelicals were suspicious of "tradition" because it obscured the pure message of Scripture, divided the church, and seemed to baptize mere human wisdom. They were also skeptical of the developments of humanist reason that gave rise to the natural sciences cultivated by the Enlightenment. They defended the Bible against the challenges posed by Darwin and interpreters who claimed that one could and should read the Bible like any other ancient document. They doubted the ability of the social sciences, as they were developed, for example, by Marx, Durkheim, Freud, Weber, and James, to interpret the dynamics of human experience—especially the kind of religious experience that brought the confidence that one had been "born again." They were also deeply suspicious of the higher criticism of the Bible—which depended on a developing tradition of reliance on historical reconstruction and the rational analysis of the texts—that gradually found a home in the academy. Although some early evangelicals adopted a posture of anti-intellectualism, others, as we have noted, developed highly rationalistic apologetics. Often drawing on nineteenth-century Princeton theologians, early evangelicals and their heirs developed doctrines of biblical infallibility. Some talked about plenary inspiration and the inerrancy of the original monographs to defend the authority of Scripture. In recent decades, this early trend toward anti-intellectualism has been widely modified. Many now recognize the significant contributions that evangelical scholars are making to intellectual life.

The mainline Protestants' approach to the touchstones of authority developed along a different course. They embraced the newer natural sciences, even fomented their development in the universities and schools they founded. They viewed the new social sciences as a close ally, recognizing that social theorists and social critics often saw dynamics and structures in human and historical experience that theologies that depended only on Scripture and experience neglected or obscured and that rationalistic fundamentalism denied.[32] Indeed, the new social sciences became the handmaidens of the Social Gospel, Christian realism, and liberation movements that would sweep mainline Protestantism in the next century. They saw the process of becoming a Christian as much a matter of nurture by socialization and acculturation experiences in the family and the Sunday school as by a distinct conversion experience. Moreover, they saw in the Enlightenment modes of reasoning fresh tools of rational analysis. They applied these to historical studies and, importantly, to the critical analysis of Scripture and tradition in order to purge them of premodern superstitions and unbelievable assumptions.

Mainline approaches to Scripture and the other points of the quadrilateral did not stand still over the course of the century. The leaders of the Social Gospel took their inspiration and guidance from the prophets and Jesus, even as they sought to illuminate the circumstances to which they spoke with the new social sciences. Reinhold Niebuhr interpreted the biblical account of the creation, fall, and redemption in light of the tradition and the discoveries of the social sciences and set forth an articulate account of human "nature and destiny." He and other Christian realists employed a biblical anthropology as a polemic against competing views of humanity and used it to guide social ethics and political possibilities or limits. Civil rights leaders recalled the doctrine of *imago Dei* in their prophetic cry for justice. They asserted that people who are equal in the eye of God should be equal in the eyes of the law and receive equal treatment in the economic and social spheres of life. These movements threw their weight on the activist side of social ministry.

At midcentury the writings of Karl Barth swept through all the mainline denominations, and they continue to exercise considerable influence in many mainline theological seminaries. Barth's focus on the threefold Word in Christ, the Bible, and preaching contributed to a renewal of biblical and doctrinal theology. However, by attacking any dependence on "natural reason" and being suspicious of too much reliance on "experience," he has contributed to a variety of fideisms. These range from naive nondisclosure of the many sources that inform one's ethical and theological thought, to an irrational, postmodern rejection of correspondence between words and the world, to several attempts to articulate a theologistic epistemology and interpretation of history that is compelling to many confessing Christians.

Toward the end of the century, liberation and feminist voices claimed that the experience of oppression conveys authoritative knowledge. They asserted that the Bible and tradition cannot be trusted since they were written, compiled, and reified by oppressors and do not reflect the experiences of the marginalized. Their witness has been accepted as bearing more than a grain of truth by most ecumenical Protestants. At the same time, the tendency to rely on experience alone as the criteria by which to judge Scripture and tradition and reason is simultaneously resisted, for the simple reason that these other touchstones of authority also contain the testimony of the experience of the millions of faithful who have gone before the present generation of voices.

Evangelicals have long been critical of mainline Protestantism's neglect of the primal authority of Scripture and of its reservations about the accounts of the miraculous birth, the many healings, and especially the bodily resurrection of Jesus Christ. Many mainline clergy and theologians would rather speak of the poetic meaning of Christmas, which signals the love of God for humanity and the presence of the divine in the midst of human life, of the power of psychosomatic changes when one has faith, and the "empty tomb" which implies a promise that even though death and entropy confront us, hope is possible and meaning does not end. But such human-focused interpretations, prompted by scientific reasoning, seldom satisfy evangelicals. In recent times they have been joined by Orthodox and Catholic voices that are also suspicious of the mainline's excessive dependence on humanistic and scientific modes of reasoning with affinities to the Enlightenment. A number of Protestant efforts are under way to try to show that the ecumenically oriented mainline can be both open to these corrections and yet right in accepting the insights of the modern natural and social sciences, and taking them into account when interpreting biblical stories and traditional doctrines.[33]

As we face the future, it is important to recall that Protestantism developed concurrently with the development of new printing techniques. These techniques made the Bible available to the laity in the vernacular and demanded literacy for all believers. It is hard to imagine that the Bible would have come to hold such a highly regarded and influential place in American culture apart from these technological developments. As the new millennium dawns, evangelical and mainline Protestants are in the midst of a new digital technological revolution that promises to transform public discourse, interaction, and epistemology. It is not yet clear what the new digital technology will mean for people who have put such great emphasis on the Book, but it is likely that film, TV, and video will influence public consciousness about religion generally and marginalize those groups that do not use it to advance their message artfully.

Positive Lessons

I. Theological Guidance

One of the significant strengths of twentieth-century mainline Protestantism has been its perennial willingness to retrieve biblical and theological themes and recast them to provide guidance in engaging society. The seminal thinkers of the various movements that have influenced the mainline churches' approach to social engagement believed that they were faithful to the spirit of the original biblical message, but they also knew they were not simply restating, verbatim, the Bible or their immediate ecclesiastical and theological predecessors. In many communions the Reformation watchwords "reformed and always being reformed" supported this retrieval.

II. Common Cause

Another strength of the mainline Protestant ecumenical spirit is its willingness to build coalitions to bring about the kinds of social change that embody justice. In the early stages, the idea that America was a white Protestant experiment tended to limit this engagement, but interaction with slavery and with the labor movements began to modify that. Later, the identification with the suffrage movements for women, still later with the Jews who were victims of the Nazis (which made many begin to think of the "Judeo-Christian" tradition as the heritage of the nation), and the belated civil rights movement with the African-Americans, built the foundations for what people today sometimes call the "rainbow coalition." Mainline Protestants have sought to penetrate society with Christian values, but they have not sought to make America a nation only for Christians. Today one of the great challenges has to do with how to think of Islam—the third of the "Abrahamic traditions"—which raises all sorts of questions about the nature of revelation and prophetic action.

Cautionary Tales

I. Speaking without a Base

Far too often in the last century, leaders have spoken from lectern or pulpit (or demonstration podium) without due attention to the split between the pew and denominational spokespersons. Some have evidenced the attitude that the church has completed its prophetic task when it has "spoken truth to power." A strength of evangelicalism, in contrast, has been its awareness of the need to convert individuals and to build grassroots communities of commitment willing to shape life not from the top down or from the bottom up, but from the center out, in civil societies where it is lived. A social ministry that is to be effective in the future will have to reconstruct a "united front" in the hearts and minds of the believers.

II. Doing without Transformation

A second flaw in mainline social engagement is the propensity for many mainline Protestants to think that God calls the church to do, rather than to be. We have seen that the insistence upon engagement has supported an activist faith that has made significant contributions to American life. However, a preoccupation with social issues has also led the church to live beyond its spiritual means. It has often viewed piety as suspect and has been unwilling to minister to the widespread, palpable desire among many in our culture to discover a spiritual life in the midst of a disenchanted world, shorn of meaning by consumerism and materialism. Rather than looking upon this hunger as opportunity for transformation and inviting people to participate in God's reign, mainline Protestants have often dismissed this hunger as an individualistic disengagement from the larger, more pressing issues of justice. This emphasis on doing is associated with other problems faced by the mainline, namely an inability to self-replicate by passing the faith on to the next generation and a fear that evangelism cannot be respectful of the autonomy of others.

III. Neglect of Institutions

The noted social ethicist James Luther Adams used to say, "If you do not incarnate, you will dissipate." Many mainline leaders favored movements not institutions, change not order. They have been genuine Protestants, in the sense that the core concept is "protest," rather than true Reformers, for whom the core concept is "ever forming." Corporations and parties, families and schools, the media and the arts need constant rebuilding, and only a broad-gauged theology and a deep set of commitments can guide these prospects. Today, for these reasons of neglect, mainline Protestants look to the future with a great deal of trepidation. For most of the twentieth century, they were "mainline" because they dominated the cultural centers of American life and many cultural leaders looked to them to provide the theological basis for the ethical norms of the common life. Today many fewer pay them any attention. This awareness has led to considerable soul-searching and the exploration of alternative options to respond to the new situation of cultural disestablishment. Some advocate a new fideism and withdrawing entirely from the public spheres of society; others describe the mainline church's situation as a new exile and respond by issuing a radical critique of society. Still others seek to renew the ecumenical church and emerging global society by articulating a compelling public theology. But that is another story.

5

Insights from Catholic Social Ethics and Political Participation

Kristin E. Heyer

IN AN ERA of renewed religious tensions, many secularists in the contemporary North American context remain concerned that most forms of public religion pose a threat to democratic values. Furthermore, amidst a culture of violence, consumerism, and relativism, even many Christians remain unclear about whether and how religion should attempt to influence or contribute to the nation's public life. Given the tensions between our identities as believers and citizens, how exactly are Christians called to live, at once members of the City of God and of the earthly city? The Roman Catholic stance essentially holds that in spite of the risks and tensions that exist for a pilgrim people, discipleship requires faithful citizenship.[1] Catholic social teaching contributes its basic affirmation that human beings are created in God's image, are social and political by nature, and are endowed with inviolable dignity and human rights. At its best, Catholic engagement grounded in this vision proceeds with a spirit of humility, dialogue, and mutual respect. Rather than inherently posing dangers to our pluralist context or religion itself, Christian political engagement can contribute to the wider society while remaining faithful to its convictions. Any Christian civic engagement entails ongoing risks, however,

101

and must remain careful to avoid co-optation on the one hand or complete withdrawal on the other.

The following reflections on insights the Catholic tradition might offer to an evangelical public ethic will proceed in three parts: We first briefly trace the theological foundations of Catholic public engagement and current political advocacy practices; we next suggest three sets of methodological insights from Catholic social teaching and political participation; and we finally conclude with some ongoing challenges for any Christian public witness.

Background: A Roman Catholic Perspective on Public Engagement

Different attitudes about Christian public engagement have expressed themselves in the American context as elsewhere within the Roman Catholic theological and social tradition. However, particularly post–Vatican II, a pastoral concern for public affairs and for the governance of nations and the international community has prevailed. While various expressions of public Catholicism exemplify a range of attitudes toward secular society and modes of civic involvement, the Catholic social tradition and legacy of Catholic political activity yield a stance of engagement with the world on the model of a "public church." We have witnessed this clearly in the travels, symbolic actions, and multilingual addresses of Pope John Paul II to many different nations, and even in acknowledgments of past errors in relations with persons of various nationalities and faiths and in actions of reconciliation.

Broadly understood, Catholic social thought and action are grounded in a theology of the fundamental goodness of creation, the mediation of the divine through the human (incarnation, sacramental principle), and the Catholic insistence on the universality of God's concern.[2] This Catholic emphasis on mediation highlights more of a continuity between nature and grace, reason and faith, this world and the kingdom of God, without denying some discontinuity. Since human understanding and religious faith are not opposed (though not identical either), constructive dialogue and interaction can ensue between the Catholic community and wider culture.

One consequence of this understanding is the centuries-old tradition of Catholic social teaching. While the official corpus of statements by popes and bishops typically designated as the Catholic social tradition spans from Pope Leo XIII's *Rerum novarum* (1891) to the present, efforts by the church to relate the fullness of the tradition to the social realties of the times reach back to Christianity's earliest encounters with surrounding cultures. Charging different Catholic communities with this ongoing task of relating the tradition to the "signs of the times," Pope Paul VI wrote, "It is up to Christian communities to analyze with objectivity the situation which is proper to their own country, to shed on it the light of the Gospel's unalterable words and to draw principles of reflection, norms of judgment and directives for action from the social teaching of the Church."[3]

At the Second Vatican Council (1962–1965) in particular, the Catholic Church moved this social tradition to the center of its mission. *The Pastoral Constitution on the Church in the Modern World* (*Gaudium et spes*) exemplifies the conciliar shift toward calling for dialogue with the world and an examination of social, cultural, and political realities in the light of the gospel. The document makes this new relationship to the world clear from the beginning: "The Council can provide no more eloquent proof of its solidarity with the entire human family with which it is bound up, as well as its respect and love for that family, than by engaging with it in conversation about these various problems."[4] Here the church's social teaching was bolstered with ecclesiological grounding; no longer was the social teaching considered only as a narrow category within moral theology, but rather it came to be chiefly conceived of as a means of fulfilling the church's very mission.[5] *Gaudium et spes* presents the human person as the bond between the church and the world, and the task of the church as safeguarding the dignity of the person (no. 76).[6] Here the council urges Christians, as "citizens of two cities," to attend to temporal duties in light of the spirit of the gospel, condemning attitudes of otherworldliness that deemphasize earthly duties on the view that our only abiding city is that which is to come.[7] Another major council document, *Dignitatis humanae*, further sustains a public role for the church by affirming that within the meaning of religious liberty lies the freedom for religious groups to make explicit the human and social implications of theological doctrine.[8] While the particular challenges of negotiating how and when the church should involve itself while remaining independent are ongoing, the post–Vatican II church has joined its personal and sacramental ministry to a social and public presence, thereby legitimizing a "public church" on the whole.[9]

In addition to these council documents, Catholic social encyclicals over the past century explicitly encourage social and political participation and outline key principles to guide such engagement. This body of documents affirms the link between faith and civic responsibility,[10] the moral function of government in protecting human rights and securing basic justice for all its citizens, and the government's connection to the common good. The Catholic conception of government in these documents generally reflects a Thomistic understanding of Christians and the political order, based upon (considerable) trust in human reason and optimism concerning the potential of natural humanity to establish a just and peaceful political order governed by law.[11] While American Catholics inevitably debate the size and role of the state in society and the economy, Catholic teaching insists that government should play an active role, particularly in defense of the poor.[12] Further, while Catholic social teaching and the principle of subsidiarity always encourage the works of mercy and working for justice on the community level, there is also a clear affirmation of the need to advocate for justice at the structural level as well.

Explicit in Pope Pius XI's articulation of the principle of subsidiarity is not only his encouragement for solving injustices at the local level when possible, but also his affirmation that ". . . owing to the change in social conditions, much that was formerly done by small bodies can nowadays be accomplished only by large organizations."[13]

In the Catholic tradition, the political order is not merely remedial of sin; it serves to achieve the common good. By emphasizing the common good, Catholic teaching urges us not to seek only our own interests or the interests of our own group, but to see all people, including the poor, immigrants, and members of other racial and ethnic groups, as members of the community of God's care and participants in the common good. The government plays a unique role in protecting the human rights of all for full participation in the life of the community. Yet Catholic thought also affirms the role of smaller groups and voluntary associations in meeting needs and pursuing the common good. Pope Pius XI articulated this principle of *subsidiarity* in *Quadragesimo anno* as the idea that the government should not replace or absorb smaller forms of community, but should provide them with help (*subsidium*) when they are unable or unwilling to contribute to the common good on their own. The government directs and coordinates the activities of these smaller units or voluntary associations as needed.[14]

For the last several decades, the U.S. bishops have issued quadrennial statements on faithful citizenship, in which they link the gospel's social mission with political responsibility.[15] As they wrote in their 1995 statement, "We hope American Catholics, as both believers and citizens, will use the resources of our faith and the opportunities of this democracy to help shape a society more respectful of the life, dignity, and rights of the human person, especially the poor and vulnerable."[16] Such documents typically outline basic principles at the heart of the Catholic social tradition that should guide policymaking, such as the life and dignity of the human person; human rights and responsibilities; family and community life; the dignity of work and rights of workers; the option for the poor; and global human solidarity.[17] The political responsibility documents in turn apply such principles to issues relevant to that particular election year, from abortion to welfare reform, capital punishment to conflicts in the Middle East. Thus in the documents of Vatican II and the social tradition since, we encounter a Catholic call to social engagement with political dimensions.

In the service of bringing this commitment and these social principles to bear upon national policy issues, the U.S. Catholic Church has maintained a presence in Washington, DC, since the National Catholic Welfare Conference was established just after World War I.[18] Today its successor, the United States Conference of Catholic Bishops, works in part to advocate for the vulnerable and apply Catholic teaching to major social and political issues. Yet the Catholic lobby extends beyond this official arm of the U.S. church, including a variety of membership organizations, religious orders, and other associations. While these groups in most cases do not directly oppose the work of the bishops' conference, there does exist a range of differences in emphasis and approach. The political patterns of Catholic advocacy generally defy typical partisan divisions due to their "progressive" stances on social welfare and labor and "conservative" positions on abortion and education policy (often serving as a bridge between evangelical and liberal Protestant approaches), yet various Catholic groups fall across the typical ideological spectrum.[19] Associations of Catholic hospitals and parochial schools lobby largely to protect their own ministries and concerns. Finally, some groups are sustained by significant Catholic memberships although they are not chiefly Catholic organizations, such as National Right to Life (the oldest antiabortion group in the U.S.), JustLife (lobbies for the "seamless garment" agenda), and Bread for the World (the Christian hunger lobby).[20]

In their comprehensive study of religion and politics in the U.S. context, political scientists Robert Booth Fowler, Allen D. Hertzke, and Laura R. Olson name several strengths of the American Catholic lobby: "a theological comfort with politics, a scholastic tradition of serious reflection on issues, clear lines of leadership, and a potentially strategic position in broader political alignments."[21] The ways in which Catholic groups approach public life are also shaped significantly by the fact that theirs is a world church and by their connection to Catholic institutions such as hospitals, schools, charities, and universities. The explicit connections between discipleship and citizenship in Catholic social teaching have given rise to this sustained national political presence in the U.S. context.

Insights from Catholic Social Ethics and Political Participation

Thus Catholic engagement is grounded in theological foundations and a rich social tradition, and it includes a history of institutional and political activity. Catholic tradition and experience offer three sets of methodological insights for evangelical engagement in the areas of (a) the overall Catholic stance toward the world; (b) the methodology of Catholic social ethics; and (c) the range of social and political issues addressed. We now briefly turn to each feature of the Catholic ethic that may prove instructive for an evangelical approach.

The Catholic Posture: A Complex Public Church

As we shall show, the multifaceted or complex nature of the basic "public church" Catholic posture helps guard against risks such as an engagement that verges on co-optation; too optimistic or too pessimistic a view of the wider world; or disproportionate reliance upon a particular theological "canon within the canon." While the aforementioned theological emphases on creation, incarnation, and mediation direct the church toward engagement with the world overall, other theological emphases temper that public mandate and lead to differences in how its social mission plays out. Discontinuities between this world and the next, the pervasiveness of sin, and the gospel call to peacemaking mitigate against an unequivocal embrace of the world and lead some Catholic scholars and practitioners to live out the social dimension of their faith in ways distinct from the dominant public church model. In fact, Ernst Troeltsch noted that the genius of the Catholic Church was the way it incorporated both "church" and "sect" types, co-opting the sectarian impulse into religious orders as a "sect" within the wider "church."[22]

Today, however, those embodying "sect" within the Catholic landscape are not limited to clergy or religious, but include laity living in the world who feel that the mainstream church model is insufficiently countercultural or attentive to gospel mandates.[23] Thus, the prevailing Catholic posture is that of a "public church," because its basic understanding of pastoral responsibility includes participation in the wider civil society.[24] Given the tensions entailed in worldly activity and distinct emphases within the whole Christian canon (incarnation *and* crucifixion, mercy *and* rigor, justice *and* faith), however, a range of Catholic approaches persists, some more prophetic than public, others aiming to impact the surrounding culture rather than legislation. Taking the cross or the incarnation as the primary lens, for example, significantly shapes a Christian's public ethic in distinct ways.[25] Where the tension among these different approaches remains creative, it helps the Catholic witness to remain faithful to the whole of the tradition in its engagement.

In the contemporary United States context in particular, the dominant stance in Catholic social ethics and political participation remains the "public church" model, with differing methodologies[26] and a degree of internal pluralism.[27] Some critics on both the left and the right, however, find a public church model like this insufficiently prophetic and countercultural. The left objects that such a *via media* between witnessing chiefly in contrast to society and co-optation with the power of the state is insufficiently prophetic in its critique of society; the right objects that the approach risks secularizing the church.[28] Objections from the left often arise around the issues of war, capitalism, and consumerism, highlighting the "inherent tension between modern war and Christian convictions, between accepting the ongoing premises of global capitalism, and between living the sort of standard American consumerist life, and discipleship."[29] Thus such critics would object that a "public church" model risks compromising too much on such issues. On the right, critics generally focus on issues like abortion, sexual standards in society, and secularism. Such critics warn that "there is a great gulf between what Catholics would expect or should expect and what goes on in the wider culture and society and therefore, the chance of common ground is very slim."[30]

The voices and witness of these other groups within the American Catholic landscape assist the dominant public church model in constantly testing on what issues and by what justification Christians engage.[31] A more rigorist ethic that prefers a witness model like that of Dorothy Day and the Catholic Worker Movement, for example, helps prevent overly optimistic participation, helping ensure Catholic engagement remains attentive to sin and to the gospel's countercultural demands, particularly amidst the violence and consumerism that pervade American culture. In one sense, the tensions exhibited by divergent scriptural themes and theological emphases or these consequent diverse approaches must remain as constitutive of life "between the times," and the diversity contained within the Catholic witness helps strike a faithful balance for pilgrims in this world.

A significant contribution of Catholic methodology that helps to retain and balance these contending positions is the relative care taken to identify levels of authority. Often when the bishops issue a statement, a clear differentiation is made between (1) "thus saith the Lord" (for example, moral absolutes such as intentionally attacking noncombatants is absolutely forbidden), (2) "this is official Catholic teaching," and (3) "this is our prudential judgment, and it depends upon our careful reading of the social realities and the best experts we have consulted, but reasonable people may disagree."[32] In their recent book *Kingdom Ethics: Following Jesus in Contemporary Context*, evangelical scholars Glen Stassen and David Gushee highlight some of the particular contributions this multidimensional Catholic methodology might yield:

- a church that acts on behalf of the well-being of society regardless of whether the society is particularly appreciative or not—as opposed to a public witness marred by a sense of aggrieved entitlement to both respect and privilege;
- a church that offers sophisticated Christian moral instruction in a respectful public language that communicates its values in a way that a wide variety of people can understand and embrace (Weigel, *Soul of the World*, chap. 4; cf. Audi and Wolterstorff, *Religion in the Public Square*, 34–35, 111–12)—as opposed to either a withdrawn sectarianism or a hateful attack-dog politics of either left or right (see Wallis, *Soul of Politics*, chap. 2);
- a church that focuses its activism on the well-being of the whole society, in particular those trampled on by the current cultural and political order, rather than on its own narrow interests;
- a church that respects religious liberty and appropriate church-state boundaries in a pluralistic democracy rather than yearning for establishment or theocracy (Hollenbach, *Justice, Peace and Human Rights; Claims in Conflict; The Common Good and Christian Ethics*); or
- a church that lays down its life for its society, like a mother for her children—or like a pastor—rather than fighting religious culture wars to the bitter end.[33]

Stassen and Gushee add that a key element in the transformation of the Catholic moral witness has been "the Church's coming to terms with its role as a disestablished participant in a pluralistic liberal democracy," noting John Courtney Murray's role in "helping the American Catholic Church make the transition to seeing disestablishment as a blessing rather than a curse."[34] On balance, then, while divergent approaches coexist within the Catholic witness,[35] the dominant "public church" model and its differentiated levels of teaching authority provide a framework for engagement that continually strives to avoid dangers of accommodation and withdrawal.

Multidimensional Theoretical and Practical Methodologies

Following from this complex stance, the Catholic Church employs a multidimensional approach in its theoretical methodology as well as its advocacy efforts. That is, a Catholic public ethic incorporates both charity *and* advocacy, public theology *and* natural law arguments, and it engages wider society at once intellectually, institutionally, politically, and personally. Catholic social teaching and advocacy combine theological, philosophical, and empirical resources and methods in a way that marries fidelity to the tradition with respect for the realities of the world and the pluralistic nature of the wider society.

Theoretical Methodology

While internal methodological debates persist, on the whole Catholic ethics combine theological and philosophical approaches. Catholic social principles themselves reflect and flow from biblical and theological foundations. For example, the tradition grounds its fundamental commitment to human life and dignity in the sacredness of all human persons as revealed in their creation in *imago Dei* and the consecration of humanity in the incarnation. A commitment to human rights flows from this fundamental human dignity, including a strong commitment to protecting human life at its vulnerable beginning and end. Catholic principles of justice are grounded in the fundamental Christian norm of love of God and neighbor, for charity must manifest itself in just structures that respect human rights and facilitate human development.[36] The option for the poor is rooted in the special concern God shows for the poor and vulnerable as revealed in the Hebrew Scriptures (e.g., prophetic texts and the context of God's liberation of and covenant with Israel), and in Jesus' own practice of seeking out the powerless during his time on earth as well as his teachings regarding attention to suffering and material wealth.[37]

At the same time, Catholic social principles are also rooted in philosophical natural law arguments, for such arguments are intended to be more universally accessible and therefore apt norms for cooperating with others of goodwill toward solving common problems.[38] For example, human dignity is also rooted in assumptions about humans' rationality and moral agency. Most social en-cyclicals rely to varying degrees upon natural law reasoning, particularly those written prior to Vatican II. Thus these principles have *both* theological and secular warrants, and the two types of warrants relate positively, following from the Catholic understanding of faith and reason. For the Catholic tradition generally understands human reason as reflecting the *imago Dei*, such that faith and reason (and in this case, theological and philosophical warrants) are not understood to be radically incompatible, reflecting a Thomistic commit-ment to reasonable moral order knowable in principle by all humans. The ways Catholic social principles relate to biblical and theological foundations or the extent to which they comprise unacceptable philosophical translations remains disputed by some theologians. Yet on balance the social principles that generally guide Catholic political engagement have both theological and secular warrants that relate positively on the whole.[39]

Some Catholic theologians insist that the church's public voice should rely on a primarily philosophical style of discourse in the tradition of John Court-ney Murray, S.J., and John XXIII's *Pacem in terris* to ensure its accessibility to the wider public. They believe that the church's effectiveness and credibility at the level of complex policy recommendations depend upon its ability to understand relevant empirical data from disciplines outside of theology (e.g., data on the economy or foreign policy) and that when coercive laws are at stake, language used in advocacy efforts should be accessible beyond one's religious tradition.[40] Others, however, employ biblical and theological language and symbols in such discourse with the understanding that they may in fact be no less publicly accessible than natural law language.[41] David Tracy has praised Catholic social ethicists' use not only of methods that make their case on ac-cessible grounds amidst pluralism, including historically conscious natural law arguments, but of their "appeals to inner-Christian resources," such as their use of biblical symbols (creation in the image of God, covenant, kingdom of God) to disclose understandings of the human person, community, and political realm.[42] For as David Hollenbach, S.J., puts his optimism in the resonance of this more publicly theological approach, the same God in whom Christians believe is the God of all creation, and "for this reason it is possible to hope that the Christian story as told in the scriptures is not entirely foreign or strange to those outside the church. It can raise echoes and perhaps recognition among all who share in the quest for the human good."[43] A clear signal of this direction is Pope John Paul II's encyclical, *Veritatis splendor*, The Splendor of Truth.[44] It begins with "Jesus Christ, the True Light that Enlightens Everyone," and it is replete with Scripture, including much from the Sermon on the Mount, "the *magna charta* of Gospel morality."[45]

This Catholic integration of both theology and philosophy in its social ethic helps enable the public deliberation necessary to test competing conceptions of the good; it also better respects the "fact of reasonable pluralism" than does restriction to public philosophy. The integration of *both* theologically explicit language and symbols in public debate *and* philosophical and empirical arguments helps to ensure that Christian engagement not only is "thick enough" to evoke the loyalties and imagination required to address the contemporary American cultural inadequacies,[46] but also retains resources to address public issues amidst pluralism in accessible ways. Yet efforts to communicate in accessible ways—whether by a natural law approach or political advocacy organizations' reliance upon the experiences of the poor and empirical data—also remain necessary for genuine and fruitful engagement to ensue. Taken as a whole, the Catholic approach conveys the belief that fidelity to the tradition and responsibility to the signs of the times call for a fully theological and fully public approach.

Beyond an approach that joins theological and more mediated forms of discourse, the Catholic approach at its best is marked by a spirit of "confident modesty." For in line with *Gaudium et spes*, the church strives to engage the world in "a spirit of dialogue and service," in a reciprocal manner, mindful that the church both teaches and learns from the world.[47] This spirit derives in part from the methodological willingness to take seriously empirical knowledge from other fields in policy analysis,[48] but also grows out of the coalition work Catholic lobbyists do (and the collaboration many Catholics engage in at every level), evidencing an active openness to the presence of God outside of the church and to learning from the other.

While contentious debate has ensued within the church over the degree of specificity that should characterize ecclesial policy statements, the characteristically broad nature of Catholic principles avoids the dangers of remaining too abstract for concrete social applications or too specific in their policy recommendations. For, while the Catholic approach typically leaves room for disagreement about concrete applications (depending upon the issue at hand),[49] as Hehir has argued, the significance and illuminative power of moral principles appear fully only as they are incarnated in the fabric of concrete social problems, and stating such principles too abstractly risks engendering "wildly divergent conclusions" among people all claiming to support the same principle.[50]

Practical Methodology

John Paul II exegetes the dialogue of Jesus with the rich young man and says, "People today need to turn to Christ once again in order to receive from him the answer to their questions about what is good and what is evil."[51] We need a response of love to God's grace. "The good is belonging to God, obeying him, walking humbly with him in doing justice and in loving kindness (cf. Micah 6:8)."[52] This requires a change of heart, and it also requires doing of justice:[53]

> In the face of serious forms of social and economic injustice and political corruption affecting entire peoples and nations, there is a growing reaction of indignation on the part of very many people whose fundamental human rights have

been trampled upon and held in contempt, as well as an ever more widespread and acute sense of *the need for a radical* personal and social *renewal* capable of ensuring justice, solidarity, honesty and openness.[54]

That is, Jesus' primary message calls for repentance and interior conversion, yet working to bring about a more just society also depends upon changing structures. The two dimensions are interrelated, for changing institutions to better reflect charity and justice, human dignity and freedom, and the full range of human rights cannot ensue without a change of heart. For example, John Paul II's remarkable role in opposing totalitarianism and tyranny is noted not only by Catholics but by many others worldwide.

A related strength of the Catholic witness lies in its multitiered approach to social engagement: from local to national to international levels; from the direct provision of human services to academic discourse on religious dimensions of public issues; from grassroots organizing to the implicit and explicit advocacy of direct service organizations like Catholic Charities USA and institutional organizations such as the Catholic Health Association. Another growing trend in political advocacy is the influence of intellectual discourse played out in elite journals, think tanks, and policy institutes.[55] In myriad ways, church members work in concert to relate theological principles to social issues in attempts to directly influence policy and culture. The U.S. bishops have noted that the Catholic community of faith brings particular assets to American political life and public discourse: a consistent set of moral principles (tradition of Catholic social teaching, consistent ethic of life); long-term, broad experience in serving those in need (Catholic schools, hospitals, social service agencies, shelters) that occasions practical expertise and everyday experience that enrich public debate; and the diverse community of citizens that Catholics comprise, ranging as they do across the political and socioeconomic spectra, and yet sharing a common commitment to stand with the poor and vulnerable. The diversity of overall stances toward engagement (outlined above) and strategies for involvement appropriately reflects the full range of the Christian tradition and strengthens Catholic witness.

Thus through personal and institutional efforts to meet direct needs and by lobbying for more structural change, the multidimensional Catholic approach carries out its social commitment. In embodying both direct aid through a network of service agencies and institutions as well as efforts at systemic change, Catholic engagement responds to immediate needs as well as continually asks why those needs persist. As Anne Curtis, R.S.M., a lobbyist at the NETWORK Catholic Social Justice Lobby, notes, the Scriptures do not call us to meet immediate needs alone, for we must attend to both the parable of the Good Samaritan *and* Exodus: "We always need people like Moses to liberate us from structures of enslavement as well as Samaritans to respond to people on sides of the road," and it is insufficient for the church to approach the problems of injustice by one method alone.[56] Catholic strategies of engagement, then, suggest some pluralism of modes and strategies at the practical level as well. As the U.S. bishops characteristically assert in their recent statement, *A Place at the Table: A Catholic Recommitment to Overcome Poverty and Respect the Dignity of All God's Children*, government *and* business, faith-based organizations *and* families and individuals all have important roles to play in countering poverty and working for a more just society.[57] In the end, these multidimensional theoretical and practical methodologies allow Christians to remain at once "vigorous in stating our own case and attentive in hearing others in public life."[58]

Comprehensive Range of Issues

In concert with a stance and methodology that reflect the wide-ranging scope of Christian concern, Catholic theology and praxis suggest that Christian political engagement should be guided by a commitment to addressing a comprehensive range of social issues. While U.S. Catholic political advocacy (particularly at the level of electoral politics) has weathered an uneven history in this regard, its developments in recent decades, on balance, suggest that churches should strive to address a comprehensive range of social issues and avoid single-issue politics. The Catholic social tradition has applied the gospel message to a fairly wide range of social issues throughout the past century, and the U.S. bishops' political responsibility statements similarly incorporate a wide-ranging gamut of political issues. For example, in recent decades the U.S. Conference of Catholic Bishops has addressed abortion, welfare reform, housing, communications policy, immigration policy, civil rights matters, criminal law, family policy, farm policy, labor legislation, and military and foreign policy. This commitment to a comprehensive range of issues yields a Catholic stance that is at once pro-life, pro-poor, pro-family, pro-sexual responsibility, and pro-environmental and racial justice. As John Carr, longtime secretary of the bishops' Office for Social Development and World Peace, recently characterized the Catholic perspective, "Every life is precious, whether in the World Trade Center or Baghdad, a fetus or a person on death row, rich or poor."[59] While more specialized advocacy groups will appropriately persist,[60] and at times, the starkness of certain issues or overwhelming injustices will require a special focus, a comprehensive range of social issues should constitute an important goal of the church's social mission as a whole amidst the fullness of the Christian tradition.

To be certain, expansion beyond a narrow range or single-issue politics is a lesson the U.S. Catholic Conference learned in the 1980s.[61] Joseph Cardinal Bernardin's subsequent consistent ethic of life framework rests on moral and ecclesiological foundations that compel a comprehensive range:

> Ecclesiologically, there is the responsibility of the church to set a tone and an atmosphere in the civil life of society which it cannot do by focusing exclusively

on a single issue. Such a posture risks depicting the church as simply an interest group in a political struggle. The effect of single-issue voting strategies is to reduce the chance that parties and candidates will be judged by standards which test their vision of society and their capacity to address the basic needs of the common good. Morally, a single-issue strategy forfeits many of the resources of the moral teaching of the church. To highlight one question as the primary and exclusive objective in the policy process is to leave too many issues unattended and risks distortion of the single issue itself.[62]

Not all Catholics accept the consistent life ethic, seeing a distinction between innocent life and attackers in war, for example. Some also note that some issues involve such serious injustice as to demand special focus. But all humans are indeed created in the image of God, and the consistent life ethic's emphasis on the interrelatedness of social issues and the connection between breadth and credibility are underscored by Catholic theology and contemporary practice. For with a more restricted focus, the church's credibility is weakened and it becomes more difficult to counter distortion from within, given the temptation to skew the rest of a particular agenda to ensure allies' support on a single issue. Single-issue agendas of any stripe can blind Christians to the fact that our social doctrine is rooted in the dual reality of human life: Humans are both sacred *and* social, so that we are called both to protect human life and foster its development at every stage *and* ensure that social institutions foster such development.[63]

Finally, the transcendence of the Christian faith, the multivocal nature of the fullness of the Christian tradition, and the church-state boundaries in the U.S. context compel a nonpartisan approach. If we are "in the world but not of it," Christians should remain uncomfortable within either political party and institutionally independent from any. In their political responsibility documents, the U.S. bishops call Catholics to be a "community of conscience within the larger society." At the same time, the bishops are careful to avoid endorsing partisan platforms or candidates.[64] On this necessary balance between political participation and the dangers of politicization, they write, "The challenge for our church is to be principled without being ideological, to be political without being partisan, to be civil without being soft, to be involved without being used."[65] Addressing a comprehensive range of issues will help a Christian witness remain faithful to the fullness of the tradition and its wide-ranging social implications and to avoid partisanship.

Conclusions: Ongoing Challenges for a Christian Public Ethic

While these methodological insights from Catholic tradition and practice may provide useful resources for an evangelical public ethic, challenges certainly persist that compromise Catholic witness efforts. In particular, the need for various internal reforms poses significant challenges to the church's public witness.[66] The recent clergy sexual abuse scandal has seriously compromised the credibility of the overall Catholic witness and the work of different Catholic advocacy groups to varying degrees. It poses challenges to the institutional church's ability to communicate its social message persuasively and with the bishops' full attention.

These ongoing challenges underscore the imperative that Christian public engagement both embody and advocate the values it advances. Although this connection is explicitly expressed in *Justitia in mundo*'s maxim that "anyone who ventures to speak about justice must first be just,"[67] it presents an ongoing challenge to the Catholic witness itself. Reinforcing this connection between how churches model justice, peace, and Christian discipleship and how they communicate the implications of those values to the wider society, bringing them to bear upon our shared life together, will enhance the integrity of any Christian social engagement.

We further suggest the value of the characteristically Catholic "both-and" presented here—both nature and grace, both church and sect, both theology and philosophy, both charity and advocacy, both the sacred and the social dimensions of the human—with the understanding that the different methods and approaches do not always harmoniously interact in mutually reinforcing ways in practice. A destructive tension has sometimes characterized intra-Catholic debates on public engagement in general and specific moral judgments in particular. At their best, however, the different approaches give rise to a creative tension that helps avoid the twin dangers of a politicized church and a church in retreat, for "the first erodes the transcendence of the gospel; the second betrays the incarnational dimension of Christian faith."[68]

In terms of limits, then, Catholic social ethics and political participation suggest that public engagement must guard against co-optation with the state, partisanship, total withdrawal, and overly specific or emptily abstract principles. Within those limits, the Catholic example reveals rich possibilities for a range of forms of faithful public engagement, stemming from a complex stance toward society and incorporating multidimensional methodologies at both the theoretical and practical levels. This diversity of approaches suggests that "thick" theological particularism and cooperative peace and justice efforts are not mutually exclusive. In a recent address on "Evangelical Protestants in the Public Square," Richard Mouw echoed this synthesis, joining a more evangelical sense of Christians as exiles with a sense of responsibility to the shared good.[69] In general the methodological lessons sketched here enable the same goal Mouw has written about in terms of Christian civility—working toward the common good of wider society without sacrificing our Christian convictions.[70] Our hope is that these Catholic insights help yield an evangelical approach of prophetic engagement that models gospel values *and* engages the wider world on issues that touch human life and dignity.

Part II

Toward an Evangelical Methodology

6

Toward an Evangelical Ethical Methodology

David P. Gushee and Dennis P. Hollinger

DEFINING A "UNIQUE evangelical approach to doing ethics," the official task of this chapter, is a formidable challenge. It is not clear whether there is or should be a unique evangelical approach to doing ethics. Much depends on how one defines the nature and purpose of the evangelical movement. Much also depends on how one understands the work of Christian ethics. Let us take each issue in turn. That will prepare us for proposing the contours of an "evangelical" ethic by considering the work of some of our leading thinkers in various traditions.

What Is Evangelicalism?

To get started, let us try to locate evangelical ethics historically and institutionally, and mean by it something like "the moral convictions of those associated with the evangelical movement within Western Protestant Christianity."

Usually the story of evangelicalism is told as beginning with the Protestant Reformation, in which those who accepted Protestant beliefs were sometimes denigratingly called "evangelicals" by critics—and eventually chose to wear the title as a badge of honor. The Puritans, originally a reform movement within British and North American Christianity, are generally identified as being located within the evangelical tradition. The Pietist movement on the Continent and later in the Colonies attempted to revivify slumbering German Protestantism and exemplified what many called an "evangelical faith." During the First Great Awakening in North America, the term was frequently employed to describe the evangelistic and revivalist efforts of Wesley, Whitefield, and Edwards. The nineteenth century saw the development of many evangelical associations in North America, both within the historic denominations and in parachurch activist groups, most attempting to bring the gospel to bear on some aspect of society.

These groups and movements, while different in many ways, generally shared beliefs such as salvation by grace through faith in Jesus Christ, emphasis on a personal and vibrant religious experience through the transforming work of the Holy Spirit, the supreme authority of the Bible for Christian faith and practice, and a fierce commitment to the spread of the gospel through evangelism, missions, and social reform. Notice that evangelicalism as seen in these varying movements had little explicit shared moral content, other than whatever might be derived from a return to biblical authority and careful biblical exegesis, as well as the motivation provided by vibrant personal faith. Movement leaders offered moral teaching that varied considerably in emphasis and approach (consider the differences between Luther, Wesley, and Edwards, for example) while still being located in a common evangelical camp emphasizing the authority of Scripture for morality and the significance of earnest moral effort as an aspect of Christian personal and social existence.

An heir to this diverse and coherent line of tradition, the contemporary American evangelical movement can be understood more immediately as a mid-twentieth-century reaction to the rigidity, separatism, and anti-intellectualism of fundamentalism as it emerged in early twentieth-century American religion. Fundamentalism itself was a reaction to the accommodation of American Protestant Christianity to modernism and theological liberalism as these made their way across the ocean from Europe in the early twentieth century.

Fundamentalism was a reactionary movement that responded to dramatic intellectual and social changes with a pessimistic withdrawal from the broader culture. The postmillennial optimism and moral/political reformism of the nineteenth century now gave way to a darker dispensationalist understanding of history that held little hope for this world and hence offered virtually no social ethic. Fundamentalists argued for many classical, orthodox Christian doctrines, as evangelicals always have done, but they pursued a highly defensive posture evidenced in ecclesiastical separatism and the development of their own Bible schools, publishing houses, and denominations. The good life was the separated life hunkered down against a corrupt world, and a rancorous spirit was targeted toward the perceived evils of their day: liberalism, the Social Gospel, Communism, and general worldliness in lifestyle and morals. Fundamentalism survives today, and if the institutional context of this project demanded a treatment of "fundamentalist ethics," this spirit, and these motifs, would certainly remain central.

But by the 1940s, a growing number of leaders within fundamentalism began to challenge the ethos of the movement. Asserting that they were essentially one with fundamentalism in theology, leaders like Harold John Ockenga, Carl F. H. Henry, and Edward J. Carnell began to dispute fundamentalism's separatism, anti-intellectualism, legalism, and lack of a social conscience. To differentiate themselves from their fundamentalist parentage, they tended to employ the term "evangelical," or Ockenga's term, "neo-evangelical." In 1947, Carl Henry's *The Uneasy Conscience of Modern Fundamentalism* chided his cohorts for their failure to address the culture and the needs of contemporary society. Henry wrote: "The problem of Fundamentalism then is basically not one of finding a valid message, but rather of giving the redemptive word a proper temporal focus."[1] Whether Henry was correct in calling evangelicalism an attack merely on fundamentalism's *application* of theology, rather than on fundamentalism's truncated theology itself, is arguable. In any case, the differences were profound, the split between fundamentalism and evangelicalism irreparable. In an effort to articulate their evangelical message clearly, and to solidify its institutional impact, evangelical leaders of the 1940s and 1950s formed several organizations that remain influential today, including the National Association of Evangelicals, Fuller Seminary, and *Christianity Today* magazine.

While the evangelicals of the 1950s and '60s were breaking with fundamentalism by calling for a Christian social ethic, most renditions of "evangelical" ethics offered at the time tended to be both highly individualistic and politically conservative.[2] Evangelical ethics, then, was characterized by an emphasis on a strict code of personal morality and a general tendency to oppose social change and progressive social movements. (This is all the more true if we include Southern Baptists among evangelicals, an identification that makes sense *ideationally* by the 1960s though not *institutionally* until the 1980s and 1990s. Most Southern Baptists, leaders and laity alike, had little contact with, or understanding of, self-identified evangelicals until the late 1980s and early 1990s, when a variety of factors converged to open Southern Baptists to the wider evangelical world.) The tendency toward a rigorous personal morality could be clearly grounded in Scripture, which remained central for evangelicalism, but opposition to social change was often more cultural than biblical, resulting in both victories for Christian fidelity (such as opposition to the sexual revolution), and grave defeats (such as resistance to racial integration and the civil rights movement).

By the 1970s, in the context of the Vietnam War and Watergate, new evangelical voices began to emerge, challenging the conservative and individualistic proclivities of evangelical social thought and calling for a "holistic biblical" (and politically independent) ethic combining rigorous personal and social morality in keeping with the full witness of the Bible. This movement, represented by such voices as Ron Sider and his group Evangelicals for Social Action, expressed opposition both to abortion on demand and to world hunger, both pornography and militarism, both euthanasia and environmental destruction, in the name of a "consistent ethic of life" drawn from Scripture (and influenced by Roman Catholic ethics). This both-and strand of holistic evangelicalism remains active today, and its influence extends far beyond those most visibly associated with its organizations. The openness of this group to "progressive" commitments on some major social issues also created new opportunities for interaction with Christian ethics as an academic discipline, which had developed along a separate track and was largely cut off from evangelicalism (see below).

On the other hand, it would be only a matter of time until an even more explicit tie to political conservatism within the evangelical world would emerge in the Moral Majority and then later the Christian Coalition and successor groups. These movements were led for the most part by people who only a decade earlier were self-proclaimed separatist fundamentalists, but who were now coming to use the term "evangelical" with the recognition of its significant political clout among "born-again Christians" (another label that confuses more than it clarifies). These new activists continued to articulate the strict personal morality of historic evangelicalism and fundamentalism but in their vigorous social and political engagement took their cues from their evangelical coreligionists rather than their more otherworldly fundamentalist brethren—and in political terms aligned themselves almost exclusively with the socially conservative wing of the Republican Party.

It was increasingly clear that despite institutional and theological commonalities, evangelicals did not (and do not) speak with one voice on social or political ethics. The diversity has been manifest not just in the various denominational traditions associated with evangelicalism, but also in its ever-proliferating parachurch institutions that devalue ties to particular denominations and instead are linked to common causes (family, poverty, race, abortion) or charismatic personalities (Billy Graham, James Dobson, Beth Moore, Chuck Colson, Tony Evans, Tony Campolo, Jim Wallis, etc.).

Today many wonder whether there really is a coherent movement called evangelicalism, and others ask what could possibly hold it together. As George Marsden has noted, "It is remarkable that American Evangelicalism has the degree of coherence it does. Little seems to hold it together other than common traditions, a central one of which is the denial of the authority of traditions."[3]

Yet this historical review shows that one thing does hold evangelicalism together other than common traditions: *a commitment to the authority of Scripture that motivates a reformist agenda whenever biblical truth is believed to be compromised or endangered.* From the Protestant Reformation to the rise of postwar neo-evangelicalism, each movement we have identified as "evangelical" shares this biblical reformist instinct. Thus we believe *it is best to understand evangelicalism as a renewal movement within Christianity that continually calls the churches back to deeply committed biblical faith and practice.*

This understanding of evangelicalism helps us make sense of its history and places its institutional forms into proper perspective. It fits better with historic Christian ecclesiology. And it helps us make sense of evangelical ethics. If there were no drift from classic, orthodox, biblical Christianity or vital Christian faith, there would be no need for evangelical reforms in the churches. Thus evangelicalism should be seen as "contingent" rather than necessary, temporary rather than eternal, a tool in God's hands to bring about the reform, reclamation, and revivifying of the churches.

This understanding also helps us answer the questions posed at the beginning of this chapter. Is there (or should there be) a unique evangelical approach to doing ethics? No. There are varieties of orthodox and committed Christian ethics located in various historic Christian communions. These find their commonality in their submission to the authority of Scripture, their deep personal commitment to Jesus Christ, and, to varying degrees, in their respect for and attention to the historic orthodox Christian tradition. Practitioners of orthodox ethics in this sense can be found in Roman Catholic, Eastern Orthodox, mainline Protestant, *and* self-identified evangelical circles. Those approaches to Christian ethics that are commonly called "evangelical" are called this (a) because they are and always have been actually "orthodox," or (b) because they are reformist (attempting to bring Christian ethics in some context back into conformity with biblical norms after a period of drift), or (c) because they are being undertaken by self-identified evangelicals. We are now claiming that those of us who have worn the label "evangelical" in doing our ethics have given up altogether too much ground from the start—it is those who *break with* historic biblical faith and practice who should wear some special label, not those of us attempting to work within it. In reifying the label "evangelical," we have also separated ourselves unnecessarily from orthodox Christians doing faithful biblical ethics in various churches and denominations all over the world. Despite real differences, we are all orthodox Christians, undertaking our work within the parameters of biblical authority. Everybody else—everyone who breaks with the classic orthodox model of consensual Christianity grounded in the authoritative Scriptures—should simply be viewed as *unorthodox*, rather than labeling orthodox or reformist Christians as *evangelicals*.[4]

What Is Christian Ethics?

To ask whether there is a unique evangelical approach to *doing Christian ethics* also demands consideration of the practice of Christian ethics as an academic discipline. The fact of the matter is that self-identified evangelicals historically have had little to do with Christian ethics. Indeed, evangelicals sometimes dismiss the field altogether.

In the September/October 2001 issue of *Books and Culture*, theologian Stephen Webb opened an article provocatively entitled "Danger! Christian Ethics" with the following claims, among others:

- Christian ethics is nothing more than simply being a good Christian.
- Christian ethics becomes just another name for Christian theology.
- What Christianity teaches about ethics is nothing different from or more than what Christianity teaches about Jesus Christ.
- Christian ethics is not only an empty idea; it is also a dangerous one.
- The study of religious ethics is one of the last strongholds of liberal Protestantism in the academy.[5]

While there is a grain of truth in Webb's claims, they generally reflect misunderstandings that have contributed to the marginalization of Christian ethics in evangelicalism. We believe that this is a significant mistake at every level. Tracing how it has taken place is an important part of our task. We need to understand the discipline of Christian ethics and the relation of evangelicals to it if we would develop a healthy evangelical approach to doing ethics for the twenty-first century.

When most self-identified Christian ethicists say "the academic discipline of Christian ethics," what they mean is that discipline practiced by those who (a) have earned a Ph.D. or equivalent degree in Christian ethics, moral theology (the preferred Catholic term), or a closely related field; (b) identify themselves as Christian ethicists; (c) author scholarly and professional publications in the field; (d) teach Christian ethics in college, university, or seminary settings or engage in full-time professional work that is closely related to the field; and (e) find one of their primary professional/institutional homes in the organization called the Society of Christian Ethics (SCE).

Yet as mainline ethicist Edward L. Long of Drew University himself put it in his 1984 history of the Society of Christian Ethics, "It is important not to equate the history of the Society [of Christian Ethics] with the history of an academic discipline. Christian ethics is as old as Christianity itself and even has roots in Old Testament thought . . . A history of Christian ethics resembles a history of Christian thought and is integrally related to it."[6] At one level, then, there is no discrete history of Christian ethics. It is simply the moral/ethical aspect of historic Christian thought. Let's call this historic Christian moral thought "Christian ethics A" because it was here first—it can be witnessed in Scripture and every era of church history. Christian ethics A is the church's reflection on the Scripture, on its own moral life, and on its engagement with society. It is a perennial task of the church. Until the twentieth century, it was usually undertaken within the parameters of biblical orthodoxy. Evangelicals should have no problem with Christian ethics A but instead should be participating in it with vigor.

The precursor of modern North American Christian ethics can be found in the late nineteenth century. Both universities and seminaries began to offer classes in contemporary social problems in the 1880s and 1890s, at the very origins of the Social Gospel movement with its deep concern for the very real injustices created by unfettered laissez-faire industrial capitalism. Let's call this "Christian ethics B." Its goal was to help students in what remained a "culturally Christian" nation translate Christian moral principles into action in the context of urbanization, industrialization, and attendant social ills. The first and most influential of these classes was an 1883–1884 course at Harvard taught by Francis Greenwood Peabody. Long rightly points out that the "social passion" of these early practitioners of so-called "applied Christianity" or "social Christianity" has always been a central characteristic of the field that later came to be called Christian ethics. It has also contributed to the conservative backlash against the discipline that has existed within fundamentalist, and sometimes evangelical, Christianity—sometimes because this "social passion" led to or was rooted in genuinely unbiblical moral teachings, but often because it challenged the economic and political practices of many conservative Christians.

Despite the steady existence of courses in "social Christianity" or "applied faith" in the period between the late nineteenth century and World War II, it was not until the 1950s that the contemporary discipline of Christian ethics began to take shape. This third stage of the development of Christian ethics can be called "Christian ethics C." What eventually became known as the Society of Christian Ethics was founded in 1959 after several years of precursor activities. Over time its agenda has evolved to include various aspects of the entire moral tradition of the Christian faith (Christian ethics A). At its heart the discipline retains the social passion of the nineteenth-century "social Christianity" that was such an important part of its birth as a discipline. That social passion has been and sometimes is misdirected by unbiblical ideologies, such as Marxism and secular feminism. But just as often it fully reflects God's passion for justice and peace, as revealed in the Scriptures, leading to profoundly important studies of a variety of contemporary moral themes and issues—most of which are completely ignored by self-identified evangelicals.

Evangelical disengagement from the mainstream discipline of Christian ethics has been obvious from the discipline's very origins. This disengagement clearly is linked to the context in which Christian ethics B was born—the Social Gospel. Though evangelicals were vigorously engaged with urban social reform efforts when that movement began, theological drift in the Social Gospel movement, the related fundamentalist-modernist controversy of the 1920s, and the ideological captivity of many fundamentalist churches sheared conservative Christians away from social engagement for a long season. This season unfortunately coincided with the consolidation of mainstream Christian ethics as an academic discipline, a development primarily led at the time by mainline Protestant scholars located in the elite northeastern divinity schools.

One of Carl Henry's signal postwar contributions was his effort to offer evangelical reflection on both "personal" and "social" Christian ethics. But his careful, even magisterial works in this area did not signal his own integration into the emerging discipline of Christian ethics or lead many other evangelical thinkers to beat a path in that direction. Today evangelical treatments of Christian ethics, including courses in ethics at Christian universities and seminaries, are often undertaken by those not trained in any tradition of Christian ethics as defined above. If contemporary evangelicals want to move into the twenty-first century with a clear, fully biblical, and richly informed Christian ethic, they will need to move into dialogue with the field of Christian ethics in a way they have not before.

When they get there, they will find a number of orthodox (and self-identified evangelical) voices already there waiting for them. These do not offer a single "unique evangelical approach to doing ethics." Instead, they share the essentials of biblical orthodoxy but work out the details of their ethical theories in ways that reflect the spirit, ethos, and history of their particular ecclesiastical and intellectual traditions as well as their own individual scholarly interests and commitments.

Varieties of Evangelical Ethics

Though contemporary evangelicals have been generally unaware of it, there have been a number of orthodox and self-identified evangelical ethicists doing substantial work within the guild of Christian ethics. They have been trained in the major graduate schools granting degrees in Christian, religious, or social ethics and have been in dialogue with the larger contours of ethical thinking. Their impact within evangelicalism has been modest, and most significant among clergy trained in seminaries. If we include orthodox and not just self-identified evangelical voices among them, we can see that their influence within the Society of Christian Ethics has been fairly significant in the last twenty years or so, especially given their numbers.[7] To unpack the varieties of evangelical moral thinking, we will examine several strands that reflect specific theological and ecclesiastical traditions, but with a clear evangelical flavor that does reflect some coherence. To explore these various strands, we will examine the thinking of one representative thinker as a paradigm of that tradition. Clearly there are other strands and thinkers that could be added to the list.

Mainstream Evangelicalism: Carl F. H. Henry

As noted earlier, Carl Henry played a significant role in the emergence of contemporary evangelicalism as a movement distinct from fundamentalism. His early writings propelled him as a young man into significant leadership positions in church and academy. And when *Christianity Today* magazine was founded in 1956, it was Carl Henry to whom the board turned for its editorial leadership. In that role and in his other voluminous writings, he became a major theological voice for evangelical causes. Henry was an American Baptist, but his primary identity was in representing what we might term mainstream evangelicalism—thinking that embodies a broad spectrum of the evangelical movement, and particularly its theological center.

In 1957, Carl Henry wrote *Christian Personal Ethics*, a substantial six-hundred-page treatise that demonstrated his ability to navigate the ethical and theological waters of contemporary thought. In this work, Henry sets forth a revelation-based ethic over against "speculative moral quests" such as various naturalisms and idealisms so prevalent in contemporary secular ethics and philosophy. While he believes that there is some merit to general ethics garnered through reason and human experience, he insists that "general ethics is ethics in revolt,"[8] due to the fall. In contrast to an ethic of human insight, Henry argues for an ethic in which the content, sanction, and dynamic come from God. He takes the voluntarist position that "the good is what God does and wills," and "there exists no intrinsic good that is distinguishable from the will of God and to which God must conform."[9]

Precisely because ethics is essentially the will of God, it is dependent upon God's self-disclosure. Part of that disclosure is found in reason and general revelation, but the primary revelation comes in special revelation, Christ, and the written Word. Henry accepts general revelation as long as it is understood in the context of divine initiative and grounding. But it is in the revelation of the Scriptures that Henry believes we find the primary source of truth and the only final alternative to speculative moral relativism, which threatens to unglue contemporary culture.[10] As he puts it:

> Because Christianity does not give up its basis in a transcendent revelation it need not surrender its moral requirements to the cultural prejudices and corruption of the day. A religious ethics may simply endorse the accepted patterns of behavior. If its gods are already a reflection of the social environment, the religion serves as a cosmic basis for individual conformity to the prevailing social code. Only the ethics of special revelation dares stand in judgment upon much that passes for the "highest morality" of the age.[11]

For Henry, ethics is not, however, a mere repetition of divine commands. It can be summarized (as Jesus did) in one word, love. Love is the divine imperative in personal relations, and because it is redemptive love rooted in Christ's atonement, it is a love to the stranger and enemy, a love of the body as well as the soul. But Henry is quick to remind us that "love, as the Bible exposits it, is not something as nebulous as moderns would have us think. The New Testament knows nothing of lawless believers in Christ. No believer is left to work out his moral solutions by the principle of love alone." Rather, Henry continually reminds us that the "content of love must be defined by Divine revelation."[12] The content of love in the Scriptures is a particularization of the will of God and is most visibly manifest in the person and work of Jesus. Jesus "was more than the great teacher of ethics. He was its great liver."[13] But the moral example of Jesus can never be isolated from the larger redemptive history revealed in Scripture and then rationally expounded in theology. For Henry, this was the failure of modernism and the Social Gospel, in which Jesus was treated primarily as an idealist moral teacher because of discomfort with the supernatural dimension of the biblical narrative and with the classic doctrine of the atonement.

Christian ethics is not only rooted in a transcendent revelation; it also needs a transcendent dynamic or empowerment. For Henry, this is the role of the Holy Spirit. He devotes an entire chapter to the Spirit, though clearly the Spirit's function is less about moral discernment of the moral good and much more about motivation and empowerment. "The Spirit is the dynamic principle of Christian ethics, the personal agency whereby God powerfully enters human life and delivers . . . from enslavement to Satan, sin, death and law."[14] And this transcendent dynamic is not void of a human dimension and response, for Henry ends the book with an entire chapter on prayer.

Because Christian ethics is rooted in God's will, known by divine revelation, and empowered by a transcendent presence, Henry reminds us that this is not an ethic for everyone. It is the ethics of the believing church. "Christian ethics is . . . the ethics of the church against the world, it is not a living possession of the unbelieving community, but of the community of faith."[15]

Does Henry then have a social ethic—Christian moral guidance for life within the world or for that world itself? It is noteworthy that the title is *Christian Personal Ethics*, and for the most part that it is. But Henry did not forget his earlier assaults on fundamentalism's failure to engage culture, and so in 1964 he wrote the companion volume, *Aspects of Christian Social Ethics*. This work, however, is less about how society itself should operate and more a strategy for Christian influence within a fallen world. Henry evaluates four main social strategies: revolution, reform, revaluation, and regeneration.

Revolution, the first strategy, is "the radical change of social patterns, in their essential constitution, through violence and compulsion."[16] Henry deems this approach a failure because it denies the existence of divinely mandated structures and norms within society. The second strategy is reform, the "gradual but pervasive amendment of particular abuses which secures a decisive improvement of prevailing social character."[17] Reform fails because its philosophical underpinning (evolutionary developmentalism) is flawed. The third social strategy is revaluation, "a fresh intellectual comprehension and direction, whereby social life and structures are critically reassessed in the light of transcendent moral norms."[18] While closer to the biblical truth, Henry believes that this kind of rethinking of social values and practices ultimately fails due to its inability to "exhibit a cosmic justification (as revealed theology does) for unchanging norms and values"[19] and in its inattention to the root social problem of sin.

In contrast to these social strategies, Carl Henry commends another approach, which he calls regenerational, the "transformation by supernatural impulse in individual lives whereby the social scene is renewed through a divine spiritual motivation."[20] He goes on to explicate the regeneration strategy in the realms of work and politics. Ultimately, for Henry, social change is rooted in personal redemption through Jesus Christ, and redeemed individuals are then called to live that transformation and bear witness to a better way in their various callings in life. Primarily what we find here is an individualistic strategy for renewed individuals, and only secondarily a theological paradigm for the social order itself. For much of the twentieth century, this kind of individualism was dominant in most evangelical social thinking, and it remains deeply influential.[21]

The Reformed Strand: Richard Mouw

Richard Mouw has exercised significant leadership within evangelicalism, first as a professor at Calvin College and Fuller Theological Seminary, and now as the president of Fuller. His writings have bridged the academy and the church.[22] He has been a frequent contributor in the pages of *Christianity Today* and has also been an evangelical spokesperson within the larger ecumenical dialogue.

Coming from the Reformed tradition, Mouw follows the lead of John Calvin in asserting that Christian ethics is ultimately the command of God. Like most evangelicals, Mouw says that the command of God is rooted in Scripture, but unlike Carl Henry and some other evangelicals, Mouw wants to insist that this command comes in much broader forms and genres than is often perceived. There is a broader sense "in which a divine command morality is coextensive with all systems of thought that view God as the supreme moral authority. In this more comprehensive sense, virtue ethics and agapism and an emphasis on a divinely implanted sense of justice can all be seen—along with the ethics of 'external law'—as diverse proposed strategies for exhibiting a pattern of moral surrender to the divine will."[23] Mouw contends that the broader understanding of divine command is itself evidenced in the Bible, and we will miss many divine imperatives if we give attention only to its grammatical imperatives. "The Bible is much more than a compendium of imperatives: the sacred writings contain historical narratives, prayers, sagas, songs, parables, letters, complaints, pleadings, visions, and so on. The moral relevance of the divine commandments found in the Scriptures can only be understood by viewing them in their interrelatedness with these other types of writings."[24]

It should be noted here that Mouw's concern about the breadth of the biblical moral witness and the need for a sophisticated interpretation of that witness characterizes much evangelical ethics today. Any tradition, such as our own, that places such great stock in the written Word must attend to developing the best, most accurate, most nuanced, and most comprehensive interpretation of that Word that it can. Here evangelical ethicists have found ready companions among evangelical (and some non-evangelical) biblical scholars doing fresh work at the intersection of canonical Scripture and both ancient and contemporary ethics. Ethicists who are well versed in biblical studies, such as Glen Stassen and Allen Verhey, here encounter biblical scholars who are well versed in ethics, such as Richard Longenecker and Richard Hays. This "Bible and ethics" literature, which has been developing in both depth and breadth over the last three decades, now plays a major role in the best scholarship in evangelical ethics. It has helped demonstrate how much easier it is to claim a high view of biblical authority than to agree on the best interpretation of the biblical witness.

One of the ways Mouw works out the broader notion of divine command is in relation to a biblical worldview, another critical concept in contemporary evangelicalism. The Bible is authority not only in its direct statements, but in the larger story implicit in the Bible, insofar as it addresses the essential worldview questions such as: Who am I? What's wrong? What is the remedy? He is thus interested "in the ways in which the broad 'oughts' of the good life are related to the even larger Christian vision of what it means to live and move and have our being in a world created by God."[25] The role of worldview can be particularly seen in his ethical analysis of political life. Such "worldviewish" thinking has only grown in popularity in evangelical circles in recent years, as evidenced in popular treatments such as Chuck Colson and Nancy Pearcey's *How Then Shall We Live?* as well as in the vast literature of Christian higher education.

In *Politics and the Biblical Drama*, Mouw argues that the Scripture does not often give us direct, systematic guidance for social life; but nonetheless, "The Bible has spoken to us in the 'wholeness' of our lives, including our political lives. We must attempt to speak about political matters out of minds and hearts disciplined by the word from God. Our political thoughts must be developed to the point where they are fitting ones for people who confess obedience to the will of God."[26] Drawing on a biblical theology paradigm that is widely used in Reformed circles, Mouw sets out to address political life through the biblical drama of creation, fall, redemption, and eschaton. From each part of the biblical drama, he seeks to articulate an understanding of the political sphere and the Christian's calling therein. For example, from the creation paradigm, we understand that "human beings were created for positive social cooperation with each other, to perform certain tasks with respect to the rest of creation, in obedience to the will of the Creator."[27] From this we can contend that the state, as a key agent of such social cooperation, has not only a negative restraining or remedial function, but a positive contribution to make to human social life. From the biblical understanding of the fall and sin, we come to understand that all injustice and oppression stem from personal rebellion against the Creator. Furthermore, there are "institutionalizations of the personal sinful project [that] can come to have a life of their own. For this reason it is not enough to insist, as many conservative evangelical Christians have done, that 'changed hearts will change society.'"[28] But due to the nature of sin, we must also recognize the temptation for politics to usurp God's domain and in so doing become oppressive and manipulative. These are examples then of the ways in which a larger understanding of God's commands and biblical directives can guide our thinking and actions within the social order and impact even the social order itself.

Divine command ethics, as Mouw envisions it, need not be set over against virtue or character ethics. While many virtue ethicists question the decision-focused and principle-focused orientations of traditional divine command theories, Mouw believes that the two approaches are not antithetical and in fact need each other. Any divine command theory that sets forth propositional statements of truth and moral goodness needs to recognize "that they are but distillations from a much richer and more textured drama—and that to distance them for too long from that narrative context is to deprive them of the source of their life-directing power."[29] For as Mouw notes, even the Decalogue is set in its narrative context: "I am the LORD your God, who brought you out of the land of Egypt, out of the house of bondage" (Exod. 20:2 NKJV). Virtue then will manifest itself in obedience to divine directives, but obedience to those directives will play a role in the development of virtue. And in similar fashion, he contends, moral character and moral decisions must go hand in hand.

While Christian ethics is rooted in God's commands, situated in the larger framework and worldview of the biblical story, in good Reformed fashion Mouw insists that this is not a sectarian ethic. Christians are called to show forth the rule of God in all spheres of human activity, not only in the church or personal life. But Mouw is acutely aware of the tension this brings to the Christian ethics enterprise, namely the tension between the particularities of God's commands rooted in Scripture and the pluralism of the larger society. Thus he asserts that Christians should not attempt "to promote legislation whose primary purpose is to force non-Christians to conform to specifically Christian patterns." Moreover, Mouw asserts, "A concern to promote justice must be based on a desire that human beings be free to pursue the interests and projects that flow from their fundamental life commitments, however regrettable those choices may be from a Christian point of view."[30] Such is not an acquiescence to the pluralisms of our age, but a recognition that commitments to truth and moral particularism must be commended with civility and a repudiation of triumphalism, a tendency he finds too often among his evangelical cohorts. After all, as Mouw reminds us, "The conflict [between competing systems of thought and morals] is real: truth and righteousness must someday vanquish all falsehood and oppression. The triumph, however, will belong to God. Our appropriate creaturely response to that victory will be one of humble gratitude and not smug vindication."[31]

The Anabaptist Strand: John Howard Yoder

Anabaptists make for an excellent example of the distinction between orthodoxy and evangelicalism that we have proposed in this chapter. Historically, Anabaptists are certainly orthodox in their doctrine and ethics, but they have not always been comfortable with the label "evangelical," and from the earliest days they have sometimes seen themselves as neither Protestant nor Catholic, due to opposition on both fronts.[32] Thus, while the late John Howard Yoder always had some ambivalence about being called an evangelical, his thinking has seemingly found its greatest home in evangelical environs. On more than one occasion, he noted that he wrote *The Politics of Jesus* for realists in the Reinhold Niebuhr tradition, but the book found its greatest reception in evangelical seminaries and colleges. He was acutely aware that the language of discipleship was the language of evangelical Christians. But of course Yoder's influence went far beyond that sphere—because, we now see, discipleship is a biblical/orthodox concept, not an "evangelical" one.

The essential thrust of Yoder's thinking is well known. The primary argument against which he wrote was "that Jesus is simply not relevant in any immediate sense to the questions of social ethics."[33] Mainstream ethics had for years, in Yoder's reading of the situation, argued from a theology of the natural in which the right is discerned from the realities around us. In contrast, he sets forth the thesis "that the ministry and the claims of Jesus are best understood as presenting . . . not the avoidance of political options, but one particular social-political-ethical option." And that option understands Jesus "to be not only relevant but also normative for a contemporary Christian social ethic."[34]

Large segments of *The Politics of Jesus* seek to demonstrate that this thesis is compatible with the rest of the Bible and the thinking of biblical theology, a pattern of justifying their claims toward which evangelicals feel intuitively compelled, as we have seen. Yoder works directly and thoroughly with the biblical texts in a way that was most unusual in Christian ethics in 1972. Moving from a creative exegesis of the Gospel according to Luke, to analyses of hard Old Testament texts, to exposition of Pauline passages, Yoder attempts to argue his thesis and answer his critics. In contrast to a spiritualizing of Jesus, an interim ethic, or other avoidance mechanisms, he argues that "Jesus was in his divinely mandated (i.e., promised, anointed, messianic) prophethood, priesthood, and kingship, the bearer of a new possibility of human, social, and therefore political relationships. His baptism is the inauguration and his cross is the culmination of that new regime in which his disciples are called to share."[35] What Jesus has established through the work of the cross is a new society, a countercommunity that in its very way of life stands in contrast to the prevailing politics of all societies, and this most clearly in our refusal to control history through the use of violence.

Yoder and the Anabaptists in general are accustomed to the charge of sectarianism—that if the politics of Jesus is primarily evidenced in the new community, the church, it is therefore irrelevant to the rest of society. But Yoder is adamant that this is not a pietistic sectarianism of withdrawal, despite the fact that kingdom ethics cannot be immediately translated into the political structures of this world. "What needs to be seen is rather that the primary social structure through which the gospel works to change other structures is that of the Christian community."[36] The particulars of how this is accomplished are probably better seen in some of Yoder's other works. For example, in *The Christian Witness to the State*, published eight years earlier, Yoder writes: "The church is herself a society. Her very existence, the fraternal relations of her members, their ways of dealing with their differences and their needs are, or rather should be, a demonstration of what love means in social relations. This demonstration cannot be transposed directly into non-Christian society, for in the church it functions only on the basis of repentance and faith; yet by analogy certain of its aspects may be instructive as stimuli to the conscience of society."[37]

The witness to the state, however, is more than mere embodiment of Jesus' social ethic within the church. The believing community can speak a word of conscience to the state and economic order. In *Christian Witness*, a very early work for Yoder (1964, as we have seen), he adopts the term "middle axioms" from then-contemporary Christian ethics to speak of communications between the church and the state. These middle axioms, such as democracy, education, liberty, equality, and human rights, can "mediate between the general principles of christological ethics and the concrete problems of political application. They claim no metaphysical status, but serve usefully as rules of thumb to make meaningful the impact of Christian social thought."[38] In his later writings, such as *Body Politics* (1992), Yoder shifts to a more richly biblical approach in advocating normative Christian practices that have clear, analogous implications for public ethics. For example, the church practices the Lord's Supper, which has clear implications for feeding the hungry and for economic justice (cf. 1 Cor. 11:21–34).[39]

A significant part of Yoder's argument for the relevance of Jesus' ethic, manifest within the life and witness of the church, is a historical argument. Namely, when the church has garnered power to control society, it has come to be controlled by society itself. As he puts it in *The Priestly Kingdom*, "Once we dominate society, the way we want things to go is the way they might very well be able to go. . . . The rightness or wrongness of behavior can now be translated or interpreted in terms of good and bad outcomes,"[40] and the distinctiveness of Jesus for ethics is lost. This not only impacts the ability of the church as a minority community to be relevant to society, it also renders the church powerless in its own faith journey.

The distinctiveness of the church as a believing community from the world is a persistent theme in evangelicalism—as it was in pre-Constantinian orthodoxy. We have seen it in Henry, in Mouw, and now in Yoder, though each in his own way. To some it seems to imply a dualism: The church has one ethics, the world has another, or the church attends to its own ethics, and not to what is happening in the world. Yoder acknowledges the *distinctiveness* of the church both in identity and ethics, while carefully avoiding the language of *dualism*, when he writes:

> There is still a sense in which the Christian community can and must "do ethics for the world," i.e., cooperate in ethical discourse beyond the borders of faith, or in language not dependent on faith. But that is a different kind of discourse from the ethical deliberation of the believing community. Such discourse beyond the bounds of faith may differ in its conclusions about the propriety of certain kinds of action which would be excluded from integral Christian discipleship but would be less easily excluded from the wider society in which faith in the crucified and risen Lord is not affirmed. I can, for instance, expect pacifism of a fellow believer who is committed to the same Lord, as I cannot expect it of other fellow citizens in a value-pluralistic nation.[41]

This vision is often set over against other types of evangelical social engagement that might appear to engage the world more forthrightly, such as the Reformed strand. But we do well to recall that some years ago John Howard Yoder and Richard Mouw together wrote an article seeking to overcome such false polarities. Against individualistic and pietistic patterns, they rejected "a dualism that either ignores or deprecates this-worldly obligations." They contended that for both the Reformed and Anabaptist traditions, "Following Jesus has an inescapably corporate dimension. . . . And the corporateness here is not fully contained within the 'internal' patterns of Christian community. The church serves in turn as a paradigmatic society—an eschatological sign of God's communal designs for the New Creation."[42]

The Wesleyan Strand: Stephen Mott

In nineteenth-century America, the energetic evangelical social reform movements were to a significant degree propelled by Wesleyan ideals. These believers took to heart the pronouncement of John Wesley that "solitary religion is not found [in the gospel]. 'Holy solitaries' is a phrase no more consistent with the gospel than 'holy adulterers.' The gospel of Christ knows of no religion but social; no holiness but social holiness."[43] Today among Wesleyan evangelicals the commitment to spread "holiness throughout the land" (including a social holiness) is still alive and is evident in the writings of Stephen Mott, among other Methodist voices (such as Stanley Hauerwas, Christine Pohl, and Sondra Wheeler). An ordained United Methodist minister, Mott taught for a number of years at Gordon-Conwell Theological Seminary and is currently pastoring a United Methodist Church near Boston.

Though Mott rarely uses the language of holiness in his writings, the concept is implicit. We perhaps get the flavor of his Wesleyan sentiments (and the implicit commitments to holiness, personal and social) best through the preface of his major work, *Biblical Ethics and Social Change*:

> It is in memory of my father, Royden Cross Mott, that I dedicate this book. From him and from my mother, Katherine Hyde Mott, I learned the natural association of faith and social compassion. Much of my father's pastoral ministry was spent with those whose lives were lived on the edge of the community: across the river, on the other side of the tracks, on the back country roads. . . . My father battled the liquor industry which took his people's money and fueled their weaknesses, and he challenged the YMCA which would not let them in. The Psalmist, the prophets, Jesus, John Wesley, Charles Dickens, Mom, and Daddy are blurred together in these memories; some taught the others so that they all taught me. My father combined active social love with a ministry of revival. Why? Because he lived his sermons, and his sermons received their life from the wrinkled pages of the Word of his God—and mine.[44]

The essential thesis of Mott's work is that "the heart of biblical thought mandates efforts to correct economic and social injustices in our communities" and that "the use of political authority to achieve justice should complement the stress upon the witness of the church as counter-community which is found in many recent writings."[45]

The first part of *Biblical Ethics and Social Change* seeks to build a biblical theology of social involvement. He works with five biblical themes to establish this grounding, each carefully derived from exegetical treatments of biblical texts and reasoned from broader biblical theology constructs: the social reality of sin, God's grace as a grounding for human acts of goodness, God's love as the essential expression of grace and a basis for human rights and dignity, God's justice in continuity with divine love as the basis for an egalitarian disposition toward the oppressed, and the reign of God as the ongoing presence of Jesus' earthly ministry and the impetus for our own impact upon social realities.

Mott establishes his grounding for social ethics the way most orthodox and evangelicals do, through the use of the Bible. But just how does Scripture work for him in establishing a social ethic? In a small work entitled *Jesus and Social Ethics*, Mott contends that the Bible serves as a moral guide in various ways: through basic directions for our lives, motivation for action, the formation of character, the development of a worldview to guide our perceptions of reality, as well as the direct statements of Scripture itself (such as commands and principles). In these various forms, "the Bible contributes substantial content to the following structural components of a social ethics among others: justice, the nature of humanity, the concept of history, the nature of society and groups, the understanding of power and property, and the purpose of government."[46] Though we must always guard against turning the Bible into an ethical code or systematic ethics text, the Scripture has the ability to address us today in concrete ways. "The transcendent ideas are addressed to concrete situations of another time. This fact affirms the importance of history but also creates difficulties in understanding both their transcendent character and their application to a different age." For Mott, such difficulties are not insurmountable, for we must seek "to understand the meaning for another period of that very concreteness which makes God's Word relevant to a particular moment of history."[47]

For Mott, social ethics cannot stop with the Bible. It must always seek concrete paths to biblically warranted social change, and in the last part of *Biblical Ethics* he explores five paths to justice in the world: evangelism, the church as countercommunity, strategic noncooperation, the possibility of the use of force, and creative reform through politics. In this part he seeks to utilize paths that most evangelicals have long accepted (i.e., evangelism, embodiment), paths about which evangelicals (at least of an earlier generation) have been cautious (i.e., noncooperation and politics), and paths that evangelicals have debated (i.e., the use of force). He believes that these paths can come "together to provide a road to justice. It is a road that can most easily be followed by those who at the beginning meet One who gives them in place of oppression a yoke that is easy and a burden that is light."[48]

The Anglican Strand: Oliver O'Donovan

The Anglican Church has often been called the "broad church," which unfortunately has often meant the toleration of overly broad boundaries in theology and ethics. However, within that breadth there has long been an orthodox and self-identified evangelical presence, especially in England and a number of the British commonwealth countries. Though it is sometimes labeled low-church Anglicanism, the evangelical movement is actually much broader than such a designation. Anglican evangelicalism clearly has a different flavor than the more revivalistic brands of American evangelicalism, but in recent years British and American evangelicals have had significant interaction through bridge scholars such as John Stott, J. I. Packer, and Alister McGrath. Among Anglican evangelicals there have historically been strong voices for social reform, particularly evident in the likes of the Clapham Sect in eighteenth-century England, a group of well-known public figures such as William Wilberforce who played a key role in abolition and various other reform movements. And there have been significant voices seeking to provide a theological foundation for ethics, a foundation that is much broader than the mere statements of Scripture itself, but that build from Scripture and the order of reality in God's good creation. In recent years one of the most significant voices in that tradition, and some would argue in all of Christian moral thinking, has been Oliver O'Donovan, the Regius Professor of Moral and Pastoral Theology at the University of Oxford, and Canon of Christ Church, Oxford.

In 1986, O'Donovan wrote his seminal work, *Resurrection and Moral Order: An Outline for Evangelical Ethics*. Using a classic Augustinian/Reformed definition of the word "evangelical," from the opening pages O'Donovan claims that "the foundations of Christian ethics must be evangelical foundations;

or, to put it more simply, Christian ethics must arise from the gospel of Jesus Christ. Otherwise it could not be *Christian* ethics."[49] Christian faith and Christian morality can never be severed,[50] for to the very nature of the gospel there belong certain ethical and moral judgments. For O'Donovan, this evangelical ethic is worked out not merely by specific texts of Scripture (though clearly they count and are binding), but rather by the intricacies of theological understandings rooted in the Divine Word. "It is the task of theology to uncover the hidden relation of things that gives the [biblical] appeal force. We are driven to concentrate on the resurrection as our starting-point because it tells us of God's vindication of his creation, and so of our created life."[51]

In affirming the resurrection as the starting point of an evangelical ethic, O'Donovan is not seeking to isolate it from other aspects of the work of Christ or other theological affirmations. Indeed, he believes that the debate between a creation ethic and a kingdom ethic is a misplaced debate. Rather, he argues, "In the resurrection of Christ creation is restored and the kingdom of God dawns."[52] The resurrection of Christ is an affirmation of creation and thus "the reality of a divinely-given order of things in which human nature itself is located."[53] Though that order is badly flawed by the fall, it remains a reality, and without it we are left with essentially a "voluntarist" approach, which assumes morality to be the creation of the human will. But an evangelical ethic not only looks back to creation, it looks forward to the eschatological hope of transformation in which the created order will reach its *telos* or fulfillment. Holding creation and eschatology together through the resurrection of Jesus Christ means for O'Donovan a repudiation of historicism in which the moral good is mediated through the developing culture. Rather, he argues, morality is our "participation in the created order. Christian morality is [the] glad response to the deed of God which has restored, proved and fulfilled that order, making man free to conform to it."[54] This, then, forms the objective reality in which ethics is grounded.

But morality is not complete with the objective reality alone. There is also a subjective reality that enables the moral agent, and this is the gift of Pentecost, the work of the Holy Spirit. O'Donovan asserts, "The Spirit makes the reality of redemption present to us," and "The Spirit evokes our free response as moral agents to the reality of redemption."[55] However, the freedom to respond to Christ in the Spirit is not a normless freedom; it is freedom to the ordered reality of the world and a freedom expressed in love. "Love is the overall shape of Christian ethics, the form of the human participation in created order." It is both the fulfillment of the moral law and the form of the moral virtues. O'Donovan is quick to add, however, "*Agape* cannot exercise its own creativity independently of God's creativity, which has gone before it and given the universe the order to which it attends."[56]

Love therefore can only be understood within the framework of an evangelical ethic in which the resurrection of Christ vindicates the order of reality from creation, points us toward the fulfillment of that order in the eschaton, and allows us to participate now in the Christ who himself makes love intelligible. Such love will be manifest in both actions and character, but in good evangelical fashion O'Donovan reminds us: "Though settled dispositions and character, though the record of good things done or not done, are important features in human morality, they take second place to this formative moment, the meeting with the divine presence in Jesus which stamps the life with the mark of love."[57]

Other Voices and Strands

We have briefly surveyed five main strands of evangelical moral thought with an acute awareness that there are other voices and other strands that could have been included. Some would think that the most grievous omission is Karl Barth. Though Barth's magisterial theology is rich with ethical import, his neo-orthodox perspective has often been questioned by those in the contemporary evangelical movement, so we have not included him here.

One can hardly think of evangelicals without mentioning Baptists, in their varying expressions. It is hard to define a baptistic ethic per se, for some have tended more in an Anabaptist direction and others in a more Reformed direction. One attempt to define a Baptist vision describes it this way: "The awareness of the biblical story as our story, . . . mission as responsibility for costly witness, . . . liberty as the freedom to obey God without state help or hindrance, . . . discipleship as life transformed into obedience to Jesus' lordship, and . . . community as daily sharing in the vision."[58] Among evangelical Baptist ethicists we could include Henlee Barnette, James McClendon, Glen Stassen, Michael Westmoreland-White, T. B. Maston, Joe Trull, Barry Harvey, and Stanley Grenz.

There is also within evangelicalism a Lutheran strand, usually found in groups like the Missouri Synod Lutherans, and attempting to carry on Luther's tradition of justifying faith active in love. Among the evangelical Lutherans we might note Milton Rudnick and Gilbert Meilaender, the latter of whom attempts a synthesis of character ethics with Lutheran formulations and has offered profoundly important work, especially in bioethics. Meilaender is certainly orthodox, though whether he would like to be called "evangelical" in the sense under discussion here is unclear.

In the African-American community we find many thinkers doing ethics in ways quite similar to evangelicals (in other words, they are orthodox), even if they operate outside the institutional spheres of (largely white) evangelicalism. These seek direct guidance from Scripture and envision the moral life flowing from a deep, personal awakening through faith in Christ and the presence of the Holy Spirit, but always manifest in a social ethic that addresses the oppression and injustice that the community, and the oppressed generally, have for too long borne. Good examples include Cheryl Sanders and Samuel Roberts—and one must not forget Martin Luther King Jr., himself trained in liberal Protestant Christian social ethics (Christian ethics B), which King brought into creative and society-changing interaction with his deeper roots in the black church tradition.

We can also hardly mention evangelicalism without noting the growing strand of Pentecostal and charismatic Christians. To date, these bodies have produced little by way of academic ethics, but given their worldwide growth and impact, it is only a matter of time until they produce a full-fledged Pentecostal ethic. Early signs of such can be seen in Murray Dempster and Douglas Petersen.

Common Themes in Evangelical Ethics

The dizzying variety of thinkers who could be called "evangelical" helps confirm the thesis that what makes ethics evangelical is essentially what makes it orthodox: a commitment to biblical authority and a consequent willingness to develop ethical norms within the parameters established by biblical teaching. In this sense, the number of ethicists who self-identify as evangelicals is insignificant. What really matters is whether they do their work under the authority of Scripture and a call to deep personal awakening through faith in Christ and the presence of the Holy Spirit. If that is the test, the tent grows much larger, and we find allies and co-laborers not just within historic evangelicalism but also within renewal movements in mainline Christianity, and among Catholic and Eastern Orthodox thinkers as well. This also helps us clarify the very real differences that exist between any orthodox Christian version of ethics and the competing visions to be found in other faith traditions, in unorthodox Christianity, and in secular moral philosophy. These other ethical systems do not undertake their work under the final authority of the canonical Scriptures and/or are not experientially grounded in faith in Christ and the presence of the Holy Spirit.

Our discussion of representative thinkers demonstrates that certain commonalities can be identified in evangelical ethics. Yet the same commonalities can almost always be identified within a broader biblical orthodoxy. Though exceptions to the generalizations listed below are not hard to find, a list of the most significant commonalities in what we have called evangelical ethics includes the following:

- Commitment to the rooting of ethical reflection and practice in a personal relationship with Jesus Christ, our Savior and Lord, a relationship rooted in personal conversion and the experience of regeneration by God's grace.
- Confidence in the entire canonical Bible as the eternal and always applicable Word of God, leading to a special-revelation-based ethic that attempts to attend deeply and carefully to issues of hermeneutics and

biblical theology and searches the length and breadth of Scriptures for moral direction.

- Belief in the authority not just of the broad principles or motifs of biblical moral teaching, such as love and justice, but also of its particular commands and injunctions—indeed, the whole of Scripture.
- Emphasis on the centrality of Jesus Christ for ethics, both his concrete moral teachings and practices and the entire range of classic orthodox christological claims about his person and work.
- Recognition of the illuminating and sanctifying work of the Holy Spirit as central to moral discernment and empowerment.
- Emphasis on rigorous moral effort as an aspect of Christian discipleship, while guarding carefully against the development of legalism or works-righteousness.
- Commitment to a holistic vision of ethics including moral decisions, principles, character, practices, and vision, rather than an isolation of one or another element as decisive.
- A focus on the believing church as the context of Christian moral formation, a body of disciples that is faithful, distinctive, and visibly different from the world.
- A stress on the church's missionary engagement with the world in the hope of social reform and transformation until the kingdom of God is fully consummated, and careful reflection on the possibilities and limits of various strategies of engagement, while recognizing that the church awaits the return of Jesus Christ when, and only when, all shall be made right.

Conclusion

In the Farewell Discourse in John, Jesus says, "If you love me, you will keep my commandments. And I will ask the Father, and he will give you another Advocate, to be with you forever. This is the Spirit of truth" (John 14:15–17a). The Christian moral life begins with God's grace in Jesus Christ. But it continues with the grateful response of a church that loves its Savior, a response of obedience that is directed and empowered by the Holy Spirit.

This grateful obedience to God-in-Christ has been incarnated by the church in some of its finest moments. Consider the martyr-witnesses of the early church, and of today, who have died under persecution rather than renounce their Lord; the abolitionists—and the slaves they freed—who risked everything for justice and liberation from bondage in the nineteenth-century South; the Christian resisters and rescuers under Nazism in the 1940s who found in the Scriptures the guidance needed to resist the murderous evils of Hitlerism; the Koinonia community, led by Clarence Jordan, which lived out racial reconciliation in pre–civil rights south Georgia despite brutal persecution.

In a culture no longer confident that moral truth even exists or can be known, and in a church riven by bitter differences over many issues, including the authority for making moral judgments, evangelical/orthodox Christian ethics, centered on the obedience of disciples to the lordship of Christ and grounded in the authority of the Bible, is looking better and better.

7

Theological Foundations for an Evangelical Political Philosophy

Nicholas Wolterstorff

OUR TOPIC CAN be approached from a number of different directions. A good many Christian theologians have included reflections on government as part of their comprehensive theology. We could develop "theological foundations for an evangelical political philosophy" by engaging in dialogue with some of the more important of these theologians. Since every Christian theology is grounded, more or less directly and in one way or another, in the Christian Scriptures, this approach would lead us sooner or later to Scripture. Alternatively, we could start with the relevant Scriptures and move from there to a theology of the political order. On this occasion I will follow the latter procedure: Instead of starting with theology we will start with Scripture.

Starting with Scripture still leaves options. We could first assemble a large collection of relevant passages and then try to arrive at some synthesizing conclusions. Alternatively, we could take a few central passages and allow them to lead us to others. I will follow the latter procedure.

Nothing much hangs on this particular way of going about things; any of these different approaches would lead eventually to the same issues. My reasons for choosing the approach indicated are that it will prove more efficient, and

140

evangelicals rightly want to be assured that the theologian's appeal to Scripture is not an afterthought but that his or her theology is genuinely rooted in, and inspired by, Scripture.

Paul's Advice to the Roman Christians Concerning the State

It was not obvious to the early Christians what stance they should take toward the institutions of Hellenistic society. The radical quality of Jesus' teaching, combined with the fact that he apparently never addressed the issue with full generality, made it problematic for them how they should relate to the extant domestic, economic, and political institutions. Should they reject those institutions and migrate to some place where they could dwell by themselves, establish alternative institutions, and within those alternative institutions live out the radical way of life taught by Jesus? Or, religious institutions excepted, should they live and act within the extant institutions in the manner of everyone else, contenting themselves with living out the radical way of Jesus within the church? Or, religious institutions excepted, should they live and act within the extant institutions but attempt there to live out Christ's new way? Or—yet a fourth possibility—should they live and act within the institutions of polity and economy in the manner of everyone else, while living out the way of Jesus in their households as well as in the church?

Because the answer was not at once obvious, the apostles and their associates regularly gave the members of the new churches advice on the topic, some of this advice being preserved for us in the New Testament. Two of the most extensive passages are found in Paul's letter to the Christians at Ephesus (5:21ff.) and in his letter to the Christians at Colossae (3:18ff.). In these passages, Paul gives advice to his readers on how they should relate to the institutions of marriage, family, and slave economy. He does not give advice on how they should relate to the political order. By contrast, in Romans 12:19–13:7 Paul gives advice on how to relate to the political order but says nothing about marriage, family, or slave economy.

The question arises whether we should interpret the Romans passage in conjunction with those other passages, on the ground that Paul is giving a unified body of advice and that it may well prove illuminating to read them in the light of each other, or whether we should treat the Romans passage by itself. Ever since Luther, the passages in Ephesians and Colossians have been called *Haustafeln*—literally, "house tables"—on the ground that they give advice concerning the household. Very often, using this name for these passages reflects the interpreter's view that Paul's attitude toward the institutions of the household is significantly different from his attitude toward political institutions.

I think there are two cogent reasons for not adopting this latter approach. In the first place, advice concerning the institutions of the household is not always separated in the New Testament from advice concerning political institutions—which makes it seem likely that what accounts for their separation in Paul is nothing more than the focus of his interest in the passages in question. The writer of 1 Peter moves seamlessly from advice to his readers concerning their relation to political institutions to advice concerning their relation to household institutions. Let me quote a bit of what he says.

> For the Lord's sake accept the authority [*krisis*] of every human institution, whether of the emperor as supreme, or of governors, as sent by him to punish those who do wrong and to praise those who do right. . . . Honor everyone. Love the family of believers. Fear God. Honor the emperor. Slaves, accept the authority of your masters with all deference, not only those who are kind and gentle but also those who are harsh. For it is a credit to you if, being aware of God, you endure pain while suffering unjustly. . . . Wives, in the same way, accept the authority of your husbands, so that, even if some of them do not obey the word, they may be won over without a word by their wives' conduct. . . . Husbands, in the same way, show consideration for your wives in your life together, paying honor to the woman as the weaker sex, since they too are also heirs of the gracious gift of life.
>
> 1 Peter 2:13–3:7

Secondly, the pattern of advice given in all the passages mentioned is strikingly similar. Nowhere are Christians urged to go off by themselves to set up their own social institutions. With the exception, of course, of religious institutions, they are to participate side by side with non-Christians in the institutions of their society: marriage, family, economy, and polity. They are to do so with a difference, however, a difference both in how they understand the significance of those institutions and in how they conduct themselves within them. This, as I say, is the structure of the advice given in all the passages, no matter whether it is household institutions that the writer has in view or political institutions. Of course, what we learn from history is that as Christians became more numerous, as they came into positions of power and those already in positions of power became Christian, and as they thought through the implications of Christ's teaching, the institutions themselves began to change.

Let us now have before us Paul's instructions to his readers in Rome concerning their relation to the political order—keeping in mind that this is part of that larger body of advice in the epistolary literature of the New Testament concerning the relation of members of the new Christian movement to extant social institutions. The Romans passage is, of course, one of the great classical passages for Christian reflection on the political order.

> Beloved, never avenge [*ekdikeō*] yourselves, but leave room for the wrath [*orgē*] of God; for it is written, "Vengeance [*ekdikēsis*] is mine, I will repay, says the Lord." No, "if your enemies are hungry, feed them; if they are thirsty, give them

something to drink; for by doing this you will heap burning coals on their heads." Do not be overcome by evil, but overcome evil with good.

Let every person be subject to the governing authorities; for there is no authority except from God, and those authorities that exist have been instituted by God. Therefore whoever resists authority resists what God has appointed, and those who resist will incur judgment [*krima*]. For rulers are not a terror to good conduct, but to bad. Do you wish to have no fear of the authority? Then do what is good, and you will receive its approval; for it is God's servant [*diakonos*] for your good. But if you do what is wrong, you should be afraid, for the authority does not bear the sword in vain! It is the servant [*diakonos*] of God to execute wrath [*orgē*] on the wrongdoer. Therefore one must be subject, not only because of wrath [*orgē*] but also because of conscience. For the same reason you also pay taxes, for the authorities are God's servants [*leitourgoi*], busy with this very thing. Pay to all what is due them—taxes to whom taxes are due, revenue to whom revenue is due, respect to whom respect is due, honor to whom honor is due.

Romans 12:19–13:7

Almost every word in this passage has been the subject of intense and extended controversy. Several of the most important points seem obvious, however. The stance that one is to take toward one's government is the same that 1 Peter enjoins. We are to obey or be subject to our rulers (the Greek verb can mean either of these) "for the sake of conscience." Or to put it in 1 Peter's words, we are to obey or submit to the emperor and his governors "for the Lord's sake." All by itself, Paul's verb, translated in the NRSV as "be subject to," might mean buckling under as a matter of prudence. That interpretation becomes implausible, however, when Paul goes on to say to his readers that they are to obey or be subject not only because of governmental power (wrath), but because of conscience (*suneidēsis*). Doing what is commanded or required is the *right* thing to do, not merely the prudential thing. What this implies is that "the authorities" have genuine authority, not just power. And so we are to "honor" them—which of course is quite different from merely fearing them. Honor the emperor, says 1 Peter, honor the authorities, says Paul. The Greek word used (noun *timē*, verb *timaō*) is the same in both cases as that which Paul uses in Ephesians 6:2 when he instructs children to "honor your father and mother."

What is also clear in both Paul and 1 Peter is the goal, the *telos*, of government. Its *telos*, in the words of 1 Peter, is "to punish those who do wrong and to praise those who do right." Paul goes on to describe the relation of God to the *telos* of government. It is *God* who has instituted or appointed governing authorities for the purpose of punishing wrongdoers and praising or approving those who do good. Government must not be thought of as some purely human artifact, nor must it be thought of as a work of the devil.

These points, I say, seem obvious; the interpretation of other points will require some work on our part. But before we get to that, another *locus classicus* for the Christian understanding of government must be laid on the table. In the thirteenth chapter of Revelation we get a vivid reminder of the painful fact that government, like everything else in this world, is fallen. Though instituted or appointed by God to punish the wrongdoer and praise the one who does good, government itself becomes a wrongdoer, sometimes to an utterly appalling degree. The great beast of which the passage speaks has traditionally been interpreted as a symbol for Rome at a time of widespread persecution of Christians—most likely under Domitian (81–96), though possibly under Nero (54–68). The beast has "authority over every tribe and people and language and nation." Everyone "whose name has not been written . . . in the book of life of the Lamb" worships it, saying, "Who is like the beast, and who can fight against it?" The beast utters "blasphemies against God," having been "allowed to make war on the saints and to conquer them." Another beast, this one with horns like a lamb, acts on behalf of the first, making "the earth and its inhabitants worship the first beast." It causes everyone who does not worship the image of the first beast to be killed; and after causing everybody to be stamped with its mark on their right hand or forehead, it orders that nobody without the mark be allowed to buy or sell.

The Old Testament Background to Paul's Advice

Paul's advice in Romans 12 and 13 was not a bolt out of the blue. Paul was deeply steeped in rabbinic Judaism; and the advice he gives to the Christians in Rome concerning their relation to the governing authorities not only echoes some of the things Jesus said, but directly quotes two passages from the Old Testament and employs two lines of thought prominent in the Old Testament.

The first passage quoted comes from Deuteronomy 32. Let us have it before us in its context. God is speaking:

> Vengeance is mine, and recompense . . . ;
> because the day of their calamity is at hand,
>   their doom comes swiftly.
> Indeed the LORD will vindicate his people,
>   have compassion on his servants.
>
> Deuteronomy 32:35–36

For the purpose of understanding Paul's thought, it is worth also having before us a passage to which he may have been alluding without directly quoting—Leviticus 19:17–18. Again, God is speaking:

You shall not hate in your heart anyone of your kin; you shall reprove your neighbor, or you will incur guilt yourself. You shall not take vengeance or bear a

grudge against any of your people, but you shall love your neighbor as yourself:
I am the LORD.

The other passage Paul quotes comes from Proverbs 25:21–22:

> If your enemies are hungry, give them bread to eat;
>   and if they are thirsty, give them water to drink;
> for you will heap coals of fire on their heads,
>   and the LORD will reward you.

Those were the passages Paul quoted. Now for the lines of thought that he
was employing. Prominent in the witness of the Old Testament is its presentation of God as *loving and executing justice*. Here is just one of many passages
that could be cited.

> Mighty King, lover of justice,
>   you have established equity;
> you have executed justice
>   and righteousness in Jacob.
>
> Psalm 99:4

Justice, as we all know, comes in two basic forms. One form can be called
corrective justice. Someone has done something unjust, or is alleged to have
done something unjust; corrective justice consists of rendering what is due
the various parties in that situation. But such justice presupposes a more basic
type of justice, call it *primary* justice. In doing something unjust, the person
has violated the requirements of primary justice; if there were no such requirements, there would be no such thing as corrective justice. Probably we should
hear the psalmist, in the passage quoted above, as alluding to both types of
justice, primary and corrective.

Confronted with a violation of primary justice, God "executes justice" or
"renders judgment." Such rendering of judgment has two components: God
vindicates the one wronged, and God *pronounces verdict and sentence* on the
wrongdoer. Dozens of passages could be cited in which God is described as
rendering judgment; the passage just quoted from Deuteronomy, from which
Paul quotes, is just one example. God judges that his people have been wronged,
thereby "vindicating" them; and he pronounces and carries out sentence on
the wrongdoers. "The day of their calamity is at hand."

God renders judgment both concerning that which transpires within
Judah and Israel and that which transpires between them and the surrounding powers. But God also renders judgment on what transpires within and
among those surrounding powers. The opening chapters of the book of Amos
are the most vivid illustration of the latter point. The prophet, speaking in
the name of the Lord, pronounces sentence on Damascus (Syria), Gaza,

Tyre, Edom, Ammon, and Moab. The sentence pronounced on Ammon is representative:

> Thus says the LORD:
> "For three transgressions of the Ammonites,
>   and for four, I will not revoke the punishment;
> because they have ripped up women with child in Gilead,
>   that they might enlarge their border.
> So I will kindle fire in the wall of Rabbah,
>   and it shall devour her strongholds,
> with shouting in the day of battle,
>   with a tempest in the day of the whirlwind;
> and their king shall go into exile,
>   he and his princes together,"
> says the LORD.
>
> Amos 1:13–15 RSV

Having pronounced God's sentence on six of the surrounding powers, the prophet then turns to Judah and Israel (i.e., the Northern Kingdom). The denunciation of Israel is far lengthier than any of the others, and filled with a pathos lacking in the denunciations of the surrounding powers. Israel, along with Judah, has been God's favorite. He delivered them from slavery in Egypt:

> "I brought you up out of the land of Egypt,
>   and led you forty years in the wilderness, . . .
> Is it not indeed so, O people of Israel?"
> says the LORD.
>
> Amos 2:10–11 RSV

And he gave to them, and them alone, his Torah:

> Thus says the LORD:
> "For three transgressions of Judah,
>   and for four, I will not revoke the punishment;
> because they have rejected the law of the LORD,
>   and have not kept his statutes."
>
> Amos 2:4–5 RSV

The fact that God renders judgment on the surrounding powers implies that even without Torah those nations knew, or could have known, what God's justice required. Amos does not develop the point, but Paul does in a passage near the beginning of his letter to the Christians in Rome. Speaking of Christ's eschatological judgment, he says, "All who have sinned without the law will also perish without the law, and all who have sinned under the law will be judged by the law." Clearly by "law," here, Paul means Torah. But he continues: "When Gentiles who have not the law do by nature what the law requires, they are a law to themselves, even though they do not have the law. They show that what the law requires is written on their hearts, while their conscience also bears witness and their conflicting thoughts accuse or perhaps excuse them on that day when . . . God judges the secrets of men by Christ Jesus" (Rom. 2:12–16 RSV).

This passage has traditionally been cited, though not without controversy, as a biblical basis for the doctrine of natural law. Though the Gentiles do not *have* the law, that is, Torah, they nonetheless are a law to themselves—or better, they are *in themselves* a law. The very same things that Torah requires have been written on their hearts; their conscience bears witness to those things. It is for this reason that God's rendering judgment on their actions, and pronouncing and carrying out sentence, is not unjust; they knew better, or could have known better.

The other theme in the Old Testament that we must recover if we are to understand Paul's thought in Romans 13 is that God's rendering of judgment is in good measure mediated by human beings and human institutions. One mode of mediation was prophetic speech. In the denunciations he uttered, Amos was mediating God's judgment. It was not Amos but God who was pronouncing judgment on Judah, Israel, and the surrounding nations; Amos was simply speaking on behalf of God. But God's judgment was also seen as mediated by judges and rulers. Indeed, God's judgment was more fully mediated by judges and rulers than by prophets—though not more reliably! Prophets were not authorized to carry out sentence; rulers were. In Deuteronomy, God is reported as enjoining Israel to "appoint judges and officials" to "render just decisions for the people" (16:18–20). And from a good many other passages it becomes clear that such judges and officials were to be seen as rendering judgment on behalf of God. Consider, for example, the *locus classicus* description of the good king in Psalm 72:1–2 (RSV):

> Give the king thy justice, O God,
>   and thy righteousness to the royal son!
> May he judge thy people with righteousness,
>   And thy poor with justice!

No doubt it was Judah's king, and/or Israel's, that the psalmist had in view. But Amos' denunciations of the surrounding nations implies that God also requires of the rulers of the Gentiles that they render just judgment, and not themselves perpetrate injustice.

Paul's thought in Romans 13, when placed within this context of its Old Testament references and antecedents, now seems eminently clear. The task of the ruling authorities is to mediate God's judgment; they have been instituted or appointed by God for this purpose. They are God's deacons, God's liturgetes. Their task is to put a stamp of approval on those who do right and to subject the wrongdoer to wrath, *orgē*—this to be seen as the executing of God's wrath, God's *orgē*. Given the Old Testament background, it seems obvious that what Paul means is that the state is authorized to employ retributive punishment on God's behalf.

In short, in his letter to the Romans, Paul took Israel's understanding of the task of its rulers and applied this understanding to ruling authorities in general. His doing so had antecedents within the Old Testament itself—in the psalmist's praise of God as King of Kings, in Amos' denunciations of the surrounding powers, and so forth.

John reminds us in Revelation that rulers all too often do not do what they were appointed by God to do. Rather than rendering just judgment on God's behalf, they render unjust judgment on their own behalf. They become a terror to good conduct rather than to bad; they affirm and praise the one who does wrong rather than the one who does right. They are no longer God's servants and ministers. Or shall we say that they are *false* servants and *unruly* ministers—that they stand to the true ruler described in Psalm 72 as the false prophet stands to the true prophet?

Paul knew that this is how governments behave. He knew it from the Old Testament; more poignantly, he knew it from personal experience, and from his memory of Jesus' crucifixion. So we have to understand him as talking about *properly functioning* government. He is speaking normatively, not descriptively.

As part of his providential rule of humankind, God renders judgment, executes justice. Some of God's judgment is rendered at the end of the ages, some is rendered within this present age; some is direct, some is mediated through human beings; sometimes the mediator is no more than an instrument of God's causality, sometimes the mediator exercises authority on God's behalf. Government is assigned the awesome task in God's providential order for this present age of mediating God's judgment in the latter manner, vindicating those who have been wronged and convicting and carrying out retributive punishment on those who have done the wronging.

By contrast to what he says about the task of government, Paul tells his readers that they are not to avenge (*ekdikeō*) themselves; they are not themselves to execute vengeance (*ekdikēsis*). They are to leave the execution of wrath, *orgē*, to God. What this has to mean, when the passage as a whole is read in the context of its Old Testament quotations and allusions, is that retributive punishment is exclusively a function of duly authorized authorities. Paul's readers are not to take retribution into their own hands. They are to break with the old cycle of tit-for-tat vengeance—to break with it to the radical extent of giving even their enemies, the ones who have wronged them, food and drink.

Government as Part of the Creation Order

But is this approach to our topic, from what Paul and 1 Peter say about the task of government, not too confined? The task of government, they say, is to secure justice in society by affirming those who do right and pronouncing sentence and exercising retributive punishment on those who do wrong. Does this not give us a theology of just one among the several functions of government, namely the judicial function?

My response is that it is a mistake to interpret what Paul and 1 Peter say as relevant only to the judicial function of government. The judicial function cannot be exercised without the legislative function; no laws, no judges. And if those who do right are to be affirmed and those who do wrong, convicted and punished, it is not sufficient that the judicial function be exercised properly; the legislative function must also be exercised properly. The laws themselves must be just. It was not a point that escaped the Old Testament writers. They bewail not only unjust judicial decisions but unjust laws.

And now for an important point concerning a just system of law. By virtue of the sanctions it attaches to disobedience to the law, a just system of law discourages wrongdoing and encourages rightdoing. But more fundamental than the discouraging and encouraging effect of sanctions is the fact that a just system of law is, as such, a guide toward just action. Law performs an inescapable educative function. The Torah was God's guide for Israel's life until the Messiah arrived.

There is a long-standing debate among Christian thinkers whether government, in God's order of things, is simply a "remedy for sin." There can be no doubt that this is prominent in what Scripture says about the task of government. But just now we have caught a glimpse of something more. A just system of law not only places inhibitions on our sinful inclination to wrongdoing, by instituting a system of sanctions. It also instructs us in what justice requires—and reminds us when we become forgetful. In that way, properly functioning government represents God's providential care for us as finite, limited creatures, not just as fallen sinful creatures. Properly functioning government is part of God's providential care for his creation *qua creation*.

And perhaps the proper function of government goes even beyond justice—beyond establishing and applying a system of just law. Or so, at least, many theologians in the Christian tradition have suggested; and I agree. I must confine myself to one example. In the last chapter of his *Institutes of the Christian Religion*, John Calvin develops a theology of government. His emphasis falls on the calling of government to promote justice. But he culminates his articulation of the "appointed end" of civil government by saying that government is meant by God "to promote general peace and tranquillity" (IV, xx, 2). He gives an indication of what he has in mind with his remark, a bit later, that civil government "embraces" such activities as seeing to it that "men breathe, eat, drink, and are kept warm . . . when it *provides for their living together*"

(IV, xx, 3; italics added). The idea is that it belongs to the task of government to serve the common good—the *shalom*, the flourishing, of the people. Of course, in promoting justice, government is already serving the flourishing of the people. And let us not forget the lesson of history, that when governments go beyond promoting justice and aim at serving *what they regard* as the common good, they all too often wreak appalling injustice. Nonetheless, I think it is impossible to deny that, in addition to promoting justice, government serves an indispensable coordinating function; and that this coordinating function, when properly exercised, aims at the common good, the general welfare. Zoning regulations and trade agreements, to take just two examples from the contemporary world, are for the welfare of the community.

The points I have been making, about the educative function of law and about government serving the common good in its coordinating activities, have traditionally been put by saying that government belongs, in part, to the "order of creation." There would have been government even had there been no sin. Government represents a blend of God's providential care of his creation *as created*, and of God's providential care of his creation *as fallen*. To which must again be added the point, already made several times, that government is itself also fallen.

The Two Rules

Governmental authority belongs to God's providential care for human beings as the peculiar sort of creatures that they are, and to God's providential care for human beings as fallen. Romans and 1 Peter instruct their readers on how to live under such authority—when it functions as it ought to function. But their addressees were also members of the church, as are most of those who will be reading this essay. And as such they participated not only within God's creational/providential order, but within God's order of redemption—participated in a special way. They lived, and we live, at a unique point of intersection of God's order of creation/providence with God's order of redemption. We are both subjects of a state and members of the church.

This duality of the Christian's location in history has been the cause of much perplexity and the subject of much discussion over the centuries. If the church were merely a club organized for the purpose of conducting religious exercises and evoking religious experiences, there would be no perplexity. The club would often have to fight for its independence from the state. But that would be a political problem, not a source of perplexity.

The church is not a club. The New Testament represents its membership as "elected" rather than self-selecting; and it represents Christ as head of the church. The metaphor of "head" carries a number of connotations; among them being that Christ is the ruler, the "lord," of the church. The church thereby has an inherent political dimension. The Christian lives under two rules: as a citizen, under the rule of some state; and as a member of the church, under the rule of Christ.

Even living under two rules need not, as such, cause perplexity. A person holding dual citizenship may well have to negotiate some difficult situations; but there is no particular perplexity produced by having dual citizenship in, say, the United States and Canada, and thus being under the rule of both. The root of the perplexity caused by the dual rule under which Christians find themselves is that the rules for how one ought to live as a member of the one institution seem so different from those for how one ought to live as a member of the other. To a good many Christians, the rules have seemed not just different but incompatible.

The root of the perplexity is right there in Romans 12 and 13. Abolish from your lives the tit-for-tat vengeance system, says Paul to his readers. Seek the good of others, even of those who have wronged you; feed them if they are hungry, give them something to drink if they are thirsty. That on the one hand. On the other hand, regard governmental authority as mediating God's justice when it promotes justice by, among other things, properly exercising retributive punishment on wrongdoers. And obey or submit to its laws and judicial declarations out of conscience and not just out of prudence.

Down through the centuries many Christians have found this to be exceedingly perplexing advice: What sense does it make to approve the punishment of the criminal at the hands of the authorities while at the same time bringing him love-baskets? The perplexity gained poignancy when, after New Testament times, those in governmental positions began to convert to Christianity and those who were already Christian began to occupy governmental positions. It is one thing to visit the criminal in prison while declaring one's approval of the government's putting him there. It is quite another thing—or so it has seemed to many—for oneself to be the government official who puts him in prison and *then* to visit him there.

An additional consideration of great importance must be introduced at this point. Not only is Christ the head of the church. In this present era it is not God the Father but Christ whose authority is mediated by the state. That is the clear implication of the teaching of the New Testament concerning Christ's authority. At the end of Matthew's Gospel we read that "all authority in heaven and on earth has been given to me" (28:18). All by itself, this could be interpreted as meaning *all authority to teach*. But when we add the following passage from Paul's first letter to the Corinthians, we have to conclude that the authority given to Christ includes political authority: "Then comes the end, when he [Christ] delivers the kingdom to God the Father after destroying every rule and every authority and power. For he must reign until he has put all his enemies under his feet. . . . When all things are subjected to him, then the Son himself will also be subjected to him who put all things under him, that God may be everything to every one" (1 Cor. 15:24–28 RSV). To this we can add Ephesians 1:22–23: God the Father "has put all things under [Christ's] feet, and has made him the head over all things for the church, which is his body, the fullness of him who fills all in all."

Christ is not only head of the church but also head of the state. The Christian is under the rule of Christ not only in the church but also in the state. The judge who sentences the criminal to jail and acts justly in so doing is thereby mediating *Christ's* authority. Now suppose that he is also a member of the church and that, in obedience to Christ's rule of the church, he visits the criminal in jail. What sense does that make? Let it be noted that the perplexity is yours and mine. There is no evidence in Paul's words that he found anything perplexing in the advice he gave to his readers in Romans 12:19–13:7. In Romans as a whole, Paul raises and addresses one perplexity after another; he gives no evidence of finding any here.

A full discussion of this perplexity would require far more space than I have available to me here. I can do no more than articulate what seems to me the heart of the answer given by most Christian thinkers down through the centuries. Whatever their disagreements on detail, the majority of Christian thinkers have held, sometimes explicitly, usually tacitly, that the clue to the solution of the perplexity lies in distinguishing between acting in one's capacity as the holder of some office or position, and acting in one's own person. When the judge declares someone guilty and sentences him to prison, he is acting in his official capacity; in his own person he lacks the "power" to make that declaration and to issue that sentence. In turn, to act in his capacity of judge is to act on behalf of the state. Strictly speaking, it is the state that makes that declaration and issues that sentence. And what we have seen is that, in the biblical view, the state in so acting is mediating Christ's judgment—assuming that justice was done. On the other hand, when the person who occupies the position of judge goes to the prison to visit the man whom he, in his capacity as judge and on behalf of the state, pronounced guilty, he is doing so in his own person. It is because the main tradition of the church has operated with this distinction that it has seen nothing contradictory in one and the same person faithfully mediating Christ's rule as head of the state by sentencing the criminal to retributive punishment and faithfully following Christ's rule as head of the church by visiting the criminal in prison.

Yoder's Alternative

The understanding of political authority that I have articulated, starting from Romans and 1 Peter and moving out from there, is that of the preponderance of Christian theologians. Naturally some of these, while agreeing with the main line of thought that I have developed, would want to put things somewhat differently—add things that I have not mentioned, alter the emphasis, and so forth. But there have also been theologians whose disagreement would not be over details but over the basic line of thought. Probably the most important alternative line of thought is that characteristic of the Anabaptist tradition. And almost everybody would agree that the most important formulation on the contemporary scene of the traditional Anabaptist understanding is that of John Howard Yoder. So, all too briefly, let me sketch out Yoder's alternative understanding, the basic source being his now-classic book *The Politics of Jesus*.

I have assigned central position in the line of thought I have developed to two New Testament passages, Romans 12–13 and 1 Peter 2–3. Yoder also gives central position to Romans; but he makes 1 Peter subordinate. And whereas I have interpreted Romans in conjunction with other New Testament passages concerning extant social institutions, as well as in the context of Paul's Old Testament quotations and allusions and in the light of his teaching that all authority has been handed over to Christ by the Father, Yoder interprets Romans through the lens of what the New Testament, and Paul in particular, has to say about "thrones and dominions and rulers and powers" (Col. 1:16)—usually now just called "powers" for short. In Colossians 2:15, for example, Paul says that God "disarmed the rulers and authorities and made a public example of them, triumphing over them in [the cross]." The Greek word translated here as "authorities" is *exousiai*. It is the same word that is translated as "authorities" in the opening of Romans 13.

So what is Yoder's understanding of the New Testament teaching concerning the powers? The powers, Yoder says, are the intellectual, ethical, religious, political, and social structures that give order and stability to human existence. Though supra-individual, we need not think of them in personal or angelic terms. They "were created by God" (*Politics* 142). For "there could not be society or history, there could not be humanity without the existence above us of religious, intellectual, moral, and social structures. *We cannot live without them*" (*Politics* 143).

Though created good, these "powers have rebelled and are fallen. They did not accept the modesty that would have permitted them to remain conformed to the creative purpose, but rather they claimed for themselves an absolute value. They thereby enslaved humanity and our history. . . . To what are we subject? Precisely to those values and structures which are necessary to life and society but which have claimed the status of idols and have succeeded in making us serve them as if they were of absolute value" (*Politics* 142). "Our lostness consists in our subjection to the rebellious powers of a fallen world" (*Politics* 144). Prominent among these fallen rebellious powers to which we are enslaved is the state.

How are we to understand the fact that even after Christ's crucifixion and resurrection, there remain such fallen powers as the state? We are to understand it as a sign of God's providential care for humanity in this time of the divine patience (*Politics* 149). Recall that these structures, including political structures, are *necessary* for human existence; they provide the *order* without which there could not be human existence. "Even tyranny . . . is still better than chaos" (*Politics* 141). Had God abolished these structures, he would thereby have abolished human existence. "Our lostness and our survival are inseparable, both dependent upon the Powers" (*Politics* 143).

This perspective both yields and is based upon a very different reading of Romans 13 from that which I have articulated. We are not to obey the state because it issues legitimate commands that place us under obligation; we are simply to subject ourselves to it, in the way that Russians subjected themselves to Stalin. The state is not the servant or minister of God in the sense that it mediates God's authority; it is simply an instrument of God's causality. And though there is some wavering on the point in some of his later essays, in *The Politics of Jesus* Yoder states unambiguously that "the function exercised by government is not the function to be exercised by Christians. However able an infinite God may be to work at the same time through the sufferings of his believing disciples who return good for evil and through the wrathful violence of the authorities who punish evil with evil, such behavior is for humans not complementary but in disjunction. Divine providence can in its own sovereign permissive way 'use' an idolatrous Assyria (Isaiah 10) or Rome. This takes place, however, without declaring that the destructive participation in it is incumbent upon the covenant people" (*Politics* 198).

A response that does justice to Yoder's thought would require an essay of its own. Yet the reader will rightly expect that I not move on as if Yoder had said nothing worth paying attention to. So let me express my difficulties with Yoder's position, in good measure in the form of questions. What I have to say will be much too brief and undeveloped to persuade the convinced Yoderian. It may, though, serve to locate some of the basic issues.

Paul, as we have seen, quotes from and alludes to a rich Old Testament body of teaching concerning the role of government in God's providential order; I think that we impose an untenable breach between the New Testament and the Old if we ignore this background. The role of government, according to Israel's witness, is not just to secure order and stave off chaos; its role is to promote justice. Paul echoes this. He does not say that God appointed or instituted governmental authority to secure order. He says that God did so in order that rightdoing might be affirmed and wrongdoing punished. The corollary of this is that when Paul says that the governing authorities are deacons or liturgetes of God, we must understand him as meaning not merely that they are instruments of divine causality (Assyria), but that they are mediators of divine authority. Thus it is that Paul says we are to obey or be subject "not only because of *orgē* but also because of conscience" and that 1 Peter says we are to do so "for the Lord's sake." And let us recall the point made earlier, that the Greek word that both Paul and 1 Peter use for the honor that we are to pay to government is the very same word that Paul uses in Ephesians to describe the honor that children are to give their parents.

An additional point is this. Recall Yoder's description of a fallen power: something that "harms" and "enslaves" us, something that "absolutizes" itself, makes us serve it as if it were of "absolute value," demands from us "unconditional loyalty," something to which we are "unconditionally subjected." Now consider Paul's language: Rulers "are not a terror to good conduct but to bad." Can Paul plausibly be interpreted as talking about one of Yoder's fallen powers? I don't see how.

It is said by some critics of Yoder that he has no doctrine of creation or providence; everything is Christology. That seems to me not correct. The issue pivots rather on his understanding of the fall. States, he says, are *fallen powers*. As one reads along, it gradually dawns on one that what he means is not that states *act unjustly under the influence of* "powers"; he means that states are themselves fallen powers. And by this he means, in turn, that they are themselves *intrinsically evil powers*. Necessary, but intrinsically evil. An analogue would be the view that the fall of humankind consisted not in human beings *acting wrongly under the influence of* powers, but *themselves becoming intrinsically evil powers*.

Obviously this is not Paul's teaching when it comes to human beings; quite the contrary. And I find no textual evidence that his teaching was any different when it comes to social institutions. From his *Haustafeln* it is obvious, for example, that he did not regard the social institutions of marriage and of the family as intrinsically evil powers to which we must all submit on pain of creating total chaos. Of course Paul thought that there were plenty of things that go wrong in marriages and families; but he did not think of those institutions as themselves intrinsically evil powers. We would need very clear evidence indeed if we were to understand what Paul says about the institution of government differently.

Lastly, is there really the intrinsic conflict that Yoder suggests between willing the good of someone and imposing retributive punishment on him or her? To move to the theological plane: Is there really the sharp dichotomy that Yoder suggests between Christ's authority in the church and his authority in the state? Yoder speaks of the authorities as punishing "evil with evil" and of employing "wrathful violence," contrasting this with the believing disciples who return "good for evil." But this is Yoder's description, not Paul's. Paul does not say that authorities do "evil" to the wrongdoer, nor does he mention violence. What he says is that the authorities pronounce judgment (*krima*) and execute anger (*orgē*) on him, this latter meaning, so I have argued, applying retributive punishment. And it is clear, not just from Romans 13 but from the book of Romans as a whole, that Paul most definitely did not regard retributive punishment as "doing evil" but rather as the exercise of justice.

Earlier I used the example of a judge who imposes sentence on a criminal and then visits the criminal in jail. Consider now a parent who punishes her child for some infraction—the family being a social institution, one among those necessary structures that Yoder regards as fallen powers. I take it to be an extrapolation from Paul's thought that it is in the parent's "office" of parent, not in her own person, that she rightly imposes retributive punishment on the child. Is there anything incompatible between the parent's loving the child and also imposing retributive punishment? May she not even impose the punishment *out of* love?

The Application to Us

In addressing the Christians in Rome, Paul was speaking to people who had no voice in government; his instructions were for mere subjects. The empire of which they were subjects was presumably not yet the murderous and totalitarian regime that the writer of the Apocalypse was familiar with. Had the empire fallen to those depths, Paul's advice surely would have been different. Rather than talking about the proper function of political authority and the relation of its subjects to such authority, he would have instructed his readers on how to relate to a regime that had departed so far from God's purpose as to have lost its legitimacy.

You and I are not mere subjects. By virtue of our right to vote, to mention nothing else, all of us have a voice in our government. And a good many of us are government functionaries. So what would Paul have said had he been addressing us?

He would have said everything he did say: Obey or be subject to the authorities, pay the taxes they justly assess rather than questioning their authority to raise taxes or trying to evade one's taxes, honor and respect their positions rather than bad-mouthing them, remember that their calling is to be servants and ministers of God mediating God's judgments. All this Paul would have said. But he also would have said something more.

The main burden of what he would have added is surely that it is your and my calling as citizens rather than mere subjects to encourage the state to live up to its task of promoting justice and serving the general welfare. When all around are saying that the state is nothing more than an arena for negotiating power relationships, the Christian will never weary of insisting that the task of the state in God's creational and providential order is to promote justice and serve the common good. The Christian will not conform to the world by organizing power blocks to negotiate special favors for Christians or anyone else.

Perhaps the principal way in which Christians of the modern world have called the state to its proper task is by initiating and supporting efforts to set structural limits to the scope of state authority, so as thereby to diminish the risk of overreaching by the state. But before I identify some of the forms these efforts at limitation have taken, let me call attention to two ways in which, in addition to overreaching, states fail to fulfill their proper calling—ways all too frequently overlooked.

The state often fails in its task of promoting justice by overlooking or refusing to acknowledge the occurrence of injustice, insisting on calling it something else instead or insisting that the injustice in question is none of its business.

Sometimes this happens because the state is in the grip of some ideology: the ideology of private enterprise, the ideology of nationalism, whatever. Often it happens because the state is in the control of rich and powerful persons who see to it that they remain free to go about their unjust ways. In such situations it is the calling of the Christian to denounce the ideologies, bring the injustice to light, name it for what it is, namely injustice, and insist that the state not shirk its task. The state fails in its God-given task not only by doing too much, but by doing too little.

In this identification of injustice, the Christian will be guided by what may be called *the biblical contour of justice*. The contour of justice that the biblical writers had in mind is very different from that to be found, say, in Plato, and from that to be found in libertarian writers of the twentieth century. To mention just one point: Whereas the impoverished and the alien are prominent in the biblical contour of justice, they are invisible in both Plato's contour of justice and the contemporary libertarian contour.

Second, though the state fails to promote justice when the judiciary is so corrupted that it knowingly pronounces the wrongdoer innocent, it also fails to promote justice when, after vindicating the innocent and convicting the wrongdoer, it metes out punishment that is inequitable, excessively harsh, humiliating to the point of being dehumanizing, incompatible with respecting the wrongdoer as a person made in the image of God. The Christian will insist that punishment always be of such a sort as to be compatible with visiting the wrongdoer in prison and giving him food and drink.

And now for some of the ideas that have emerged from the seedbed of the Christian tradition for securing a duly limited government, some being ideas for the internal structuring of government, some being ideas for restraining the tendency of government to aggrandizement. In saying that these ideas emerged from the seedbed of the Christian tradition, I mean to suggest that not all of them are to be found, as such, in Scripture. Though John of the Apocalypse was confronted with a government that was aggrandizing to an appalling degree, neither he nor any other biblical writer proposed, for example, a division of powers within government so as to make such overreaching less likely in the future. I should add that in saying that these ideas emerged from the seedbed of the Christian tradition, I do not mean to suggest that they did not have other roots as well; on this occasion I simply want to highlight their Christian roots.

(1) The most important idea, and also the one that emerged first, was the idea of government as the rule of law rather than of the mere will of the sovereign. The idea of law as opposed to sovereign will is omnipresent in the Old Testament. The king is to see to it that God's judgments are mediated to the people, these judgments being known to the king and his judiciary from their knowledge of God's law, whether in the form of Torah or in the form of the writing on one's heart. And the mediation is to take the form of a body of historically posited law that enshrines God's law, along

with a judiciary that interprets and applies that law. Such law transcends the personal will of rulers and abides amidst their coming and going. Furthermore—this is crucial—the rulers and their judiciary are themselves to be subject to this law.

(2) A second development, strictly speaking an aspect of the first but worth singling out for special attention, was the rise of constitutionalism. A constitution lays down a system of government by providing for various "offices," specifying the conditions under which persons are entitled to enter those offices and required to leave them, and specifying the scope and limits of the "powers" and privileges attached to those offices. In its sharp differentiation of persons from offices, in its making the holding of office a matter of procedure rather than of power or happenstance, and in its setting of limits to what a person is authorized to do in office, a constitution goes beyond the role of law as such. Furthermore, a constitution typically makes the revision of most of these stipulations far more difficult than the revision of ordinary law.

Constitutionalism did not arise as an intellectual force until late medieval times; nonetheless, I think there can be no doubt that the core idea was there already in Paul's instructions to the Roman Christians and in the Old Testament line of thought to which he was giving expression. Only those in authority are authorized to impose "vengeance," that is, retributive punishment. The old vengeance system, in which private parties take it on themselves to pay back the wrongs done them, is to be abolished.

(3) A third development, strictly speaking a development within constitutionalism but again worth singling out for separate attention, was the emergence of the idea that government should be so structured that there is a division of powers—in particular, a division of legislative, judicial, and executive powers. The most influential argument in favor of a division of powers was apparently the argument from human sinfulness. The temptation of those in power to expand their power is among the strongest and most dangerous temptations to which human beings are subject. Best then to specify a division of powers in the constitution, thereby setting up a system of checks and balances. The result will often be postponement, compromise, inaction, lack of clarity, and so forth; but better those flaws than the totalitarian beasts of Revelation 13.

(4) A fourth development has been the slow working out of the implications of the idea that the human person, on account of being an image of God, is of such worth that he or she must never be violated. The view of government held by most Christians in medieval times was that it was the task of government not just to promote justice but to cultivate moral and religious virtue in the subjects; the magisterial Reformers perpetuated this view. It is my own judgment that this view comes closer to the views of Plato, Aristotle, and the other philosophers of pagan antiquity than it does to the views of the biblical writers. But be that as it may, every reader is

aware that this view of the task of government resulted in appalling cruelty. Those who did not have the approved moral or religious views, or did not exhibit the approved moral or religious virtues, were tortured, burned at the stake, beheaded.

As I read the history of the matter, the conviction slowly sank in that whatever may be the worth of cultivating moral and religious virtue, it cannot come at the price of such violation of the person. Such cruelty is incompatible with recognizing the worth of the person as an image of God. It was in good measure from this conviction that there emerged the rights and liberties of the liberal democratic polity as we know it today—especially the right and liberty to worship God according to the convictions of one's own conscience.

(5) Closely connected to the preceding is the emergence of the idea of natural human rights as a protection against tyrannical government. I am aware that some have argued in recent years that the idea of natural human rights emerged not from the seedbed of the Christian tradition but from the supposedly individualistic philosophies of the late medieval nominalists and the Enlightenment philosophers. My own view is that the history here is mistaken. When such great church fathers as Chrysostom and Ambrose declared that if the poor person has no shoes, then the shoes in the closet of the wealthy person *belong to* the poor person, not by virtue of any extant laws but simply by virtue of the fact that he is an impoverished human being, then they were expressing in their own way the idea of natural human rights.

(6) Though the last development I have in mind has been less influential than the preceding, in my judgment it is no less important. In both Catholicism and Dutch neo-Calvinism of the latter part of the nineteenth century there emerged the idea that the scope of state action is to be limited not only by the requirement that the state not violate the individual person nor allow other persons or institutions to do so, but also by the requirement that the state not absorb into itself the manifold institutions of civil society. Rather than absorbing them, the state is to confine itself to seeing to it that the demands of justice are satisfied, both by how these institutions interact with each other and by how they treat their members.

Abraham Kuyper, the most creative and influential of the Dutch neo-Calvinists, developed the point by arguing that the emergence of social institutions, each with its own authority structure, is part of God's providential care for humankind and for its progress over the course of history. The authority of the various institutions of civil society is not delegated to them by the state but exercised directly before the face of God by each of them. The totalitarian temptation of the state to absorb all competing authority structures and turn them into branches of the state must thus be vigorously resisted. The state is but one authority structure among many—albeit unique in that it is, as it were, the court of last resort for society as a whole in the promotion of justice and the rendering of just judgment.

Other Issues

There are many elements of a comprehensive evangelical political philosophy that I have not had time to discuss. I have not discussed the limits of our obligation to political obedience; I have simply taken for granted that there are such limits. There is no obligation to obey the ravenous state of Revelation 13 when it demands that we worship it; our duty is to not obey. Neither have I discussed the limits on what Christians may do when functioning in some governmental office. All too often Christians in government assume that there are no such limits—either that, or they assume that the limits are so wide that it's not worth taking note of them. In government one just does what everybody else does: tells lies, bears false witness against one's opponents, pursues power, goes to war for nationalistic reasons, and so forth. These are both exceedingly important issues. My not having discussed them is not to be construed as implying otherwise.

One final remark. The reader must also not conclude from the foregoing that the state is the only institution that has the task of rendering just judgment by establishing a system of just rules or law and applying those justly. All institutions render this sort of judgment, and all must do so justly. Other institutions do so, however, in the course of carrying out their primary task of providing education, organizing recreation, manufacturing computers, investing funds, or whatever. It would be a calamity if just judgment were exclusively the province of the state. When just judgment is being rendered by the various institutions of civil society, the state is required to "keep its nose out of it." What is unique about the state is that rendering just judgment is among its *primary* tasks and that it is entitled to use strong coercive measures in carrying out that task.

Basic Theses

In conclusion, let me state some theses concerning government that a broad range of evangelicals can agree on—acknowledging that at some points, those representing the Anabaptist tradition would disagree.

1. Government is not a merely human creation, nor is it a work of the devil. Government is instituted by God as part of God's providential care for his human creatures.
2. The task assigned by God to government is twofold: to promote justice, both primary and corrective, and in its coordinating activities to enhance the common good.
3. Government, thus understood, belongs both to God's providential care for us as creatures and to God's providential care for us as fallen.
4. When government acts as it ought to act, it acts with genuine authority. That authority is to be understood as not merely human but as mediating Christ's authority.

5. The corollary of the exercise by government of genuine authority is that its subjects are obligated to obey that authority.

6. Among the things that governments are authorized to do is apply retributive punishment to wrongdoers—provided that the punishment is itself of a just sort.

7. Though government, along with such other social institutions as marriage, family, and economy, is instituted by God as part of his providential care for human beings as creatures and as fallen, government, along with these other institutions, is itself fallen. That is to say, government and other social institutions never fully carry out the tasks assigned them by God.

8. Though not every failing on the part of government—or any other social institution—justifies disobedience, all too often governments do fail to such a degree that disobedience is required. The starkest examples of such obligatory disobedience are those cases in which government demands that something other than God be worshiped.

9. The Christian may serve in the offices of government; in doing so, he is mediating the rule over the state of that very same Christ who is the ruler of the church.

10. When the Christian occupies some governmental office, he or she must not be guided by customary practice but by the God-assigned task of government: to promote justice and the common good.

11. It is the duty of the Christian always to call his or her government to its proper task. Especially is this true for those of us who have some degree of voice in our governments.

12. Such calling of government to its proper task will ordinarily include proclamation. But whenever possible, it will also include the promotion of governmental structures that make it less likely that the government will fail in, or violate, its task.

13. Christians will honor and respect government; they will not talk and act as if government has no right to exist. And they will support government by paying taxes. They will not talk and act as if government, in assessing taxes, is forcefully taking from its subjects "their money." Financial support is *owed* government.

Bibliography

Aquinas, Thomas. *On Princely Government (de regimine principum)*, in R. W. Dyson, ed. and trans., *Aquinas: Political Writings* (Cambridge: Cambridge University Press, 2002).

Calvin, John. *Institutes of the Christian Religion*. Translated by Ford Lewis Battles. Philadelphia: Westminster, 1960.

Chrysostom, John. *On Wealth and Poverty*. Translated by Catherine P. Roth. Crestwood, NY: St Vladimir's Seminary Press, 1984.

Kuyper, Abraham. *Calvinism: The Stone Lectures 1898–1899*. New York: Fleming H. Revell, n.d.

O'Donovan, Oliver. *The Desire of the Nations*. Cambridge: Cambridge University Press, 1996.

O'Donovan, Oliver, and Joan Lockwood O'Donovan. *From Irenaeus to Grotius: A Sourcebook in Christian Political Thought 100–1625*. Grand Rapids: Eerdmans, 1999.

Tierney, Brian. *The Idea of Natural Rights: Studies on Natural Rights, Natural Law and Church Law 1150–1625*. Atlanta: Scholars Press, 1997.

Yoder, John H. *The Politics of Jesus*. Grand Rapids: Eerdmans, 1972.

8

Justice, Human Rights, and Government

Toward an Evangelical Perspective

Ronald J. Sider

A CONTEMPORARY POLITICAL philosophy[1] dealing with justice, human rights, and government must answer at least the following big questions. What is the ultimate source of justice, human rights, and governmental authority? Is it finally governmental fiat backed by power, a social contract among free citizens, or divine law? Is justice exclusively or primarily procedural (e.g., fair courts), or is it also concerned with fair distribution? Are valid human rights primarily or exclusively civil/political (freedom of speech, religion, etc.) or also socioeconomic (right to food, job, etc.)? Is government only necessary because of sin? What is the relationship between justice and love? Is the primary or exclusive role of government to restrain evil and set procedural rules (very limited government), or is it also to promote the common good by nurturing fair distribution (a more activist government)?

This last question points to one of the major contemporary debates among evangelicals. To what extent should the government tax wealthier citizens in order to make basic services (food, health care, education, etc.) available to poorer citizens? At one extreme would be some who argue that all care for the poor should be done by nongovernmental voluntary organizations. At the other extreme would be those who see government as the first and primary agent to care for the poor. In the middle would be large numbers of folk who argue for some mix of public and private programs to help the poorer members of society. In this chapter, I will try to see what light the biblical material throws on this crucial debate.

Justice and Human Rights

Since the time of Aristotle, political thinkers have agreed that justice exists when persons receive what is due them. Persons, of course, live in groups and institutions, and something is also owed these different societal institutions. Therefore evangelical philosopher Nicholas Wolterstorff says: "Justice is present among persons, groups and institutions when their right, their legitimate claims, are honored."[2] That can happen only when persons and groups fulfill their responsibilities.

What is the ultimate foundation of the obligation to give persons and institutions their due? For most of Western history, the nearly universal answer was God and the order the Creator embedded in nature. God is just and commands persons to be just. Therefore human laws are just and to be obeyed because they reflect, however imperfectly, divine law and justice. In the last two centuries, however, modern thinkers have rejected the notion of a divine standard of justice underlying actual laws, arguing instead that human laws are merely human products designed by the powerful for their own self-interest. The result of this legal positivism, Emil Brunner has argued persuasively, is modern totalitarianism: "If there is no divine standard of justice, there is no criterion for the legal system set up by the state. If there is no justice transcending the state, then the state can declare anything it likes to be law. . . . The totalitarian state is the inevitable result."[3]

From the biblical perspective, God is clearly the ultimate foundation for justice. Numerous biblical texts say that God loves and does justice ("I the LORD love justice" (Isa. 61:8 RSV; cf. also Ps. 37:28; 103:6). Persons made in God's image are called to reflect God's justice in our actions ("He [God] executes justice for the fatherless and the widow, and loves the sojourner, giving him food and clothing. Love the sojourner therefore . . ." (Deut. 10:18–19 RSV). If we respect the image of God in other persons, we must give them what is their due.

But what is due to persons and institutions? The most basic theological answer is the order of creation established by God. "The rights of man are rights which, so to speak, God gives men at their birth. The rights of communities are rights which go back to a definite relationship between men based on the order of creation—for instance that of man and woman in marriage. In the last resort all justice means these constants of creation as a basis on which every human being receives his due."[4]

But we need more specificity. We need more detailed guidance to spell out what is due persons and institutions. Political thinkers have often done this by talking about commutative justice, retributive justice, procedural justice, and distributive justice.

Commutative justice "requires fairness in agreements and exchanges between private parties."[5] Weights and measures should be the same for everyone. Contracts should be kept.

Retributive justice defines what is due to persons when they have done wrong. It defines what is appropriate punishment for someone who has broken the law.

Procedural justice defines the procedures and processes that must be fair if justice is to prevail. Procedural justice requires a transparent legal framework, unbiased courts, the rule of law, freedom of speech, assembly and the vote, honest elections, and so on.

Distributive justice refers to how the numerous goods of society are divided. What is a just division of money, health care, educational opportunities—in short, all the goods and services in society? Who owes what of all these things to persons and institutions? What role if any does government have in guaranteeing that there is a "fair distribution" of these goods? Is it enough for government to ensure fair procedures (unbiased courts, etc.), or should government seek to promote "fair outcomes"?

Obviously, if society (whether families, businesses, governments, etc.) is to distribute goods and services fairly, we need criteria to define what is owed to each. Over the centuries, various criteria have been used: need, contribution, effort, ability, the market value of supply and demand, equality, and utilitarian judgment about what serves the public interest.[6] Merit, equality, and need have been the most common. Distribution based on merit would allocate social goods on the basis of the person's merit (whether work effort, skillful productivity, or aristocratic worth). Distribution based on equality would allocate social goods on the basis of either equal outcomes (Communism, at least in theory) or equal access (e.g., John Rawls). Distribution based on need would allocate goods largely on the basis of deficiency in basic needs of specific persons and groups and would pay special attention to correcting past injustice.

One of the most vigorous debates of the last century has been about whether justice exists if the procedures are fair regardless of the resulting distribution of social goods or whether justice requires some "fair outcome." Political philosophers like Robert Nozick, particularly concerned to advocate very limited government, argued for the former. According to Nozick, justice is whatever emerges from a just situation by just steps.[7] If the procedures are fair, the outcome is just. Some evangelicals have agreed with Nozick.[8]

Other evangelicals, on the other hand, have argued that justice requires at least some attention to "just outcomes" so that everyone in fact enjoys, or at least has genuine access to, what is needed to earn a certain level of physical and social well-being. Mainline Protestants, Roman Catholics, and many evangelicals insist on this understanding of distributive justice.

Closely related to this debate about procedural and distributive justice is the heated twentieth-century debate about human rights. Are they primarily civil/political or primarily socioeconomic or both?

Western democracies, rooted in liberal political theory going back to John Locke, have especially emphasized civil/political rights: freedom of religion, speech, and assembly; the right to possess property; a system of laws and courts that are transparent; and unbiased, free elections. All of these rights are grounded in individual liberty—"the most precious of human values in liberal thought."[9] According to Locke, the natural state of humanity was one where all persons possess "perfect freedom to order their actions and dispose of their possessions and persons, as they see fit."[10]

Marxists emphasized socioeconomic rights: an adequate standard of living (food, clothing, housing); the highest attainable standard of health care; education; and social security for the elderly and others unable to work. Since Marxists believed that "purely formal" rights such as freedom of speech are relatively useless unless people enjoy basic socioeconomic rights, they argued that civil liberties could be suspended or ignored in the effort to implement key socioeconomic rights.

A Christian understanding of human rights must help us answer this debate between twentieth-century Liberals and Marxists. Are there valid human rights claims in both the civil/political and the socioeconomic areas or just in one? We also need criteria for deciding how to determine what to do when the claims of differing human rights collide.

To search for answers to the questions raised about the nature of justice and human rights, I want to examine the biblical material in several different ways: first, a discussion of aspects of the biblical story; second, a study of the key Hebrew words for justice and righteousness; third, the close connection between love and justice; fourth, the dynamic, restorative character of biblical justice; fifth, biblical teaching about God's concern for the poor; sixth, the emphasis on restoration to community; seventh, access to productive resources; and finally, care for those who cannot care for themselves.

The Biblical Story

The first thing the biblical story tells us is that the material world around us is very good.[11] It is finite, limited, not divine. But it is not an illusion. It is so real and so good in its finite glory that the Creator of the galaxies became flesh, trod the dusty paths of this little planet, rose bodily from the dead, and promised to return to this earth to complete the restoration of this material, physical world to wholeness. Furthermore, until his return, he has given us the task of creating wealth, building civilizations, and nudging history in the direction of that coming wholeness.

At the heart of the biblical story is the teaching that persons are created in the very image of God, formed as body-soul individuals designed for community, and called to be God's stewards to have dominion over the nonhuman world and trace the Creator's footsteps in reshaping the material and social world to create wealth and fashion civilizations of beauty and goodness.

According to Genesis, persons alone are created in the divine image (Gen. 1:27). God gave each person freedom and summoned each person to respond freely to God's call to obedience and fellowship with the Creator. When we rebelled, God loved persons so much that the Second Person of the Triune God became flesh and then died and rose again to save every person who will believe and trust in the Savior. Every single person is invited by the almighty Creator to live forever with the living God. That is how immeasurably important and valuable, how full of dignity, every individual person is.

That is also why human beings have rights and responsibilities. If the Creator of all things declares that persons are that important, then we must treat them with the same respect. Every person's human right to life, freedom, and all the other things the Creator reveals as human rights flows from God's creative design.[12]

The theological foundation of human rights also reveals the one-sidedness of much modern discussion of human rights that neglects duties and responsibilities. The same Creator who extends such astonishing dignity to persons summons them to obey his commands and submit to the moral order embedded in the universe. Human rights and human obligations are inseparable.

According to Genesis, persons are body-soul unities. Made from "dust from the ground" (Gen. 2:7 RSV), we are solidly material, designed in our very essence as a part of the physical world, and therefore unable to be what the Creator intended without a generous sufficiency of material things. God also breathes into us "the breath of life" and gives us a freedom not possessed by the rest of creation. Does the very fact that the Creator designed us as body-soul unities suggest that understandings of human rights as primarily civil/political (focused on human freedom) or primarily socioeconomic (focused on material needs) are unlikely to capture the biblical story's full understanding of the nature of persons?

The biblical story also holds together the inestimable worth of each individual person and the communal nature of human beings. Both the radical individualism of contemporary Western liberal democracies and the totalitarian communalism of twentieth-century Fascist and Communist societies are one-sided perversions of a profound biblical balance. The Creator made us individual persons so completely designed for community that we cannot be whole unless we enjoy mutual interdependence with others.

Until Eve arrived, Adam was restless. God created them to discover mutual fulfillment as they became one flesh. This communal nature is grounded in the nature of God. Since we are created in the very image of the triune personal God who is Father, Son, and Holy Spirit, being a person means being united to other persons in mutual love.[13]

Therefore justice from a biblical perspective must pay equal attention to the rights of individuals and the common good of all. Political and economic systems dare not either sacrifice individuals and personal freedom on the altar of some abstract common good nor absolutize individual freedom of choice without regard to the impact on the well-being of everyone.

The fact that we are created for community suggests that "government" in some sense is necessary even apart from the fall. Even if sin had never entered the human family, creating violence and evil that government rightly restrains, human beings would have needed processes and institutions to nurture the common good and arrange society so that all could live in wholesome mutual interdependence.

Nothing, unfortunately, on God's good earth has escaped sin's marauding presence.[14] Sin has twisted both individual persons and the ideas and institutions they create. Rebelling against their Creator's instructions, people either exaggerate or belittle the significance of history and the material world. Exaggerating their own importance, they regularly create political and economic institutions—complete with sophisticated rationalizations—that oppress their neighbors. Workable political and economic systems must both appeal to persons' better instincts that sin has not quite managed to obliterate and also hold in check and turn to positive use the pervasive selfishness that corrupts every act.

Even this very brief exploration of key aspects of the biblical story shows how it provides significant components of a normative Christian framework for political engagement.[15] We can obtain further important help from a careful analysis of the Hebrew words for justice and righteousness.

The Hebrew Words for Justice and Righteousness

The two key words are *mishpat* and *tsedaqah*, which very often appear together in Hebrew parallelism. Amos 5:24 is typical: "Let justice [*mishpat*] roll down like waters, and righteousness [*tsedaqah*] like an ever-flowing stream" (RSV).

The noun *mishpat*[16] appears 422 times in the Old Testament, and it comes from the verb *shapat*, which means to govern and judge. Since Israelite society did not separate legislative, judicial, and administrative aspects of governing, the noun *mishpat* can mean the act of deciding a case in court (Deut. 25:1), the actual judicial decision (1 Kings 20:40), or a legal ordinance and case law (the laws of Exodus 21–23 are simply called the *mishpatim*). If one wants to use just one English word, probably the best translation is "justice."

Tsedaqah (feminine) appears 157 times and *tsedeq* (masculine) appears 119 times in the Old Testament.[17] The basic connotation refers to that which is "straight" or matches the norm. *Tsedaqah* often means norm or standard—that is, the way things ought to be. There can be a bad law (*mishpat*) but not bad *tsedaqah*. *Tsedaqah* provides the standard for measuring specific laws because it defines the way things should be. The English word "righteousness" is a possible translation if one does not limit the word to personal relations and inner attitudes. *Tsedaqah* regularly appears with *mishpat* in Hebrew parallelism and includes the meaning of justice as the norm of the way things should be. Thus it is used to refer to accurate weights and measures (Lev. 19:36; Deut. 25:15) and straight paths (Ps. 23:3).

The first thing to underline about these two words is their theocentric foundation. The righteous, just God who commands his people to imitate his justice is the source and foundation of human justice. God is a "righteous judge" (Ps. 7:11) who gives divine justice to human rulers: "Give the king *your* justice [*mishpat*], O God, and *your* righteousness [*tsedaqah*] to a king's son" (Ps. 72:1, italics added). Human justice must imitate God's justice (Deut. 10:17–19; also 1:17).

That procedural justice (e.g., fair courts) is central to the meaning of these key biblical words is clear in many texts. "You shall not render an unjust judgment; you shall not be partial to the poor or defer to the great: with justice [*mishpat*] you shall judge your neighbor" (Lev. 19:15; see also Deut. 10:17–19; 1:17). In a long string of verses, Exodus 23 demands fair courts. Do not be a false witness even if the majority spread falsehood: "You shall not side with the majority so as to pervert justice" (v. 2). Refuse bribes (v. 8). "You shall not pervert the justice [*mishpat*] due to your poor in their lawsuits" (v. 6)—"nor shall you be partial to the poor in a lawsuit" (v. 3). Again and again the prophets pronounced divine judgment, in fact, exile and national destruction, on Israel and Judah because of their unfair courts (Amos 5:10–15). Since there is widespread agreement in evangelical circles on the importance of procedural justice, we need not spend more time on it here.

These two words, *mishpat* and *tsedaqah*, however, refer to more than procedural justice in the courts. They are also the words the prophets used to call for economic justice—a point less widely understood by evangelicals and therefore needing much more attention. Immediately after denouncing Israel and Judah as an unfaithful vineyard where God sought in vain for *mishpat* and *tsedaqah* (Isa. 5:7), Isaiah goes on to denounce his society's economic injustice: "Ah, you who join house to house, who add field to field, until there is room for no one but you, and you are left to live alone in the midst of the land! The LORD of hosts has sworn in my hearing: Surely many houses shall be desolate, large and beautiful houses, without inhabitant" (Isa. 5:8; see also Amos 5:11–12). Micah similarly condemned the rich and powerful who "covet fields, and seize them; houses, and take them away; they oppress householder and house, people and their inheritance" (Micah 2:2) instead of providing the justice (*mishpat*) God longs for (Micah 6:8).

These eighth-century BC prophets lived at the end of a time when the monarchies of Israel and Judah had, over the preceding two centuries, centralized land ownership in the hands of a small powerful elite. The earlier arrangement of decentralized land ownership under the judges where every family enjoyed their own ancestral land had increasingly disappeared. Modern archeologists have discovered that in the tenth century BC, houses seem to have been similar in size, but by the eighth century, there were large houses in one area and tiny houses in another. That reflects the reality that the prophets denounce. Many people have lost their land and become poor because of the oppression of the powerful.

Sometimes the oppression happened through raw royal power—witness Jezebel's seizure of Naboth's ancestral land (1 Kings 21). Sometimes it happened through unjust laws: "Ah, you who make iniquitous decrees, who write oppressive statutes, to turn aside the needy from justice [*mishpat*] and to rob the poor of my people of their right" (Isa. 10:1–2). Sometimes it happened through disobedience to laws designed to protect the poor—Exodus 22:26–27 explicitly prohibited keeping a poor person's garment overnight as collateral, but the powerful of Amos' day did precisely that and then spread these garments out to kneel on when they went to worship! (Amos 2:8a). And sometimes it happened as the powerful abused the judicial system (Amos 5:10ff.).

According to the prophets, God became so angry at Israel's and Judah's corrupt courts and unfair economic practices (as well as their idolatry) that he destroyed first Israel and then Judah, allowing foreign invaders to devastate both nations. But the prophets' final word was not destruction and despair. They looked beyond the foreign captivity to a new day, a messianic time, when *mishpat* and *tsedaqah* would be restored (Isa. 1:26–27; 16:4b–5; 32:16–17). The messianic passages of Isaiah 9 and 11 promise that the Messiah will bring righteousness and justice for all (9:7). Of the shoot from the stump of Jesse, the prophet declares that "with righteousness [*tsedeq*] he shall judge [*shapat*] the poor" (11:4). In that day, Micah declares, "They shall all sit under their own vines and under their own fig trees, and no one shall make them afraid" (Micah 4:4). Economic justice will be restored and each family will again have their own land.

In the glorious vision of messianic restoration in Ezekiel, the prophet paints a picture of an ideal, restored society with the temple at the center. The passage ends with a promise of the restoration of economic justice for the people: "And my princes shall no longer oppress my people; but they shall let the house of Israel have the land according to their tribes. Thus says the Lord GOD: Enough, O princes of Israel! Put away violence and oppression, and do what is just [*mishpat*] and right [*tsedaqah*]. Cease your evictions of my people, says the Lord GOD" (Ezek. 45:8–9). When the rulers do *mishpat*, the people who had lost their property through violence and oppression again enjoy their own land. Active promotion of economic justice is clearly a central component of the prophets' understanding of *mishpat* and *tsedaqah*.

Clearly the Old Testament words for justice and righteousness indicate that from a biblical perspective, justice is both procedural and also distributive. Four other aspects of biblical teaching strengthen this argument.[18]

Love and justice together. Some have argued that justice and love must be almost totally separated. Justice refers to fair procedures but does not require caring for the poor and needy. That is the task of love. In many texts, however, we discover the words for love and justice in close association. "Sow for yourselves justice, reap the fruit of steadfast love" (Hosea 10:12).[19] Sometimes love and justice are interchangeable: "[It is the Lord] who executes *justice* [*mishphat*] for the orphan and the widow, and who *loves* the strangers, providing them food and clothing" (Deut. 10:18, italics added; cf. Isa. 30:18).[20]

Justice's dynamic, restorative character. In the Bible, justice is not a mere *mitigation* of suffering in oppression, it is a *deliverance*. Justice demands that we correct the gross social inequities of the disadvantaged. The terms for justice are frequently associated with *yasha^c, yeshua*, the most important Hebrew word for deliverance and salvation: "God arose to establish justice [*mishpat*] to save [*hoshia*] all the oppressed of the earth" (Ps. 76:9; cf. Isa. 63:1).[21] "Give justice to the weak" and "maintain the right of the lowly" are parallel to "rescue the weak and the needy and snatch them out of the power of the wicked" (Ps. 82:3–4).[22]

Justice describes the deliverance of the people from political and economic oppressors (Judg. 5:11),[23] from slavery (1 Sam. 12:7–8; Micah 6:4), and from captivity (Isa. 41:1–11 [cf. v. 2 for *tsedeq*]; Jer. 51:10). Providing for the needy means ending their oppression, setting them back on their feet, giving them a home, and leading them to prosperity and restoration (Ps. 68:5–10; 10:15–18).[24] Justice does not merely help victims cope with oppression; it removes it. Because of this dynamic, restorative emphasis, distributive justice requires not primarily that we maintain a stable society, but rather that we advance the well-being of the disadvantaged.

God's special concern for the poor. Hundreds of biblical verses show that God is especially attentive to the poor and needy.[25] God is not biased. Because of unequal needs, however, equal provision of basic rights requires justice to be partial in order to be impartial. (Good firefighters do not spend equal time at every house; they are "partial" to people with fires.) Partiality to the weak is the most striking characteristic of biblical justice.[26] In the raging social struggles in which the poor are perennially victims of injustice, God and God's people take up the cause of the weak.[27] Rulers and leaders have a special obligation to do justice for the weak and powerless.[28] This partiality to the poor provides strong evidence that in biblical thought, justice is concerned with more than fair procedures.

The Scriptures speak of God's special concern for the poor in at least four different ways.[29]

1. Repeatedly the Bible says that the Sovereign of history works to lift up the poor and oppressed. Consider the exodus. Again and again the texts say God intervened because God hated the oppression of the poor Israelites (Exod. 3:7–8; 6:5–7; Deut. 26:6–8). Or consider the Psalms: "I know that the LORD maintains the cause of the afflicted, and executes justice for the needy" (140:12 RSV; cf. 12:5). God acts in history to lift up the poor and oppressed.

2. Sometimes, the Lord of history tears down rich and powerful people. Mary's song is shocking: "My soul glorifies the Lord . . . He has filled the hungry with good things but has sent the rich away empty" (Luke 1:46, 53

NIV). James is even more blunt: "Now listen, you rich people, weep and wail because of the misery that is coming upon you" (James 5:1 NIV).

Since God calls us to create wealth and is not biased against the rich, why do the Scriptures warn again and again that God sometimes works in history to destroy the rich? The Bible has a simple answer. It is because the rich sometimes get rich by oppressing the poor. Or because they often have plenty and neglect the needy. In either case, God is furious.

James warned the rich so harshly because they had hoarded wealth and refused to pay their workers (James 5:2–6). Repeatedly the prophets said the same thing (Psalm 10; Jer. 22:13–19; Isa. 3:14–25). "Among my people are wicked men who lie in wait like men who snare birds and like those who set traps to catch men. Like cages full of birds, their houses are full of deceit; they have become rich and powerful and have grown fat and sleek. . . . They do not defend the rights of the poor. Should I not punish them for this?" (Jer. 5:26–29 NIV).

Repeatedly the prophets warned that God was so outraged that he would destroy the nations of Israel and Judah. Because of the way they "trample on the heads of the poor . . . and deny justice to the oppressed," Amos predicted terrible captivity (2:7 NIV; see also 5:11; 6:4, 7; 7:11, 17). So did Isaiah and Micah (Isa. 10:1–3; Micah 2:2; 3:12). And it happened just as they foretold. According to both the Old and New Testaments, God destroys people and societies that get rich by oppressing the poor.

But what if we work hard and create wealth in just ways? That is good—as long as we do not forget to share. No matter how justly we have acquired our wealth, God demands that we act generously toward the poor. When we do not, God treats us in a similar way to those who oppress the poor. There is not a hint in Jesus' story of the rich man and Lazarus that the rich man exploited Lazarus to acquire wealth. He simply neglected to share. So God punished him (Luke 16:19–31).

Ezekiel's striking explanation for the destruction of Sodom reveals the same point: "Now this was the sin of your sister Sodom: She and her daughters were arrogant, overfed and unconcerned; they did not help the poor and needy. . . . Therefore I did away with them" (16:49–50 NIV). Again, the text does not charge them with gaining wealth by oppression. They simply refused to share.

The Bible is clear. If we get rich by oppressing the poor or if we have wealth and do not reach out generously to the needy, the Lord of history moves against us. God judges societies by what they do to the people at the bottom.

3. God identifies with the poor so strongly that caring for them is almost like helping God. "He who is kind to the poor lends to the LORD" (Prov. 19:17 NIV). On the other hand, one "who oppresses the poor shows contempt for their Maker" (14:31 NIV).

Jesus' parable of the sheep and goats is the ultimate commentary on these two proverbs. Jesus surprises those on the right with his insistence that they had fed and clothed him when he was cold and hungry. When they protested that they could not remember ever doing that, Jesus replied: "Whatever you did for one of the least of these brothers of mine, you did for me" (Matt. 25:40 NIV). If we believe his words, we look on the poor and neglected with entirely new eyes.

4. Finally, God demands that his people share God's special concern for the poor. God commanded Israel not to treat widows, orphans, and foreigners the way the Egyptians had treated them (Exod. 22:21–24). Instead, they should love the poor just as God cared for them at the exodus (Exod. 22:21–24; Deut. 15:13–15). When Jesus' disciples throw parties, they should especially invite the poor and disabled (Luke 14:12–14; Heb. 13:1–3). Paul held up Jesus' model of becoming poor to show how generously the Corinthians should contribute to the poor in Jerusalem (2 Cor. 8:9).

The Bible, however, goes one shocking step further. God insists that if we do not imitate God's concern for the poor, we are not really God's people—no matter how frequent our worship or how orthodox our creeds. Because Israel failed to correct oppression and defend poor widows, Isaiah insisted that Israel was really the pagan people of Gomorrah (1:10–17). God despised their fasting because they tried to worship God and oppress their workers at the same time (Isa. 58:3–7). Through Amos, the Lord shouted in fury that the very religious festivals God had ordained made God angry and sick. Why? Because the rich and powerful were mixing worship and oppression of the poor (5:21–24). Jesus was even more harsh. At the last judgment, some who expect to enter heaven will learn that their failure to feed the hungry condemns them to hell (Matthew 25). If we do not care for the needy brother or sister, God's love does not abide in us (1 John 3:17).

Jeremiah 22:13–19 describes good king Josiah and his wicked son Jehoiakim. When Jehoiakim became king, he built a fabulous palace by oppressing his workers. God sent the prophet Jeremiah to announce a terrible punishment. The most interesting part of the passage, however, is a short aside on this evil king's good father: "He defended the cause of the poor and needy, and so all went well. *'Is that not what it means to know me?'* declares the Lord" (v. 16 NIV; italics added). Knowing God is *inseparable* from caring for the poor. Of course, we dare not reduce knowing God only to a concern for the needy as some radical theologians do. We meet God in prayer, Bible study, worship—in many ways. But if we do not share God's passion to strengthen the poor, we simply do not know God in a biblical way.

All this biblical material clearly demonstrates that God and God's faithful people have a great concern for the poor. Earlier I argued that God is partial to the poor but not biased. God does not love the poor any more than the rich. God has an equal concern for the well-being of every single person. Most rich and powerful people, however, are genuinely biased; they care a lot more about themselves than about their poor neighbors. By contrast with the genuine bias of most people, God's lack of bias makes God appear biased. God cares equally for everyone.

How then is God "partial" to the poor? Because in concrete historical situations, equal concern for everyone requires special attention to specific people. In a family, loving parents do not provide equal tutorial time to a son struggling hard to scrape by with D's and a daughter easily making A's. Precisely in order to be "impartial" and love both equally, they devote extra time to helping the more needy child. In historical situations (e.g., apartheid) where some people oppress others, God's lack of bias does not mean neutrality. Precisely because God loves all equally, God works against oppressors and actively sides with the oppressed—in order to liberate both whom he loves equally!

We see this connection precisely in the texts that declare God's lack of bias: "For the LORD your God is God of gods and Lord of lords, the great, the mighty, the terrible God, who is not partial and takes no bribe. He executes justice for the fatherless and the widow, and loves the sojourner, giving him food and clothing" (Deut. 10:17–18 RSV). Justice and love are virtual synonyms in this passage. There is no suggestion that loving the sojourner is a benevolent, voluntary act different from a legal demand to do justice to the fatherless. Furthermore, there is no indication in the text that those needing food and clothing are poor because of some violation of due process such as fraud or robbery. The text simply says they are poor and therefore God who is not biased pays special attention to them.

Leviticus 19 is similar. In verse 15, the text condemns partiality: "You shall not be partial to the poor or defer to the great." The preceding verses refer to several of the Ten Commandments (stealing, lying, blasphemy [v. 11]). But special references to the poor are in the same passage. When harvesting their crops, God's people must leave the grain at the edge of the field and not pick up the grapes that fall in the vineyard: "You shall leave them for the poor and the alien" (v. 10). This is a divine command, not a suggestion for voluntary charity, and it is part of the same passage that declares God's lack of bias.[30]

Precisely because God is not biased, God pays special attention to the poor. Consequently, an understanding of justice that reflects this biblical teaching must be concerned with more than procedural justice. Distributive justice that insists on special attention to the poor so they have opportunity to enjoy material well-being is also crucial.

Justice as restoration to community.[31] Restoration to community—and to the benefit rights necessary for dignified participation in community—are an important part of what the Bible means by justice. Since persons are created for community, the Scriptures understand the good life as sharing in the essential aspects of social life. Justice includes helping people return to the kind of life in community that God intends for them. Leviticus 25:35–36 describes the poor as being on the verge of falling out of the community because of their economic distress. "If members of your community become poor in that their power slips *with you*, you shall make them strong . . . that they may live *with you*" (Lev. 25:35–36).[32] The word translated as "power" here is "hand" in the Hebrew. "Hand" (*yod*) metaphorically means "power." The solution is that those who are able correct the situation and thereby restore the poor to community. The poor in fact are their own flesh or kin (Isa. 58:7). Poverty is a family affair.

In order to restore the weak to participation in community, the community's responsibility to its diminished members is "to make them strong" again (Lev. 25:35). This translation is a literal rendering of the Hebrew, which is the word "to be strong" and is found here in the causative (Hiphil) conjugation and therefore means "cause him to be strong." The purpose of this empowerment is "that they may live *beside you*" (v. 35); that is, be restored to community. According to Psalm 107, God's steadfast love leads God to care for the hungry so they are able to "establish a town to live in; they sow fields, and plant vineyards. . . . By his blessing they multiply greatly" (vv. 36–38). Once more the hungry can be active, participating members of a community. The concern is for the whole person in community and what it takes to maintain persons in that relationship.

Community membership means the ability to share fully within one's capacity and potential in each essential aspect of community.[33] Participation in community has multiple dimensions. It includes participation in decision making, social life, economic production, education, culture, and religion. Also essential are physical life itself and the material resources necessary for a decent life.

Providing the conditions for participation in community demands a focus on what are the basic needs for life in community. Achieving such justice includes access to the material essentials of life, such as food and shelter. It is God "who executes justice for the oppressed; who gives food to the hungry" (Ps. 146:7). It is the Lord "who executes justice for the orphan and the widow, and who loves the strangers, providing them food and clothing" (Deut. 10:18). "Food and clothing" is a Hebraism for what is indispensable.[34]

Job 24, one of the most powerful pictures of poverty in the Bible, describes the economic benefits that injustice takes away. Injustice starts with assault on a person's land, the basis of economic power (v. 2). It moves then to secondary means of production, the donkey and the ox (v. 3). As a result the victims experience powerlessness and indignity: "They thrust the needy off the road; the poor of the earth all hide themselves" (v. 4). The poor are separated from the bonds of community, wandering like wild donkeys in the desert (v. 5). They are denied basic needs of food (vv. 6, 10), drink (v. 11), clothing, and shelter (vv. 7, 10).[35] Elsewhere in Job, failure to provide food and clothing for the needy is condemned as injustice (22:7; 31:19). Opportunity for everyone to have access to the material resources necessary for life in community is basic to the biblical concept of justice. Does that not suggest that human rights must include not just civil/political rights but also socioeconomic rights?

As we shall see at greater length in the following section, enjoying the socioeconomic benefits crucial to participation in community goes well beyond "welfare" or "charity." People in distress are to be empowered at the point where their participation in community has been undercut. That means restoring their productive capability. Therefore, restoration of the land, the basic productive resource, is the way that Leviticus 25 commands the people to fulfill the call to "make them strong again" so "they may live beside you" in the land (v. 35). As the poor return to their land, they receive a new power and dignity that restores their participation in the community.

Other provisions in the Law also provide access to the means of production.[36] In the sabbatical years, the lands remain fallow and unharvested so that "the poor may eat" (Exod. 23:10–11). Similarly, the farmer was not to go back over the first run of harvesting or to harvest to the very corners of the field so that the poor could provide for themselves (Lev. 19:9–10; Deut. 24:19–22).

There are also restrictions on the processes that tear people down so that their "power slips" and they cannot support themselves. Interest on loans was prohibited; food to the poor was not to be provided at profit (Lev. 25:36ff.). A means of production like a millstone for grinding grain was not to be taken as collateral on a loan because that would be "taking a life in pledge" (Deut. 24:6 RSV). If a poor person gave an essential item of clothing as a pledge, the creditor had to return it before night came (Exod. 22:26). All these provisions are restrictions on individual economic freedom that go well beyond merely preventing fraud, theft, and violence. The Law did, of course, support the rights of owners to benefit from their property, but the law placed limits on the owners' control of property and on the quest for profit. The common good of the community outweighed unrestricted economic freedom.

The fact that justice in the Scriptures includes socioeconomic human benefits means that we must reject the notion that biblical justice is merely procedural, merely the protection of property, person, and equal access to the procedures of the community. That is by no means to deny that procedural justice is important. A person who is denied these protections is cut off from the political and civil community and is not only open to abuse, but is diminished in his or her ability to affect the life of the community. Procedural justice is absolutely essential to protect people from fraud, theft, and violence.

Biblical justice, however, also includes socioeconomic benefits, which are the responsibility of the community to guarantee (*who* in the community has an obligation to guarantee these benefits is a separate question to be discussed below). Biblical justice has both an economic and a legal focus. The goal of justice is not only the recovery of the integrity of the legal system. It is also the restoration of the community as a place where all live together in wholeness.

The wrong to which justice responds is not merely an illegitimate process (like stealing). What is wrong is also an end result in which people are deprived of basic needs. Leviticus 19:13 condemns both stealing *and* withholding a poor person's salary for a day. Isaiah 5:8–10 condemns those who buy up field after field until only the rich person is left dwelling alone in his big, beautiful house. Significantly, however, the prophet here does not denounce the acquisition of the land as illegal. Through legal foreclosing of mortgages or through debt bondage, the property could be taken within the law.[37] Isaiah nevertheless condemns the rulers for permitting this injustice to the weak. He appeals to social justice above the technicalities of current law. Restoration to community is central to justice.

From the biblical perspective, justice demands more than fair procedures. It demands both fair courts and fair economic structures. It includes both freedom rights and benefit rights. Precisely because of its equal concern for wholeness for everyone, it pays special attention to the needs of the weak and marginalized.

The Content of Distributive Justice

None of the above claims, however, offers a norm that describes the actual content of distributive justice. The next two sections seek to develop such a norm. I will argue that from a biblical perspective, distributive justice demands adequate access to productive resources for those able to earn their own way and a generous sufficiency for those who are too old, too disabled, or otherwise unable to earn their own way.

Justice as adequate access to productive resources. Equality has been one of the most powerful slogans of the twentieth century—and one of the most popular definitions of distributive justice. But what does it mean? Does it mean equality before the law? One person, one vote? Equality of opportunity in education? Identical income shares? Or absolute identity—facial equality—as described in the satirical novel *Facial Justice?*[38]

History shows that full equality of economic results is not compatible with human freedom and responsibility. Free choices have consequences; therefore when immoral decisions reduce someone's earning power, we should, other things being equal, consider the result just. Even absolute equality of opportunity is impossible unless we (wrongly) prevent parents from passing on any of their knowledge or other capital to their children.

So what definition of equality–or better, equity–do the biblical materials suggest?

Capital in an agricultural society. The biblical material on Israel and the land offers important clues about what a biblical understanding of equity would look like. The contrast between early Israel and surrounding societies was striking.[39] In Egypt, most of the land belonged to the Pharaoh or the temples. In most other Near-Eastern contexts, a feudal system of landholding prevailed. The king granted large tracts of land, worked by landless laborers, to a small number of elite royal vassals. This feudal system did not exist in early Israel, except in their relationship to Yahweh. Yahweh the King owned all the land and made important demands on those to whom he gave it to use. Under Yahweh, however, each family had their own land. Israel's ideal was decentralized family "ownership" understood as stewardship under Yahweh's absolute ownership. In the period of the judges, the pattern in Israel was free peasants on small land holdings of approximately equal size.[40]

Land was the basic capital in early Israel's agricultural economy, and the Law says the land was divided in such a way that each extended family had the resources to produce the things needed for a decent life.

Joshua 18 and Numbers 26 contain the two most important accounts of the division of the land.[41] They represent Israel's social ideal with regard to the land. Originally the land was divided among the clans of the tribes so that a relatively similar amount of land was available to all the family units. The larger tribes got a larger portion and the smaller tribes a smaller portion (Num. 26:54). In Ezekiel's vision of a future time of justice, the land is said to be divided "equally" (47:14, literally, "each according to his brother").

Several institutions had the purpose of preserving a just distribution of the land over the generations. The *law of levirate* served to prevent the land from going out of the family line (Deut. 25:5). The provision for a *kinship redeemer* meant that when poverty forced someone to sell his land, a relative was to step in to purchase it for him (Lev. 25:25).

The picture of land ownership in the time of the judges suggests some approximation of equality of land ownership—at least up to the point where every family had enough to enjoy a decent, dignified life in the community if they acted responsibly. Decentralized land ownership by extended families was the economic base for a relatively egalitarian society of small landowners and vinedressers in the time of the judges.[42] Israel's ideal called for each family to have enough land so they had the opportunity to acquire life's necessities.

"Necessities" is not to be understood as the minimum necessary to keep from starving. In the nonhierarchical, relatively egalitarian society of small farmers depicted above, families possessed resources to earn a living that would have been considered reasonable and acceptable, not embarrassingly minimal. That is not to suggest that every family had exactly the same income. It does mean, however, that every family had an equality of economic opportunity up to the point that they had the resources to earn a living that would enable them not only to meet minimal needs of food, clothing, and housing, but also to be respected participants in the community. Possessing their own land enabled each extended family to acquire the necessities for a decent life through responsible work.

The Year of Jubilee. Two astonishing biblical texts—Leviticus 25 and Deuteronomy 15—show how important this basic equality of opportunity was to God. The Jubilee text in Leviticus demanded that the land return to the original owners every fifty years. And Deuteronomy 15 called for the release of debts every seven years.

Leviticus 25 is one of the most astonishing texts in all of Scripture.[43] Every fifty years, God said, the land was to return to the original owners. Physical handicaps, death of a breadwinner, or lack of natural ability may lead some families to become poorer than others. But God does not want such disadvantages to lead to ever-increasing extremes of wealth and poverty with the result that the poor eventually lack the basic resources to earn a decent livelihood. God therefore gave his people a law to guarantee that no family would permanently lose its land. Every fifty years, the land returned to the original owners so that every family had enough productive resources to function as dignified, participating members of the community (Lev. 25:10–24). Private property was not abolished. Regularly, however, the means of producing wealth was to be "equalized"—not fully, but up to the point of every family having the resources to earn a decent living.

What is the theological basis for this startling command? Yahweh owns it! "The land shall not be sold in perpetuity, for the land is mine; for you are strangers and sojourners with me" (Lev. 25:23).

The assumption in this text that people must suffer the consequences of wrong choices is also striking. A whole generation or more could suffer the loss of ancestral land, but every fifty years the basic source of wealth would be returned so that each family had the opportunity to provide for its basic needs.

This passage prescribes justice in a way that even the most well-intentioned private philanthropy can never deliver. The Year of Jubilee was intended to be an institutionalized structure that affected all Israelites automatically. It was to be the poor family's right to recover their inherited land at the Jubilee. Returning the land was not a charitable courtesy that the wealthy might extend if they pleased.[44]

Interestingly, the principles of Jubilee challenge modern extremes of both the Left and Right. Only God is an absolute owner. No one else has absolute property rights. The right of each family to have the means to earn a living takes priority over a purchaser's "property rights." At the same time, Jubilee affirms not only the right but the importance of property managed by families (normally extended families) who understand that they are stewards responsible to God. This text does not point us in the direction of the Communist model where the state owns all the land. God wants each family to own the resources to produce its own livelihood. Why? To strengthen the family (this is a very important "pro-family" text!). To give people the freedom to participate in shaping history. And to prevent the centralization of power—and the oppression and totalitarianism that almost always accompany centralized ownership of land or capital by either the state or small elites.

The teaching of the prophets that we explored earlier in the section on *mishpat* and *tsedaqah* underlines the principles of Leviticus 25. In the tenth to the eighth centuries BC, major centralization of landholding occurred. Poorer farmers lost their land, becoming landless laborers or slaves. The prophets regularly denounced the bribery, political assassination, and economic oppression that destroyed the earlier decentralized economy described above.

They also expressed a powerful eschatological hope for a future day of justice when "all shall sit under their own vines and under their own fig trees" (Micah

4:4; cf. also Zech. 3:10) and the leaders will guarantee that all people again enjoy their ancestral land (Ezek. 45:1–9).

In the giving of the land, in the denunciation of oppressors who seized the land of the poor, and in the vision of a new day when once again all will delight in the fruits of their own land and labor, we see a social ideal in which families are to have the economic means to earn their own way. A basic equality of economic opportunity up to the point that all can at least provide for their own basic needs through responsible work is the norm. Failure to act responsibly has economic consequences, so there is no assumption of absolute equality of outcome. Central, however, is the demand that each family have the necessary capital (land in an agricultural society) so that responsible stewardship will result in an economically decent life.[45]

The sabbatical year. God's law also provided for liberation of soil, slaves, and debtors every seven years. Again the concern is justice for the poor and disadvantaged (as well as the well-being of the land). A central goal is to protect people against processes that would result in their losing their productive resources or to restore productive resources after a time of loss.

Hebrew slaves also received their freedom in the sabbatical year (Deut. 15:12–18). And when they left, their masters were commanded by God to give them cattle and other products from the farm (Deut. 15:13–14; see also Exod. 21:2–6). As a consequence, the freed slave would again have some productive resources so he could earn his own way.[46]

The sabbatical provision on loans is even more surprising (Deut. 15:1–6) if, as some scholars think, the text calls for cancellation of debts every seventh year.[47] If followed, this provision would have protected small landowners from the exorbitant interest of moneylenders and thereby helped prevent them from losing their productive resources.

As in the case of the Year of Jubilee, this passage involves structural justice rather than mere charity. The sabbatical release of debts was an institutionalized mechanism to prevent the kind of economic divisions where a few people would possess all the capital while others had no productive resources.

The sabbatical year, unfortunately, was practiced only sporadically. Some texts suggest that failure to obey this law was one reason for the Babylonian exile (2 Chron. 36:20–21; Lev. 26:34–36).[48] Disobedience, however, does not negate God's demand. Institutionalized structures to prevent poverty are central to God's will for his people.

Does the biblical material offer a norm for distributive justice today? Some would argue that the biblical material on the land in Israel applies only to God's covenant community. But that is to ignore both the fact that God chose Abraham and his descendants to be a witness to the nations and also that the biblical writers did not hesitate to apply revealed standards to persons and societies outside Israel. Israel was to be a priest to the nations (Exod. 19:6), disclosing the Creator's will for all people and thus blessing all nations (Gen. 26:24). Amos announced divine punishment on the surrounding nations for their evil and injustice (Amos 1–2). Isaiah condemned Assyria for its pride and injustice (Isa. 10:12–19). The book of Daniel shows that God removed pagan kings like Nebuchadnezzar in the same way he destroyed Israel's rulers when they failed to show mercy to the oppressed (Dan. 4:27). God obliterated Sodom and Gomorrah no less than Israel and Judah because they neglected to aid the poor and feed the hungry. The Lord of history applies the same standards of social justice to all nations.

That does not mean, however, that we should try to apply the specific mechanisms of the Jubilee and the sabbatical release to twenty-first-century global market economies. It is the basic paradigm that is normative for us today. Appropriate application of these texts requires that we ask how their specific mechanisms functioned in Israelite culture, and then determine what specific measures would fulfill a similar function in our very different society. Since land in Israelite society represented productive power, we must identify the forms of productive power in modern societies. In an industrial society, a central area of productive power is the factory, and in an information society it is knowledge. Faithful application of these biblical texts in such societies means finding mechanisms that offer everyone the opportunity to share in the ownership of these productive resources; that is, guaranteeing, in an information society, that every child has genuine opportunity to receive quality education. If we start with the Jubilee's call for everyone to enjoy access to productive power, we must criticize all socioeconomic arrangements where productive power is owned or controlled by only one class or group (whether bourgeois, aristocratic, or proletarian)—or by a state or party oligarchy. Indeed, we saw that the prophets protested the development of an economic system in which land ownership was shifted to a small group within society. And we must develop appropriate intervening processes in society to restore access to productive resources to everyone.

The central normative principle about distributive justice that emerges from the biblical material on the land and the sabbatical release of debts is this: *Justice demands that every person or family has access to the productive resources (land, money, knowledge) so they have the opportunity to earn a generous sufficiency of material necessities and be dignified participating members of their community.* This norm offers significant guidance for how to shape the economy so that people normally have the opportunity to earn their own way.

But what should be done for those—whether the able-bodied who experience an emergency or dependents such as orphans, widows, the elderly, or the disabled—who for shorter or longer periods simply cannot provide basic necessities through their own efforts alone?

Generous care for those who cannot care for themselves. Again the biblical material is very helpful. Both in the Old Testament and the New Testament, we discover explicit teaching on the community's obligation to support those who cannot support themselves.

The Pentateuch commands at least five important provisions designed to help those who could not help themselves:[49]

1. The third-year tithe goes to poor widows, orphans, and sojourners as well as the Levites (Deut. 14:28–29; 26:12).
2. Laws on gleaning stipulate that the corners of the grain fields and the sheaves and grapes that dropped were to be left for the poor, especially widows, orphans, and sojourners (Lev. 19:9–10; Deut. 24:19–21).
3. Every seventh year, fields must remain fallow, and the poor may reap the natural growth (Exod. 23:10–11; Lev. 25:1–7).
4. A zero-interest loan must be available to the poor, and if the balance is not repaid by the sabbatical year, it is forgiven (Exod. 22:25; Lev. 25:35–38; Deut. 15:1–11).
5. Israelites who become slaves to repay debts go free in the seventh year (Exod. 21:1–11; Lev. 25:47–53; Deut. 15:12–18). And when the freed slaves leave, their temporary "master" must provide liberally, giving the former slaves cattle, grain, and wine (Deut. 15:14) so they can again earn their own way.

In his masterful essay on this topic, John Mason argues that the primary assistance to the able-bodied person was probably the no-interest loan. This would maintain the family unit, avoid stigmatizing people unnecessarily, and require work so that long-term dependency did not result.

Dependent poor such as widows and orphans received direct "transfer payments" through the third-year tithe. But other provisions such as those on gleaning required the poor to work for the "free" produce they gleaned. The widow Ruth, for example, labored in the fields to feed herself and her mother-in-law (Ruth 2:1–23).

It is important to note the ways that the provisions for helping the needy include a major emphasis on the role of nongovernmental actors. Not only did Ruth and other poor folk have to glean in the fields; more wealthy landowners had responsibilities to leave the corners of the fields and the grapes that dropped. And in the story of Ruth, Boaz as the next of kin took responsibility for her well-being (Ruth 3–4).

The texts seem to assume a level of assistance best described as "sufficiency for need"—"with a fairly liberal interpretation of need."[50] Deuteronomy 15:8 specifies that the poor brother receive a loan "large enough to meet the need." Frequently God commands those with resources to treat their poor fellow Israelites with the same liberality that God showed them at the exodus, in the wilderness, and in giving them their own land (Exod. 22:21; Lev. 25:38; Deut. 24:18, 22). God wanted those who could not care for themselves to receive a liberal sufficiency for need offered in a way that encouraged work and responsibility, strengthened the family, and helped the poor return to self-sufficiency.

Were those "welfare provisions" part of the law to be enforced by the community? Or were they merely suggestions for voluntary charity?[51] The third-year tithe was gathered in a central location (Deut. 14:28) and then shared with the needy. Community leaders would have to act together to carry out such a centralized operation. In the Talmud, there is evidence that the proper community leaders had the right to demand contributions.[52] Nehemiah 5 deals explicitly with violations of these provisions on loans to the poor. The political leader calls an assembly, brings "charges against the nobles," and commands that the situation be corrected (Neh. 5:7; cf. all of 1–13). Old Testament texts often speak of the "rights" or "cause" of the poor. Since these terms have clear legal significance,[53] they support the view that the provisions we have explored for assisting the poor would have been legally enforceable. "The clear fact is that the provisions for the impoverished were part of the Mosaic legislation, as much as other laws such as those dealing with murder and theft. Since nothing in the text allows us to consider them as different, they must be presumed to have been legally enforceable."[54]

The sociopolitical situation is dramatically different in the New Testament. The early church is a tiny religious minority with very few political rights in a vast pagan Roman Empire. But within the church, the standard is the same. Acts 2:43–47 and 4:32–37 record dramatic economic sharing in order to respond to those who could not care for themselves. The norm? "Distribution was made to each as any had need" (Acts 4:35 RSV—i.e., up to the point of an adequate sufficiency for a decent life). As a result, "there was not a needy person among them" (v. 34).

The great evangelist Paul spent much of his time over several years collecting an international offering for the impoverished Christians in Jerusalem (2 Corinthians 8–9). For his work, he found a norm (2 Cor. 8:13–15)—equality of basic necessities—articulated in the Exodus story of the manna where every person ended up with "as much as each of them needed" (Exod. 16:18).[55]

Throughout the Scriptures we see the same standard. When people cannot care for themselves, their community must provide a generous sufficiency so that their needs are met.

Summary

How should we summarize the implications of this vast amount of biblical material for our understanding of justice and human rights?

Procedural justice is very important. So is commutative justice—God wants honest weights and measures (Lev. 19:35–36; Prov. 11:1; Ezek. 45:10; Amos 8:5) and insists that persons keep their promises—so that a fair, honest exchange of goods and services is possible.

At the same time, fair distribution is also central to the biblical understanding of justice. This is clear from the meaning of the biblical words *mishpat* and *tsedaqah*, the close connection of justice and love, the restorative character of justice, the special concern to empower the weak and needy, and the emphasis on restoring people to community. The biblical material also provides significant content for our understanding of fair distribution: The able-bodied must have genuine access to the productive resources of their society so they can earn their own way and be dignified members of their community; and those unable to care for themselves must receive a generous sufficiency of life's necessities.

The biblical material points to an answer to the long dispute about whether human rights are primarily civil/political, primarily socioeconomic, or both.

The importance of civil/political human rights is clearly supported by the biblical material. Legal procedures must be transparent and fair. The right to own private property (subject, of course, to the will of God, the absolute owner) is assumed and explicitly affirmed throughout Scripture. No biblical texts talk directly about freedom of speech, a secret ballot, or democratic process. But history has shown that religious and political freedom and democratic processes seem essential if we want to respect the inestimable dignity and worth of every individual. It is not surprising that civil/political human rights have become one of the most esteemed treasures of Western societies that have been shaped for many centuries by biblical values.

It is equally clear that biblical norms contain a moral demand that all persons have access to socioeconomic benefits, although evangelicals as well as others disagree about whether we should use the language of rights when speaking of these socioeconomic benefits. In the subsequent section on government, I will discuss the question of who (family, civil society, government?) has the responsibility to guarantee the right to things like work, food, health care, and housing. But it is surely the case that the same biblical materials that emphasize and give content to distributive justice clearly call biblical Christians to affirm the importance of socioeconomic human rights.[56]

What do we do when various human rights collide? What do we do when the implementation of socioeconomic rights seems to require less concern for or even abandonment of civil/political rights? If the last century of Nazi and Marxist totalitarianism has taught us anything, it has shown that we dare not trade freedom for bread. Human beings are created for both. Evangelical political voices must be faithful advocates of those who seek to create societies that treasure both and refuse to play one against the other. Among other things, that means recognizing that a great deal of governmental activity to promote a high level of economic equality will undermine freedom and also that some restriction on the economic freedom of the powerful will be necessary to move toward equality of opportunity. In every society, at every juncture, prudential wisdom informed by biblical norms and historical experience will face the difficult, imprecise task of discerning which set of human rights is most endangered at a given moment and designing wise ways to correct the imbalance. There is no way to avoid the complexity and ambiguity of that task. But biblical voices should not seek to avoid this difficult problem by arguing that one set of rights is more important or basic than the other.

In his discussion of how the claims of different human rights collide, Roman Catholic scholar David Hollenbach suggests three "strategic moral priorities" that I believe flow from the biblical emphasis on corrective action to restore justice for the weak and needy:

1. The needs of the poor take priority over the wants of the rich.
2. The freedom of the dominated takes priority over the liberty of the powerful.
3. The participation of marginalized groups takes priority over the preservation of an order which excludes them.[57]

Implementing these priorities by no means suggests returning to a Marxist neglect of civil/political rights. They remain basic and must apply to everyone, rich and poor. But does not the loud, persistent biblical claim that economic empowerment of the poor is a central component of justice mean that *some* restriction of the freedom of the rich and powerful (as, for example, in progressive taxation) is legitimate in order to guarantee access to basic necessities for the poor and neglected? Surely that follows from the biblical truth that one of the central ways God measures societies is by how they treat the people on the bottom.

Society and Government

"The one great heresy," according to William Temple, one of the great twentieth-century archbishops of Canterbury, is to equate society and the state (or government).[58] The government is only one of many important institutions in society.

The very first institutions to appear in the biblical story are marriage and family. The Creator made persons male and female, designed for the divinely ordained institutions of marriage and family. Only when Eve arrives is Adam's heart satisfied. The social institutions of marriage and family are embedded in the very order of creation—at the very beginning. Only later does the text discuss the institution of government.

In the history of Israel, we see the slow emergence of different societal institutions.[59] In Abraham, a leader of an extended family, we detect hardly any distinction between the roles of parent, priest, and king. In the course of Israel's history, however, the institutions of the priesthood and the prophets emerge as distinct from both family and government. With the early church, as Christianity breaks the narrow bonds of ethnic religion and becomes a universal faith embracing people of every tribe and nation, the church becomes a powerful institution clearly distinct from—and often in sharp conflict with—the state.

Increasing differentiation of societal institutions continues over the course of human history as more and more institutions emerge as distinct entities independent of government. Independent economic institutions—both business corporations and unions—become powerful. A vast variety of educational, cultural, and civic institutions flourish with very little dependence on government. "The great array of differentiated social cohesions, which represent in their totality the free society of modern civilization, and from which the authority and force embodied in the state have withdrawn themselves, furnish the individual with that great variety of choice which constitutes real freedom."[60]

Surely one of the clearest lessons taught by the history of the last one hundred years is that human freedom and flourishing collapse when the state refuses to accept its role as just one of many important societal institutions and instead seeks to dominate and control all others. As both Nazi and Communist totalitarian governments sought to obliterate every other independent societal institution, human freedom largely disappeared—thus devastating for a time the kind of free flourishing that the Creator intended for persons made in his image. Both because the centralization of power is dangerous in a fallen world and because totalitarianism prevents individuals from responding to their Creator's call to freedom and the creative, personal shaping of history, the vast variety of societal institutions independent of the state are an essential ingredient of a good society. The state or government is not society.

The state is "society acting as a whole, with the ultimate power to compel compliance within its own jurisdiction."[61] To prevent disorder and promote the common good of the entire society, we need an institution that has the authority and power to provide a good, accepted framework in which all the other institutions can both enjoy their own freedom and also work together effectively. Hence the need for governmental legislators to write the laws, administrators to implement them, and judges to enforce them.

What is the source of government's limited yet still awesome authority? The answer of historic Christianity differs sharply from modern contract theory. In the latter, sovereign individuals living in a state of nature freely choose to form a social compact with other free individuals, surrendering some of their freedom to create the state. Government, consequently, derives its authority from this original contract between free individuals. As William Temple notes, contract theory is "not even good myth."[62] As a matter of historical fact, the state emerged in a far more organic way. And in terms of government's ultimate authority, it comes not from some choice of individual persons but from God.

Jesus bluntly informed Pilate: "You would have no power over me unless it had been given you from above" (John 19:11). And Paul boldly declared that "there is no authority except from God, and those authorities that exist have been instituted by God" (Rom. 13:1). The Creator who made us communal beings needing mutual interdependence with others, and therefore the institutions to mediate that interdependence, is the ultimate source of all governmental authority.

That does not mean that, secondarily, human agreements to write and accept constitutions that provide for the democratic election of governmental officials are unimportant. Nor does it mean that the democratic claim is wrong that in some important sense, the "people are sovereign" and governments derive their authority from the choices of people in free democratic elections. But it does mean that the vote of the majority does not make something right. God is the ultimate source of all governmental authority, and God wills that "the people" and governments do justice. "The fact that political authority stems not from the people but from God shows that government does not have the right to do what it wills, and neither do the people."[63]

The purpose of government. Is it only to restrain evil or also to do good?

It does not take much historical observation to notice that there is plenty of evil to restrain. Sin, and the oppression and violence to which it leads, are universal. Throughout the Scriptures, we see government (the king, the courts, etc.) called to restrain evil and punish evildoers. Paul summarizes a vast amount of biblical teaching with his simple statement that governmental authority "is the servant of God to execute wrath on the wrongdoer" (Rom. 13:4).

Over the course of Christian history, many theologians have understood the role of government as largely or exclusively negative. Government comes only after the fall, and its essential purpose is to restrain evil. Many others, however, including Thomas Aquinas and John Calvin, while accepting this purpose of government, also endorse a positive purpose—the promotion of the common good. Calvin denounced those who regarded magistrates "only as a kind of necessary evil." Civil authority, Calvin believed, is "the most honorable of all callings in the whole of life"—government's function among people being "no less than that of bread, water, sun and air."[64]

In fact, in Romans 13, Paul specifies a positive role for government before he refers to its negative function. Government is "God's servant for your good" (v. 4).[65] God approved and blessed the kings of Israel for leading their societies in positive activities. David brought the ark of the covenant to Jerusalem and Solomon organized the nation in a massive, lengthy societal project to build the temple.

Does the absence of specific reference to government before the fall mean that government is necessary only because of sin? Probably not. If God had created persons as the kind of isolated individuals imagined by contract theorists, then probably the answer would be yes. But the Trinitarian God who exists in mutual, loving fellowship among Father, Son, and Holy Spirit created us in the divine image. We are made for mutual interdependence, not individualistic isolation. Quite apart from the fall, we reach our God-given destiny only when we interact with others in cooperative tasks and loving fellowship. Even without the fall, a growing human population would have needed cooperative efforts and leaders to organize that cooperation in order to carry out God's mandate to exercise dominion and stewardship in creating human civilization. Government's positive purpose—promoting the common good—flows directly from the fact that we are created in the image of the Triune God.

The fact that government comes into the biblical story explicitly only after the fall does not prove that it is necessary only because of sin. Music is also first mentioned after the fall (Gen. 4:21), but that hardly means that it results from sin.[66] Furthermore, "the fact that the book of Revelation says that kings will bring their glory and the honour of the nations into the New Jerusalem suggests that the political enterprise has its own intrinsic merit apart from the effects of sin" (see Rev. 21:24–26).[67]

Limited government. There are many reasons why government should have major limitations put on its reach and power.

Probably the most crucial limitation on government flows from widespread recognition of the theological truth that all governmental authority flows from God. And God insists that all state action conform to the divine standard of justice. Thus we can always condemn specific governmental decisions by appealing to the higher law of divine justice.

Jesus and the early church's attitude toward Roman imperial power underlines how the knowledge of God's ultimate sovereignty relativizes and challenges all earthly governmental power. At his trial, Jesus bluntly reminded Pilate that his (and Caesar's) authority and power came from God. At a time when Roman emperors were beginning to claim to be divine, Paul says they are *God's servant*! "Paul relativizes the Roman Imperial order. He refuses to accept the Emperor's ultimate authority and says that the Emperor is *under* God, a servant."[68] Again and again throughout Christian history, Christians have limited governmental power by giving their ultimate allegiance to God alone, thus relativizing the power of every earthly ruler.

The fact that God creates each individual person as a free, creative being called to trace the Creator's steps by freely choosing to mold the material world, shape history, and create things never seen before also demands limited government. Individuals simply cannot carry out their creation mandate if an all-powerful government makes all the decisions.

The dreadful reality of omnipresent evil underlines the importance of limited government. History has confirmed the truth of Lord Acton's comment that power tends to corrupt and absolute power corrupts absolutely. Sinful persons almost always use immense power for their personal, selfish advantage. The Scriptures are full of stories about oppressive kings and overpowerful, evil governments (e.g., 1 Kings 2; Revelation 13). There are also warnings about what powerful rulers will do (1 Sam. 8:11–17; cf. also Deut. 17:14–20). Only if governmental power is significantly limited is there any hope of avoiding gross evil on the part of the state.

Finally, the fact that God has divinely instituted other institutions in society (the family, the church) also demands limited government. God, not the state, creates and establishes family and church and gives them freedom and authority to carry out their responsibilities independently of government. Only if government is appropriately limited can the other institutions in society flourish as God intended.[69]

Fortunately, democratic societies have discovered numerous ways to implement the vision of limited government. The constitutional separation of powers (legislative, judicial, and administrative); the several substantially independent spheres of federal, state, and local government; regular, free democratic elections; recognition of the importance and freedom from government of a vast range of nongovernmental institutions; acknowledgment that government officials are under, not above, the law; freedom of speech, assembly, and dissent—in these and other ways, we implement limited government.

When we understand the importance of limited government, we see why it is crucial not to immediately turn to government to solve every social problem. Other institutions—family, church, schools, business, unions—all have obligations to solve societal problems. In every case, we need to ask what institution in society and at what level of that institution we can best solve a particular problem.

We can see this principle at work in the biblical text where at different points it is clear that the family has the first obligation to help needy members.[70] In the great text on the Jubilee in Leviticus 25, the first responsibility to help the poor person forced by poverty to sell land belongs to the next of kin in the extended family (Lev. 25:25, 35). But the poor person's help does not end with the family. Even if there are no family members to help, the poor person has the legal right to get his land back at the next Jubilee (25:28). Similarly, 1 Timothy 5:16 insists that a Christian widow's relatives should be her first means of support. Only when the family cannot help should the church step in. Any policy or political philosophy that immediately seeks governmental solutions for problems that could be solved just as well or better at the level of the family violates the biblical framework that stresses the central societal role of the family.

On the other hand, that does not mean that there is no role for government to promote the common good. Government is an instrument of community and is inherent in human life as an expression of our created social nature.

Sin also makes government action necessary. When selfish, powerful people deprive others of their rightful access to productive resources, the state rightly steps in with intervening power to correct the injustice. When other individuals and institutions in the community do not or cannot provide basic necessities for the needy, government rightly helps.

Frequently, of course, the state contributes to the common good by encouraging and enabling other institutions in the community—whether family, church, nongovernmental social agencies, guilds, or unions[71]—to carry out their responsibilities to care for the economically dependent. Sometimes, however, the depth of social need exceeds the capacity of nongovernmental institutions. When indirect approaches are not effective in restraining economic injustice or in providing care for those who cannot care for themselves, the state must act directly to demand patterns of justice and provide vital services—always, of course, in a way that does not further weaken but restores and strengthens the other nongovernmental institutions.

The objective of the state, however, is not merely to maintain an equilibrium of power in society. Its purpose is not merely to enable other groups in the society to carry out their tasks. The state has a positive responsibility to foster justice. The nature of justice defines the work of government so fundamentally that any statement of the purpose of government must depend upon a proper definition of justice.

That is why our whole discussion of the biblical paradigm on distributive justice is so important. "He [the Lord] has made you king to execute justice and righteousness" (1 Kings 10:9; cf. Jer. 22:15–16). And these two key words, *justice* and *righteousness*, as we have seen, refer not only to fair legal systems, but also to just economic structures.

The positive role of government in advancing economic justice is seen in the biblical materials that present the ideal monarch. Both the royal psalms and the messianic prophecies develop the picture of this ideal ruler.

Psalm 72 (a royal psalm) gives the following purpose for the ruler: "May he defend the cause of the poor of the people, give deliverance to the needy, and crush the oppressor" (v. 4). And this task is identified as the work of justice (vv. 1–3, 7). In this passage, justice includes using power to deliver the needy and oppressed.

According to Psalm 72, there are oppressors of the poor separate from the state who need to be crushed. State power, despite its dangers, is necessary for society because of the evil power of such exploiting groups. "On the side of their oppressors there was power," Ecclesiastes 4:1 declares. Without governmental force to counter such oppressive power, there is "no one to comfort" (Eccles. 4:1). Whether it is the monarch or the village elders (Amos 5:12, 15), governmental power should deliver the economically weak and guarantee the "rights of the poor" (Jer. 22:15–16; also Ps. 45:4–5; Jer. 21:12).

Prophecies about the coming messianic ruler also develop the picture of the ideal ruler. "With righteousness he shall judge the poor, and decide with equity for the meek of the earth; he shall strike the earth with the rod of his mouth, and with the breath of his lips he shall kill the wicked" (Isa. 11:4).

This ideal ruler will take responsibility for the needs of the people as a shepherd: "He shall feed them and be their shepherd" (Ezek. 34:23). Ezekiel 34:4 denounces the failure of the shepherds (i.e., the rulers) of Israel to "feed" the people. Then in verses 15–16, the same phrases are repeated to describe God's promise of justice:

> ". . . and I will make them lie down," says the Lord GOD. "I will seek the lost, and I will bring back the strayed, and I will bind up the injured, and I will strengthen the weak, but the fat and the strong I will destroy. I will feed them with justice."

This promise will be fulfilled by the coming Davidic ruler (vv. 23–24). Similarly in Isaiah 32:1–8, the promised just and wise monarch is contrasted with the fool who leaves the hungry unsatisfied (v. 6).

This teaching on the role of government applies not just to Israel but to government everywhere. The ideal monarch was to be a channel of God's justice (Ps. 72:1), and God's justice extends to the whole world (e.g., Ps. 9:7–9). All legitimate rulers are instituted by God and are God's servants for human good (Rom. 13:1, 4). Romans 13 is similar to Psalm 72:1 in viewing the ruler as a channel of God's authority. All people everywhere can pray with the Israelites: "Give the king thy justice, O God" (Ps. 72:1 RSV).

Daniel 4:27 shows that the ideal of the monarch as the protector of the weak has universal application. God summons the Babylonian monarch no less than the Israelite king to bring "justice and . . . mercy to the oppressed." Similarly, in Proverbs 31:9, King Lemuel (generally considered to be a northern Arabian monarch) is to "defend the rights of the poor and needy." The general obligation of the Israelite king to guarantee that the weak enjoy fair courts and the daily necessities of life is, in the biblical perspective, a duty of all rulers.[72]

The teaching on the ideal, just monarch of Israel, whether in royal psalms or messianic prophecies, cannot be restricted to some future messianic reign. God demanded that the kings of Israel provide in their own time what the messianic ruler would eventually bring more completely: namely, that justice which delivers the needy from oppression. God's concern in the present and in the future within Israel and outside of Israel is that government promote the common good, especially for the weak.

Emil Brunner is probably correct in suggesting that the more healthy a society, the more nongovernmental institutions will be able to handle problems without government intervention.[73] On the other hand, the greater the moral decay, the more government must act. One can see this with clarity in the way that moral decay and resulting family breakdown today have led to greatly expanded government activity to care for children abandoned by parents. As long as that government intervention is done in a way that aims to restore the nongovernmental institutions (e.g., the family) so they can again as quickly as possible play their proper role, that governmental action is justified.

No general principles about the proper role of limited government in solving problems can replace the necessity of prudential wisdom at every specific moment. We can agree[74] (in parallel with the Catholic principle of subsidiarity) that social problems should be dealt with at as local a level as is effective; that government action should strengthen, not undermine, the vitality of nongovernmental institutions; that sometimes social problems are so sweeping that government must play a significant role; that some things by their very nature are done better by a higher level of government (e.g., minimum-wage laws and laws requiring companies to prevent or pay for the costs of pollution are necessary because without them, companies that freely choose to pay fair wages or not pollute will find themselves at a comparative disadvantage with companies that do not). But there is no mathematical calculus for determining how such a mix of principles applies to any given governmental proposal. Always, we must make finite human judgments about how things are currently unbalanced and what correction of what magnitude is needed. Since our best judgments may be wrong, we must maintain a fundamental humility and tentativeness about all our concrete political conclusions.

Christians should respect and treasure government as a good gift ordained by God to promote the good and restrain evil. But if it is to be helpful rather than harmful, it must be limited. We must recognize that society is much larger than the state and contains many crucial nongovernmental institutions that have their own independence and worth. At the same time, government must act not only to maintain commutative, retributive, and procedural justice, but also to promote distributive justice, especially in order to empower the poor and weak.

Conclusion

In conclusion, I want to outline what I hope are principles that a broad range of evangelicals from many diverse political persuasions can embrace as commonly accepted principles that flow from and are consistent with a faithful reading of both Scripture and history.

1. The principles that shape evangelical political thought and engagement should flow from both a normative framework rooted in biblical revelation and also a careful socioeconomic, historical examination of human experience.
2. The ultimate foundation of government, justice, and human rights is the Creator who is just.
3. Justice defines what is due persons and institutions. What is due them is based in the order of creation established by God.
4. God demands commutative, retributive, procedural, and distributive justice.
5. The biblical story tells us many things relevant to political engagement, including that:
   a. persons are created by God to create wealth and shape history;
   b. all human rights and responsibilities flow from the fact that every person is created in the image of God and treasured immeasurably by the Creator; and
   c. persons are body-soul unities made for community.
6. The biblical words for justice show that justice requires both fair, honest legal systems and also fair economic structures.
7. Biblical justice includes a call to correct oppression and restore justice to the needy.
8. Precisely because God is not biased and loves the rich and poor equally, God acts in history to lift up those who are oppressed by the powerful or who lack access to the necessities of physical life.

9. Hundreds of biblical texts demonstrate that God and God's faithful people exhibit a special concern to empower the poor.
10. The biblical understanding of justice requires that:
    a. the able-bodied have access to the productive resources so that if they act responsibly, they can earn a decent livelihood and be dignified members of their community; and
    b. those unable to care for themselves receive a generous sufficiency from society.
11. As we integrate biblical norms and careful study of history, we see that God demands that people enjoy certain benefits—both civil/political benefits (e.g., fair courts, freedom of speech, religion) and socioeconomic benefits (e.g., access to food, shelter, health care)—and we dare not sacrifice one to the other, although evangelicals disagree about whether not only the first but also the second area should be designated "rights" that governments must enforce.
12. We recognize a certain tension between different rights and believe that the needs of the poor take priority over the wants of the rich.
13. Society is much larger than the state and contains many crucial non-governmental institutions (family, church, business, unions, etc.) that must be largely independent of government.
14. Government is ordained by God, derives its authority from God, and is obligated to reflect God's justice.
15. The purpose of government is both to restrain evil and to promote the good.
16. Both biblical truths and historical experience demonstrate that good government is limited government.
17. Societal problems should be solved at as local a level as can handle them properly and effectively.
18. Nongovernmental institutions (e.g., family, church) are often better places to solve social problems than government, and when government rightly intervenes, it should do so in a way that strengthens, rather than undermines, nongovernmental institutions.
19. The biblical understanding of justice and the role of government teaches that government rightly plays a role in solving social problems and promoting economic justice, helping the poor gain access to productive resources, and guaranteeing that those unable to care for themselves receive a generous sufficiency.

9

Citizenship, Civil Society, and the Church

Joseph Loconte

IF THE EVENTS of the last few years demonstrate anything, it's that the appeal and influence of Christianity in public life—even in a nation as religious as the United States—is a fragile thing.

Beginning in the early 1990s, many academics were calling for the revival of "civil society"—the families, churches, charities, neighborhood groups, and voluntary organizations of all kinds that shape and sustain democratic culture. A leading group of scholars summarized the issue this way: "No nation on earth has so thoroughly staked its success on the functioning of free and voluntary associations. Our most important challenge is to strengthen the moral habits and ways of living that make democracy possible."[1] Many agreed that the human, financial, and moral resources of Christian churches—especially those in the evangelical tradition—make them crucial to the project of cultural renewal. Soon a wave of conferences, books, and organizations appeared to examine their influence. Even media elites acquired an ear for stories illustrating the transforming effects of faith. A cover story in *U.S. News and World Report*, for example, carried this headline: "Can Churches Save America?" A report about religious groups tackling crime, welfare, and other social problems, it answered mostly in the affirmative. The social power of religion also became a

194

major theme in the 2000 presidential race. Candidate George W. Bush made the work of religious charities the engine of his "compassionate conservatism" campaign. Speaking to the evangelical Salvation Army, Vice President Al Gore pledged to "put the solutions that faith-based organizations are pioneering at the very heart" of his administration.

Today, however, it's hard to remember a time when the influence of Christianity in America was under greater assault. President Bush's faith-based agenda has been crippled in the Congress and lambasted by the press. The massive cover-up of child sexual abuse continues to damage the integrity of the Catholic Church. A roiling debate over gay "marriage" threatens to envelop the Episcopal Church, while supporters of traditional marriage are increasingly vilified as bigots and hate mongers. Finally, there's the fallout from the attacks of September 11, 2001, and the ongoing terrorism associated with them. Many seem convinced that fanaticism and violence are the natural fruit of religious commitment. Christian fundamentalism, Catholicism, orthodox Judaism, Islamism—all are lumped together as symptoms of the same illness. Writing in the *New York Times Magazine*, Andrew Sullivan diagnosed the problem as traditional belief in God: "If you take your beliefs from books written more than a thousand years ago, and you believe these texts literally, then the appearance of the modern world must truly terrify." His conclusion: "It seems almost as if there is something inherent in religious monotheism that lends itself to this kind of terrorist temptation."[2] Though Christianity's fiercest critics are found in elite intellectual circles, a general skepticism about traditional religion seems to be on the rise.

All of this suggests an urgent need for Christian believers to recover—in theory and in practice—their commitment to a set of civic ideals that once guided the American democratic tradition. They include virtue, service, justice, and love. Compared to other nations, Christians in the United States have enjoyed a wide field in which to apply these ideals in the public square. The reason goes back to America's most distinctive contribution to Western democracy: freedom of religion as the brick and mortar of civic and political life. The ability to worship God according to one's conscience, and the moral commitments this freedom makes possible, is the most important reason for the success of the American experiment. Rather than fighting amongst themselves for government favoritism and largesse, the nation's faith traditions have focused on serving their own communities, as well as reaching out to their neighbors. That's the civic side of religion's contribution. The political side is the way in which these religious ideals have sustained—and reformed—democratic government since the founding era. This is the two-sided nature of Christian activism: the believer as prophet (challenging social and political evils) and Good Samaritan (caring for those in need).

True, the Christian church often has neglected these roles, or exercised them in ways that grossly compromised aspects of the gospel. These dangers are still with us, but they are aggravated by another problem: widespread historical amnesia. Partisans on the left and on the right have forgotten the lessons of the nation's experience in Christian cultural engagement. Political philosopher Jean Bethke Elshtain points to the fact that young people learn American history not as a story of a society struggling to live out its high principles, but as a sorry tale of broken promises. "We have failed to offer the young a strong civic story to hold on to," she says. "The interweaving of faith with civic life is central to this narrative."[3] James Billington, librarian of Congress, agrees. "The large American universities, media, and foundations that largely control our public intellectual agenda have in the late twentieth century generally thought religion to be both unimportant and unrelated to progress," he says. "We have let our collective memory fade."[4]

It is vital that Americans, especially evangelical Christians, recover this collective memory. Why? Not because of any alleged "covenant" between God and America. The quality of our Christian obedience isn't somehow bound up with the health or even survival of American democracy (as important as its survival is to freedom around the world). Neither does the final and full arrival of the kingdom of heaven depend on a democratic culture that is friendly to biblical revelation. Rather, at stake is the most basic civic response to Christ's call to love our neighbors as ourselves. The weight of Christian teaching doesn't allow us to forget that until Jesus returns, his followers have dual citizenship: preeminently in the kingdom of heaven, yet significantly here on earth. Our engagement as citizens, as members of civil society, offers one of the most consequential arenas of Christian discipleship. Since such a large part of our lives of faith must be lived in this realm, how could it be otherwise?

In recent years, three arenas of activity have emerged in which the potential for Christian influence is great, yet the challenges to such influence are equally strong. The areas I have in mind are education, social welfare, and politics. All involve our common lives as citizens and as disciples of Christ. The health of each depends on believers who vigorously apply the Christian ideals of virtue, service, justice, and love. And yet in each area Christians have been of two minds: to withdraw into a completely privatized faith (churches that preach orthodoxy but fail to connect faith to their public lives, for example) or to publicly condemn sin without performing acts of mercy (the response of some Christian leaders, for example, to the appearance of AIDS). Christ's call to live out our discipleship with both wisdom and integrity—"as shrewd as snakes and innocent as doves"—argues for a better response. In a world of individuals and institutions darkened by the fall, we must chart a course that brings biblical truth into our common lives, but with uncommon charity and grace.

Madison's Religious Revolution

American Christians would do well to reflect on the debt they owe to one of America's greatest Enlightenment figures: James Madison. Scholars acknowledge

Madison as the architect of the U.S. Constitution but tend to ignore the driving passion of his political career, his zeal for religious liberty. "Madison's views on religious freedom," writes historian Gary Wills, "are the inspiration for all that was best in his later political thought."[5] Indeed, no statesman understood better the link between faith, civil society, and republican government. Over a career that spanned four decades, he laid the groundwork for a secular democracy that nonetheless would depend decisively on religious belief and religious institutions. If the influence of Christianity in America could be linked to the political career of any single person, it would be James Madison.

Consider, for example, the debate in 1776 in Madison's home state of Virginia over a new constitution. The proposed document contained a Declaration of Rights with a clause on religious liberty, written by George Mason. It declared that "all men should enjoy the fullest toleration in the exercise of religion, according to the dictates of conscience . . ." The bookish, twenty-six-year-old Madison didn't like it. He objected to Mason's use of the word "toleration" because it implied that the exercise of faith was a concession from government, not a gift from the Creator and thus an inalienable right of every individual. Madison's substitute—"all men are entitled to the full and free exercise" of religion—won the day. He pushed this concept of freedom for the rest of his political life. In *Memorial and Remonstrance*, a peerless argument against religious establishments, Madison called religious liberty "precedent, both in order of time and in degree of obligation, to the claims of Civil Society." By placing the right of conscience superior to all other rights and duties, he gave it the strongest political foundation possible.

One reason for Madison's emphasis was that he presupposed the sacred nature of religious conviction. "Religion or the duty which we owe to our Creator and the Manner of discharging it," he wrote, "can be directed only by reason and conviction, not by force or violence." Contrary to some revisionists, what Madison abhorred was not organized religion, but its temptation to enlist the power of government to oppress minorities. Another reason for Madison's pursuit of religious freedom is that he considered faith the firmest foundation for republican virtue. He once called belief in God "essential to the moral order of the World." A final reason is that Madison saw cultural and economic progress as the fruit of religious liberty. That was his conclusion, for example, when he looked at the state of religious pluralism in Pennsylvania. "You are happy in dwelling in a Land where those inestimable privileges are fully enjoyed and the public has long felt the good effects of their religious as well as Civil Liberty," he wrote his friend William Bradford. "Industry and Virtue have been promoted by mutual emulation and mutual Inspection, Commerce and the Arts have flourished . . ."

Madison's assumptions about the importance of religious belief were endorsed almost universally by America's founding generation. Indeed, they form the backdrop to the religion clauses in the First Amendment. George Washington called religion and morality "indispensable supports" to American democracy.

Even Thomas Jefferson, among the most unorthodox of the founders, argued that "no nation has yet existed or been governed without religion—nor can be." In this, they went way beyond European Enlightenment icons who often sneered at religion and hoped to stigmatize its full and free expression. Each of Madison's ideas about religion—its privileged and sacred status, its link to republican virtue, and its contribution to social progress—helped propel the expansion of the Christian gospel in the early days of the Republic.

A Virtuous Education

Nevertheless, each of these ideas is now under sustained attack, threatening the viability both of religion and of civil society. Don Eberly, an intellectual leader in the civil society movement, warns of continued cultural breakdown absent faith commitment. "When society can't draw moral meaning and direction from religious belief," he writes, "it draws it from other sources."[6]

We've already begun to see what those other sources are. Consider the strategic area of public education. Americans have viewed their schools as the first institution of democracy, and at one time couldn't conceive of a proper education divorced from religious ideals. Benjamin Rush argued that "the only foundation for a useful education in a republic is to be laid in religion." The signers of the Northwest Ordinance of 1787, concerned about the moral development of the northwestern United States, wrote this provision into the law: "Religion, morality and knowledge, being necessary to good government and the happiness of mankind, Schools and the means of education shall forever be encouraged."[7] The standard elementary school textbook until about 1830 was *The New England Primer*, heavy with Christian doctrine. By the early nineteenth century, shortly before the rise of public education, the Sunday school movement emerged as a massive ecumenical effort to promote basic literacy and moral instruction. Initiated by laypeople, the schools welcomed children of all denominations. A Massachusetts newspaper estimated in 1827 that roughly two hundred thousand children attended Sunday schools in America.[8]

The appearance of a system of public education was, in many ways, an extension of the local church, finally disestablished from state governments. Indeed, what America's "common schools" shared was a commitment to the central theological and moral tenets of Protestant Christianity. Even the National Teachers' Association (the forerunner of the National Education Association) declared in 1869 that "the Bible should not only be studied . . . but devotionally read, and its precepts inculcated" in all elementary schools.[9] This often was done in a way that trampled the rights of Jews, Catholics, and other religious minorities; it fueled no small amount of civic strife. Nevertheless, the purpose of education, says scholar Warren Nord, was to make children faithful, virtuous, and good Americans. "The common schools were officially nonsectarian," Nord observes, but "the idea of a truly nonreligious education was unimaginable."[10]

It would not be long, however, before the essentially religious mission of public schools would begin to erode. Humanistic ideas about morality, severed from Christian theology, provided the solvent. "Where churches and sects and nations divide . . . the schools can unite by becoming temples and laboratories of a common democratic faith," argued educators such as Horace Mann.[11] By 1900, there was little substantive religion left in schools, and their once lofty purpose was replaced by a host of earthly objectives.

Today the idea that a democratic education ought to be anchored in religious values is considered subversive. This was one of the arguments, for example, in *Locke v. Davey*, the 2004 Supreme Court case in which a college student was denied a state scholarship because he intended to use it to pursue a theological degree. Detractors envisioned nothing less than a civic apocalypse once college education vouchers began flowing to students attending religious schools. "Today's case is part of an ongoing effort to lower the wall between church and state," intoned the *New York Times*. "In a time of great sectarian conflict worldwide, moving further in that direction would be a serious mistake."[12] It was the same dark subtext in the 2002 school voucher case decided in *Zelman v. Simmons-Harris*. The Court ruled 5–4 that poor parents in Cleveland could use publicly funded vouchers to send their children to private and religious schools. Justice Stevens argued in dissent that the ruling allowed public funds "to pay for the indoctrination of thousands of grammar school children in particular religious faiths." Justice Souter complained that the only alternative to the public schools in Cleveland was a religious alternative—and that, he said, was a "Hobson's choice." Not to be outdone, Justice Breyer warned ominously of "religiously based social conflict" that would shred the social fabric by pitting "sect against sect."

None of the critics paused to reflect on the secular assumptions of public education—or that such assumptions might be deeply offensive to millions of religious Americans. Few seem to believe that a religiously based education actually qualifies as an education. And few can imagine that such an education might fulfill the government's goal of producing responsible, self-governing citizens. Think of it: The *New York Times* said the *Zelman* ruling "undermines one of the public school system's most important functions: teaching democracy and pluralism."[13] They and other critics predicted that school vouchers would instigate a decline in citizenship and the Balkanization of American civic life. The general consensus among liberal thinkers could be boiled down to this: The greater the influence of religion over children and families, the less interested they are in public education or in promoting the public goals of civility and citizenship.

The evidence, however, points in the opposite direction. Survey data from the U.S. Department of Education show that families involved in Catholic, Protestant, and other private schools are consistently more engaged in civic activities than public school families.[14] A 2000 national survey shows that evangelical Protestants are more likely to be involved in public schools than are nonreligious Americans—whether it be in the form of school boards or PTAs. "Despite their sense of alienation from public schools," concludes sociologist David Sikkink, "evangelicals are not disengaged from civic participation within schools."[15] Is there any evidence that a neutral aid program of private choice sparks interreligious conflict in America? Child-care vouchers, which poor parents use to send their children to church-based programs, have been an integral part of federal programs since 1990. Religious colleges already receive federal aid through grants and loans. Students have been using Pell Grants at religious schools for over twenty years. All of this has been going on without a hint of civic rancor. Justice Rehnquist summarized the alleged danger of a voucher system this way: "The program has ignited no 'divisiveness' or 'strife' other than this litigation." Like other school voucher programs around the country, the Cleveland program has produced thousands of satisfied parents—and literate, educated, civically engaged students.

Among cultured elites, however, even a public school system that is manifestly failing to educate its citizens is a better alternative than religious institutions. As education scholar Charles Glenn describes it, public schools have become "islands of secularity" that are distorting both the function and meaning of public education. Ethnic and religious pluralism made the unofficial establishment of Protestant Christianity impossible to sustain in public education. Educators should have realized that no single belief system could replace the old certainties and serve the needs of parents. They could have found ways to preserve religiously rooted education as a vital part of the mix. Instead, a secular orthodoxy has been enthroned at the heart of public education. Its new sources of meaning include self-esteem, consumerism, feminism, and relativism. "It is not an exaggeration to say," Glenn writes, "that pupils who relied exclusively on what they were told in school . . . could come out after twelve or thirteen years unaware that such a thing as religion existed in the contemporary world, much less that it continues to play a major role in American life."[16] As the sorry condition of public schools suggests, this state of affairs is not advancing the goal of preparing young people for responsible citizenship.

There are numerous ways that faithful Christians can help remoralize education in America. The expansion of private schools, the growth of the home-schooling movement, and the involvement of Christian parents in charter schools are all important endeavors. Christians are also engaged in civic education efforts such as the "Finding Common Ground" curriculum on religion developed by scholar Charles Haynes. "For most of history the sacred and the secular were pervasively entwined, and religion pervaded all of life," writes Haynes. "If students are to understand history they must understand religion. This is not controversial."[17] Finally, there's a profound need for churches and religious groups to work intensively with needy students. Many of the most impressive tutoring and mentoring programs in public schools are led by evangelical Christians. Kids Hope USA, for example, sends church-based volunteers into public elementary schools in twenty-seven states. Their mentors are paired with about four thousand at-risk children, and the organization gets requests every month from *public school principals* for more volunteers. "God never left the public schools, but he's calling many of us back into them," says Virgil Gulker, the organization's founder and director. "There is within the church a growing awareness that it is distinctively called and equipped to reach out and serve these neighbors that Christ has called them to love."[18]

The Armies of Compassion

Another major area in which religion's contribution is contested is the nation's social safety net. President Bush's faith-based initiative, an effort to enlist religious charities in helping the needy, has sparked an unprecedented argument in the history of church-state relations in America. The debate is not over the appearance of religious symbols or religious speech in public life; rather, it's about whether the tools of government—tax incentives, regulatory reform, and financial support—should be used to extend the compassionate work of the nation's Good Samaritans.

The initiative raises legitimate constitutional concerns, but much of the criticism is overheated. Helen Thomas, UPI reporter and the dean of the White House press corps, was aghast at the proposal. "The mixing of religion and government for centuries has led to slaughter," she scolded the president. "You are a secular official, not a missionary."[19] Boston University professor Richard Landes worries that the "creedal zealotry" of religious believers will become "a recipe of social strife" unless it's carefully restricted.[20] Cornell University professors Isaac Kramnick and R. Laurence Moore, writing in the *American Prospect*, insist that the secular state is more competent at addressing social ills. The reason, they claim, is that "faith has not kept our streets clean or safe, housed our homeless, or healed our sick."[21]

It seems reasonable to wonder if some academics are spending too much time in the faculty lounge. For it's an observable fact that in many parts of inner-city America, virtually the only institution engaged in the community is the church. There are more than 325,000 churches, synagogues, and mosques in the United States, most of which have at least one program for the poor. Indeed, recent academic studies suggest that more than 85 percent of all houses of worship offer desperately needed social services, attacking problems ranging from juvenile delinquency to drug addiction. A University of Pennsylvania study of congregations in six U.S. cities found that 91 percent offered at least one social service, and many offered five or more.[22] Another study of 401 congregations in Philadelphia reported similar results and calculated the annual value of services at $103,000 per church. Where does it go? The typical person helped is an at-risk child whose family does not attend the church.[23] Add to this the literally thousands of religious charities engaged in social outreach: crisis pregnancy centers, prison programs, day-care programs, drug treatment centers, shelters for the homeless, programs for young fathers, outreach to juvenile offenders, and community development programs that rebuild blighted neighborhoods.

None of these efforts, now so much a part of the civic landscape, came about by accident. When Madison helped secure religious liberty in the First Amendment as the "first freedom," he made possible a civil society energized and reformed by people of robust faith. At the same time, disestablishment of religion removed the main obstacle to Christian unity: government endorsement of one sect over another. "Now that state support of ministers had come to an end . . . the door was thrown open to joint action on behalf of common social ends," writes historian John West.[24] Lyman Beecher, a Connecticut Congregationalist who strongly opposed disestablishment, later called it "the best thing that ever happened to the state of Connecticut." Why? Because it cast churches on their own resources and on God, and extended their influence "by voluntary efforts, societies, missions, and revivals."[25] Beecher emerged as one of the century's most important social reformers, founding scores of church-based groups to confront a wide range of social evils. It was this brand of civic activism that so impressed French observer Alexis de Tocqueville during his 1830s tour of the young nation: "Nothing, in my opinion, is more deserving of our attention than the intellectual and moral associations of America." Organizations to assist widows, curb drunkenness, discourage dueling, promote literacy, distribute Bibles: Tocqueville judged these associations to be the real source of America's civic vitality and political stability. He is worth quoting at length on this point:

> The political and industrial associations of that country strike us forcibly; but the others elude our observation, or if we discover them, we understand them imperfectly because we have hardly ever seen anything of the kind. It must be acknowledged, however, that they are as necessary to the American people as the former, and perhaps more so. In democratic countries the SCIENCE of association is the mother of science; the progress of all the rest depends upon the progress it has made.[26]

Too many critics of religion seem happy to whitewash America's remarkable record of social progress: Missing is the way in which charity, philanthropy, and economic growth have been deeply marked by the activism of orthodox Christians. As numerous historians have observed, America's frontier was tamed largely by the influence of evangelicalism. In the small towns and emerging cities, churches taught hard work, sobriety, thrift, and family responsibility.[27] Writes church historian William Sweet: "A random turning of the pages of any of the old record books of the early frontier churches will soon convince one that the church was a large factor in maintaining order in these raw communities."[28] Faced with new problems caused by the growth of the cities, Christians also led the major social movements throughout the nineteenth and twentieth centuries. Scholars such as Joel Schwartz and Marvin Olasky have documented the impressive help that religious organizations delivered to destitute women in urban America, offering real alternatives to poverty, prostitution, and abortion. In the 1840s, for example, Robert Milham Hartley joined with other prominent Christian merchants in New York to found the New York Association for Improving the Condition of the Poor. It set up medical clinics, established a model tenement house, and sent church volunteers into the homes of poor families to offer practical and moral support.[29]

The Young Men's Christian Association (YMCA), backed by the philanthropy of wealthy church members, aimed at easing poverty by promoting "the welfare of the whole man—body, soul and spirit."[30] Joined by the YWCA, they functioned practically as a Protestant denomination: Job training was offered alongside Bible classes, while gymnasiums doubled as worship halls.[31] By 1900 there were nearly 1,500 local YMCA chapters with 250,000 members. Likewise, the Salvation Army, imported from Britain in 1880, brought its philosophy of "soup, soap and salvation" to some of the most destitute areas of the country. Within twenty years the group had spawned over 900 chapters, which combined shelters, stores, and workshops. Its employment bureaus were placing about 4,800 people a month.[32] Food, shelter, medical assistance, vocational training, prison ministry, legal aid for the poor, the provision of cheap coal in the winter—by offering these and other services, the Salvation Army soon became the most comprehensive Christian outreach to the cities.[33] "Late nineteenth-century Americans who read the Bible regularly did not see God as a sugar daddy who merely felt sorry for people in distress," writes Olasky in *The Tragedy of American Compassion*. "They saw God showing compassion while demanding change, and they tried to do the same."[34]

It's this kind of faith-based activism that the White House is trying to integrate into government's social-service regime. Critics assume base political motives at work, but the deepest reason for engaging religious groups is a moral one. Simply put, secular approaches to solving social problems, enthroned in government policy for decades, have failed. They produce after-school programs that teach self-esteem but not character, family services that ignore marriage, and drug treatment strategies that substitute one addiction for another. Secularism offers a worldview that is profoundly fatalistic: It treats people in need as "clients," not as individuals made in God's image who, with divine grace, can make better choices for their lives. It is this outlook that justifies various initiatives under the guise of compassionate government: programs to combat the AIDS pandemic, for example, that offer condoms to prostitutes and clean needles to drug users—and nothing more. The Christian vision sees this for what it is: death on the installment plan. President Bush calls it "the soft bigotry of low expectations."

It's precisely at this point where faith-based organizations, guided by Christian ideals, can make a real difference. A study I conducted with researcher Lia Fantuzzo found that the 37 ministries we examined, most driven by volunteers, were reaching more than 23,000 at-risk youth—delivering tough love along with tutoring and job training.[35] Drug-treatment programs such as Teen Challenge help about 2,700 individuals each year escape addiction and prepare for work or school. Manhattan's Bowery Mission is ranked by the city as its most effective program to get homeless addicts sober and into full-time employment. Chuck Colson's Prison Fellowship ministers to roughly 219,000 inmates, or about 10 percent of the total U.S. prison population, drawing on church volunteers to help offenders break the cycle of crime. This is what President Bush means by the "armies of compassion." If advanced with great care, his faith-based initiative could help reverse decades of hostility to social programs rooted in religious belief. If the initiative is taken to its logical conclusion, no social problem would be immunized from the works of mercy and humanity that typify Christian charity.

What, after all, would many neighborhoods in America be like without the influence of churches and religious organizations? Religion is not the only source of morality and social stability, but it's obviously one of the most important.

A crucial finding among social scientists over the last twenty years is that belief in God, and the presence of religious institutions, are closely linked to lower rates of crime, drug use, and out-of-wedlock births. A recent Manhattan Institute review of forty quantitative studies of urban youth, for example, uncovered at least one major theme: Higher levels of religiosity appear to reduce delinquent behavior. "These findings provide evidence that church attendance itself has its own unique effect on deviance among inner-city black youth."[36] Such evidence, both quantitative and anecdotal, has persuaded many to take religious belief seriously as a force for good. Don Browning, professor at the Divinity School of the University of Chicago, admits to being stunned by the civic energy of a black Pentecostal church in his neighborhood. "I am not arguing for the truth or superiority of Christianity as such," he writes. "Rather, as a longtime liberal, I am saying we can learn a great deal from this conservative church about how local religious expressions, feeding on commanding religious traditions, can support the revitalization of civil society."[37] James Q. Wilson, professor of public policy at UCLA and a self-proclaimed secularist, reaches a similar conclusion. "Religion's chief contribution to morality is to enable people to transform their lives," he writes. "The evidence, though not conclusive, does suggest rather strongly that religion can make a difference in the lives of people about whom we worry, and ought to worry, the most."[38]

Prophets and Politics

A final arena that needs more mature Christian influence is politics. To listen to some critics, one might think the greatest threat to America's democratic system is the orthodox Christian voter. Twenty years ago, on the eve of the 1984 presidential election, journalist Sidney Blumenthal warned that the activism of the "Evangelical New Right" threatened to disrupt the country's two-party system. He feared the political zeal of Christians who take seriously the Bible's teachings about God's judgment of the wicked, Satan's final defeat, and the full establishment of the kingdom of heaven. "In preparing for the universal apocalypse, the movement Evangelicals are eagerly pursuing an ideological apocalypse," he wrote. "The business of soul winning has become the politics of takeover."[39] Similar warnings have surfaced during every presidential election since. In *The Fundamentals of Extremism*, Kimberly Blaker accuses Christian political leaders of indoctrinating "an army of puppets who will kill—and even die—for their predetermined cause."[40]

Some liberal thinkers recognize such hyperventilating for what it is. Yale law professor Stephen Carter has described a "culture of disbelief" engulfing his liberal colleagues and criticized them for "treating the religious impulse to public action as presumptively wicked."[41] Indeed, this antagonism completely overlooks the role of Christianity in challenging state-sponsored evils and ultimately reforming American law and politics.

Go back to the 1830s, for example, when the U.S. government began to forcibly remove Native Americans from their homes in Georgia and elsewhere. The problem, of course, was that Indian tribes such as the Cherokees owned the land. More than that, they had become a nation of agrarian republicans, with farms, schools, stores, and settlements. To uproot them meant that treaties would be violated, and many Indians would perish during the relocation. Who stood in the way? Christian missionaries. Evangelicals such as Jeremiah Evarts fought the plan—unsuccessfully—for a decade. Petitions flooded Congress. Ministers were harassed and jailed. "The Cherokees are human beings," Evarts argued, "endowed by their Creator with the same natural rights as other men." In what ranks as a criminal act on the part of the American government, religious believers raised the most important voice of protest.[42]

Now go back further, to the emergence of the African-American church. In the last quarter of the eighteenth century, evangelical Baptist and Methodist congregations, guided by biblical views of human dignity, were the first to grant black men licenses to preach. This was no small matter, for it challenged the slave-owning status quo. For free blacks in the North, churches quickly became the single institution controlled by black communities and even enjoyed some autonomy in southern states. "These black churches formed the institutional structure for the development of free black communities," writes historian Albert Raboteau. "Without the activism of free black communities in the North, the antislavery movement would have been weakened."[43]

It's no accident that for decades the political and cultural battle against slavery was led almost exclusively by Bible-based dissenters. As early as 1758, Quakers in Philadelphia ruled that any Friend buying or selling slaves would be excluded from church affairs. In 1780, the Methodist General Conference in Baltimore condemned slavery as "contrary to the laws of God, man, and nature."[44] In 1834, evangelical businessman Lewis Tappan helped launch the American Anti-Slavery Society, which became the nation's most important antislavery organization. Charles Finney, the leading revivalist of the 1830s, made Oberlin College, his preaching base, a hotbed of abolitionist rhetoric and a center for the underground railroad.[45] Harriet Beecher Stowe, daughter of evangelical minister Lyman Beecher, used popular literature as an instrument of religious conviction. According to historian Mark Noll, her novel, *Uncle Tom's Cabin*, ignited antislavery sentiment because of its "forceful summation of Christian revivalism . . . and Christian abolition."[46] In 1854, more than three thousand New England clergymen signed a petition opposing passage of the infamous Kansas-Nebraska Bill, which would extend slavery into the Northwest Territory. The spread of slavery, in their view, would reduce the region to a moral and religious wasteland. "The question ceases to be whether black men are forever to be slaves," argued Baptist leader Francis Wayland, "but whether the sons of Puritans are to become slaves themselves."[47] U.S. Senator James Mason, from the slave state of Virginia, denounced the ministers as "the most encroaching, and . . . arrogant class of men."[48] Such criticism, observes historian Richard Carwardine, reflected the growing involvement of evangelicals in national political debates. "Once explicitly moral questions entered national, state and local arenas . . . the evangelical temper—crusading, unyielding, principally responsive to appeals to conscience—gave politics a new and distinctive character."[49]

The moral-religious character of American politics would continue into the next century, propelled this time through the Social Gospel movement. Though rejecting traditional biblical doctrines, Social Gospel leaders tried to hold on to the ethical imperatives of Christianity; they spoke often about personal and social responsibility as they confronted the problems of urban life. Walter Rauschenbusch described their reform agenda as "the progressive transformation of all human affairs by the thought and spirit of Christ."[50] Evangelist Billy Sunday dismissed it as "godless social service nonsense."[51] Nevertheless, the social gospelers did supply some of the moral capital of Progressive politics. By 1912, the Progressive platform had embraced several of their causes, including women's suffrage and laws against child labor. Teddy Roosevelt drew in part on the Social Gospel tradition to oppose corporate monopolies and intervene for the rights of workers. "The thought of modern industry in the hands of Christian charity is a dream worth dreaming," he said. "The thought of industry in the hands of paganism is a nightmare beyond imagining."

In the last half of the twentieth century, no political reform movement was more momentous than the struggle for racial equality. Once again, rebellious churchgoers formed the strategic center of the movement. Consider the story of Fannie Lou Hamer, a devout evangelical Christian, who was the guiding voice of the Mississippi Freedom Democratic Party. Her organization led a campaign to get an integrated slate of delegates to the 1964 Democratic National Convention—a controversy that rattled President Lyndon Johnson. Vice president in waiting Hubert Humphrey was dispatched to buy off Mrs. Hamer. Instead, she shamed him with these words: "If you take [the vice presidential nomination] this way, why, you will never be able to do any good for civil rights, for poor people, for peace or any of those things you talk about. Senator Humphrey, I'm gonna pray to Jesus for you."[52]

The Reverend Martin Luther King Jr. embodied like none other this relentless commitment to social justice. A Baptist minister, King unashamedly drew on his Christian convictions to challenge the conscience of a nation awash in racial discrimination. He summoned those same convictions to reject both the complacency of the moderates and the hatred of the black nationalists. "There is the more excellent way of love and nonviolent protest," he wrote in his Letter from Birmingham Jail. "I am grateful to God that, through the influence of the Negro church, the way of nonviolence became an integral part of our struggle."[53] It's difficult to imagine the civil rights movement succeeding as it did—and remaining nonviolent—apart from its Christian roots. "In the middle years of the twentieth century," writes Yale professor Stephen Carter, "no social movement was more plainly religious, in both its inspiration and its message."[54]

Economist Robert Fogel, in *The Fourth Great Awakening and the Future of Egalitarianism*, says it's impossible to understand America's commitment to social justice without the moral influence of Christianity. Churches and the lay movements they spawned have often served as "critics of state policy and as advocates of individual rights," he says. "They . . . were principal vehicles through which the common people have been drawn into the process of shaping American society."[55] They still can be. Although collaborating with advocacy groups across the political spectrum, evangelicals have made the strongest moral arguments for directing international attention on a range of human rights issues. As political science professor Allen Hertzke observes, evangelical Christians have become "the grassroots vanguard" of the drive to elevate human rights as a major aim of American foreign policy.[56]

Just consider the efforts of socially minded Christians in opposing genocide in Sudan, challenging international sex trafficking, ministering to street children, or mobilizing to fight global AIDS. "Prodded by its conservative evangelical base," writes Holly Burkhalter in *Foreign Affairs*, "the Bush Administration has pushed AIDS to the forefront of its international agenda."[57] Dr. Edward Green, of the Harvard Center for Population and Development Studies, has singled out the work of Christian charitable groups in Uganda in stemming that country's AIDS epidemic. Indeed, Uganda's church-based model for combating HIV, now a vital ingredient in the administration's Global AIDS Initiative, has sparked intense political debate over U.S. AIDS policy. "Many faith-based organizations have been working patiently, compassionately and effectively for years in AIDS mitigation and prevention," writes Green. "It makes little sense to mobilize only secular resources in such countries."[58]

Standing in the Breach

Indeed, secular institutions have rarely shown the ability to inspire comparable social or political reform. "Secularism . . . possesses no inherent power for heroic action," writes Don Eberly. "It is hard to imagine American secularism summoning Americans to engage in public argument with a redemptive spirit, to fight for social change with humility and self-sacrifice, or to consistently acknowledge the humanity of others through an attitude of mercy."[59] Nevertheless, for the better part of the last century, America has been experimenting with what might be called the Milli Vanilli approach to democratic life. Remember the pop duo? They won a 1989 Grammy Award for their CD *Girl, You Know It's True*. It wasn't true: Milli Vanilli didn't sing a note on their own CD. They lip-synced their way to the Grammies, were exposed as frauds, and sheepishly gave back their award.

We cannot lip-sync our way to a stable and healthy democratic society. Democratic institutions—such as direct elections, the separation of powers, an impartial judiciary—are essential. So are a free press and a free market economy. Yet none of this is sufficient, by itself, to sustain freedom over the long haul. Without self-governing citizens, without free and vibrant Christian institutions, there are only two possibilities: social chaos or, as government intervenes to prevent social chaos, tyranny. As John Adams once warned: "There never was a democracy yet that did not commit suicide."[60] No force on earth has proven more powerful than Christian conviction in avoiding these outcomes.

Christian conservatives understand the connection in theory, but not always in practice. For they sometimes act in ways that betray their historic commitment to religious liberty and misplace the strength of religious belief. Why, for example, are some so intent on hanging the Ten Commandments in government buildings, reintroducing formal prayers in public schools, or slipping Nativity scenes onto public property? These are the trappings of faith, not the substance of it. They serve as fiery political symbols, but they fail to challenge conscience, forge character, or reclaim broken lives. Preserving the phrase "under God" in the Pledge of Allegiance may be worth a fight, but what about reintroducing students to America's religious history in the public school curriculum? Likewise, a constitutional amendment to protect the definition of marriage may be a worthy goal, but it won't do much to reverse the trends in family disintegration ravaging communities everywhere—evangelical churches included.

By expecting the state to lead the charge for faith and virtue, Christians become disillusioned: They end up with a watered-down civil religion, or a puffed-up view of government and politics. This explains the somewhat angry book *Blinded by Might*, cowritten by former Moral Majority leaders Cal Thomas and Ed Dobson. The authors scold Christian activists for pursuing political influence at the expense of piety. "It's time to admit that because we are using the wrong weapons, we are losing the battle," they write. "We have confused political power with God's power."[61]

If Christian conservatives sometimes blur the roles of church and state, liberals have lurched in the opposite direction: They confuse the separation of church and state with the separation of faith from life. Liberalism treats

traditional religion not as a civic virtue, but as a civic virus—a source of oppression and social strife. Theda Skocpol, professor of government at Harvard,
complains that her peers have utterly distorted the role of religious charities
in assisting the needy. "The academic literature on 'social welfare policy' has
been so dominated by leftist secularists that it has written out of the record
positive contributions from religiously inspired service to the poor," she writes.
"If noted at all, such ministry has transmuted into machiavellian acts of class or
racial domination."[62] It is now clear that certain religious ideals are no longer
welcome in public life. Just consider the ongoing attacks on the Boy Scouts
of America, who uphold traditional marriage and reject openly gay men as
Scoutmasters. In the 2000 Supreme Court case *Boy Scouts v. Dale*, several
justices sided with liberal activists by accusing the organization of faith-based
bigotry. "Unfavorable opinions about homosexuals 'have ancient roots,'" wrote
Justice Stevens in dissent. "Like equally atavistic opinions about certain racial
groups, these roots have been nourished by sectarian doctrine." This is where
modern liberalism has arrived: Conventional, religious teachings about sexuality and marriage—views held by tens of millions of Americans across religious
traditions—are the result of dark and irrational prejudice. The remedy, they
say: Outlaw these views wherever possible.

Banned as well, it seems, would be any connection between good citizens
and good government. "Liberals have always taken the position that democracy
can dispense with civic virtue," writes Christopher Lasch in *Revolt of the Elites*.
"According to this way of thinking, it is liberal institutions, not the character
of citizens, that make democracy work."[63] One of the obvious reasons for
skepticism about religion is the growing agnosticism about moral truths. For
millions of Americans, the question is not, Can we be good without God?
Rather, the question is, Why worry about being good at all? We're still wak-
ing up to the consequences of this shift. "A central problem of contemporary
political philosophy," writes James Q. Wilson, "is whether a liberal democratic
society can sustain the culture necessary for the good life."[64] It was the same
problem that confronted America's Founding generation. Without a monarchy
or a state church, what social forces would hold American society together?
The founders believed that human nature, left to itself, couldn't be counted
on. Like most of his peers, James Madison inherited a profound appreciation
for the tragedy of human nature: bearing the image of God, yet stubbornly
and deeply fallen. He often worried that there might not be sufficient virtue
among citizens to sustain America's bold experiment in liberty. "Had every
Athenian citizen been a Socrates," he argued in the *Federalist Papers*, "every
Athenian assembly would still have been a mob."[65]

The French observer Alexis de Tocqueville likewise feared that selfish individualism, unrestrained by religious ideals, would poison civic life in America.
It's what he called "democratic despotism," a situation where individuals and
groups relentlessly pursue their interests at the expense of charity, or faith, or
even common sense. "How is it possible that society should escape destruction

if the moral tie is not strengthened in proportion as the political tie is relaxed? And what can be done with a people who are their own masters if they are not submissive to the Deity?" he asked. "Despotism may govern without faith, but democracy cannot."[66]

Would the reassertion of Christian ideals in education, social welfare, and politics undo the damage this despotism already has accomplished in civic life? It would be a beginning. It almost certainly would produce a more just society. Surely this is a proper aim of Christian engagement, even if it isn't the only aim. "In the Christian view," writes political philosopher Glenn Tinder, "while every individual is exalted, society is not." The boundless exaltation of society, even the most egalitarian society, amounts to apostasy. Nevertheless, Tinder adds, we meet our fellow human beings in civil society or not at all. "Hence we cannot stand wholly apart from society without failing in our responsibilities to the human beings whom God has exalted. So far as we are responsive to God, we must live within human kingdoms as creatures destined to be fellow citizens in God's kingdom."[67]

The "human kingdoms" discussed in this chapter offer special opportunities for Christians to bring the ideals of virtue, service, justice, and love to their fellow citizens. The absence of their decisive influence is becoming increasingly difficult to bear. Evidence abounds, for example, that an education system divorced from religious commitment is a breeding ground for moral chaos. In contrast, an education grounded in a biblical anthropology provides the strongest basis for defending human rights. It instructs the next generation in the classic Christian virtues such as humility, forgiveness, and compassion. Likewise, a system of social welfare that marginalizes religious organizations guided by these virtues is a system in crisis. Any social-service regime that denies the moral and spiritual dimension to human life can offer material help—but not much else. It cannot help those in need with the grace that truly uplifts and ennobles. Finally, when the public square excludes the redemptive influence of the faithful, every issue is reduced to calculations about power. The losers are the social outcasts, the vulnerable minorities, the voiceless weak. A political system cleansed of any Christian vision makes an idol out of politics, an idol that breaks the hearts of its worshipers. For heaven's sake, and for the sake of their neighbors on earth, evangelicals are called to stand in the breach.

Part **III**

Central Themes for an Evangelical Framework

10

The Sanctity of Life in the Twenty-first Century

An Agenda for Homo sapiens *in the image of God*

Nigel M. de S. Cameron

As CHRISTIANS CONFRONT the pressing moral agenda of the twenty-first century, their loyalties and energies are pulled in many directions. On every side lie problems and threats, a continually growing list of questions on which the Christian worldview is threatened and subverted. Among the several areas of concern lie issues in bioethics, old threats and new assaults on the sanctity and dignity of human life. Yet the seeming disparity of these many questions is misleading. They share a common focus. For whether we are discussing sexuality, drug policy, crime, media, poverty, religious freedom, or international human rights, we are merely unpacking the implications for our generation of a single question: How should we treat human beings? And that question arises, in turn, from another: What does it mean to be human? Every one of these many, sometimes highly complex, discussions resolves finally into one. This is no accident, though it is a sign of the general failure of the contemporary church to bring a coherent worldview to bear on the culture of our day that we tend almost invariably to handle these questions *seriatim*, one by one. This is a crucial point to grasp as we enter the arena of bioethics. It can be expressed in a slightly different fashion.

At the fulcrum of every human culture lies a set of assumptions about human nature—what it means to be a member of the tribe. These assumptions are typically unstated. They are self-evident to members of the group—so basic they are rarely noted or discussed—and therefore almost invisible in their common life. It is only under two conditions that their explication becomes the norm: in engagement with other cultures, and in the context of cultural revision and reconstruction. Both of these forces have begun powerfully to affect the "West" and its self-understanding, and therefore to begin to flesh out our grasp of what it means to be one of us.

That is why the self-evident assumptions of the "West" have so long been hidden from view, and why they are now so suddenly in crisis. The vision of human dignity, founded on the biblical doctrine of the creation of human being "in the image of God," has served as the major taproot of the Western concept of human nature. Through the so-called Enlightenment of the eighteenth century it blossomed into secularized yet recognizable notions of human rights and the dignity of the individual. Its seemingly unstoppable force led soon to the abolition of slavery, and then to the civil rights movement; with more ambiguity, and evidence of the distortions to come, it led to feminism and more recently—the refraction now substantial—to the movement for "children's rights" and of course the "gay rights" agenda. Its subversion in the "animal rights" movement, itself the stepchild of a distended version of environmental stewardship (a further secularized and therefore distorted biblical doctrine) has parallels in the distortions of radical feminism with its entailment of "abortion rights." "Pro-choice" feminists, "black power" racists, "gay" activists, "children's rights" radicals, and "animal rights" extremists are all alike the legatees of the Judeo-Christian vision of human dignity, even though in their various hands the tradition has folded back on itself and begun to eat its own young. The distinctive character and context of the biblical idea of the image of God has ceased to exercise control, and in its place we see the luxuriant growth of excrescences on the Western tradition that, while claiming to take its principles to their next logical stage, succeed only in demonstrating the final poverty of the enlightenment project with its vision of the rights of man divorced from the glory of the Creator God (Psalm 8).

Nevertheless, the flowering in our generation of the concept of human rights as a keystone of international law and the deep public revulsion at the idea of human cloning alike demonstrate the continuing potency of the Christian understanding of human nature—what it means to be one of us—and its capacity to frame both popular imagination and public policy. At the same time, as this survey of some of the major cultural movements of the past two centuries makes plain, the story is not simple. On every hand we see the distortions of good, exaggerated responses to evil, amalgams of virtue and vice. The tendency of our politics, and sometimes our specifically Christian engagement in politics, to seek simplicity at all costs meets head-on a picture that is anything but simple. We need to note that this is the context for our consideration of the sanctity of life and the Christian worldview.

Biblical Foundations

Biblical anthropology—the Christian idea of what it means to be human—has many roots in Scripture and rests on the two most fundamental of biblical doctrines: creation and incarnation. It is an interesting comment on evangelical use of Scripture that in seeking to argue against abortion, pro-life evangelicals have searched the Psalms and the Prophets for their many references to human life before birth, which vividly illustrate the humanity of the fetus and the continuity of human life unborn and born. They have rarely brought to bear the major resources available in these foundational doctrines, which set a framework for every consideration of human nature and offer a substantive basis for an evangelical bioethics that has yet to be seriously explored. As the biotechnology agenda has begun to unfold in a manner that is set to eclipse abortion as the great moral issue of the day, it is urgent to return to the bases of the biblical worldview and reassert the fundamental ground of human dignity in the *imago Dei*.

First, creation. Genesis 1 unambiguously lays out a taxonomy of the created order, in which humankind—man, male and female—is set at its head, as "God's last work" (Tennyson), made "in his image." The contrast with the other creatures is striking, since in the repeated refrain they are to reproduce "after their kind." That phrase is not used of humankind, which is made, as it were, after "God's kind," in the Maker's very likeness, even if also profoundly unlike him in the warp and woof of space and time. The bearing of the divine image and likeness is coterminous with humankind; membership in *Homo sapiens* entails nothing less. Every product of human conception is therefore a being after God's kind.

This foundation for human dignity offers a radical starting point for every discussion of human dignity and rights—especially of the equal dignity of women, and of men and women of all races and conditions. Yet it has remarkable application to the context of bioethics. While not addressing every problem in contemporary bioethics debate, its radical assertion of the unity and common dignity of the human race in the Maker's image establishes a framework of understanding within which many questions are immediately resolved, and those that remain unclear may be addressed.

Second, incarnation. The preeminent significance among Christian beliefs of the extraordinary doctrine of the incarnation is often obscured or downplayed in evangelical circles. There are several evident reasons. It is sometimes, often unconsciously, seen as a rival to the focus on the cross. It is seen as somehow encouraging the "liberal" idea that imitating Christ will bring salvation. The corrective intent is understandable: old-time liberal Christianity surely discounted the atoning sacrifice of Calvary and laid its focus on the doing of good works, as if the Jesus of Nazareth, who did them and told us to do likewise, was not also the Savior who died and rose again. Yet the discounting of the incarnation, as if it were mere stage setting for Calvary, is one of the major areas of weakness in contemporary evangelicalism. The incarnation is key to our understanding of the Christian life. And its teaching of God in human form, in humiliation in the Palestine of the first century and in glory today, lies at the heart of the highly distinctive character of the Christian vision of God. It is also rich in significance for the questions addressed in contemporary bioethics. For not only did God take human form, he did so in the form of a blastocyst, as an early embryo. Not only did he sanctify human nature by his life as a Palestinian Jew, he sanctifies it today in his continuing, glorified humanity.

The Bioethics Agenda

We can group the major questions arising in bioethics in three categories. The term "bioethics" was first coined in 1971,[1] and its introduction into the language served two purposes. From one perspective, it offered a useful category in which to bring together the various parties to discussions of what had traditionally been seen as "medical ethics," the ethical issues that arise in the practice of the profession. The older term both suggested, and often meant, that ethics in medicine was a matter for physicians, and physicians alone. The rise of "bioethics," in name and in practice, was the result of what one eminent writer termed at the time "The Unmasking of Medicine."[2] At the same time, another more sinister and ultimately destructive process was afoot. For the coinage of "bioethics" both represented and aided the development of an interdisciplinary academic field that was essentially disconnected both from medicine itself and from the history of medical ethics discussion. "Bioethics" as an academic enterprise is both novel (bioethics texts make only rare reference to earlier discussions of medical ethics) and postmodern. This term "postmodern" can be used in several ways; it is used here in two. The focus of contemporary bioethics is largely on the development of procedures to enable people to make private decisions—there is little interest in the forging of consensus on the basis of commonly held truth. Moreover, the field operates through articles and papers, conferences, and *ad hoc* centers and has produced few monographs and academic departments. It carries little baggage, historical or institutional, and that absence profoundly conditions the character of its discussions.

Christian engagement in the field has been precariously limited. As I have shown elsewhere,[3] the history of specifically evangelical engagement, in what one would have thought to be issues of prime consequence to the evangelical view of the world, has been and remains notoriously weak. Mainline Protestants have engaged in bioethics, though in general they have accepted the broad terms of the secular writers who lead the field. (Paul Ramsey, the major figure in the field during the decade of its beginnings, wrote as an unapologetic Christian but has been followed by few.) The Roman Catholic church's participation has proved complex, with a spectrum of responses all the way from those who reflect the highly distinctive voice of the *magisterium* to individual bioethics writers who are hard to distinguish from their secular colleagues in method or conclusions.

Bioethics 1: Abortion, Euthanasia, and Experimentation

Evangelical participation has been conditioned by several factors. For one thing, the general disinterest in public and intellectual issues that characterized much evangelicalism in the twentieth century persists and has made bioethics no more interesting to Christians in general than, say, literary criticism or jurisprudence. Moreover, engagement in the abortion debate, which came slowly and late to evangelicals, has failed to catalyze broader interest in the questions underlying support for liberal abortion (for example, the focus on autonomy), let alone the wider bioethics agenda. Even end-of-life issues, and euthanasia in particular, have been little addressed. The most substantive evidence of this systemic disinterest lies in evangelical institutions, especially colleges and seminaries, where with only one or two exceptions these questions have claimed only a marginal place in the curriculum. Meanwhile, a series of related debates has addressed questions of experimentation on human subjects, all the way from the Tuskegee syphilis experiments (in which syphilitic men were systematically untreated for purposes of research)[4] to the experimental use of human embryos (obtained from *in vitro* procedures or, perhaps, through cloning). The question of experimental use of the embryo has tended to be viewed as a subset of the abortion debate, but it is equally related to wider discussions about the ethics and policy of human subject research.[5]

Thirty years after Roe, the debate about abortion has shifted into a fresh mode. Time was when the chief focus of public disagreement centered on whether and at what point and for what purposes the product of human conception should be regarded as a "human life" with moral weight. The many discontinuities in the human procreative and maturing process offered points at which it might be held either that "life began" or that the developing fetus could make a greater claim on the moral attention of the human community. Historically, the great point of discontinuity was held to be "quickening," the point at which the mother becomes aware of movement on the part of the fetus. With our growing awareness of embryology, other points have suggested themselves—such as implantation, the onset of brain activity, and viability—the capacity of the child to survive outside the womb. Quickening we now know to be subjective; women often perceive it earlier in later pregnancies than in their first—though for centuries in English law, for example, it marked the point after which a woman could not be hanged. Viability has exercised a powerful pull on the imagination, though it is of course also in some degree subjective—dependent on the level of medical care available to support the newborn and on advances in neonatal skills. The development of an artificial womb—on which research continues to progress after many decades—will of course render it nugatory. The development of ultrasonic scans and intra-uterine video photography have combined to erode the significance of any such discontinuities and to underline the radical continuity that pervades mammalian life from its biological beginnings to its end—from fertilization through fetal growth and development, birth, infancy, childhood, adolescence, into maturity, and finally old age.

It is partly for this reason that the "when does life begin" argument should be seen as a halfway house. The defense of elective abortion has begun to evacuate the "cluster of cells" defense and to acknowledge that "in some sense" the continuity of mammalian life in the human fetus and born child must be acknowledged.[6] While the pro-life movement might have expected this to lead to the abandonment of the abortion defense, its effect has begun to prove more sinister than could have been anticipated, since it has fueled the growing move to deny not that unborn life is human life, but that human life is sacred.

The preeminent exponent of this position is the radical philosopher Peter Singer. Singer has been dubbed the world's most influential living philosopher, and there is no doubt that his highly controversial ideas represent the leading edge of contemporary opinion. Part of their sinister power lies precisely in the fact that he gives rational shape to positions that have been half-formed and essentially irrational—such as the defense of elective abortion. Singer does not deny that unborn life is human life. He simply denies that human life is sacred and seeks another basis for the preservation of the lives of (most) born persons. For him, as for the pro-life movement, abortion and the infanticide of a handicapped newborn have the same moral force.

While Singer's position on this as on other questions is controversial in the academic community and among those who defend elective abortion, its sheer rationality resonates with the commonsense view that a "fetus" is an unborn child; the view inevitably expressed by pro-choice women who have "wanted" pregnancies and then talk unself-consciously of "my baby." While Singer's candor is at one level to be welcomed, its fundamental denial of the sanctity of human life—the "doctrine" of the sanctity of life, to quote the title of his colleague Helga Kuhse's major book that attacks it[7]—takes the West one giant step in the direction of a systemic abandonment of its vision for human nature. Liberal abortion, like other historical evils such as slavery, has existed in tension with the idea of the *imago Dei* as the fundamental assumption of Western anthropology. Singer's vision is for a new coherence in which that idea has been consigned to history. He sees the development of the doctrine of the sanctity of life as a mistake, to be contrasted with the acceptance of abortion, infanticide, and euthanasia on the part of many primitive tribal peoples. He seeks to unscramble the humane anthropology of our civilization.

Singer's fundamental significance lies in his offering the most candid and influential critique of Judeo-Christian anthropology in our generation. In a context in which the direction of much recent bioethics has been to press various classes of human being to what I have elsewhere called the "margins" of the human race,[8] such that the unborn, the severely disabled, those with dementia, and those in a so-called "persistent vegetative state" come to partake of an ambiguous humanity, Singer moves to a more consistent and far more radical position.

His basic contention is, in effect, to deny the possibility of anthropology; to be human, merely, is without significance. Rather than seek to qualify human nature with life stages or competencies (as has been done in typical defenses of abortion and other taking of innocent life), Singer moves to deny the significance of human nature in itself and at the same time to absolutize the question of competencies, which he erects into a listing of (to use his term) "morally relevant characteristics." These "characteristics" include rationality, the capacity to communicate, self-consciousness, and others. Taken together they offer a useful summation of the qualities and competencies of mature and healthy human nature; indeed, they are derived from an induction of those things that we would generally take to be most characteristic of "being human." That is what gives them, in his hands, their persuasive power. Who could deny that these "characteristics" are "morally relevant"?

Yet the argument at this point depends on a logical sleight of hand. For "characteristics" in mature human flourishing that are plainly significant morally as well as otherwise are suddenly turned into necessary conditions for human dignity. We may celebrate these features of human maturity; it is something quite else to regard their denial as evidence of human absence. For if we acknowledge and celebrate them properly, they will be seen as characteristically human but conditioned precisely by the health and maturity of the subject that were the criteria employed for their selection. Singer's argument is therefore circular. His exclusion of other features and experiences that are typically human, and indeed morally relevant, such as infancy and age with their dependence, and handicap and sickness with their challenge to the caring community, destroys the credibility of a case that depends on reducing the human race to his selected group.

Singer moves on, having established his criteria, to a double use: both to exclude those who fail to possess them (hence his argument in favor of the killing of handicapped newborns as a parental choice), and to propose newfound dignity and a claim on "personhood" for intelligent subhuman creatures such as chimpanzees. Membership in the human race per se has ceased to have significance. Indeed, says Singer, to defend its intrinsic significance is to fall prey to "speciesism," which on a par with racism elevates one group at the expense of others without moral justification.

Singer's importance in the articulation of a biblical anthropology for bioethics is hard to overstate, since he develops a position that is robustly antithetical to Judeo-Christian assumptions and thereby uniquely sheds light on their significance. His central charge of speciesism may be readily shown to be specious. The unique significance of human being is indeed illustrated by the "morally relevant" features to which he draws attention, though that does not offer a listing of necessary conditions for human dignity but rather a sampling of those aspects of human experience that the healthy, mature human being will evidence. They illuminate the kind of being we are by showing how in maturity and with health human beings will flourish. This is that species which flourishes in this way rather than in other ways. Moreover, it is in fact Singer whose method closely parallels that of the racist. For the racist takes human beings—the human race—and on grounds that he or she considers "morally relevant" (skin pigmentation; ethnicity) determines that some members of this species shall be treated with human dignity while others shall not. The racist divides the human race down the middle, according to his or her own extrinsic criteria. That is exactly Singer's method.

In dramatic contrast, the biblical anthropology, set forth in the doctrine of creation and underlined with vivid power in the incarnation, asserts the unity of humankind and our unique and abiding dignity.

While most evangelical energies—caring and political—have been directed into sustaining this vision for *Homo sapiens* at the start of life, the threat to human beings in their other moment of supreme weakness, when they face chronic and terminal illness, continues to grow. Many observers have been surprised that Christians have not engaged more energetically in the political debates around euthanasia (and its surrogate, "assisted suicide") and also that they have not developed ministries that parallel the many hundreds of initiatives directed to sustain human dignity at the start of life. One reason lies in the fact that euthanasia has not yet had its "Roe," although a series of judicial decisions have begun to whittle away at the sanctity of life of those who are dependent and in need of serious medical care. The state of Oregon has now established a euthanasia regime, with "physician-assisted suicide" permitted through the prescription of lethal medications. While some European nations (especially Belgium and Switzerland) have taken steps to follow the Netherlands, the one country with an established euthanasia jurisdiction, the progress of this insidious threat to human dignity has been slow. It is also more complex to assert the pro-life position, in the face of willing candidates for "voluntary" euthanasia, for whom the "choice" is claimed to be their own and not (as in the case of abortion) that of other parties.[9] Moreover, there are substantial cost savings that may result from the premature ending of life.

Bioethics 2: Cloning and Genetics

We now confront a transition from "Bioethics 1," my term for the life issues of abortion and euthanasia that have dominated debate for a generation and will continue to prove pervasive challenges to public policy in the future, to "Bioethics 2"—questions that relate fundamentally not to the taking of innocent human life but to its manipulation and manufacture. Many questions do not sit tidily in one category or the other. *In vitro* fertilization, with its clutch of moral and clinical issues largely ignored by evangelicals in the past generation, straddles the two since it has generally operated on the principle that human embryos may be quality-tested, destroyed, and frozen. In Bioethics 2 terms, it may seem benign—for example, when enabling a couple to have their own children. Yet it has also been used to enable plainly eugenic conceptions, whether through trade in sperm and eggs, or—much more commonly—the use of "selective reduction" (the newspeak term for destroying the least attractive embryos in the petri dish, and, sometimes, supernumerary fetuses in the case of multiple conceptions).

By the same token, the debate over human cloning, the harbinger of Bioethics 2 and one of the great issues to be confronted by the human race in this century, is a debate that straddles the two. That indeed is part of its utility in this discussion, since it has awakened the pro-life movement to the significance of biotech questions: Cloning for experimental research involves making and killing embryos, and cloning that is intended to lead to live birth would build on such research the hazards of experimental pregnancies. Near-universal opposition to live-birth cloning and widespread agreement around the world that experimental cloning should not be permitted together indicate that this is no rerun of the abortion debate. Moreover, energetic engagement in attempts to ban experimental cloning on the part of some pro-choice feminists and environmentalists illustrates the fresh character of this debate.[10] Their being found in co-belligerency with the pro-life movement offers the ocular proof that the debate over the sanctity of life has undergone a sea change with the move into Bioethics 2. In tandem, the generally politically conservative pro-life movement has begun to take on issues that have generally been considered part of the "progressive" agenda, including genetic discrimination and gene patenting.[11]

With cloning, we take the first decisive step across the line that separates the kind of beings we are from the kind of things we make; thus *Homo sapiens*, who has always been *Homo faber*, man the maker, turns his making on himself—and in the sublimest of ironies in a single fateful act both elevates himself to the role of creator and degrades that same self to the status of a manufacture.

This act is stupefying in its scope. Humankind simultaneously claims the role of God while being reduced to playing the part of a mere thing, the dust of the earth out of which we were made and to which we foolish creatures choose to return ourselves; to become, in President Bush's recent phrase, commodity rather than creation.

From a theological perspective the significance of both these sides of the coin is plain. In our attempt to serve as our own creator, we are revealed as usurpers, capable only of manufacture. That Faustian bargain is the only one on offer. For the task of creator is personal to God, and his election of the interpersonal mystery of human sexuality as the context for procreation preserves his creatorhood absolutely. The most that his human creatures can do is, as we say, to "ape" his role, parody it, and reduce it to the mechanistic and industrial processes at which we are so good and for which indeed—among other things—we were made. The ambiguity of the clonal human, as both creature and product, *Homo sapiens* hijacked by *Homo faber*, moves us decisively toward what the posthumanists call the "singularity"—that state they envisage in which the distinction between human being and manufactured being is over, and a seamless dress weaves together our humankind and what we have made. It anticipates the union of "mecha" and "orga."[12]

In his famous jeremiad, "Why the Future Doesn't Need Us,"[13] Bill Joy, cofounder of Sun Microsystems, claims that genetics, robotics, and nanotechnology are the three great threats to the human race in the twenty-first century. Through some mixture of accident and intent they are likely to destroy the human species, or supplant it, through some biological or mechanical meltdown or through the triumph of machine intelligence. One does not need to buy the whole thesis to acclaim his comprehensive framing of the issues. And at the heart of this secular analysis lies what Christians recognize as a single theological issue: the threat to human nature that is posed by fallen human creativity; the dominion mandate from Genesis 1 to "subdue the earth" divorced from its biblical context—human dignity made in the image of God.

The Bioethics 2 agenda is therefore focused on the use of technology to control, design, and perhaps improve human being at the fundamental level of genetics. While in the context of the pro-life movement, in which the protection of human life is paramount, it might seem of lesser significance to be concerned with the possibility of interventions that do not destroy life, there is emerging a fresh paradigm in which it is recognized that taking a human life made in God's image may not in fact be as serious, in his eyes, as making a human being in our own. Incremental technological interventions in the process of human procreation that began with artificial insemination and, subsequently, *in vitro* fertilization and its variants, will encompass increasingly sophisticated capacities. "Genetic engineering," the blanket term used to cover interventions that make changes at the genetic level, has already begun to have limited clinical applications. While genetic alterations that benefit the individual by curing disease are to be welcomed, changes that produce "enhancements" will also be possible; and, most important of all, inheritable changes—changes in the germ line that will affect the genetic constitution of every subsequent human being in that family—will offer the ultimate challenge to humankind, whether we should seek to "improve" our human nature and take control over the kind of beings that we are.

It was of this possibility that C. S. Lewis wrote, with extraordinary prescience, in his essay *The Abolition of Man*, in which he foresaw "man's final triumph over nature" in our triumph over our own nature. Yet he asks the question, who has won? And he suggests that what appears to be "man's triumph over nature" is in fact "nature's triumph over man." By taking control of our own nature, we are subjecting ourselves to ourselves and turning ourselves into some*thing* that we can control and dominate. The general who rides in the triumphal procession is one and the same with the slave he pulls behind him.[14]

There can be no doubt that the question of the integrity of human nature will soon emerge as the greatest issue to have been faced by humankind—and the greatest threat. For biotechnology will deliver into our hands a capacity to alter what it means to be human.

Together with the immediate question of human cloning, the prospect of genetic interventions intended to enhance our power over our children and the future of the human race indicates the manner in which developments in biotechnology have raised the stakes for the human race.

Bioethics 3: A Posthuman Future?

And beyond genetics we already see advances in nanotechnology and cybernetics that offer a vision of human nature radically enhanced. The terms "posthumanist" and "transhumanist" have been coined by advocates of a reconstructed human nature in which the "cyborg" ("cybernetic organism"), a human-robotic amalgam, takes the place of humankind.[15] While much of the research in these areas of science and technology may have benign purposes, and indeed hold the prospect of vast benefit to humankind, there has been little discussion within the church of its potential significance in the reshaping of human nature.[16] The questions raised by these technologies for human dignity are precisely parallel to those focused by developments in human genetics, and there is reason to believe that some of the applications of the Bioethics 3 technologies will raise ethical and policy issues for the human race well before genetics develops the capacities to reshape our nature.

The Challenge to Evangelicals

Evangelical Christians are uniquely placed to address the unfolding questions of biotechnology, even as the "life issues" of abortion and euthanasia have slowly taken hold on their imagination.

With human cloning we cross the Rubicon and venture for the first time into the manufacture of our own kind. Until now the depth of our imaginative depravity had to be content with new forms of killing, the legacy of Cain and Abel. We confront now a new kind of sin, a fresh fulfillment of our conflicted fallen nature, the descendant of the Tower of Babel. This is our best opportunity to begin to frame public policy for biotechnology around an issue of high profile that has resonated with the public conscience.

The challenge comes to us at that time in the history of our civilization when we are least able to resist. While our churches remain full (at least here in the United States), the web of Judeo-Christian ideals and default positions that have long nourished the values of our culture and fed its moral vision is steadily being reset by our cultural elite, a process aided by the generally pietistic and withdrawn character of our Christianity. It remains to be seen whether Christian commitment to the pro-life cause, the single most striking exception, can evolve into a broad engagement with biotechnology.

Our theological rationale is clear. Human beings are made in God's image. The technological imperative that we read out of the "dominion mandate" in Genesis 1 lies in the context of the kind of being that God has made his human creatures to be.

What is more, the incarnation of Jesus Christ, in which God takes human nature for his own, declares unambiguously that *Homo sapiens* is no mere accident of history but God's own image impressed into space and time. The fact of his continuing humanity offers the surest possible guide to Christians who are perplexed in the face of technologies that have the power to reshape human nature itself. The Jesus who died, rose again, and ascended is seated in his divine-human form at the right hand of the Father; "the one who sits on the throne of the universe," as Charles Hodge, perhaps the greatest evangelical theologian of the nineteenth century, stated it boldly, "is both perfect man and perfect God."[17] His words have a fresh ring as we enter the twenty-first century, in which human nature itself is up for debate. If the evangelical church is to serve Jesus Christ in the generation to come, it will be as light-bearer and saltshaker in that generation in which the barbarities of abortion and euthanasia are not behind us, yet the new temptations of reshaping our own selves lie ahead. Let us pray that we shall prove equal to the task.

Appendix

The Sanctity of Life in a Brave New World

A Manifesto on Biotechnology and Human Dignity[18]

"Our children are creations, not commodities."

President George W. Bush

"If any one age really attains, by eugenics and scientific education, the power to make its descendants what it pleases, all men who live after are the patients of that power," slaves to the "dead hand of the great planners and conditioners."

C. S. Lewis

1. The Issue

The debates over human cloning have focused our attention on the significance for the human race of what has been called "the biotech century." Biotechnology raises great hopes for technological progress; but it also raises profound moral questions, since it gives us new power over our own nature. It poses in the sharpest form the question: What does it mean to be human?

2. Biotechnology and Moral Questions

We are thankful for the hope that biotechnology offers of new treatments for some of the most dreaded diseases. But the same technology can be used for good or ill. Scientists are already working in many countries to clone human beings, either for embryo experiments or for live birth.

In December 2002, the Raelians, a religious cult that believes the human race was cloned by space aliens, announced that a baby they called "Eve" was the first cloned human. But it is not just the fringe cults that are involved in cloning; that same month, Stanford University announced a project to create cloned embryos for medical experimentation.

Before long, scientists will also be able to intervene in human nature by making inheritable genetic changes. Biotechnology companies are already staking claims to parts of the human body through patents on human genes, cells, and other tissues for commercial use. Genetic information about the individual may make possible advances in diagnosis and treatment of disease, but it may also make those with "weaker" genes subject to discrimination along eugenic lines.

3. The Uniqueness of Humanity and Its Dignity

These questions have led many to believe that in biotechnology we meet the moral challenge of the twenty-first century. For the uniqueness of human nature is at stake. Human dignity is indivisible: the aged, the sick, the very young, those with genetic diseases—every human being is possessed of an equal dignity; any threat to the dignity of one is a threat to us all. This challenge is not simply for Christians. Jews, Muslims, and members of other faiths have voiced the same concerns. So, too, have millions of others who understand that humans are distinct from all other species; at every stage of life and in every condition of dependency they are intrinsically valuable and deserving of full moral respect. To argue otherwise will lead to the ultimate tyranny in which someone determines those who are deemed worthy of protection and those who are not.

4. Why This Must Be Addressed

As C. S. Lewis warned a half-century ago in his remarkable essay *The Abolition of Man*, the new capacities of biotechnology give us power over ourselves and our own nature. But such power will always tend to turn us into commodities that have been manufactured. As we develop powers to make inheritable changes in human nature, we become controllers of every future generation.

It is therefore vital that we undertake a serious national conversation to ensure a thorough understanding of these questions, and their answers, so that our democratic institutions will be able to make prudent choices as public policy is shaped for the future.

5. What We Propose

We strongly favor work in biotechnology that will lead to cures for diseases and disabilities, and are excited by the promise of stem cells from adult donors and other ethical avenues of research. We see that around the world other jurisdictions have begun to develop ethical standards within which biotech can flourish. We note that Germany, which because of its Nazi past has a unique sensitivity to unethical science and medicine, has enacted laws that prohibit all cloning and other unethical biotech options. We note that the one international bioethics treaty, the European Convention on Human Rights and Biomedicine, outlaws all inheritable genetic changes and has been amended to prohibit all cloning.

We therefore seek as an urgent first step a comprehensive ban on all human cloning and inheritable genetic modification. This is imperative to prevent the birth of a generation of malformed humans (animal cloning has led to grotesque failures) and the establishment of vast experimental embryo farms with millions of cloned humans.

We emphasize: All human cloning must be banned. There are those who argue that cloning can be sanctioned for medical experimentation—so-called "therapeutic" purposes. No matter what promise this might hold—all of which we note is speculative—it is morally offensive since it involves creating, killing, and harvesting one human being in the service of others. No civilized state could countenance such a practice. Moreover, if cloning for experiments is allowed, how could we ensure that a cloned embryo would not be implanted in a womb? The Department of Justice has testified that such a law would be unenforceable.

We also seek legislation to prohibit discrimination based on genetic information, which is private to the individual. We seek a wide-ranging review of the patent law to protect human dignity from the commercial use of human genes, cells, and other tissue. We believe that such public policy initiatives will help ensure the progress of ethical biotechnology while protecting the sanctity of human life.

We welcome all medical and scientific research as long as it is firmly tethered to moral truth. History teaches that whenever the two have been separated, the consequence is disaster and great suffering for humanity.

11

Caring for the Vulnerable

Clive Calver and Galen Carey

Introduction

Christians are called to care for the vulnerable. As beneficiaries of God's loving providence, grace, and mercy, we show our gratitude by loving both God and our neighbors. Jesus taught in the parable of the Good Samaritan that neighbor is defined by need, not geography.

Throughout the history of the church, Christians have cared for the vulnerable. The church has sponsored schools, orphanages, hospitals, and rescue missions. Through evangelism and discipleship ministries, the church cultivates commitments, disciplines, and virtues that promote responsible caring for self, family, and community. Numerous economists and sociologists have documented the contributions of Christianity to the creation of strong, caring communities.[1]

In this chapter we will look at dimensions of vulnerability and caring, briefly consider the rich history of evangelical care for the vulnerable, review some of the theological and missiological issues, and examine pitfalls to avoid. We will then consider the appropriate roles for individual Christians, for churches, and for government. We will conclude by surveying some of the main areas of consensus among evangelicals.

Although the word "vulnerable" does not appear in most English Bibles, the concept is found throughout the Scriptures—in both Old and New Testaments and in every genre. Terms such as poor, needy, oppressed, afflicted, sick, prisoner, blind, suffering, persecuted, widow, and orphan convey various dimensions of vulnerability.

Likewise, the concept of care is widespread in the Scriptures. It is captured in the many injunctions to love, protect, give, serve, nurture, and the like. A central theme of Scripture is represented by God's care for the vulnerable, and the repeated exhortation to God's people to reflect a similar care and concern. Such a commitment extends beyond compassion to embrace the themes of both justice and mercy.

Biblical teaching on political philosophy when related to caring for the vulnerable is both less prominent and more complex. The Bible does not present a model constitution, nor does it offer any detailed prescriptions on how the institutions of human government should be organized. There are substantial hermeneutical hurdles in moving from the narrative passages about human government in general, and the evolving Israelite theocracy/monarchy, to prescriptions for twenty-first-century politics.

It is always important to avoid what Haddon Wilmer calls "concordance work" that looks only at passages containing explicit references to government. Rather, a political philosophy on caring for the vulnerable that seeks a biblical justification must rely more on basic principles and deductions from those principles, rather than on explicit teachings.

Who Are the "Vulnerable"?

The dictionary tells us that our English word "vulnerable" comes from the Latin *vulnus*, or wound, and refers to one who is "without adequate protection; open to emotional or physical danger or harm."[2] In one sense, all of us are vulnerable, as Moses eloquently stated in Psalm 90:

> For a thousand years in your sight
>   are like yesterday when it is past,
>   or like a watch in the night.
>
> You sweep them away; they are like a dream,
>   like grass that is renewed in the morning;
> in the morning it flourishes and is renewed;
>   in the evening it fades and withers.
>
>   Psalm 90:4–6

Whether we like it or not, all of us are subject to the aging process and eventually to death. No one can predict or control their moment of final judgment. No one is invulnerable in the face of death. Jesus himself spoke of the serious sense of false security that the rich farmer had placed in his wealth:

> "You fool! This very night your life will be demanded from you. Then who will get what you have prepared for yourself?" This is how it will be with anyone who stores up things for himself but is not rich toward God.
>
> Luke 12:20–21 NIV

Furthermore, all of us, both rich and poor alike, know what it is to be rejected. We are all able to feel the emotional pain of broken human relationships. The recognition of our mutual vulnerability can go a long way toward developing a healthy compassion for the vulnerable.

In another sense, however, vulnerability is distributed very unevenly among humankind. Simply put, some are more vulnerable than others. There are those for whom inherited and earned wealth, education, secure employment, family relationships, and a generous social safety net provide multiple hedges against physical, social, and emotional harm. And when harm does come, there are doctors, counselors, and insurance policies to fall back on.

By contrast, the vast majority of people are forced to survive from day to day, not knowing where they will find their next meal. Globally, more than 1.2 billion people live on less than one dollar per day.[3]

Groups at Risk

There are many dimensions of vulnerability. In most societies the vulnerable will include women, especially widows; children, especially orphans; immigrants and refugees; the poor and unemployed; the sick and disabled; the addicted; and those persecuted and imprisoned. Each of these groups has distinct needs for protection and support.

1. *The poor.* As a generic term, "the poor" includes both the chronically unemployed and those who work for very low wages. Poor people face multiple layers of vulnerability, including lack of adequate food, shelter, health care, and education. Reduced participation and a muted voice in community life act as both a cause and a result of poverty.

2. *Women.* Aside from enjoying a slightly longer life expectancy, women will usually be more vulnerable than men. Women usually earn less than men, even for comparable work. They can be disproportionately subject to abuse, including discrimination, domestic violence, trafficking, and rape. In some societies women have fewer rights, and the practice of girls being subject to sexual slavery may be condoned or ignored. Women pay taxes and do more than their share of the work but have relatively little voice in politics and resource allocation. Widows and single women are particularly vulnerable since social structures often assume patriarchal

protection. Predators can assume that they may attack or defraud a widow with impunity.

3. *Children.* Babies enter the world in a state of exquisite vulnerability. As they grow, they gradually learn how to survive on their own. However, they remain dependent on parents and communities for many years. In situations where social structures have broken down, children may be subject to hard labor, forced military recruitment, gang violence, physical and sexual abuse, trafficking, prostitution, and pornography. Those whose parents have died or abandoned them are particularly at risk.

4. *Immigrants.* Those who cross cultural and national boundaries in search of a better life face many challenges adjusting to new languages, cultures, and systems. They must deal with the pain of separation from home and all that is familiar, as well as with the indifference, fear, or even hostility of the host culture. Immigrants come from all socioeconomic strata, but those who arrive without money, education, or visas are particularly vulnerable.

5. *Refugees.* Refugees face similar struggles to those encountered by immigrants, but with the added challenge of recovering from the painful experiences of persecution, including beatings, imprisonment, torture, rape, and more. Some have been forced to watch as family members were raped or murdered. Internationally, many refugees are locked away in closed refugee camps, with no opportunity to work or lead a normal life. There may be little or no prospect of ever returning home. In other cases refugees live under the threat of being forcibly returned to their country where they will once again face their persecutors. According to the United Nations High Commissioner for Refugees, there are nearly ten million refugees in the world, as well as millions more who are internally displaced within their own countries.[4]

6. *The sick.* All people are likely to face health problems at one time or another. When serious illness strikes, people face pain, uncertainty, fear, and, often, expensive treatments. If the illness requires hospitalization, there is also separation from home and family and subjection to a regime not unlike prison in terms of the assault on human dignity. Persons infected with leprosy, the HIV virus, and other stigmatized conditions also face rejection and ostracism.

7. *Persons with disabilities.* The term "disabilities" covers a wide range of physical and mental conditions. With proper education and health care, many persons with disabilities can live and work independently. Others require continuing support throughout their lives. In addition to the difficulties intrinsic to their disability, many face misunderstanding and rejection.

8. *The persecuted.* These so often represent the forgotten people, those who are vulnerable to oppression because of their gender, ethnicity, race, or creed. The sufferings inflicted upon them may be long lasting in character and extreme in their severity.[5]

9. *Minorities.* It was George Bernard Shaw who first observed that God is usually seen to be on the side of the big battalions! Whether one is speaking of numerical disadvantage, tribal inequity, racial discrimination, or those with

either physical or learning difficulties, there will always be groups who are simply at a disadvantage within society. They can often come over as powerless in the face of the more powerful, and they can frequently be the victims of overt injustice and unfair treatment at the hands of the majority.

10. *The addicted.* Drug and alcohol addictions enslave the lives of millions throughout the world. Other addictions, such as pornography, can be equally debilitating. In its advanced stages, addiction prevents normal functioning and leads to family breakup, job loss, illness, and even death.

11. *Prisoners.* Prisons are filled with those who have committed crimes, faced trial, and been convicted and sentenced. Prisons are also home to some innocent victims who—whether mistakenly or intentionally—have been wrongly convicted. In either case prisoners face a radical loss of freedom, dignity, and self-esteem. When prisoners are released, they face major reintegration challenges, often in a climate of fear and discrimination.

Christians and the Vulnerable

Evangelicals have done much to care for the vulnerable. Through the centuries there have been practices such as sick visitation, the poor box, and a variety of medical and philanthropic endeavors. The Paulicans, Bogomils, and Albigenses, among many others, exhibited elements of a social compassion that would later be identified with the Anabaptists in their rich tradition of social involvement on behalf of the vulnerable.

This kind of emphasis would find fresh expression and a profound renaissance both during and after the Evangelical Awakening. Harry Blamires has wisely observed that the Evangelical Revival did more to transfigure the moral character of the general populace than any other comparable movement in recent history. This led to the movement for the cessation of the slave trade, a concern about Sunday observance, a commitment to education for the masses, and a desire to see radical change in spheres of public health.

The Salvation Army itself was to become legendary in the heart of London's East End. The Salvation Army offered an incarnational response to human deprivation and poverty. Today the Salvation Army has more than 1.1 million members working in 109 countries throughout the world.[6] As the twentieth century opened, an increasing evangelical awareness of the need for social justice to embody social righteousness, alongside individual acts of mercy, was evident. The compassionate outreach of groups like those associated with D. L. Moody in Chicago, the YMCA, and others demonstrated a commitment to care for the poor.

The early to middle decades of the twentieth century did witness an evangelical retreat in the face of concern over theological shortcomings in the Social Gospel movement. One observer claimed:

> Those who place a high value on salvation are conservative, anxious to maintain the status quo, and unsympathetic or indifferent to the plight of the black or the poor. . . . The data suggest a portrait of the religious-minded as a person having a self-centered preoccupation with saving his own soul, an other-worldly orientation, coupled with an indifference toward or even a tacit endorsement of a social system that would perpetuate social inequality and injustice.[7]

This is certainly an overstatement, and yet it contains enough truth to make us uncomfortable. Such a perspective would scarcely hold out much hope for the less advantaged among us, and the vulnerable have the right to expect more from the church, and from Christian people. It was Archbishop William Temple who used to observe that the church of Jesus Christ is the only society on earth that exists entirely for the benefit of its nonmembers. One could add that this should nowhere be truer than when it applies to the most vulnerable among us.

What Does It Mean to Care for the Vulnerable?

If vulnerability means being without adequate protection from danger and harm, then a key element of caring for the vulnerable will be providing access to those structures and resources that will shelter them from current and future harm. This will vary from case to case.

Those facing life-threatening circumstances such as war, famine, or disaster require immediate rescue and relief. As James argues,

> Suppose a brother or sister is without clothes and daily food. If one of you says to him, "Go, I wish you well; keep warm and well fed," but does nothing about his physical needs, what good is it? In the same way, faith by itself, if it is not accompanied by action, is dead.
>
> James 2:15–17 NIV

Similarly, those who are in prison should be visited, those who are strangers should be shown hospitality, and those who are sick should be treated. (See Matt. 25:31–46 among many other passages.) The same applies to those enduring persecution provoked by injustice. While it is true that Jesus pronounced a beatitude upon those who would suffer persecution for the sake of his kingdom (Matthew 10), this does not provide us with a legitimate or convenient excuse to ignore them in their time of need. Nor should we ignore the plight of the powerless merely because we find it difficult to identify with their sufferings.

Caring for the vulnerable must inevitably extend far beyond immediate relief. Justice demands that we also create the conditions within our society, insofar as is possible, that will militate against continuing and systemic vulnerability.

We are called, in Isaiah's words, to "loose the chains of injustice" and to "break every yoke" (Isa. 58:6 NIV). This will require wisdom to discern what private and public actions can best restrain those who are violent and oppressive, while protecting and empowering those who are most vulnerable.

Central to effective caring is the sense of interconnectedness or social solidarity. Human beings are created in the image of the Triune God (Gen. 1:27). The Trinity provides us with the archetypal relationship of interdependence that human beings are intended to image. Human solidarity begins with the marriage and family relationships, but it does not end there. God's covenant people—both Israel and the church—are referred to in Scripture more than 330 times as "brothers."[8]

When members of our family struggle, we are not at liberty to remain unaffected. If we do in fact ignore our sisters' and brothers' suffering, it calls into question whether we are really family. This recognition of the dangers of abuse must impinge upon every area of our lives in order to provide a framework for the simple but profound question, How shall we then live?

The enormous and growing contemporary gap between rich and poor—domestically and even more internationally—can appear to pose an almost insurmountable barrier to realizing the goal outlined by Paul in his letter to the Corinthians:

> Our desire is not that others might be relieved while you are hard pressed, but that there might be equality. At the present time your plenty will supply what they need, so that in turn their plenty will supply what you need. Then there will be equality, as it is written: "He who gathered much did not have too much, and he who gathered little did not have too little."
>
> 2 Corinthians 8:13–15 NIV

Paul seems to have envisioned a temporary reversal of fortunes, rather than permanent structural imbalances. The astonishing wealth of first-world Christians in the twenty-first century gives us unprecedented opportunity—and with it, responsibility—to act on behalf of the world's poor and disenfranchised. However, even what we assume to be generous sharing of our resources will barely dent the current global inequities. As will be discussed later, our wealth also distorts our relationships with the poor, risking insincerity and manipulation on both sides when we do try to connect.

These dangers notwithstanding, our care for the vulnerable must involve more than writing a check or lobbying for economic reforms, as important as both of these responses are. Unless our caring is personalized through direct contact with the poor—beginning with those in our local communities—we are unlikely to move to deeper levels of solidarity and family connection. In the light of this, policies supporting mixed-income residential patterns are highly desirable. Regardless of what the secular patterns are, Christians should consider, where feasible, living and worshiping in poor or mixed-income communities.[9]

Shalom: A Guiding Vision

The biblical concept of *shalom* captures well God's vision for humanity, and particularly for the vulnerable. Shalom is sometimes translated in English as "peace," but it entails a much more robust notion of holistic well-being than the mere absence of conflict. Shalom is translated in the NIV by the words "peace" (113 times), "all right" (9), "safe" (9), "safely" (9), "prosperity" (5), "success" (3), "good health" (2), "treaty of friendship" (2), and "peace and prosperity" (1), among others. Shalom encompasses a vision of wholistic well-being, safety, and peace. It is an attribute both of individuals and communities. It implies a state of reconciliation with God and between human beings.

Shalom includes the concepts of physical health and social reconciliation, as well as what evangelicals mean when we speak of salvation. Many scholars consider shalom to be one of the most comprehensive summaries of God's intentions for humankind to be found anywhere in the Bible. A pattern of development can be traced throughout Scripture, moving from an initial focus on physical health to include emotional, social, and spiritual components. The full development of the concept of shalom can be seen in Isaiah, where the Suffering Servant brings about shalom through his sacrificial death:

> But he was pierced for our transgressions,
>   he was crushed for our iniquities;
> the punishment that brought us peace [*shalom*] was upon him,
>   and by his wounds we are healed.
>
> Isaiah 53:5 NIV

In later chapters Isaiah paints a compelling picture of a society characterized by shalom:

> Never again will there be in it
>   an infant who lives but a few days,
>   or an old man who does not live out his years;
> he who dies at a hundred
>   will be thought a mere youth;
> he who fails to reach a hundred
>   will be considered accursed.
> They will build houses and dwell in them;
>   they will plant vineyards and eat their fruit.
> No longer will they build houses and others live in them,
>   or plant and others eat.
> For as the days of a tree,
>   so will be the days of my people;
> my chosen ones will long enjoy
>   the works of their hands.
> They will not toil in vain

or bear children doomed to misfortune;
for they will be a people blessed by the LORD,
they and their descendants with them.

Isaiah 65:20–23

As Raymond Fung observes, this is not a pie-in-the-sky utopian vision: People still must toil in order to survive; the difference is that they do not toil in vain. They can enjoy the fruits of their labor. People still eventually die; the difference is that they do not die prematurely, as children. In a society characterized by shalom, people may be vulnerable, but they will have access to the protective resources of the community.[10]

What Is the Role of the Church?

1. *Evangelism and discipleship.* It would be our contention that every person—both powerful and powerless alike—needs Jesus and the healing and salvation that he offers. Evangelism and discipleship begin in the home, as parents raise their children to know and worship God, and as they model lives of Christian caring.

Our care for the vulnerable must therefore include a sharing of both the love and the truth of Jesus. Furthermore, the church must be equipped and ready to put these principles into practice. As we have already observed, our deeds must never become divorced from our words.

2. *Comfort.* When disaster strikes, government workers can conduct needs assessments, deploy rescue teams, and issue benefits checks. But Uncle Sam does not offer a shoulder to cry on, or a hand to hold. The church, however, as the collective channel of God's providential love, is well positioned for a ministry of caring and compassion. The church offers a high-touch ministry to the hurting, drawing on the resources of group prayer, counseling, and encouragement. (See 2 Cor. 1:3–7.)

3. *Community.* Where does the unemployed factory worker turn when the search for employment becomes too discouraging? The church brings built-in networking mechanisms that can provide accountable support, both emotional and practical. The recovering addict who knows that others are praying for her is more likely to successfully resist temptation. (See Prov. 27:17; Eph. 4:13–16.)

4. *Forgiveness.* When people do fail, the church is there ready and willing to minister the grace and forgiveness of God. We learn forgiveness in the crucible of shared daily life in the community of faith. Experiencing forgiveness is central to restoring the broken and vulnerable to wholeness (Eph. 4:32).

5. *Prophetic voice.* The church speaks truth to those in power. While the church as an institution does not align itself with any specific political party,

it nonetheless exerts a powerful influence on the moral issues of the day by the way in which it brings God's Word to bear on those issues, both among its members and in the world. No oppressor can last long without at least a veneer of morality. The church, when it is faithful, exposes the lies and deceptions of those who destroy the fabric of the community (Matt. 5:13–16).

The church can also shape the values of the community with an impassioned voice that can avoid falling into the danger of being particularly strident or politically partisan.

What Is the Role of Christian Families and Individuals?

1. *Generosity.* Christians are called to share generously of their time as well as their money with those in need. Jesus' comment that the poor will be with us always (Matt. 26:11) is often used to justify inaction or complacency. Jesus, however, is quoting from Deuteronomy, where a very different conclusion is reached:

> If there is a poor man among your brothers in any of the towns of the land that the LORD your God is giving you, do not be hardhearted or tightfisted toward your poor brother. Rather be openhanded and freely lend him whatever he needs. Be careful not to harbor this wicked thought: "The seventh year, the year for canceling debts, is near," so that you do not show ill will toward your needy brother and give him nothing. He may then appeal to the LORD against you, and you will be found guilty of sin.
>
> Deuteronomy 15:7–8, 10–11 NIV

Christian generosity may not in itself wipe out poverty, much less other forms of vulnerability. However, it can have a significant impact, not least in the hearts and lives of those who give. It is also a powerful witness to the kingdom of God. "They will know we are Christians by our love." (See John 13:35.)

2. *Simplicity.* Christians are called to lives of sacrificial service. Caring for the vulnerable requires time and attention; it is easy to be distracted. The issue of simple lifestyle is anything but simple, as the extensive treatments of the topic elsewhere readily demonstrate. The complexity of the biblical material allows virtually anyone to find proof texts to make their point. Simplicity is not merely a matter of living on less; it implies a simpler living but with a much greater focus. "Seek first the kingdom of God" is the watchword.

3. *Hospitality.* The Scripture is full of exhortations to hospitality to the vulnerable. "Share with God's people who are in need. Practice hospitality" (Rom. 12:13 NIV). Christians show hospitality when they open their hearts and homes to the poor and the stranger, as well as when they support public policies that are welcoming to refugees, immigrants, and others in need. Hospitality is

a virtue particularly suited to families. Children who are raised in hospitable homes receive an invaluable lesson in caring for the vulnerable.

4. *Citizenship.* Christians who live in democracies have particular responsibilities to promote a just society that provides both opportunities and protection to each and every one of its citizens.

Far from the cozy withdrawal of opting out and adopting an apolitical stance, Christians should be prepared to study the issues and vote in both national and local elections. They should pray for their political leaders and inform them of their support for just policies that will both offer protection and care for the vulnerable. They should also see that these issues are raised in the media and in other forums where policies are debated.

Some Christians may also join political parties, contribute or volunteer in campaigns, run for office, or participate in rallies, protests, and other public actions.[11] As Richard Mouw observes, "Democratic government grants Christians the right publicly to criticize, review, debate, and challenge current procedures and policies. Under those conditions, the message of Romans 13 imposes on them the duty to make use of that right."[12]

What Is the Role of Government?

When considering a biblical view of government, many turn first to Romans 13, where Paul states that the "governing authorities" are God's servants to do and commend those who do good, and to terrorize and punish evildoers (Rom. 13:2–4). In fact, some commentators who favor a minimalist role for government focus their attention almost exclusively on this passage. Certainly having a government that actively promotes good and punishes evil will go a long way toward caring for the vulnerable.

This is true because the vulnerable both need and therefore require more than a neutral arbiter. Psalm 72 is another important biblical text on the role of government in caring for the vulnerable. In this passage the king is responsible to promote justice and righteousness, with a special focus on the poor and needy.

> He will defend the afflicted among the people
>   and save the children of the needy;
> he will crush the oppressor. . . .
>
> For he will deliver the needy who cry out,
>   the afflicted who have no one to help.
> He will take pity on the weak and the needy
>   and save the needy from death.
> He will rescue them from oppression and violence,
>   for precious is their blood in his sight.
>
> Psalm 72:4, 12–14 NIV

The active verbs used here—defend, save, crush, deliver, take pity, save, and rescue—convey something of the range of official action on behalf of the vulnerable that is contemplated. It is clear that the king was responsible not merely to create a level playing field, but to actually achieve justice for the poor and needy. It is assumed here that the suffering of the weak arises from the actions of violent oppressors.

The government has several responsibilities in caring for the vulnerable:

1. *Law.* Government is responsible to create a policy environment that will serve to protect the vulnerable by establishing enforceable standards and rights. Just laws serve to place limitations on the ability of the rich and powerful to oppress, abuse, exploit, or ignore the needs of their fellow citizens. In order for such laws to have their intended effect, proactive police alongside the judicial systems must be particularly responsive to the needs of the vulnerable.

2. *Security.* Government plays a critical role in protecting all its citizens, and especially the most vulnerable, both from outsiders and from each other. It deters aggressors with the threat of punishment. This power is certainly subject to abuse, even in a democracy, as history amply illustrates. It is nonetheless an essential role. One need only look at the plight of the modern "failed states," such as Somalia, to see what happens when government abdicates its security role. As more than one commentator has observed, the only thing worse than a brutal dictatorship is no government at all.

3. *Trade.* In our current globalized economy, trade policy represents one of the most profound levers for addressing economic vulnerability. Trade barriers can be used to protect domestic industries that would be vulnerable to foreign competition. However, in many cases protectionism is either futile or self-defeating. If trade liberalization does lead to the loss of jobs, the government can help by retraining workers for other industries.

The current terms of international trade are highly skewed in favor of first-world nations. In some cases, even the outsourcing of jobs to third-world countries does more to boost the U.S. economy than it does the third-world economy.[13]

Subsidies to first-world farmers depress agricultural commodities prices, enabling European and American farmers to sell their products at or below the cost of production, thus undercutting third-world competitors. Analysts estimate that elimination of first-world agricultural subsidies and tariffs would increase the incomes of third-world farmers by more than $40 billion per year.[14]

4. *Infrastructure.* Government is uniquely positioned to invest in roads, bridges, dams, and other expensive infrastructure whose benefits are widely diffused throughout society. It is often impractical for investors to recoup these costs through user fees. Private ownership or control of public goods also raises justice concerns. It is the responsibility of government to ensure that these investments are made equitably—for example, providing roads, schools, and health clinics in rural areas as well as in the cities. Government must also ensure that public works projects do not inadvertently leave some citizens more vulnerable than before. If a dam displaces poor farmers, they must be adequately compensated and resettled.

5. *Risk management.* In a market economy, individuals are able to protect themselves from many areas of vulnerability through the purchase of insurance products. Government provides an important service by regulating such products and requiring standards of fairness and transparency. There are, however, some areas in which market forces fail to offer adequate protection. In these cases the government must properly step in to create what is effectively a society-wide risk pool. Catastrophic health coverage and emergency relief following natural disasters would be obvious examples.

6. *Social safety net.* While families, churches, and local communities provide the first lines of defense against hunger, homelessness, and other forms of poverty, it is appropriate, and in the community's interest, to have a social safety net that protects citizens who fall on hard times and who would otherwise be without recourse. Vulnerable citizens should not be allowed to fall through the cracks. An appropriate publicly funded safety net enables all citizens to contribute to the care of the vulnerable. This need not be at odds with private charity. As Haddon Wilmer observes, "The state as systematic and extended love of neighbours is a form of the Good Samaritan. In the state, the Good Samaritan may be given a longer reach—the sign of God's love given something more of that which are characteristic of God in his heavenly fullness."[15]

The safety net should ensure first of all that those in need have access to lifesaving emergency food, shelter, and health care. Even the poorest country should do this. Prosperous countries will be able to do much more, including providing short-term cash and medical assistance to the unemployed and longer-term support for those whose disabilities prevent them from earning a living wage. All able-bodied adults should be required to work, or be actively preparing for work, as a condition of assistance. Experience has shown that government can achieve a more efficient and effective safety net by partnering with the private sector, including churches and other faith-based organizations.

7. *Education.* All children should be offered education as a basic right of life. First and foremost, parents are responsible before God for the education of their children. Parents, however, need the support of church and community, which have important roles to play in preparing children to be productive citizens who can provide for themselves, their families, and others in need. In this model, publicly supported schools should be available to all. They should complement, rather than compete with, private educational initiatives. Local ownership and control of schools is good, provided it does not lead to a system in which children are segregated by race and class.

Common Pitfalls Encountered in Caring for the Vulnerable

1. *Paternalism.* Well-meaning caregivers sometimes assume that the vulnerable can do nothing to defend themselves, thus robbing persons of the opportunity to help themselves. Beneficiaries sometimes adopt the same as-

sumption, particularly if it is reinforced over time. Caregivers may become overly prescriptive, believing that since they have the money and power, they have the right to dictate the terms of assistance to those they are serving.

2. *Entitlement mentality.* Government assistance can create a sense of entitlement. A sense of entitlement is good to a point, but this can lead to inappropriate utilization of benefits, and it can displace initiative. Why save to go to college if there are going to be plenty of scholarships and loans?

3. *Fraud.* Fraud occurs in businesses and in nonprofit organizations as well as in government programs. Fraud occurs when program administrators embezzle or misuse funds, as well as when ineligible beneficiaries collect benefits. The complicated policies surrounding many government benefits programs lead to many confusing and illogical situations in which clearly needy people are ineligible due to technicalities, whereas others are able to manipulate the rules to their advantage. This can, in turn, lead to disrespect for the rules and increased fraud.

Marketing fraud can occur in both church and nonprofit ministries, when well-intentioned fund-raisers exaggerate or misrepresent the need or virtue of their beneficiaries, or the impact of their interventions, with the aim of raising funds to extend their ministry. The inaccurate portrayal of beneficiaries as helpless victims sometimes inadvertently harms the beneficiaries by lowering either their self-esteem, if they have access to donor communications, or their standing in the community. Whatever the case, it is the vulnerable who will normally turn out to be the victims.

4. *Futility.* The magnitude of the need can sometimes overwhelm caregivers, who may feel that no amount of work on their part is going to end poverty and hunger, bring about world peace, or prevent the terminally ill from dying. This is true of taxpayers as well as volunteers. Such a realization has the potential to introduce certain important benefits by inducing an appropriate sense of humility; but if not handled prayerfully, it can also tend to immobilize and lead to cynicism.

5. *Displaced initiative.* The vulnerable may need help, but that does not mean that they are helpless. However, when help is given inappropriately, it can lead others to sit back and wait to be rescued, rather than doing what they can with their own resources. Getting it right both answers the objections to help being given and restores the dignity of those for whom such assistance is vital.

Areas of Consensus

Caring for the vulnerable requires a range of efforts including initiatives by the vulnerable themselves, personal sharing among neighbors, collective efforts by churches and associations, and actions by government at local, national, and international levels. There will inevitably be disagreements both about strategies and about the appropriate actors and modalities. However, there should not be too much difficulty in developing broad agreement among evangelicals on a number of principles:

1. *Responsibility.* Christians are responsible, both personally and collectively, for contributing to the care of the vulnerable, locally and globally, both through voluntary contributions and efforts and through advocacy for and tax support of appropriate government-sponsored initiatives.

2. *Dignity.* All people are created in God's image (Gen. 1:27). Christian care for the vulnerable must respect the dignity, freedom, and responsibility of those served. This means enabling the vulnerable wherever possible to care for and protect themselves and their neighbors. Where subsidies are required, vouchers or other systems that allow beneficiaries to select among alternative service providers provide the poor with the benefit and dignity of choice.

3. *Sustainability.* Where possible, sustainable, market-based solutions to poverty and vulnerability are preferable to those solutions that require continual subsidies, whether private or public. However, business cannot solve all social problems, and it sometimes creates other problems. A pragmatic approach is best.

4. *Faith-based initiatives.* Evangelicals have embraced the call for the creation of a level playing field where government agencies that contract with private service providers learn to give equal consideration to qualified faith-based organizations. Networks such as Christians for Faith-Based Initiatives have formed to promote greater evangelical participation in public-private partnerships to address social issues. While acceptance of government funding entails certain risks, there are many opportunities for churches and Christian organizations to harness public funds to scale up effective programs in order to help more people.

Policy Proposals

1. *Establish as a national goal the elimination of absolute poverty in the U.S.A.* History has clearly shown that disparities in relative wealth are unavoidable—whatever the governing ideology. However, in countries as prosperous as the United States, it should be possible—and therefore morally imperative—to work toward the goal that all people are enabled to enjoy:

   a. adequate food for a nutritious diet
   b. safe and decent shelter from the elements
   c. basic preventative and curative health care
   d. an education that can enable full participation in the community, both economically and culturally

There will inevitably be disagreements about methodologies and specific programs. Policies that offer flexibility and choice at the local level may appear to be generally preferable, so long as these do not prejudice the well-being of other communities. In most cases private production and distribution systems will be preferable to central planning models. It is certainly appropriate to require work, investment, and even sacrifice as a condition of benefits; entitlement without responsibility is a demonstrated recipe for social catastrophe.

However, the creation of opportunities for all people to access and provide for their basic needs must be among our highest priorities. And for those who are clearly unable to provide life necessities for themselves and their families, there must be an adequate safety net. In most cases this will be a temporary safety net designed to help individuals and communities get back on their feet. But provision must be made for assistance to the long-term sick, disabled, elderly, and others who are unable to survive on market-oriented mechanisms alone.

2. *Extend the same rights and protections to vulnerable immigrants and refugees as citizens.* Scripture is replete with injunctions to welcome and care for the stranger. While there were cultic restrictions on Gentile worship, social and legal benefits were nondiscriminatory: "When an alien [Hebrew *gerim*] lives with you in your land, do not mistreat him. The alien living with you must be treated as one of your native-born. Love him as yourself, for you were aliens in Egypt. I am the Lord your God" (Lev. 19:33–34 NIV). The Mosaic code makes no distinctions based on the legal status of the *gerim*. In fact, from the Israelite point of view, all of the *gerim* were "illegal," since the land had been promised to the Israelites by God. There are significant differences of opinion among Christians on immigration policy questions, but Christians should be united in sharing God's love and care for all *gerim*.

This commitment need not be an economic burden. There is substantial evidence that the relative openness of American society to refugees and immigrants has provided enormous benefit to the U.S. economy.[16]

3. *Integrate vulnerable individuals as fully as possible into the economic and cultural life of the community.* "Separate but equal" systems have been shown to be inherently unequal. Consideration should be given to the education of children with disabilities in regular schools and classrooms. Poor and rich children should where possible be educated together. To the extent consistent with sound treatment and public safety, the mentally ill should be treated and housed in the community, with appropriate supports, neither locked away in institutions nor dumped on our streets. Tax, finance, zoning, and other policies should encourage and incentivize mixed-income and ethnically diverse housing and education patterns, without creating rigid quota systems.

4. *Support the Millennium Development Goals, particularly the goal of achieving a 50 percent reduction in world poverty by 2015.*[17] A worldwide coalition of evangelicals coming together under the banner of the World Evangelical Alliance has launched the Micah Challenge, a bold attempt to hold the world's leaders accountable for their promises to address world poverty. Achieving this goal will require a well-orchestrated combination of aid, trade, and policy reforms. Relatively little has been done since these goals were announced in

2000. It will cost the rich countries of the world more to start now, playing catch up, than if we had taken the goals seriously in the beginning. But it will cost even more if we delay further. Recent commitments to a substantial new U.S. contribution to the fight against HIV/AIDS, and to major increases in development aid through the Millennium Challenge Account, are welcome steps in this direction. However, politicians are unlikely to find the courage to keep these commitments without widespread public pressure from concerned citizens. Further, the value of commitments to particular programs must be weighed against the trade-offs that are often made when one program is funded at the expense of another. For example, recent gains in HIV/AIDS funding have come at the expense of funding for child survival, refugees, and other key humanitarian assistance and development accounts. Churches should back these governmental initiatives while increasing their own contributions and outreach through private agencies. A particular focus should be made on efforts to work with and through the church in poor communities around the world.

Even more important than the level of international assistance is the question of trade. Poor countries must be granted more favorable access to first-world markets, while producers within poor countries must be protected from labor and environmental abuses.

The Roman Catholic Mass concludes with the words *"ite missa est,"* which could be crudely translated as "Get out." The meaning is obvious. We are dismissed to go out into the world of the AIDS sufferer, the refugee, the sick, the impoverished, and the dying. We are challenged to make a difference for the vulnerable, because that is, in reality, what Jesus would do!

Bibliography

Balswick, Jack O., and J. Kenneth Morland. *Social Problems.* Grand Rapids: Baker, 1990.

Beckman, David, and Arthur Simon. *Grace at the Table: Ending Hunger in God's World.* Downers Grove, IL: InterVarsity, 1999.

Beisner, E. Calvin. *Prosperity and Poverty: The Compassionate Use of Resources in a World of Scarcity.* Wheaton: Crossway Books, 1988.

Boerma, Conrad. *Rich Man, Poor Man—and the Bible.* London: SCM, 1979.

Cotterell, Peter. *Mission and Meaninglessness.* London: SPCK, 1990.

Donaldson, Dave, and Stanley Carlson-Thies. *A Revolution of Compassion: Faith-Based Groups as Full Partners in Fighting America's Social Problems.* Grand Rapids: Baker, 2003.

Driver, John, and Samuel Escobar. *Christian Mission and Social Justice.* Scottsdale, PA: Herald Press, 1978.

Elliot, Charles. *Comfortable Compassion?* London: Hodder & Stoughton, 1987.

Fung, Raymond. *The Isaiah Vision: An Ecumenical Strategy for Congregational Evangelism.* Geneva: WCC, 1992.

Gonzalez, Justo L. *Faith and Wealth.* San Francisco: Harper & Row, 1990.

Grand Rapids Report. *Evangelism and Social Responsibility: An Evangelical Commitment.* Exeter: Paternoster, 1982.

Griffiths, Brian. *The Creation of Wealth.* London: Hodder & Stoughton, 1984.

Harvey, A. E. *Strenuous Commands: The Ethics of Jesus.* London: SCM, 1990.

Long, W. Meredith. *Health, Healing and God's Kingdom: New Pathways to Christian Health Ministry in Africa.* Wheaton: Billy Graham Center, 1999.

Martin, David. *Tongues of Fire: The Explosion of Protestantism in Latin America.* Oxford: Blackwell Publishing, 1993.

Moberg, David A. *The Great Reversal.* London: Scripture Union, 1973.

Mott, Stephen Charles. *A Christian Perspective on Political Thought.* New York: Oxford University Press, 1993.

Myers, Bryant. *Walking with the Poor: Principles and Practice of Transformational Development.* Maryknoll, NY: Orbis Books, 1999.

Pleins, J. David. *The Social Visions of the Hebrew Bible.* Louisville: Westminster John Knox Press, 2001.

Samuel, Vinay, and Chris Sugden. *Evangelism and the Poor.* Oxford: Oxford Centre for Mission Studies, 1983.

Sheppard, David. *Bias to the Poor.* London: Hodder & Stoughton, 1983.

Sider, Ronald. *Rich Christians in an Age of Hunger.* 5th ed. Nashville: Word, 2005.

Sider, Ronald, et al. *Just Generosity: A New Vision for Overcoming Poverty in America.* Grand Rapids: Baker, 1999.

Stott, John R. W. *Decisive Issues Facing Christians Today.* London: Marshall Pickering, 1984.

Tamez, Elsa. *Bible of the Oppressed.* Maryknoll, NY: Orbis Books, 1982.

Wallis, Jim. *Agenda for Biblical People.* London: SPCK, 1986.

———. *The Call to Conversion.* San Francisco: Harper, 1992.

Wilmer, Haddon. "Toward a Theology of the State." In *Essays in Evangelical Social Ethics,* edited by David F. Wright. Wilton, CT: Morehouse-Barlow, 1979.

Wood, Chester E. *With Justice for All: The Task of the People of God: A Biblical Theology.* Nairobi: Nairobi Evangelical Graduate School of Theology, 2001.

Woolffe, John, ed., *Evangelical Faith and Public Zeal.* London: SPCK, 1995.

Wright, Christopher J. H. *Living as the People of God.* Leicester: Inter-Varsity, 1983.

Yoder, Perry. *Shalom: The Bible's Word for Salvation, Justice and Peace.* Nappannee, IN: Evangel Publishers, 1987.

12

Family Integrity

Tom Minnery and Glenn T. Stanton

It was the best of times, it was the worst of times, it was the age of wisdom, it was the age of foolishness, it was the epoch of belief, it was the epoch of incredulity, it was the season of Light, it was the season of Darkness, it was the spring of hope, it was the winter of despair, we had everything before us, we had nothing before us, we were all going direct to Heaven, we were all going direct the other way . . .

Charles Dickens, *A Tale of Two Cities*

THESE BEAUTIFULLY INCONGRUOUS words, which Dickens chose to describe the spirit of the age of the French Revolution, are the same words we could use to describe the spirit of the age regarding family in our current day. They speak of being in two contradictory conditions at the same time. For as we experience the decades bridging the end of the twentieth to the beginning of the twenty-first century, we observe that it is a time of great despair while also a time of great hopefulness. There is much to be encouraged about. There is much cause for great concern.

There has never been a golden age of family. Each generation is plagued with its own problems and bears the fruit of the fall. However, some generations have done family better than others. Our generation has not been one of them. The changes in family in the West (and developing in the East) over

245

the past four decades have been unprecedented in world history. The forms that have experienced substantial growth in recent decades are those marked by the failure of marriage, evidenced by the sharply rising divorce, remarriage, and stepparenting rates. (Fortunately, the divorce rate has leveled of late.) But we are seeing the greatest increase in families that simply forgo marriage, opting instead for cohabitation (currently our fastest growing family form) and single, never married parenthood (also our fastest growing form of single parent family)[1] (Popenoe and Whitehead 2003).

And now our nation is being engaged in a debate on the proper definition of marriage by same-sex marriage advocates who assert that fairness requires we redefine marriage to be something it has never been in any other human civilization: a moldable union between any coupling of consenting adults, regardless of gender, driven by adult desire rather than an obligation to the next generation. (And it is curious that for all the great social justice theorists from whom our world has benefited, none of them has ever hinted that marriage being confined to opposite-sex coupling was a hindrance to human equality. The question has only been raised in the last millisecond of human history by a very small handful of advocates.)

Likewise, making socially and personally ambiguous cohabiting relationships equal with marriage enjoys growing support by some important and influential legal advocates. Both the American Law Institute in its recent *Principles of the Law of Family Dissolution* as well as the Law Commission of Canada's 2001 report, *Beyond Conjugality: Recognizing and Supporting Close Personal Relationships*, advocate elevating all close personal relationships to the legal status of marriage, and as a result, eliminating marriage as the primary important domestic configuration. Leading legal theorists at prestigious universities advocate the same. Professor Nancy Polikoff encourages gay and lesbian advocates to work toward "abolishing the legal status of marriage for everyone" (Polikoff 2003). Writing in the *Family Law Quarterly*, Harry Krause says marriage "should be seen for what it has become: one lifestyle choice among many." Thus, "married and unmarried couples who are in the same factual position should be treated alike" (Krause 2000, 272, 300). There are many more who strongly advocate marriage's legal abolition (Stanton and Maier 2004, 157–68; Kurtz 2003, 26).

All of this is the result of a slow dismantling of family, and we should remember that no society has ever been able to sustain itself with a buffet-like "pick what appeals to you" mentality of family life. Strict family norms serve the needs of all societies.

Likewise, the family consisting of a husband and wife faithfully committed to their marriage for life and raising their own biological or adopted children has fallen on hard times. This form has been in sharp decline. The late Professor Lawrence Stone, a distinguished family historian from Princeton University, lamented, "The scale of marital breakdown in the West since 1960 has no historical precedent that I know of. There has been nothing like it for the last

2,000 years, and probably longer" (Stone 1989). Rutgers sociologist David Popenoe interprets the current state of family this way:

> If the family trends of recent decades are extended into the future, the result will be not only growing uncertainty within marriage, but also the gradual elimination of marriage in favor of casual liaisons oriented to adult expressiveness and self-fulfillment. The problem with this scenario is that children will be harmed, adults will probably be no happier and the social order could collapse. (Popenoe 1996, 248)

A substantial and reliable body of new research (a product of scientists observing this massive social change over decades) is telling us these changes *have* been harmful for adults and children in many unexpected and profound ways. Researchers are finding that when we move away from the family ideal where male and female commit themselves to each other exclusively in marriage and cooperatively raise their common children, men, women, and children suffer substantial declines in every important measure of well-being: mental and physical health, shorter life spans, lowered educational performance and attainment, increases in criminal and antisocial behavior, greater sexual dysfunction, alcoholism, suicide, domestic violence, and sexual abuse. Christ's command to love our neighbors will not allow us to tolerate family relativism.

By these measures, the family is in the worst of times, the season of Darkness, the winter of despair.

But the family is not without signs of hope and good news. The family has never enjoyed more positive, deliberate attention and resources focused on improving its health than it does today. The number of titles on building or repairing familial relationships between spouses and parents and children continues to grow every month, even as bookstore sections that house them have changed in name from "Marriage and Family" to the more generic and inclusive "Relationships" (Blankenhorn 2001, 4–5). The number of organizations that operate with the sole purpose of strengthening family relationships has mushroomed over the past fifteen years and are like Abraham's descendants, for it seems impossible to count their numbers.[2] Certainly, this explosive growth is initiated by the rising concern over the future and health of the nuclear family and the larger society. The sheer energy of so many organizations, working from the fields of academia, mental health, faith, and public policy, focused on improving basic family relationships is a very encouraging sign. But it is ironic that family is declining like never before at the very moment our knowledge of how to make it work has never been more extensive and widely available.

Couple this with the attitudes and actions of young people regarding family. Unlike their parents who rebelled against the family values of the '50s, they are rebelling against the family instability of the '70s and '80s. They are rebelling not exclusively out of moral conviction, but from their raw experience. They were the first generation to be largely denied a settled, intact family setting. As one young woman recalls her childhood, "Ronald Reagan was around a lot longer than some of my friend's fathers" (Howe and Strauss 1993, 53). This absence has created a deep desire for something different for themselves and their families. Claire Raines, coauthor of *Twentysomethings: Managing and Motivating Today's New Work Force*, explains, "Generations are motivated by what they are deprived of when they were kids, and for this generation, that was time with their parents" (Krueger 1994, 62). Just as the children of the Depression era created one of the greatest economic revolutions, largely as a reaction to their financially impoverished childhood, today's children of divorce could well create a new family revolution as a response to their childhood experience.

There are indicators that this generation *is* doing things differently. For the first time since the '60s, the birthrate is increasing to almost replacement level and the divorce rate is slowing. The rate of young people engaging in sexual activity before marriage is decreasing by some measures. College-educated young women are increasingly choosing homemaking as their primary career, and twentysomethings are valuing marriage as more important to a happy life than their parents did. A large study of emerging family trends found that 96 percent of young people entering adulthood today plan to marry and that 90 percent plan to have an average of three children, marking a significant increase over their parents' attitudes and expectations (Stanton 1999, 8). Research conducted at the University of Pennsylvania found that women graduates today are marrying sooner then those in the '70s did (Stanton 1999, 8). One college student admits that her attitude for a more stable future family sounds counterrevolutionary, if not downright traditional: "It's kind of a '50s mentality, but it's what feels natural, normal and rational for us." A young man communicates a similar life goal, "A happy marriage with a lifetime commitment and no divorce is the most important thing." Among all age groups, a happy family founded on lifelong marriage is listed as one of the most important goals for 93 percent of Americans (Waite and Gallagher 2000, 2–3).

With the improving attitudes of young people toward marriage and family and an arsenal of smart and helpful resources for helping them build those relationships, the future of the family looks brighter than it has in many decades. What is more, the wealth of very good research coming to press in the past fifteen years shows us that lifelong marriage and intentional, involved parenting are rich personal and social goods.[3] These interesting and changing attitudes among young adults provide the church with a powerful opportunity to encourage young people that their desires are good and attainable and to provide them help and resources for making their families and faithful, lifelong marriage work. By these measures, it is the best of times, the season of Light, the spring of hope for family.

Establishing Ideals and Motivation

In the midst of these simultaneously discouraging and hopeful changes in the family and as we seek to influence them through political and cultural engagement, it is important that we do this from the proper foundation. We must have ideals that motivate and keep us focused on the most important things.

We must ask ourselves:

- Why does the family matter?
- What is the essential nature of family?

Together, these two questions inform a third, which is the interest of this work:

- What is the family's relationship to the state and public life?

These questions help us understand what we are working *from* and working *for*.

As evangelicals, we are interested in answering these questions from an important and unique perspective. Before we discuss what this perspective is, let us make sure we are clear on what it is *not*. We are not interested in answering these questions from purely pragmatic reasons, although we believe the answers do lead to the best possible outcome for people in daily life, which love of neighbor demands we be concerned with. The reasons are larger than simply that they work, for they work because of larger realities.

Nor are we interested in answering these questions by faithfully occupying any of the various positions represented on the current culture war spectrum. While we may identify with particular points in this spectrum, Christianity should transcend and be qualitatively distinguishable from these dichotomies. As we are observed in our work, let people appraise us as good Christ-ones, rather than good liberals, conservatives, or moderates, for Christ calls us to so much more than what these programs represent and offer.

Nor are we only interested in upholding some sort of cultural traditionalism or progressiveness. Certainly the life God gives us is localized and played out in a particular culture that, by experience, we either grow to appreciate and view as normative or become dissatisfied with and react against. However, Christians are concerned with distinguishing between the transcendent rule of Christ and the cultural particulars that seem right or wrong to us by experience and tradition. Yes, our own culture will always shape our behaviors because it is what we know. However, it should never rule them.

Instead, we are interested in answering these questions in the light of a larger metanarrative, that of the historic Christian tradition, given to us in the sacred

Scriptures. This story contains important points that help us understand how the family reflects the very nature of God. Let us begin by addressing the first question.

Why Does the Family Matter? A Theology of Family

The first two parts of the story are what Christians share in common with their Jewish neighbors: *creation* and *covenant*.

Creation illuminates our understanding of why family is significant in the Christian story. It tells us something very profound about the nature of God and the nature of humanity, what we were created *out of* and what we were created *for*. Genesis 2:18 explains that God said something very curious: "Then the Lord God said, 'It is not good for the man to be alone . . .'" (NASB).

As God looked out over his perfect creation, with which he was very pleased, he saw one thing that was not as it was intended to be. It was not good for man to be alone. The superspiritual among us might have replied, "But God, I have everything I need, which is perfect communion with you! I need nothing else." The secularist might answer, "I have no need of God. I just need myself and others!" But God says that all of us need him as our Creator and we have all been designed in such a way that we need others. But why do we need others, and what *kind* of "other"?

We find the answer to this important question in Genesis 1:26–27 where we read about man's creation: "Then God said, 'Let Us make man in Our image, according to Our likeness . . .' God created man in His own image, in the image of God He created him; male and female He created them" (NASB).

It was not good for man to be alone, because he was not created to be alone. The historical Christian tradition teaches that humanity was created in the image of the Trinitarian God who is relational by his very essence. He is not solitary. He is community, marked by warm intimacy and passionate love. The core of the universe and all reality is Father, Son, and Holy Spirit, simply and eternally existing together, loving and glorying in each other (John 17:5, 24). The primary characteristics of this eternal and primary community of persons are what humanity is created *out of* and created *for*. These qualities, among many, are love, intimacy, community, cooperative creativity, communication, relational exclusivity, and permanence. These same qualities describe family life.

And God did not just give Adam another guy to hang out, work, and fish with. He gave Adam someone who was *like* him in his image-bearing humanity, but *unlike* him in her co-image-reflecting femininity. God established humanity and human culture upon marriage—the sexual, emotional, and domestic union of male and female—and family—the bringing forth of new life through sexual union and cooperative parenting. And we should also recognize here that in these verses God has declared the strongest and most important statement about gender equality known to humanity, for male and female together reflect the very image of God, and they cannot do this fully in isolation from one another. This is why it was not good that Adam was alone.

Therefore, marriage and family are inherently trinitarian. For it is the closest earthly model we have of this eternal heavenly reality. Man and woman, though separate beings both representing their unique parts of humanity, are joined together before God and become one flesh. Their relationship, in the ideal, is of love, intimacy, creativity and procreation, communication, exclusiveness, and permanence. They are a mystery, uniquely proclaiming the nature of God and his character in creation.

Perhaps this is what makes family life so paradoxical and rich. It is joyous at times and exceedingly difficult at others. That is because we are participating in something so grand, so eternal, and so primary and powerful that we cannot control it or even fully comprehend it (Stanton 2004). In its grand holiness and representational nature, it is bitterly hated by the Evil One who despises it and seeks its demise. But we must treasure it for what it is and be faithful to it.

Given all this, we cannot understand the wonder of the Christian story without understanding the mystery of family. And we cannot understand the wonder of family without understanding the mystery of the Christian story and the nature of the personal Trinitarian God who is there.

It is from this understanding that we should move out in public life and advocate for the family. We should not be motivated out of an allegiance to some moral or traditional code, for to be so motivated is to settle for something too small. Our motivation is found in something much larger. To fail to care for the family is, in a very real way, to fail to care for the very image of God on earth.

In understanding the significance of family, consider also the covenant God made with his people, Israel, through Abraham. In Genesis 17:5–7 (NASB), God says to Abram:

> No longer shall your name be called Abram,
> But your name shall be Abraham;
> For I will make you the father of a multitude of nations.
> I will make you exceedingly fruitful, and I will make nations of you, and kings will come forth from you. I will establish My covenant between Me and you and your descendants after you throughout their generations for an everlasting covenant, to be God to you and to your descendants after you.

When God promises to make a great nation from Abram and this promise is actualized, it is not the way nations are usually founded, through political power, or ideological or economic influence. Abraham did not amass a following by being powerful or persuasive, but by simply being a progenitor. He did it through family, and he is remembered by the ages as Father Abraham. God established his people, not by converts, but by family.

We are also reminded of the importance of family as we consider biblical language about God. Christian tradition has historically understood that God reveals himself to us as Father and this means something. It has not been an inducement to harsh patriarchy, but instead a correction against it. It has enriched family life and culture. God the Father, Abba, unconditionally loves and cares for his children. He is the role model for good fathering. Theologian Dianne Tennis, in her book *Is God the Only Reliable Father?* explains the benefits of God's model as father:

> Holding on to that reliable Father God can be a way of informing and challenging the status quo. For human fathers are experienced as unreliable. . . . By contrast, God as Father does not abandon. If God the Father is reliable, he surely expects reliability of earthly fathers. And therefore, so can we! A reliable Father God is a source of calling men into fathering. A reliable Father God is a source of judgment on unreliable sexual arrangements, a source of hope for women and for the fatherless, a symbol emerging out of our loss . . ." (Tennis 1985, 9)

Jurgen Moltmann adds,

> [Culturally and historically], where God as Father was emphasized, the Christian patriarchy arose, that is, paternalism tempered by compassion and love from above. Where the compassion and unconditional love were taken as the beginning, there existed a fundamental critique of the domination of father. . . . Those who set their bearings on Jesus and call out "Abba" with him have broken with law and the power systems of patriarchy. (Moltmann 1990, 3–25)

But Christians also recognize the Second Person of the Trinity, Christ, as the Son of the Father. The Holy Spirit's presence in our lives in love, correction, wooing, forgiving, and empowering us in lives of love and justice are gracious parental qualities. The imagery of family continues.

Biblical language about the kingdom of God continues the language of family. We enter the kingdom of God, as Jesus explained to Nicodemus, by being "born again." This curious phrase caused Jesus' questioner to ask how a man can enter his mother's womb a second time. Christians enter the family of God, not as direct, natural descendants of Abraham, but as adopted children, according to God's grace via this second birth. The great culmination of the kingdom of God, the parousia, will be experienced as the great wedding feast when the bride of Christ, the church, will be wed to the Bridegroom, who is Christ. The kingdom of God is powerfully and vividly communicated through and understood by the language of family.

Consider also that Christians, since their faith's founding, have intimately referred to other believers worldwide as brothers and sisters. And Paul explains that the defining mark of a Christian is not holiness, charisma, knowledge, or sacrifice. It is love, the primary component of family life and the principal quality of God.

It is not insignificant that God chose to communicate the reality and wonder of his project with humanity largely through the language of family. While Scripture uses the language of politics (the kingdom of God), commerce (tenders of the Garden), medicine (Christ is the Great Physician), and other things, the primary language of the kingdom of God is the language of family. And this language and imagery is not chosen for dramatic effect, for how it could entice people. It was chosen because it corresponds, beautifully communicating the truth about his nature and his relationship with humanity. Again, we will explore more on this point in a moment.

The Incarnation and Family

When thinking about the importance of family in Christian perspective, we must also consider what C. S. Lewis called "the central event in the history of the Earth—the very thing the whole story has been about" (Lewis 1960, 108). This is God's incarnation in Christ Jesus. At Christmas, we celebrate the birth of the Christ child, and the story is very familiar. God entered our realm, as the Savior of creation, through a common woman and a simple carpenter who were obediently reporting from Nazareth to Bethlehem to participate in the census. God entered our realm at the intersection of a common family doing the mundane things families have to do. This is very profound.

Of all the grand and glorious options at God's disposal, he chose to do the most wonderful thing in a seemingly ordinary way. The Christmas manger is an earthly trinity: a man, a woman, and a child. This family is the stage through which God transcended eternity and entered our realm. This is deeply significant, for it is an incredible stamp of approval upon the whole family enterprise: the relationships, the work, the struggles, the hardship, the love, and the comfort of family. God is telling us in a very powerful way that there is something here that matters. In our wrestling with this truth, we will never fully be able to comprehend the richness of it.

Also, think about the life of Christ as he grew. He remained in his family as a son throughout his short life. He learned a trade from his father and worked at it diligently, and it provided his living. He remained close to his mother and cared for her until his last day, even from the cross asking John, his beloved friend, to care for her. This is one of the many ways Christ stands in stark contrast to the founders of other world religions who forsook their families as a sign of spiritual enlightenment in favor of an ascetic life.

At Christian weddings, we are often reminded by the minister that Christ's first public miracle was performed at a wedding (that he was attending with his mother!). This fact is shared as an encouragement to the couple and their celebrants that Christ was recognizing the special celebration that a wedding is. Christ entered our world through family, he valued his own family, and he celebrated the joys of marriage and family.

All in all, family is central in God's interaction with humanity. It is the crown of God's creation, it has a primary place in the establishment of God's people (Abraham is blessed through a large family), it is central in the first coming of Christ (God enters humanity as an infant through an engaged couple), and it is central in Christ's second coming and our reunion with him (the marriage feast of the Lamb). You cannot understand or explain Christianity or the kingdom of God without understanding family.

The Essential Nature of Family

But what are the qualities of family that are inherent to the Christian picture and universal to humanity? As we engage the culture regarding the family, we must have some ideals to guide us. Fixing these in our minds helps us know we are working on the most important goals and not being distracted by lesser things. For as the motivational speakers would tell us, "If you don't know where you are going, everything becomes an interesting destination." There seem to be three primary qualities to the Christian ideal that should hold our focus.

Marriage

And He answered and said, "Have you not read that He who created them from the beginning made them male and female, and said, 'For this reason a man will leave his father and mother and be joined to his wife, and the two shall become one flesh'? So they are no longer two, but one flesh. What therefore God has joined together, let no man separate."

Matthew 19:4–6 NASB

For the Christian, the foundation of a family is marriage, demonstrated in a lifelong, committed relationship between a man and a woman whom God joins together and makes one flesh. Husband and wife mutually and selflessly love, respect, and serve one another before all others. God's ideal in marriage is the great cultural equalizer between men and women, both being created in the very image of God. All the other aspects of family life ideally flow from this relationship.

Sexuality

. . . and they shall become one flesh. And the man and his wife were both naked and were not ashamed.

Genesis 2:24–25 NASB

This is both a physical and spiritual activity and bond that should be, in the ideal, expressed in self-giving love, warmth, intimacy, passion, exclusivity, faithfulness, and the creation of new life. The commitment and protection of marriage are its proper context. When practiced outside of this context, it is something much less than it was intended to be. It is something else altogether. Much more than a mere physical act, the sexual union is a mystery, an earthly picture of that heavenly intimacy and communion the persons of the Trinity share from eternity.

Parenthood

God blessed them; and God said to them, "Be fruitful and multiply, and fill the earth, and subdue it . . ."

Genesis 1:28 NASB

In the ideal, the bringing of children into the family by procreation or adoption extends the love and mystery of the marriage into the world and into the next generation. Father and mother both have unique and necessary roles in raising these mutual children into their full humanity.[4] Both parents should engage in the task as a team with loving intention, providing for the physical, emotional, intellectual, social, and spiritual development of the child.

And while there is diversity to marriage and family in various human cultures, there is also great uniformity. Anthropologists tell us marriage is common to and essential in all human societies in the form of permanent, socially approved male/female pair bonding. Marriage is also ideally and universally, through various social pressures, prior to childbearing. Of course marriage is sometimes polygamous, but all cultures encourage and demand permanent unions between men and woman in order to regulate sexuality (both socially and religiously) and ensure that mothers and fathers care and provide for the resultant offspring together. No societies—advanced or primitive—until very recently, have tolerated casual sexual or domestic liaisons or same-sex domestic pair bonding.[5]

Areas of Harmony and Disagreement

There are many aspects of the family and family life that evangelicals might disagree on among themselves and with other Christians. Issues such as birth control, family size, headship and submission, corporal punishment, manner of education, and which parents should work outside the home and when are some. These are important issues, and we should endeavor to seek God's heart and mind on them in light of his sacred Word.

But as good Christians, we can debate these important issues and still love and please God. However, the above three qualities—marriage, sexuality, and parenthood—are primary and essential and should be valued as nonnegotiables in our thinking on the health and integrity of the family; for to dismiss or renegotiate one of them is to remove a necessary leg of the stool of family life. These foundational Christian family values make clear the real-world practices that Christians should universally oppose. All Christians should resist, in terms of public policy and cultural engagement:

- Affirming easy divorce, same-sex marriage and parenting (which rejects the image of God in humanity by rejecting the necessity of male and female coupling), or transforming marriage into merely a self-satisfying adult relationship.
- Policies, like tax codes or employment benefits, that either penalize the married mother-father-child triad or those that elevate other lesser domestic relationships to equal status with marriage by virtue of benefits offered. This would include both hetero- and homosexual civil unions.
- Accepting other domestic situations—cohabitation and single parenting by choice—as normal or tolerable parts of community family life.
- Policies that tend to normalize the great social divorce between human sexuality and the emotionally and physically protective confines of marriage.
- Affirming situations in which children are abandoned or separated from their biological mothers and fathers due to divorce, same-sex parenting, or unwed childbearing.
- The move by some leading family law theorists, along with the American Law Institute, seeking to remove all legal marriage and family categories in favor of recognizing all close personal domestic relationships equally.

Additionally, all Christians should support efforts that:

- Strengthen healthy, cooperative marital unions of mutual respect where husband and wife are seeking to serve the other in love and grace.
- Help young people and adults make healthy choices by confining sexuality to marriage where couples have committed exclusively to each other, physically, spiritually, and emotionally.
- Help parents lovingly and creatively raise their children together to grow to become healthy, well-adjusted, confident, intelligent, creative human beings.
- Help families and the individuals in them learn to love and serve God and others in the fullness of domestic and public life.

Given these essentials of family life, our work should center on making sure we are caring for these ideals. There is a positive and negative side to this work. The *positive* is to make sure these ideals are growing stronger and healthier in each coming generation. We should work to assure that each generation possesses the ideals, habits, and attitudes needed to keep them strong. The *negative* work is to protect these ideals from ideas, attitudes, and policies that threaten their integrity and well-being. Both postures are vital. To focus on only one to the exclusion of the other fails to recognize that we live in a fallen world where, if something is not threatened by outright challenge, it may be threatened by shortsightedness or neglect.

Our job is to serve as good stewards of these ideals and help the next generation become good stewards of them as well, protecting them from deliberate attack from without as well as careless neglect from within.

The Relationship between the Family and the *Polis*

Given our understanding of the essential nature of the family and why it matters, we now move to the question of the family's relationship to the state and vice versa. We encounter this question from the beginning of Western political philosophy with Plato and Aristotle offering foundational but differing opinions on the question.

In Plato's *Republic*, the relationship between family and state is simple: The family exists for the state. For the sake of the Republic, "all these women shall be wives in common for all these men. That none of them shall live as individuals with any of the men. That children in turn shall belong to all of them. That no parent shall know its own child, no child its own parent" (Plato trans. 2000, Book 5, 457d).

Regarding this relationship, Plato wonders, "I don't imagine there could be any disagreement about its utility. No one would deny that if it is possible, having wives in common and children in common is a major benefit" (Plato trans. 2000, Book 5, 457d). Frederick Copleston, in his discussion of Plato, forcefully explains there is at least one group who would raise objection to this ideal.

> Plato's proposals in this matter are abhorrent to all true Christians. His intentions were, of course, excellent, for he desired the greatest possible improvement of the human race; but his good intentions led him to . . . proposals . . . which are necessarily unacceptable and repugnant to all those who adhere to Christian principles concerning the value of the human personality and the sanctity of human life. . . . In the case of the human race, it does not follow that the Government has the right to apply such measures. Those who today follow, or would like to follow, in the footsteps of Plato . . . have not, be it remembered, Plato's excuse, that he lived at a period anterior to the presentation of the Christian ideals and principles. (Copleston 1962, 256–57)

The other foundational Western political thinker, Aristotle, takes a different view on the nature and essence of family and its relation to the state. In his *Politics*, there are two primary associations that are the foundation of the society. One is domestic: the coming together of male and female in marriage. The other is largely economic and municipal: the union of slave and master (Aristotle trans. 1941, Book 1, Chapter 2).

Even though the family is the most basic element of the community, it is not primary. Neither the individual nor the family, by itself, can attain the good life. For Aristotle, the family requires the participation of the state for health and vitality. On this Plato and Aristotle agree.

But Aristotle rejects Plato's Communist revisions to the family for the sake of the state, not out of any ideal of the sacredness of family, but because holding such things in common does not correspond with the motions of the human heart. Plato and Aristotle are the best representatives of the classical understanding of the relationship between family and state. It wasn't until Christian ideals came to influence society, as Copleston explained, that the family was seen as a thing in itself to be valued, rather than a utility of the state.

Let us move to an evangelical Christian understanding of the family's relation to the state as demonstrated in Abraham Kuyper. In his Stone Lectures of 1898 at Princeton University, Kuyper endeavored to apply the theological thinking of Calvin to the various spheres of life. The third of his six lectures, entitled "Calvinism and Politics," discusses the primary parts or spheres of the human community, their relation to one another, and their relation to God: the Sovereignty of the State, the Sovereignty of Society, and the Sovereignty of the Church. Each of these is sovereign, over and against the others, but subordinate to a greater Authority. This is so because they each "eradiate" from the primordial "Sovereignty of the Triune God over the whole Cosmos, in all its spheres and kingdoms, visible and invisible" (Kuyper 1931, 79).

Kuyper agrees with Aristotle that man is a political animal, a *zoon politikon*, and that the state is an intrinsic and natural good. However, he believes this in a different way for different reasons, for Kuyper's view is rooted in a creation anthropology. The impulse to participate in a state arises from man's social nature given to him, before the fall, at creation. This is rooted in humanity's Adamic origin, being "one humanity" of "one blood" (Kuyper 1931, 79) created as a reflection of that primary society of Father, Son, and Holy Spirit. As a consequent, humanity is made for community and will naturally seek it out. As such, a state did not arise solely because sin came into the world as "a disintegrating force" (Kuyper 1931, 79). If sin had not tainted creation, Kuyper asserts, a "political life, in its entirety would have evolved itself, after a patriarchal fashion, from the life of the family" (Kuyper 1931, 80). With or without sin's effect on the world, we would have a state because it was given to humanity to subdue and rule the creation. The fall did not initiate the question of whether we would have a state, but instead, what kind and to what end. But we have the fall and we have a state that exists as a consequence of the fall.

Given the reality of the disintegrating force of the fall, let us go on to look at Kuyper's thought on the nature of the state as it developed and its relation to the family. Whereas Plato and Aristotle saw the state as deeply primary, Kuyper takes another view altogether. He would have us understand, as highest importance, the difference in the *organic life* of society (where family is the primary component) and the *mechanical character* of the government in a fallen world. He explains,

> Whatever among men originates directly from creation is possessed of all the data for its development, in human nature as such. You see this at once in the family and in the connection of blood relations and other ties. From the duality of man and woman marriage arises. From the original existence of one man and one woman monogamy comes forth. The children exist by reason of the innate power of reproduction; naturally the children are connected as brother and sister. And by and by these children, in their turn, marry again, as a matter of course, all those connections originate from blood-relationships and other ties, which dominate the whole family-life. In all this, there is nothing mechanical. . . . for the vast majority of our race, marriage remains the foundation of human society and the family retains its position as the primordial sphere of sociology. (Kuyper 1931, 91)

The family is organic in its nature. It is a basic part of creation and the most basic part of human culture, existing before the fall, straight from the mouth of God, and therefore intrinsic to our basic design. As such, its basic nature, as discussed above, has seen little and short-lived variation in the history and diversity of human culture. "But the case is wholly different," according to Kuyper, "with the assertion of the powers of government." He explains,

> For though it be admitted that even without sin the need would have asserted itself of combining many families in higher unity, this unity would have internally been bound up in the Kingship of God, which would have ruled regularly, directly and harmoniously in the hearts of all men, and which would have externally incorporated itself in a patriarchal hierarchy. Thus no States would have existed, but only one organic world-empire, with God as its King: exactly what is prophesied for the future which awaits us, when all sin shall have disappeared. (Kuyper 1931, 92)

But this is not the case. Sin and its consequence in the creation necessitate a different kind of state. For out of humanity's natural desire for unity, Babel's tower was built and various peoples and nations were originated.

> These people formed States. And over these States God appointed *governments*. And thus, if I may be allowed the expression, it is not a natural head, which organically grew from the body of the people, but a *mechanical* head, which from without has been placed upon the trunk of the nation. A mere remedy, therefore, for a wrong condition supervening. A stick placed beside the plant to hold it up, since without it, by reason of its inherent weakness, it would fall to the ground. (Kuyper 1931, 92–93)

The state, therefore, is God ordained, but as a mechanical device to protect and serve the organic spheres such as family. Therefore, the family cannot be coerced to change according to the grace and will of the government as Plato proposed (and Aristotle too, no doubt, had he believed it best). For the organic cannot be directed by the mechanical. The mechanical exists as God's servant to protect and nurture the organic, as a stick placed by the gardener beside the trunk of the tree to hold it up.

But, Kuyper informs us, this does not mean the family is wholly autonomous from the state. The state must intervene in family matters when, but only when, (1) the social spheres, such as family, art, science, agriculture, industry, or commerce transgress their own boundary lines and infringe upon the others; (2) it is necessary to defend the weak ones in these spheres against the abuse of power of the strong, as in the case of domestic violence or child labor abuses; (3) we must encourage all to collectively bear the personal and financial burdens for the maintenance of the natural unity of the state (Kuyper 1931, 97). Kuyper contends that love of neighbor doesn't allow us a libertarian luxury.

Althusius and the Natural Origin of Community

Another thinker, much underappreciated, who has done some important work on the relationship between family and state is a German scholar of civil and ecclesiastical law, Johannes Althusius (1557–1638). His major work, *Politica*, was the first presentation of a comprehensive theory of federal republicanism working from a theological, covenantal view of society, making it worth a brief mention. It was first published in 1603.

Althusius, like Kuyper, agrees with Aristotle that man is political by nature, for he is designed to be so. "Politics is," he explains, "the art of associating men for the purpose of establishing, cultivating, and conserving social life among them." The end of political man is a "holy, just, comfortable, and happy symbiosis, a life lacking nothing either necessary or useful" (Althusius trans. 1995, 17).

We see this truth clearly in God's first anthropological appraisal of man, "It is not good for man to be alone." While alone, man does not fully bear the image of the Trinitarian God, and therefore he cannot accomplish the work God has given him to do. Of individuals, Althusius asks, "How can they perform the works of love [which they are created for and commanded to] when they live outside of human fellowship?" (Althusius trans. 1995, 23). As Augustine reminds us, those who rule "serve those whom they seem to command; for they rule not from love of power, but from a sense of duty they owe to others—not because they are proud of authority, but because they love mercy" (Augustine trans. 1950, Book XIX, 14).

The most basic and primary relationship of the community is the domestic. When considering the other private and public associations that make up the *polis*, Althusius tells us that "knowledge of other associations is . . . incomplete and defective without this doctrine of conjugal and kinship associations, and cannot be rightly understood without it" (Althusius trans. 1995, 31). Like spokes in a wheel, the rest of the *polis* radiates from the primary association of husband, wife, and children. The public associations grow out of this and therefore should seek to preserve the source. As Kuyper would say, the mechanical always serves the natural. This idea is found in Althusius, in that the rulers have the duty not only to leave that which is primary and natural unharmed, but to help lead and develop it to its proper end (Althusius trans. 1995, 21).

Conclusion

The state has a duty to care for the family, for the family is prior to the state. Whereas the U.S. Supreme Court less than thirty years ago recognized that marriage transcends law and the state, being a "sacred" institution "older than the Bill of Rights" (*Griswold* 1965), in late 2003 Massachusetts's Supreme Judicial Court declared civil marriage a mere *creation* of the state (*Goodridge* 2003). And if marriage is a mere creation, then it is subservient to and pliable by the state as in Plato's *Republic*.

Our society has been reshaping marriage and the family into oblivion. Nearly all of this reshaping is measurably harmful to society and human well-being, and thus something all faithful Christians should oppose. So how do we prophetically and redemptively challenge this change? What is more, how do we do this in an increasingly pluralistic society?

First is to realize that Christ has called us to engage the culture. It is a sin to remain silent (Minnery 2001). To say our task is solely to lead others to Christ and believe the rest will work itself out, as some Christians do, is shamefully simplistic and fails to recognize the fullness of the lordship of Christ over all of creation, including public and family life.

Second, a pluralistic society challenges us to learn how to persuade from common human principles. Christians do not hold to a Gnostic faith that has nothing to do with the physical world and real human life. We have an incarnational faith that indwells real flesh-and-blood life. We can persuade from the perspective of human well-being, for God doesn't make up his directives for reasons that have no impact in the lives of those he loves.

We must show that when we move away from God's ideal for family, people suffer. We can say that cohabitation is "living in sin." But in many discussions, we might more effectively demonstrate from the social sciences how cohabitation is associated with increases in domestic violence for women and children; increased drug use and abuse; lowered relational faithfulness, happiness, and durability; and dramatic increases in divorce once a marriage is entered.

We can encourage people to seek marriage as we demonstrate how married people live longer, healthier, happier lives in every way scientists know to measure these things compared to people who do not marry (Waite and Gallager 2000; Stanton 1997). We can explain that people should reserve sex for marriage because research consistently shows that the most sexually satisfied people in society are those who have only known one sexual partner in their lifetime—their spouse—and that sexual satisfaction tends to decline with the increase in number of lifetime sexual partners (Laumann et al. 1994).

It is true both that divorce offends God and that it is rarely a path to greater happiness. It typically leads to far deeper problems for adults and children for longer periods of time than people ever imagined (Wallerstein, Lewis, and Blakeslee 2000).

We must explain that our resistance to the same-sex marriage proposal is not rooted in a disdain for people who identify as homosexuals, but that it is unwise public policy because it further transforms marriage into an institution that exists solely for adult fulfillment rather than the needs of people and society—which must regulate sexual activity, socialize men by linking them permanently with women, as well as protect women from unattached males by enforcing rules of monogamy. Marriage is also the way all societies ensure that the parents who have a biological stake in a child cooperate together to raise and provide for that child through the child's life span so the community does not have to do so. Heterosexual marriage calls individuals out of love of self through an intimate and self-giving relationship with "the other." Crossing the gender divide in our most basic and primary social institution prevents "sexual apartheid." Same-sex marriage says male and female are not essential.

The importance of biologically rooted parenting is consistently supported by the sociological fact that children face serious reductions in every important measure of well-being when they are raised in a home separate from their biological parents. This is even truer for children living with stepfamilies (Booth and Dunn 1994, 6). It is never compassionate to intentionally deny a child access to their mother or father in order to satisfy adult emotional or sexual desire. This is what the same-sex family does.

As witnesses, we must help people make the connection between God's rule for family life and the way it corresponds with human and societal well-being. Our Lord's two great commandments—love God and love neighbor—demand we concern ourselves for the health of the family, at home and in the public square. God created the family to uniquely reflect his nature and the glory of his church in the world; and our neighbor's well-being is deeply rooted in the health of their family.

Bibliography

Althusius, Johannes. *Politica.* Indianapolis: Liberty Fund, 1995.

Aristotle. *Politics* Book 1, Chapter 2. In *The Basic Works of Aristotle,* translated by Benjamin Jowett. New York: Random House, 1941.

Augustine. *The City of God* Book XIX, 14. New York: Modern Library, 1950.

Blankenhorn, David. "The New Laws of Love." *Propositions.* Institute for American Values, Winter 2001.

Booth, Alan, and Judy Dunn, eds. *Stepfamilies: Who Benefits? Who Does Not?* Hillsdale, NJ: Lawrence Erlbaum Associates, 1994.

Copleston, Frederick, S.J. *A History of Philosophy, Vol. I, Part I.* Garden City, NY: Image Books, 1962.

Goodridge vs. Department of Public Health, MA, SJC-08860, 2003.

Griswold vs. Connecticut, U.S., 381 U.S. 479, 1965.

Howe, Neil, and William Strauss, *13th Gen.* New York: Vintage, 1993.

Krause, Harry D. "Marriage for the New Millennium: Hetereosexual, Same Sex—or Not at All?" *Family Law Quarterly* 34, no. 2 (2000): 271–300.

Krueger, Pamela. "Superwoman's Daughters." *Working Woman,* May 1994.

Kurtz, Stanley. "Beyond Gay Marriage." *The Weekly Standard,* August 4, 2003, 26–33.

Kuyper, Abraham. *Lectures on Calvinism.* Grand Rapids: Eerdmans, 1931.

Laumann, Edward O., John H. Gagnon, Robert T. Michael, and Stuart Michaels. *Social Organization of Sexuality: Sexual Practices in the United States.* Chicago: The University of Chicago Press, 1994.

Lewis, C. S. *Miracles.* New York: Collier Books, 1960.

Minnery, Tom. *Why You Can't Stay Silent.* Wheaton: Tyndale, 2001.

Moltmann, Jurgen. "I Believe in God the Father: Patriarchal and Non-Patriarchal Reference," *Drew Gateway* 59 (1990): 3–25.

Plato. *The Republic.* Translated by Tom Griffith. Cambridge: Cambridge University Press, 2000.

Polikoff, Nancy D. "An End of All Marriage," *Washington Blade,* July 25, 2003.

Popenoe, David. *Life without Father.* New York: Free Press, 1996.

———. "Modern Marriage: Revisiting the Cultural Script." In *Promises to Keep: Decline and Renewal of Marriage in America,* edited by David Popenoe, Jean Bethke Elshtain, and David Blankenhorn. Lanham, MD: Roman & Littlefield, 1996.

Popenoe, David, and Barbara Dafoe Whitehead. *The State of Our Unions, 2003: The Social Health of Marriage in America.* Rutgers, NJ: National Marriage Project, 2003.

"Principles of the Law of Family Dissolution: Analysis and Recommendations." American Law Institute, May 15, 2002.

Raines, Claire, et al. *Twenty Something: Managing and Motivating Today's New Work Force.* New York: Master Media Publishing Co., 1993.

Rosiers, Nathalie Des, et al. *Beyond Conjugality: Recognizing and Supporting Close Personal Adult Relationships.* Ottawa: Law Commission of Canada, 2001.

Stanton, Glenn T. "Aiding the New Family Revolution," *Current Thoughts and Trends,* January 1999.

———. *My Crazy, Imperfect Christian Family.* Colorado Springs: NavPress, 2004.

———. *Why Marriage Matters: Reasons to Believe in Marriage in Postmodern Society.* Colorado Springs: NavPress, 1997.

Stanton, Glenn T., and Bill Maier. *Marriage on Trial: The Case against Same-Sex Marriage and Parenting.* Downers Grove, IL: InterVarsity, 2004.

Stone, Lawrence. "The Road to Polygamy." *New York Review,* March 2, 1989, http://www.nybooks.com/articles/article-preview?article_id=4129.

Tennis, Dianne. *Is God the Only Reliable Father?* Philadelphia: Westminster, 1985.

Waite, Linda J., and Maggie Gallagher. *The Case for Marriage: Why Married People Are Happier, Healthier, and Better Off Financially.* New York: Doubleday, 2000.

Wallerstein, Judith, Julia Lewis, and Sandra Blakeslee. *The Unexpected Legacy of Divorce: A 25 Year Landmark Study.* New York: Hyperion, 2000.

13

Stewardship

R. Scott Rodin

As EVANGELICALS OUR theological heritage and commitment to biblical authority uniquely equip us to develop and practice a rich, holistic, and uncompromising theology of stewardship. The goal of this chapter is to look at six evangelical theological convictions that form a theology of stewardship, namely a Christocentric epistemology, the Trinity, the creation of humanity in the *imago Dei*, the fall and the corruption of all creation by sin, the incarnation and atoning work of Christ, and the call of the Christian to a life of obedience, surrender, and service. I will conclude by proposing an evangelical agenda for living as God's stewards.

Epistemology

Evangelical theology has based its epistemology on the self-revelation of God in Jesus Christ. Our relationship with God is solely by grace through faith, and it is made possible not by our innate human ability or inborn receptivity to God, but by virtue of God's desire to cross the great divide that separates us from God to reveal himself to us.

The core of evangelical theology is the good news that this event has happened as the defining moment in our human history. For this reason, our knowledge of God is not only reliable and sufficient, but it comes entirely through God's action. We know God as the God who acts, and all we can know of God is revealed in his activity toward us.

The Gospel of John speaks pointedly to the message of God's self-revelation to us, steering us away from flawed epistemologies. John claims that the Word was both with God (*pros ton theon*) and was God (*theos en ho logos*). Therefore, the *logos* is coeternal with God and is capable of revealing God. Evangelical faith depends on the validity of this truth that the *logos* of God is truly God himself. John points to Christ as the author of life through whom and by whom we were created. Finally, he switches from the language of God and *logos* and introduces the relational language that will dominate his Gospel. For the Word now becomes the one sent by the Father, full of grace and truth.

If Jesus Christ is our starting point, then our theology must always move from this concrete reality to the more abstract. It must start with what is revealed to us and from there ask the difficult theological and ethical questions. As evangelicals we reject ethics that are written backward, which begin with what we do not know, then proceed to construct a system of beliefs, laws, and regulations based on experience and end by projecting them back into God. This flawed methodology seeks solutions based on our own passion to justify ourselves and our existence. As a result, we create God in our own image.

Evangelical theology is at its best when it seeks knowledge of God only through a participation in the life of the Son's revelation of the Father in the power of the Holy Spirit. In doing so it is rightly equipped to keep all discussions of stewardship grounded in the self-revelation of God to us in Jesus Christ. If we are God's stewards, called according to his command and empowered for his service, then we must start with God's self-revelation as we look for the answers to our questions about what that service looks like or what is expected of us. To start at any other point, such as the standards of the world, our own experiences or preferences, reason and logic, our economic systems, or our society's values, is to start falsely from which can only come a defective ethic. Once we have grounded our process in the knowledge we have of our God as revealed to us in Jesus Christ, we can then appropriate the other helpful tools at our disposal such as natural law, general revelation, the testimony of the community of believers, and the church's rich historic teachings. As evangelicals, however, our process must always move us from the concrete (God for us in Jesus Christ) to the more abstract (how then should we live). In doing so we keep Christ at the center and allow God's self-revelation to us to modify the other sources of knowledge that help us come to know and understand the things of God and the world.

The Trinity

An evangelical epistemology leads us to the position that creation is through and through a trinitarian event. As a trinitarian event, creation reflects the image of the Creator and so is endowed with the inherent traits of interrelationship. "The true human community is designed to be the *imago Trinitatis*."[1] This creation is a system of mutually dependent parts that require fellowship, participation, cooperation, and even sacrifice to survive and flourish. We have learned painful lessons of disturbing ecosystems whether on the macro or micro level. We know that our bodies are comprised of a series of complex, interrelated systems that are dependent upon one another for health. Sociologists show how our family systems, relational systems, community systems, and social systems are made up of individuals who are highly interdependent and who must both give and receive appropriately, freely, and sacrificially if the individual and, consequently, the system are to survive.

A thoroughly trinitarian doctrine of creation informs our self-understanding as creatures of a wholly relational God. The God who by his very nature is fellowship (triunity) in joy (complete and whole), created us for fellowship and joy. There is a dual movement in creation that can be described as "God-Humanward" and "Human-Godward." The act of creation can be described as the work of the Father, through the Son, by the Spirit. God acts toward humanity in this trinitarian way. Conversely, we worship the Father, through the Son, and in the Spirit. This is our human response to God's work for us and in us. This is always the proper order for these two movements. These movements are thoroughly trinitarian in nature, and therefore they reflect the triune nature of God.

All of our work as the people of God comes in this trinitarian form. Our worship, our work for the kingdom, and our building of healthy relationships are triune by their very nature, or they are not reflecting the glory of God. The call to be a steward is a call that comes from the Father, through the Son, and in the Spirit. God the Father creates us in grace and commands us in love to be his faithful stewards. God the Son redeems us by his precious blood and gathers us as the body of Christ to be stewards in the kingdom of God. And God the Holy Spirit empowers and equips us for our work as stewards and unites us with Christ in our worship of the Father.

Our response is motivated by the movement of the Spirit who we believe is at the heart of all we do as stewards. Stewardship is Spirit centered work. As we work in the power of the Spirit, we seek to be stewards and to train up stewards in gracious response to the love of God in Christ Jesus. We accept by faith that we are recipients of grace by means of the covenant of God made complete in Jesus Christ. We respond with gratitude by participating in the ongoing work of the Son, in the name of the Son, and for the sake of the Son. All this is done to the glory of God the Father, who created us for this work, saved us for fellowship with him, and called us to be his children in his kingdom now and forever. The work of the steward is a trinitarian event.

Creation and the *Imago Dei*

The special, privileged work of the steward in God's kingdom is to be carried out on all four relational levels in which we were created: our relationship with God, with ourselves, with our neighbor, and with creation. Each level requires our stewarding, each was proclaimed as "very good" by God at creation, and each bears witness to our creation in the image of a Trinitarian God (Gen. 1:27–28a).

The opening chapters of the Bible proclaim that we are created first for fellowship with our Creator. There we find the purpose and meaning of our existence. We are fulfilled, content, and satisfied in our existence to the extent that we are in fellowship with our Creator. This is the first level that defines our existence and brings meaning to our life. *The Confessions of St. Augustine* open with the beautiful words, "Thou awakest us to delight in Thy praise; for Thou madest us for Thyself, and our heart is restless, until it repose in Thee."

The image of God in which we were created is witnessed to in our status as covenant partners of God. That is, God has chosen us from creation to be his people. One crucial aspect of the revelation of God's covenantal love for us in creation is the clear understanding that God created us to be "with" us and not "over" us. God created us for fellowship. This is not as equals that we may be like God, but it is also not as underlings with no real worth or value. To be created in God's image is to be created with inestimable worth and value. Our original created state was one in which we could stand to look into the face of God, walk with him in the stillness of the garden, talk with him about the affairs of our heart, and dwell with him in perfect peace. We were created for nothing less. This is the heart of God both for his original creation and for his redeemed creation.

We witness God's grace in our lives when we live out our call to be stewards. Stewardship, like discipleship, must be understood as the free and loving response to the grace of God in our lives. The relationship into which we are called as children of God in Christ Jesus is both freely given and one that requires our stewardship. We are to be caretakers of this precious gift, even though it is a gift of grace. Perhaps we should say *especially because* it is a gift of grace. This relationship is not "ours." We did not initiate it (or even want it); we did not sustain it, empower it, or bring it to fruition. We simply accepted it and thanked God for it. As it continues today we do not provide the means for it to grow stronger, nor do we control its hold over us. This is all a continued outpouring of the grace of God. We simply have a responsibility to be stewards of this relationship.

Second, we were created for personal wholeness. There is a physical, mental, and spiritual aspect to our humanity. These form a system that is mutually dependent. God created us to be whole persons, to live with strong bodies and sound minds and to be filled with the Holy Spirit. We are commanded to love God with all of these: heart, soul, strength, and mind. This personal wholeness is a reflection of our creation in the image of a Triune God. Perhaps the hardest and least talked about level of our steward responsibilities is this personal level. A major reason for this difficulty is the distortion in our understanding of the relationship between body and soul. We must avoid the Gnostic tendency to attribute sin, uncleanness, and evil to the "flesh" while elevating the soul to a higher state. This has had devastating effects on Christian ethics and stewardship and has resulted in a lack of care for things material, including our bodies and, not coincidentally, the bodies of the poor. This self-dissection can also lead us to believe that the world is "passing away," rendering our care for creation as a waste of time—the futile attempt to preserve a sinful creation that is destined for destruction. We must guard against adopting a utilitarian approach to the stewardship of creation and devaluing our care for the environment and ourselves. Moltmann comments, "If human society is to find a home in the natural environment, the human soul must correspondingly find a home in the bodily existence of the human person."[2]

Third, we are created for fellowship one with another. This need for fellowship began in Eden when God created the woman out of the need of the man for another like him. The scenario in Eden is a theological statement about our creation as male and female. The creation story teaches us, among other things, that men and women were created to be together, to live and work and play and worship together in the kind of fellowship that reflects the character of God and brings him glory. Again here we must not fall back into a dualistic heresy by seeing personal redemption as our *only* responsibility to our neighbor. While evangelism must be among our highest priorities, it does not exonerate us from serving the needs of our neighbor and, more importantly, seeing these two together as the fullest expression of our call to be stewards in God's kingdom. Ron Sider writes,

> Genuine evangelism will be an incarnational, contextual evangelism that applies the gospel to the whole context of the person addressed. Jesus did not throw words at sinners from afar. He lived among them and modeled how the Good News of the kingdom brings radical transformation of the status quo. The evangelist is a harmless peddler, not a faithful proclaimer of the gospel . . . unless she shows how the gospel challenges men and women within the whole context in which they live.[3]

Finally, we are reminded in Scripture that while we are the "crown of creation," we are also counted among the creatures in God's creation. We are part of the animal kingdom that has a place in the created world and a role with responsibilities. The animals and our environment are ours to care for like an older brother cares for a younger. While it cannot be said that the animals were created in the image of God, it must be said that all creation bears his image in the sense that its interdependence and robust vitality glorify a Triune God as the Creator of all things. Bryant Myers writes, "The calling or vocation of human beings is to be fruitful, productive stewards of God's creation. We are to make a contribution that adds value. The creation account gives every human being an identity and a vocation."[4]

Therefore, there is obligation and opportunity to glorify God in our relation to his creation. Care for creation is ultimately a reflection of our care for ourselves, and, consequently, the destruction of our environment is our own self-destruction. Again this creation is not "ours." Despite the ability to own land, buy natural resources, purchase mineral rights, and so forth, we are at no time the ultimate owners of any part of this creation. For all that science and technology have done for us, they deceive us when they lead us to believe that whatever control we may be able to harness carries with it the right to absolute ownership. One case in point is bioethics in which the stewardship questions—which would ask if we have the right to alter or clone life—are set aside in the quest to apply new technologies. When the right of absolute ownership is a given, ethics becomes a secondary and inconsequential concern.

Here we must shed some light on the problems and mistreatments of the command of God to "have dominion," "subdue," and "rule over." In doing so we must not wander from our commitment to understand the ethic of the steward in light of our epistemology. We must also be true to the dual direction we laid out for the relationship between God and us in his free and loving act of giving, and between us and God in our free and loving response. The definition of these words is given by the one who proclaimed them and no one else. Adam and Eve understood "dominion," "subdue," and "rule over" in light of their Creator. They were commanded to have dominion over the created world *just as God had demonstrated his dominion over them,* as one who sought to be *with* them rather than *over* them, who lovingly provided for them and who sought only their good. They received this command from a God who created for them an environment in which they could grow and flourish, one which worked together in harmony, and one which provided abundantly for their welfare and future.

We must avoid taking a post-fall, sin-filled definition of "dominion" and "rule" and foist it back upon God's original proclamation in a way to lend credibility to the exploitation of the planet. Only after the fall does "dominion" become "dominance," "subdue" become "exploit," and "rule over" become "abuse." At no time prior to the fall did these terms endow Adam and Eve with the right or power or authority to claim some kind of alien dominance or counterfeit rule. They simply knew nothing else but a godly, grace-filled rule and dominion.

These four levels all bear witness to a triune, loving, and free Creator. All four emerge from a wholly evangelical theology of God, Trinity, and creation. They all four are endowed with grace and call us to a life of care, love, and commitment if they are to continue to be reflective of our God.

The Fall and the Corruption of All Things by Sin

Evangelical theology holds firm to the biblical understanding of the parasitic nature of evil and its entrance into the created world through the untrusting act of the man and woman created by God. Evil had its "three moments" in the history of humankind: rebellion against God, enmity toward neighbor (and creation), and sin against self. This original sin also rent asunder the relatedness that defined the man and woman at all four levels.

On the first level, Scripture teaches that Adam and Eve had snatched from them their confident status before their Creator. They lost their precious fellowship with the one who created them solely to be *with* them. In doing so, they lost the very reason for their existence. The immediate result of their sin was their recognition that suddenly they were *apart from God*, and in that distinction, they saw how terrifying it was for them, as sinners, to stand in the presence of the holy God. Sin brings separation, brokenness, and a sense of one "over and against" another. Their response to God also shows that for the first time they began to consider themselves in a distinct way—namely, as separate, defined not by fellowship but by isolation.

On the second level, Adam and Eve, and all humanity with them, replaced that loss with the desire to create, acquire, or take by force those things that would recreate purpose and meaning in life. By doing so they accepted a new paradigm in which life taking replaced life giving, where self competed with God for sovereignty, where words like "dominion," "rule," and "subdue," which were once imbued with grace, were now redefined for use in a more human-centered world. This new state of sin would create the need to put self-interest at the center of existence, and it would raise up distortion as its one defining characteristic.

Equally devastating to humankind was the radical change in our relationships to one another, the third level. In Eden we were properly "lords and servants." In Eden the first couple understood "lordship" not in terms of power and manipulation, but in terms of servanthood. Lordship in Eden meant the cherished opportunity to care for another as God cares for all creation. In relationships this lordship was demonstrated by a constant concern for the other. It was a call to be caretaker, nurturer, provider, enabler, and empowerer. That is how Adam and Eve knew God, and that was all they knew of lordship in the innocence of holiness. To be "lord in Eden" was to act for others and all creation like God acted toward his creature and creation. To be "lord and servant" was to be "steward." In this sense we could say that Adam and Eve were not able to think of themselves *in abstacto*. That is, there was no awareness of self that could be conceived of apart from that same self *in relation*. Adam was not Adam without Eve. That is the whole theology behind the story of the creation of humanity in Genesis 2. Male and female were complete together. Male and female were complete only in relationship to the God who created them and in the work of stewarding the creation that was created for them. Being a steward in Eden was as natural as breathing. The key to this state was the lack of the autonomous, independent self as a conceivable reality.

In the act of sinful rebellion we witness the rise of the knowledge of the self. The very first moment of our fallenness did not produce an act of defiance of

God, nor an act of dominance over creation, nor even an act of enmity against another. It produced instead the shocking revelation that in sin, the creature that was created for fellowship was now defined *in isolation*. Relationships would forevermore be the product of hard work and sacrifice. Every form of evil that the created world now hosted would be borne out in this one area that, more than any other, defined the creature as being made in the image of the Creator. This is the significance of the loss of our natural relatedness at the fall.

In this rise of the autonomous, individual self, the fall brought about another movement within the creature. The effect of the fall was to refocus the creature's attention away from servant and onto a counterfeit form of lordship. The rise of the self and the search for "self-understanding" created a new standard for self-definition that is defined in terms of power, dominance, pursuit of personal happiness, self-actualization, and gratification. It is the prize that we grasp at in the fury of our frantic existence. By grasping at the chance to be like God, the creature changed from being the "servant of the Lord" to being the "Lord over servants." Barth comments, "Wanting to act the Lord in relation to God, man will desire and grasp at lordship over other men, and on the same presupposition, other men will meet him with the same desiring and grasping."[5]

Finally, on the fourth level we find that a defining mark of our fallenness is the shift in our self-understanding from steward to owner. This is a considerable shift. In defiance of the God who gives us all things freely, we become takers, usurpers actually of that which we can never ultimately own. It is not ownership per se that is wrong. It is absolute ownership. In God's economy we may own a house, a car, furniture, clothing, and the like, but this ownership can never be anything more than a pseudo-ownership, a "temporary use permit" allowing access to some resources in distinction to others. The fall corrupts this understanding on two fronts.

First, the sense of temporary ownership is very hard to maintain. It is our nature (our fallen nature) to take, to possess, to mark off our boundaries, to build our empires, and to better our own lot in life with things that promise happiness, purpose, and meaning. We get swept up in the "right" of absolute ownership and its deadly pursuit, and as we do so we return to Eden and grasp at power to choose, to control, to stand on our own over and against God.

Second, absolute ownership brings power. When we control an asset, we deny it to others. It is really *mine* in contradistinction to being either "yours" or "anybody's" or even "mine unless you need it." It is part of what I have demarcated as my kingdom, and as such, absolute ownership is a power we exhibit over others. What we own not only defines us as successful, but it defines us as powerful. We must not underestimate the lure of power that lies behind our temptation to amass and consume. In the end it is not money per se that is the allure, but the power that money can bring. And while men and women of God empowered by the Holy Spirit can and do faithfully and effectively use money in the service of God's kingdom, Jesus minced no words in speaking of the intoxicating power of money when he warned us that it is nothing less than a rival deity. "No one can serve two masters. Either he will hate the one and love the other, or he will be devoted to the one and despise the other. You cannot serve both God and Money."[6] Mammon, in the words of Jesus, is not a neutral medium of exchange but a very real spiritual power that seeks our worship, our adoration, and our very souls. Jacques Ellul writes, "He [Jesus] is speaking of a power which tries to be like God, which makes itself our master and which has specific goals."[7] Richard Foster goes further: "Discussions of stewardship, almost without exception, view money as completely neutral and depersonalized . . . What all this talk about stewardship fails to see is that money is not just a neutral medium of exchange but a 'power' with a life of its own."[8]

The result of absolute ownership is the belief that creation is to be valued only as it is able to supply us our needs, fulfill our desires, or provide us with security. We value it for its contribution to our happiness, our success, our peace, and our personal well-being, all of which are part of our new, alien definition of purpose and meaning in life. Creation ceases to have inherent value, and so stewardship ceases to make sense unless it is linked with some potential use for creation that serves our needs. Such is the predominance of sin at this and at all four levels. In the end, the sin that results from the fall has created a world of earthly kingdom builders. In every phase of life, people are building worldly kingdoms in order to find the stuff of life that will provide them with what society tells them they must have if life is to be worth living. For many evangelicals, the battle may be less with an all-encompassing consumerism than with the subtler search for earthly security. We may denounce the drive to acquire and amass more possessions, yet focus enormous energies on building a large portfolio that will assure us of a comfortable retirement. It is not the careful planning that is the problem, but the underlying quest for security that looks to any source other than the gracious provision of a faithful God. If we seek solace in the size of our investments, then the process of creating a future earthly kingdom of retirement comfort makes us earthly kingdom builders.

As evangelicals seeking to be salt and light in this world, we are called to be people of only one kingdom. Yet if we are honest with ourselves, we must admit that we all fall victim to a two-kingdom lifestyle. We desire to live as children of the kingdom of God while, at the same time, building an earthly kingdom side by side with our non-Christian neighbor. Even if we take our faith seriously, if we see "reality" as divided between that which is part of our spiritual kingdom—and thus belongs to God—and that which belongs to our earthly kingdom—and rightly belongs to us, we are living a two-kingdom lifestyle.

Evangelicals have all the tools necessary to reject this two-kingdom worldview, which is built on a deficient understanding of salvation that assumes a strict division between body and soul.[9] We affirm that Christ assumed our fallen humanity not only for a spiritual purpose, but for a holistic transformation that conforms all we are to the image of Christ. As we deal with the ethical demands of the kingdom of God, we must be clear that as evangelicals we see that the question here is not one of faith but of *lordship*. Put another way, the question is not whether we believe in God as strongly as in our earthly kingdom, but who is Lord and master here? In building our earthly kingdom we reenact the sin of Adam and Eve, grasping at power and seeking to be like God.

All four levels of our created nature are at risk here. Two kingdom people will begin to own their relationship to God, demanding that worship be done according to their standards and that the church conform to their own preferences. The moment this happens, worship ceases to be a stewardship response and becomes an ownership issue. Worship wars are often battles over ownership, not stewardship.

Two-kingdom people will lose their self-identity in Christ and seek to rediscover it in the voices of those who hold power, exhibit influence, and engender adoration. They will reject a gospel message that speaks of humility, sacrifice, and servanthood. Cheap grace is the result of a church that seeks to appease two-kingdom people.

Two-kingdom people see relationships with neighbors as means to an end. We cannot be stewards of relationships that we use to better ourselves. They cease to be gifts to be stewarded and immediately become possessions to be used. Again the question is lordship versus stewardship. Until we see our neighbors and our relationship with them as essential to our own self-identity as a child of God, we will never be stewards of our relationships with them.

Finally, two-kingdom people seek to have control in their lives as it relates to their relationship with possessions. This grasp at control and the desire to decide for ourselves is the rejection of the lordship of God in this area of our lives. It is the move from being steward to being absolute owner. When our relationship to creation is no longer defined by the characteristics of God's lordship over us, then sin will distort Scripture's intent, and we will subsume creation under our earthly kingdom and use it as was never intended. Our creation has suffered intensely from this two-kingdom thinking.

Finally, in a very specific way this two-kingdom worldview confronts us in every aspect of Christian giving. When we call two-kingdom people to godly stewardship, we are challenging them to abandon an earthly kingdom that has taken them a lifetime to build. If we fail to make this fundamental challenge, if we allow our people to remain comfortably in their two-kingdom world, then stewardship is reduced to a transfer of assets, debiting the earthly kingdom of what is "mine" in order to credit our spiritual kingdom. The primary "stewardship" question in this asset transfer is, "How much of my assets should I give to the church?" Or put another way, "How much is enough—5 percent, 4 percent, 3 percent?" Stewardship programs that speak of tithing but focus only on helping people define what is "enough" are not at all about stewardship. They are only sad vestiges of our accommodation to this two-kingdom lifestyle. In the end, stewardship makes little or no sense at all if these two kingdoms are allowed to stand side by side.

In the fall we lost our understanding of true lordship at all four levels, substituting an alien form of ownership that has been manifested in a two-kingdom view of reality. As evangelicals we must better understand this as our state and prepare to tackle this situation head-on in our desire to lead our churches to new levels of obedience and discipleship. The weapon for this battle is found in the proclamation of the fullness of God's work for us in Jesus Christ.

The Restoration of All Things in Christ

As evangelicals we understand that everything that was lost in the fall was restored and redeemed in the incarnation, life, death, and resurrection of Jesus Christ. That is the basis of our entire theology and faith. It is important here that we not focus so singularly on the restoration of our relationship to God that we lose the radical nature of redemption in the other three levels of our created relationship. It is in the work of the incarnate Christ that we understand our transformed nature as we stand before God and our transformed responsibility as we stand by our neighbor, with ourselves, and in our created world.

Evangelical theology holds to the Chalcedonian formula concerning the two natures of Christ upholding both Christ's divinity and Christ's true humanity. This is critical for our understanding of the steward. Tim Dearborn writes, "Salvation is possible not only because Jesus was fully divine, but precisely because Jesus was fully human. Jesus is not just the revealer of authentic humanity, he ontologically establishes it. His humanly divine life is not just the model for others' lives. His life is the basis for other's life."[10]

This is the joyful and complete understanding of the great statement, "God was in Christ reconciling the world to Himself" (2 Cor. 5:19 NASB). Ray Anderson reminds us, "The humanity of Christ brings all humanity under the judgment in order to bring it under the gracious work of renewal and reconciliation through resurrection."[11] Evangelicals affirm the great words of the Cappadocian divines, "The unassumed is the unredeemed." If there was any part of our human nature that Christ did not assume fully in the incarnation, then it remains outside of his redemptive work for us. Praise be to God that Christ assumed it all! Therefore, Anderson can conclude, "The humanity of the church is thus grounded ontologically, not merely ethically, on the humanity and ministry of Jesus Christ."[12]

This understanding of the work of Christ tells us that the reconciling work of God for us in Jesus Christ has been fulfilled. When we as evangelicals speak of stewardship, we must draw on this rich theological understanding that nothing in all creation is left outside of God's redeeming work in Christ. This is the theological basis for a holistic theology of the steward.

Our role is purely that of joyous and grateful respondents to the free grace of God. As we do so, we participate in the work of Christ as the body of Christ, and our work is not apart from but in and through Christ. Everything that transpires between us and God in this new covenant does so solely through our participation in the already completed work of Christ. This is why we pray to the Father, in the name of and for the sake of the Son, and in the power of the Spirit. That is why our worship is directed to the Father, in the name of the Son, and in the Spirit. Our relationship to God is trinitarian. It has direction and it calls us to a life of service as servants of God in Christ.

Our call to be stewards is based on our acceptance of a gracious gift and our rejection of the lure to play the owner. On all four levels we were created for fellowship with God, we lost that fellowship through sin, and now we have been given back that precious fellowship through the atoning blood of Jesus Christ. Therefore, relationships at each level are gifts that we are to accept with humility and participate in with joy and gratitude. This is the foundation for a theology of the steward.

By redeeming our relationship to God, Jesus offers back to us the meaning of our existence and the promise of an eternity with the one who created us for fellowship. In short, Jesus offers us back our own self-understanding. We can once again know who we are because we know *whose* we are. We are invited back into a right relationship with ourselves through our participation in the ministry of the one who redeemed us and through whom we have access to our Creator. By redeeming our relationship to God, Jesus also calls us into a right relationship with our neighbor. The enmity and strife that were evidenced immediately in Eden, that were confirmed just as immediately by Cain, and that now characterize our nation and our world were also assumed by Christ. His "becoming flesh" meant his assumption of this discord. His death for the sins of the world meant his overcoming this strife. His resurrection meant that we can now participate in his work of reconciliation. He has taken back our brokenness, assumed it, redeemed it, and now calls us to himself to be children in his kingdom where we are empowered to live in right relationships with our neighbor.

By redeeming our relationship to God, Jesus also calls us into a right relationship with the created world in which we live. Ron Sider writes, "It is precisely the bodily resurrection of Jesus and the fact that the Incarnation continues that is the capstone of an incredible Biblical truth: Creation is so good that God intends to purge it of evil and bring it to perfection."[13]

We have become kingdom people in Christ. We are a new creation. To be a steward in the kingdom of the Triune God of grace means we pay homage to only one Lord. Stewards serve in only one kingdom. Stewards have died to the things of this world and have become a new creation. They serve only one Master, and as a result, stewards are joyous, stewards are people of hope, stewards are free. For this reason stewardship is ultimately an act of worship. Being a steward in God's kingdom is not an activity we do alongside our other roles as Christians, but it *defines our roles as Christians*. We must no longer split the terms "Christian" and "steward" as if the latter were one of many options available to the believer. The very term "steward," understood as we have developed it here, carries with it the essence of what it means to be a follower of Jesus Christ.

And the evidence of this new kingdom is found in the lives of the people of the kingdom who live as stewards in a world of owners. We are called to be stewards in God's kingdom on all four levels. Our evangelical tradition brings us to this conclusion and gives to us the biblical and theological tools to preach, teach, and encourage this fundamental truth of the Christian life. In this way stewardship is almost synonymous with discipleship. They are both holistic in their calling to an absolute commitment of everything we have and everything we are to Jesus Christ.

Toward an Evangelical Agenda for Stewardship

We will conclude by proposing four points that should make up an evangelical agenda regarding stewardship.

The Response to Systems

No earthly economic system can incorporate the ethics of the steward in God's kingdom. In our fallenness we can only at best construct systems that appropriate the spirit of such an ethic, and even then we will constantly be at risk of giving in to our nature as kingdom builders. In regard to our relationship to the world, Scripture and the history of the church instruct us to reject both isolationism and the establishment of a new Christendom. Instead, we are to live as critical and cautious participants in the economies and social systems of our day. To be "in" the world but not "of" the world obligates us to cooperate within these systems but never to be conformed to them.

Therefore, we must seek to be one kingdom stewards in a milieu that promotes two-kingdom living as the norm. In doing so, we must understand our responsibility as evangelicals to speak and live in a way that defines us as nonconforming participants. To do so we must understand the socioeconomic systems in which we live in order to operate as godly stewards within them. For those of us who live in a capitalistic system, we must acknowledge that capitalism is based on the premise of ownership and the power that comes with it. Buying and selling are the foundations of capitalism, and by definition, every buying and selling transaction requires ownership. Positively, capitalism promotes a strong work ethic and a system that links consequences with behavior. Perhaps no other economic system has the potential to lift the poor and create opportunities for those willing to work, invest in good ideas, and create businesses that produce needed goods and services while gainfully employing others in the process. In the hands of good and honest people, capitalism can bless a society.

However, capitalism has also brought about the dominance of *having* over *being*. Financial and societal pressures can turn godly capitalists into kingdom builders perpetuating a system fueled by an ideology of profit as the ultimate determiner of success. In this system money—and the power behind it—becomes a moral value, an ethical standard. The Enrons we have suffered in our recent history are testimonies of the corrupting power of kingdom building fueled by capitalism unchecked. Michael Novak gives us an important reminder that such scandals are "three times evil," harming the perpetrator, his peers, and the poor worldwide whose hope lies, in part, on a strong, expanding free economy.[14] Therefore, while the freedoms and respect for human choice and free will in a capitalistic system are certainly closer to kingdom ethics than either socialism or Communism, as Christians serving only one Master, we cannot adopt the capitalistic system uncritically. Any sense of the merging of evangelicalism with capitalism should be increasingly troublesome to one-kingdom stewards. Capitalism may be the best we can produce this side of heaven, but we must operate within it as a cautious and critical and even begrudging and sometimes rebellious participant.

The challenge for evangelicals is to preach and teach biblical, one-kingdom stewardship to a people living in the midst of a society that is based fundamentally on the pursuit of building a second, alien, counterfeit kingdom. We cannot let our theology become the predicate of our society. As evangelicals, let us rise to the challenge of speaking against those aspects of our systems that are an anathema to the ethics of the kingdom of God and to its people. As evangelical churches, let us reject the old dichotomy between soul and body and see the whole person as fallen, saved by grace, and called to one-lordship service in God's kingdom even if it means we find ourselves in an uneasy and often antagonistic relationship to the economic systems in which we live.

The Response to Wealth

As evangelicals, we must adopt a right attitude about wealth. Such an attitude will require us to address the inconsistencies in evangelical theology's understanding of the relationship between wealth and obedience. If we are truly stewards of all four levels of relationship, then we must treat everything as gifts from a gracious and loving God. And as gifts *of grace*, they are unmerited and freely given. Where Scripture seems to point to wealth as a reward for godly living, we must understand that it is God's wealth. That is, wealth may be a sign to us of God's favor and blessing, but as a sign its sole purpose is to point us to what is being signified—namely, our gracious God who gives gifts as he chooses and who seeks our praise and service in response. Problems arise when we value the sign over the thing signified. Wealth, given by God as a gracious gift to his people, is both a sign of his love and grace and also the means by which God asks us to be gracious and free in being a blessing to others. To use the sign to ungodly ends is the greatest of offenses. And these ends include hoarding it, lording it over others, using its power to subordinate others, spending to increase our abundance in an age of hunger and poverty, and allowing it to become our purpose in life, supplanting our daily trust and dependence upon the God who gives all gifts freely.

We must also not fall into the false logic that if blessings from God sometimes equal wealth, then wealth always equals God's blessing. The "prosperity gospel" is, in this ethic, nothing short of an abomination. It equates material wealth with the best God intends for us. It measures grace in economic terms. And it divides the body of Christ in the exact opposite way that Scripture would by associating God's favor with the rich instead of the poor. If God blesses us with wealth, it is a gift with enormous responsibilities. Nowhere in Scripture are we ever directed to ask for it. When it is given, it is always grace, and it always is meant to point to the Giver.

We must also be keenly aware that in Scripture wealth is attributed to the wicked more than the godly. Wealth is more often the sign of the oppressors, the haters of the poor, the lost, those headed for destruction, and those held up as the example of greed and godlessness. (See Deut. 8:13–14; Job 21:7–15; 31:24–28; Ps. 52:7; 62:10; 73; Prov. 28:20; Matt. 19:23; Mark 4:19; Luke 6:24; 1 Tim. 6:9; and James 5:1 for just a few examples.) If we read Scripture carefully, we will live at great dis-ease with our wealth. As the wealthy, we hear Scripture telling us that our salvation is in grave danger. The temptations we face are profoundly greater as a result of our riches, and the responsibility for our use of our wealth is measured on an eternal scale. We cannot close our ears to the recurrent cry of prophets, disciples, and of Jesus himself, "Woe to you who are rich."

As evangelicals we value grace above all else. It is the basis of our salvation and hope. Let us use the same graciousness in God's provision of wealth in ways that demonstrate to the world that we have only one Lord, live according to the values of only one kingdom, and give as graciously and generously as our God has graciously and freely given to us.

The Response to the Environment

Given our theological heritage and commitments, it is surprising that evangelicals have not been more at the forefront in the cause of saving and preserving our environment. No other world religion or spiritual movement has such a rich and full theological tradition to draw upon with regard to the goodness of creation as do evangelicals. This may be due in part to the view taken by many evangelicals that the world is passing away, so there is no reason to take care of it. This position formed partly as a reaction against a liberation theology that taught that care of creation was one part of a scenario that would itself usher in the new kingdom. Both of these views are problematic given the ethics that result from an evangelical theology of creation and the redemption of all things in Christ.

There is ample room, however, for evangelicals to distance themselves from both the panentheistic tendencies of so many environmentalist extremists on the one hand, and the liberation/process theologians on the other. We must reject both the identification of creation with God and the idea that we somehow are preparing and perfecting the earth as a requisite for the second coming. However, we have too often jettisoned a solidly biblical position in the process. This we must reclaim.

Evangelicals can speak of the goodness of creation and God's love of creation without straying into either of these extremes. We can provide a corrective that will keep creation care in its proper context. We must recapture our stewardship responsibilities with regard to creation. Van Dyke, Mahan, Sheldon, and Brand offer four aspects of a Christian view of caring for creation: (1) *knowledge* of what creation is and how it works; (2) *concern* for the plight of God's creation that moves us to act; (3) *sacrifice* that requires us to make lifestyle changes; and (4) the work of the *redemption* of creation because that is God's ultimate goal for it.[15]

Our care for creation is an extension of our care for ourselves and our neighbor and ultimately speaks profoundly to our love for the God who created all things. We love God's creation because we love the God who created it. We tend it and care for it out of pure obedience and with great joy whether or not we believe it is passing away. We need not come down on one side or the other in the debate over the meaning of the "new heaven and the new earth" in order to heed our call to be stewards of God's creation. It is a call to all God's people and it is unequivocal.

As evangelical leaders we need to step up to our responsibilities to be leaders in the fight for clean air and water, to stop the burning of rain forests, cruelty to animals, overuse of pesticides, and the countless other issues that result from our consumer-oriented lifestyles. We must be vocal in the face of technological and scientific advances that speed faster than the careful, ethical consideration of their consequences. We must create theological responses to the issues of population growth, global warming, and species extinction, among others. We must speak to the links between public policy, private land ownership, a market-driven economy, and our environment. We must speak out on the issues of the cost of a clean environment, the promotion of technologies that enhance environmental protection, and an evangelical position on economic progress, understanding the complex relationship between the three.[16] And we must be teachers and preachers who help our people understand that God's call to be stewards involves redemption in our relationships with God, our selves, our neighbor, and God's creation. In the helpful words of "An Evangelical Declaration on the Care of Creation," "The presence of the kingdom of God is marked not only by renewed fellowship with God, but also by renewed harmony and justice between people, and by renewed harmony and justice between people and the rest of the created world."[17]

The Response to the Poor

We have left this issue for the end in order to let it have the final word on the issue of stewardship. Evangelicals in America not only have to deal with the challenges of being ranked with the wealthiest people in the world, but they also must contend with the poor. We have said above that Scripture pronounces a judgment against the rich. The condemnation is broad and unrelenting, and it must command more of our attention as those called to be humble stewards of a gracious God. Yet here more must be said, for as vociferous as Scripture is in its pronouncements against the rich, it is equally if not more powerful in its association of the kingdom of God with the poor. There simply can be no doubt that the poor have a very special place in God's economy. They are preached to first, they are lifted up as examples of how we should live our lives, they are the blessed, and they are given special protection and prominence in God's kingdom. (See 1 Sam. 2:8; Job 36:6; Ps. 12:5; Isa. 41:17; Luke 4:18–19; 6:20; and James 2:5 for a few examples.) Most importantly, Jesus identified himself with the poor and their cause against the rich who would oppress them. Our acts of service to our neighbor who is in prison, sick, homeless, or naked is identified with serving Christ himself, and with eternal consequences (Matthew 25).

In addition, Scripture calls upon the rich to "maintain the right of the poor" (Prov. 31:5). Our responsibility toward the poor is unequivocal. The very existence of the poor is a constant question that is put to us at every turn. They are the church's living conscience asking us, "Who is my neighbor?" "If your neighbor has need and you say to him 'be well,' what good is it?" It is God's question to us in human flesh. It is the presence of Jesus looking to us who "have" to see if we are truly one-kingdom people. The poor we will always have with us, and for this reason we will always have this question before us.

As evangelicals we must not allow ourselves to look away from the poor in an attempt to deflect the question from our ears. As evangelical leaders and pastors we must keep the question in front of our people. We must be willing to be uncomfortable, convicted, and moved to tears with our people. If we believe that our love for our neighbor is a direct reflection of our love for ourselves, and ultimately our love for God, then how can we as God's redeemed creation shrink away from hearing this question put to us?

Two final things must be said. First, our response must be both individual and corporate. Christ calls us to encounter the poor on a very personal basis. It is far too easy for us to write checks to food banks and drop off clothes at Goodwill. Bryant Myers writes, "Talking about the poor as an abstract noun invites well-intentioned people of compassion to speak for the poor and to practice the latest fads in social engineering. The poor become custodians of the state, objects of professional study, or a social group to be organized. Whenever we reduce poor people from names to abstractions we add to their poverty and impoverish ourselves."[18]

God calls us to presence and involvement with the poor. Again our giving needs to reflect our own priorities of "being" over "having." When we express our care for the poor only through giving of our possessions, we fail to follow the Savior who identified himself with the poor. We cannot stand afar off and love the poor. They need our advocacy, our presence, and our participation in the systemic solution to what entraps them as much or more than they need our financial gifts. As evangelical leaders we need to provide our people with more than giving opportunities. We need to involve them in immersion experiences that put them in direct contact with the poor. But beyond this, we need to invite the poor to be with us. We need to destroy the wall that we have built around the church and open our doors to the very people we are most called to love and serve.

Second, our response must be Christlike. This is the final step in following a God who became incarnate and dwelt among us. Caring for the poor is not an activity, it is a lifestyle. It requires an attitude of deep, godly humility and a sacrificial spirit. It is far too easy for us to patronize the poor or to address the symptoms and disregard the root problems. The issues of fair taxation, employment rights, discrimination, systemic injustice, family breakdown, oppression, exploitation, and abuse are much harder to address than taking food and clothes to a shelter. Both are needed, but the former is what God requires of us if we are to do more than tip our hand to the poor. Evangelicals need to step forward to become leaders in the pursuit of economic justice, job training, public policy reform, the strengthening of family life, and a host of other issues that go to the core of the plight of the poor. We need participation both personally and corporately in the systemic solution to what entraps them. We need to let the world see that we understand God's love for the poor and our supreme responsibility to be stewards of the abundance God has given to us.

If we are to be stewards in the kingdom of the Triune God, who seek to be obedient to the God who saved us and redeemed our relationships on all four levels, then we must move these four items to the top of our evangelical agenda.

Bibliography

Anderson, Ray. "Christopraxis: Christ's Ministry for the World." In *Christ in Our Place*, edited by Trevor Hart and Daniel Thimell. Exeter: Paternoster Press, 1989.

Augustine. *The Confessions of St. Augustine*. Oxford: John Henry Parker, 1838.

Barna, George. *Virtual America*. Ventura: Regal Books, 1994.

Barth, Karl. *Church Dogmatics* 4.1. Edited by G. W. Bromiley and T. F. Torrance. Edinburgh: T & T Clark, 1956.

Benne, Robert. *The Ethic of Democratic Capitalism: A Moral Reassessment*. Philadelphia: Fortress Press, 1981.

Clapp, Rodney. *The Consuming Passion: Christianity and the Consumer Culture.* Downers Grove, IL: InterVarsity, 1998.

Dearborn, Tim. "God, Grace and Salvation." In *Christ in Our Place,* edited by Trevor Hart and Daniel Thimell. Exeter: Paternoster Press, 1989.

Dodd, C. H. *The Interpretation of the Fourth Gospel.* Cambridge: Cambridge University Press, 1953.

Ellul, Jacques. *Money and Power.* Downers Grove, IL: InterVarsity, 1985.

Foster, Richard. *The Challenge of the Disciplined Life.* San Francisco: Harper Collins, 1989.

Gunton, Colin. *The Promise of Trinitarian Theology.* Edinburgh: T & T Clark, 1991.

Hall, Douglas John. *The Steward.* Grand Rapids: Eerdmans, 1990.

Ladd, George Eldon. *A Theology of the New Testament.* Grand Rapids: Eerdmans, 1974.

Moltmann, Jurgen. *God in Creation.* London: SCM Press, 1985.

Myers, Bryant. *Walking with the Poor.* Maryknoll, NY: Orbis Books, 1999.

Novak, Michael. *The Spirit of Democratic Capitalism.* New York: Simon & Schuster, 1982.

Rieger, Jeorg. *Liberating the Future: God, Mammon and Theology.* Minneapolis: Fortress Press, 1998.

Rodin, Scott. *Stewards in the Kingdom.* Downers Grove, IL: InterVarsity, 2000.

Romanowski, William. *Eyes Wide Open.* Grand Rapids: Brazos Press, 2001.

Shaw, Vera. "The Ecology of Eden." *Green Cross* 1, no. 2 (Winter 1995): 4–5.

Sherrard, Philip. "Sacred Cosmology and the Ecological Crisis." *Green Cross* 2, no. 1 (Fall 1996): 8–14.

Sider, Ronald J. *Good News and Good Works.* Grand Rapids: Baker, 1993.

Van Dyke, Fred, David Mahan, Joseph Sheldon, and Raymond Brand. *Redeeming Creation: The Biblical Basis for Environmental Stewardship.* Downers Grove, IL: InterVarsity, 1996.

Van Leeuwen, Ray. "Enjoying Creation—Within Limits." In *The Midas Trap,* edited by David Neff. Wheaton: Victor Books, 1990.

Wood Lynn, Robert. "Faith and Money," *Inside Information,* Spring 1997.

Wuthnow, Robert. *God and Mammon in America.* New York: Free Press, 1994.

14

The Ethics of War and Peacemaking

Glen H. Stassen

CHRISTIAN ETHICS HAS three approaches to violence, war, and peacemaking: just war theory, pacifism/nonviolence, and just peacemaking theory. Christian ethics, reflecting differences among theological traditions, is divided over which one (or which combination) best displays faithfulness to Jesus in a sinful world. I will begin by considering Jesus' way of peacemaking and its link to Isaiah's prophecies of the kingdom. Then I will present just war theory and pacifism in their best forms, as well as just peacemaking. I will not attempt to resolve the just war/pacifism debate, but will supplement them with their implicit commitment to just peacemaking. I urge that every church teach the three models so that Christians are not blown about by every shifting wind and accommodated to secular forces (Eph. 4:14ff.).

The Basis for All Three Ethics: Jesus' Way of Peacemaking

In this section, I argue that Jesus fulfilled Isaiah's prophecies that the deliverer who would come would bring peace. The next section then will present

Adapted from Glen H. Stassen and David P. Gushee, *Kingdom Ethics: Following Jesus in Contemporary Context* (Downers Grove, IL: InterVarsity: 2003), 149–74. Copyright © 2003 by Glen H. Stassen and David P. Gushee. Used by permission of InterVarsity Press, P.O. Box 1400, Downers Grove, IL 60515, USA. www.ivpress.com

just war theory. It will not try to support just war theory by arguing that Jesus did not teach peacemaking. Major nonpacifist theologians like Karl Barth and Reinhold Niebuhr also agreed that Jesus taught peacemaking and the way of nonviolence. They argued that some wars are just not by trying to deny Jesus' peacemaking, but by arguing that in an "emergency situation" or in some contexts violent coercion is needed pragmatically. Therefore, the present section does not argue for one of the three kinds of ethics over the other; it simply seeks to be clear about Jesus' teaching. The argument for each of the three kinds of ethics will come later, in the other sections.[1]

The prophet whom Jesus quoted far more than any other is Isaiah. Isaiah's prophecies consistently emphasize peace and peacemaking as characteristics of God's deliverance. Isaiah 26:12 prophesies, "O LORD, you will ordain peace for us." Isaiah 31:1–5 pronounces judgment on Israel for trusting in Egypt for military help, and trusting in horses, chariots, and horsemen, instead of the Lord. Egypt was notorious for encouraging an ally to join with them in fighting a war and then leaving the ally to fight alone and thus be betrayed into destruction. Instead, Israel should trust in the powerful Spirit of the Lord, "poured upon us from on high" (Isa. 32:15 RSV). This does not mean being passive; it means being empowered to do God's will actively.

Isaiah teaches again and again that God's will is deeply committed to justice for the downtrodden. Once "the Spirit is poured upon us from on high . . . then justice will dwell in the wilderness, and righteousness abide in the fruitful field. And the effect of righteousness will be peace, and the result of righteousness, quietness and trust forever. My people will abide in a peaceful habitation, in secure dwellings, and in quiet resting places" (Isa. 32:15–18 RSV). In Hebrew, "righteousness" (*tsedaqah*) is synonymous with "delivering justice"; it means the kind of justice that delivers the downtrodden from domination and brings the outcasts into community. Peace, justice, and compassion come as a single package; they depend on each other because they are part and parcel of God's will and God's action of deliverance: "I will appoint Peace as your overseer and Righteousness as your taskmaster. Violence shall no more be heard in your land, devastation or destruction within your borders" (60:17–18). "Comfort, comfort my people, says your God. . . . And cry to her that her warfare is ended" (40:1 RSV). "How beautiful upon the mountains are the feet of him who brings good tidings, who publishes peace" (52:7 RSV).

God's reign and mercy will bring peace through God's suffering servant, who will be so committed to peacemaking that he will do no violence: "He will not cry or lift up his voice, or make it heard in the street; a bruised reed he will not break, and a dimly burning wick he will not quench" (42:2–3 RSV). He will bring peace through his suffering and death: "Yet he did not open his mouth; like a lamb that is led to the slaughter, and like a sheep that before its shearers is silent. . . . By a perversion of justice he was taken away . . . although he had done no violence, and there was no deceit in his mouth" (53:7–9). God brings peace by delivering justice, by nonviolent suffering, and by including the Gentiles in community rather than by hating and excluding them: "I will give you as a light to the nations [i.e., the Gentiles], that my salvation may reach to the end of the earth" (49:5). "Let not the foreigner who has joined himself to the LORD say, 'The LORD will surely separate me from his people' . . . these I will bring to my holy mountain, and make them joyful in my house of prayer . . . for my house shall be called a house of prayer for *all* peoples" (56:3, 7 RSV; italics added).

Did Jesus fulfill Isaiah's prophecies that a mark of the kingdom of God will be peace and peacemaking? In Jesus' time intense Jewish hatred of Rome often boiled up into insurrections against Roman rule. Jesus wept over Jerusalem, saying, "Would that even today you knew the things that make for peace! But now they are hid from your eyes" (Luke 19:42 RSV).

Accordingly, Jesus prophesied—five times in the New Testament—that the temple would soon be destroyed. The very hatred that Jesus was trying to correct led his opponents to accuse him of seeking to destroy the temple, and so the high priest and the council decided to seek his crucifixion (Matt. 26:61–66; Mark 14:58–64). They got the hated Romans to crucify the one who taught and practiced peacemaking toward the Romans. The hatred of enemies continued after he was crucified and boiled over into massive revolt in the year 66. Rome responded by crushing the revolt, destroying Jerusalem, and demolishing the temple in the year 70, thereby proving Jesus' prophecies true.

Jesus had prophesied not only that the temple would be destroyed, but that people should flee into the mountains rather than waging war (Mark 13:14–23, 30). Because of Jesus' teachings and peacemaking practices, the Jesus movement became a Jewish peace movement, and so Christian Jews did not participate in the revolt but instead did flee Jerusalem.[2] They were delivered from warmaking, and by their love they spread the gospel among the very Romans who were so hated. In the book of Revelation, the followers of the Beast do violence, but the followers of the Lamb do not. Instead, they do the deeds that Jesus taught (Rev. 2:2, 19, 23, 26; 3:8, 10; 9:20–21; 12:17; 14:4, 12; 16:11; 19:10; 20:12–13; 22:11), and they are delivered from the destruction. Christians are given a clear teaching for endurance, for faith, and against doing violence, echoing Matthew 26:52: "Whoever takes the sword to kill, by the sword he is bound to be killed" (Rev. 13:10 NEB). Perhaps the most perceptive New Testament scholar on the book of Revelation, Richard Bauckham, concludes:

No doubt in the Jewish circles with which John and his churches had contact . . . ideas of eschatological holy war against Rome, such as the Qumran community had entertained and the Zealots espoused, were well known. . . . Therefore, instead of simply repudiating apocalyptic militancy, [John] *reinterprets* it in a Christian sense, taking up its reading of Old Testament prophecy into a specifically Christian reading of the Old Testament. He aims to show that the decisive battle in God's eschatological holy war against all evil, including the power of

Rome, has already been won—by the faithful witness and sacrificial death of Jesus. Christians are called to participate in his war and his victory—but by the same means as he employed: bearing the witness of Jesus to the point of martyrdom.[3]

Hence when in Revelation 6:10 the martyrs cry out, "Sovereign Lord, holy and true, how long will it be before you judge and avenge our blood on the inhabitants of the earth?" they are "each given a white robe and told to rest a little longer" (v. 11). This fits Romans 12:19–20, where we are told never to avenge ourselves but to leave vengeance to God. The martyrs are told to wait patiently for God's victory, rather than seeking to avenge themselves. They receive white robes that symbolize their innocence, in contrast with those who killed them.

Similarly, in Revelation 11:5, the two witnesses, modeled after the prophets Moses and Elijah, slay with fire that comes *from their mouth*, as Christ in 19:15 slays with a sword that comes from his mouth. From their mouth comes the prophetic word, a figurative sword, like "the sword of the Spirit, which is the word of God" in Ephesians 6:17. So Christ in Revelation 19:13 is named "The Word of God." The sword coming from the mouth is the prophetic word in Revelation 1:16; 2:12, 16; 19:15, 21; 4 Ezra 13:25–39; Isaiah 11:4; and Jeremiah 5:14, which says: "Because you have spoken this word, behold, I have given my words in your mouth [as] fire . . . and it will consume them."[4]

Jesus' antagonists who thought the right response to Roman enemies was to make war on them did have some support in the Old Testament. See, for example, Exodus 17:10–14: "So Joshua fought the Amalekites as Moses had ordered. . . . Then the LORD said to Moses, "Write this on a scroll as something to be remembered and make sure that Joshua hears it, because I will completely blot out the memory of Amalek from under heaven" (NIV).

Or 1 Samuel 15:3, where the people of Israel are commanded to "utterly destroy all that they have; do not spare them, but kill both man and woman, child and infant, ox and sheep, camel and donkey." But other passages in Isaiah, Jeremiah, Hosea, Jonah, and Micah command peacemaking toward the other nations. The prophets—especially Jeremiah—proclaim that unless Israel does justly toward others, God will drive them out of the land. And Isaiah prophesies again and again that peace will be a crucial mark of the kingdom of God. Jesus repeatedly quoted and cited and affirmed these prophetic teachings, but he never quoted Old Testament passages that call for killing or war. Even when he cited "eye for eye and tooth for tooth," he omitted "and life for life."

How are we to understand the fact that some Old Testament passages call for killing every man, woman, and child in a city, while prophets call for making peace? How are we to understand the fact that Jesus cites the prophetic teachings often, and never the passages that call for killing? Good Christians give a variety of answers. (1) The Hebrew Scriptures are a rich and diverse narrative.

The people of Israel were a diverse people—originally an idolatrous people who worshiped and served many gods, including gods of war—who debated with each other how to interpret God's word to them.[5] Jesus shows how to interpret that rich narrative. He never quotes passages that favor killing, war, or national supremacy. He quotes only the passages that favor peacemaking. Our method of interpretation is to affirm Jesus Christ as fully Lord and fully Savior and as the key to interpreting the Scriptures. (2) The central message of the Old Testament is that the exodus and conquest, and the security of Israel, are gifts of God; God did the fighting, usually by scattering or drowning the enemies, and not by our own strength and prowess. God calls us to be faithful to God's will, not to rely on our own horses and chariots and alliances with Egypt and Assyria.[6] (3) God was doing a special work in bringing the chosen people out of Egypt and into the Promised Land, and Jesus is saying this phase of God's work of redemption is not the same as God's calling for Christians now. (4) Jesus' teachings about the calling for Christians applies to Christians in Jesus' time but does not apply to what governments do in our time. (This last answer has the great liability of marginalizing Jesus' lordship so that it has nothing to say about life in the midst of today's struggles; it leads to secularism in public life.)

Whichever alternative—or another variation—that one adopts, we urge that it not reduce down to an ethic that says, "Whatever the government does, Christians should support it." It may be right for governments sometimes to make war, but that is far from saying governments never sin, or Christians should give over all discernment of what is right to Caesar. That, pure and simple, is idolatry. "We must obey God rather than men" (Acts 5:29 RSV). Jesus Christ is Lord of all of life, and we do not have some other lord such as Caesar, or Mars, the god of war.

In the Sermon on the Mount (Matthew 5–7), we see Jesus' way of deliverance through transforming initiatives of peacemaking. When something causes anger and divides us from another, we are to take the initiative of going to make peace. Do not retaliate revengefully by evil means, but instead take transforming initiatives of peacemaking. In Jesus' day, to be slapped on the right cheek was a backhanded slap of insult, as to a slave or a nonperson; to turn the other cheek was to turn the cheek of equal dignity. Turning the other cheek does not mean mere passivity, but surprising the insulter with nonviolent confrontation, as Gandhi and Martin Luther King Jr. did. When the Roman soldiers demand that we carry their pack a mile, the transforming initiative is not simply to comply with the demand, but to surprise them by taking an initiative of reconciliation on our own. When sued (in court) for one's shirt, we are to give our cloak as well. This means we stand there naked, revealing the greed of the suitor in all its nakedness before the whole law court, thus confronting the injustice nonviolently and pressing for justice. When a beggar or a borrower asks for money, thereby nonviolently confronting us, to give aid is to take an initiative to remove some of the gap between rich and poor. Each of these initiatives takes an action to oppose injustice, to stand up for human dignity, and to invite to reconciliation. We are to love our enemies as God does.[7]

Some traditions argue that Jesus' teachings in the Sermon on the Mount are "high ideals" limited only to individual relations. Making peace with one's brother, carrying the Roman soldier's pack a second mile, giving "to everyone who begs from you" and "lov[ing] your enemies and pray[ing] for those who persecute you" are only about relations with individuals and not about political or economic matters in first-century Palestine.

David Gushee and I have sought to show that Jesus' way is not high ideals but the way of deliverance in the midst of a world of sin.[8] Jewish ethics was not about ideals, and not only for individuals, but about practical life in covenant community. Jesus explicitly affirmed the Old Testament and especially the prophets, above all Isaiah. He should be interpreted in Jewish context. Nowhere does Jesus or the Old Testament split individual relations from the rest of life. Jesus was directly countering the resentful teaching of major political movements, including many Pharisees. Furthermore, we argue, the danger of the dualistic split is that it fences off most of life as forbidden territory for Jesus' lordship and creates another lord over life in society.

It is better to understand Jesus as disclosing God's will in the context of his time, which has *analogous* but sometimes not identical meaning for different contexts. No Roman soldier will compel us to carry his pack a mile, but we will encounter other unjust kinds of domination. We will need to seek God's analogous way of deliverance in our context with creativity. Thus, in 1 Corinthians 7:15, in a different Greek context from Jesus' Jewish context, the apostle Paul approves of a divorce or a separation when an unbelieving spouse wants it. (Exactly what this means is rightly debated, but it does seem that Paul sees an analogous but not identical meaning in a different context; he does not simply repeat the exception clause in Matthew 5:32 but interprets creatively.) Different spheres of authority and responsibility will lead us to interpret or apply the Sermon differently, or analogously, but not to go completely against it.

Some traditions make an argument from silence, saying Jesus welcomed a centurion and was silent about telling him to put up his sword. But in Jesus' day, the question was not whether his followers should join the Roman army; his followers were Jews and certainly not invited to join the Roman army. The question for Jesus' followers was whether to make war on the Romans. Jesus taught them not to kill their enemies but to love them. He praised the faith of Gentiles, prostitutes, Samaritans, tax collectors, and even a centurion. He was not advocating that his followers become Gentiles, prostitutes, Samaritans, tax collectors, and centurions; he was advocating that they welcome all these people forgivingly into the community.

Richard Hays has written what is widely regarded as the best New Testament ethics book. Besides presenting much evidence in line with the above, he deals with the two verses (Matt. 10:34 and Luke 22:36) in which Jesus warns the disciples that they can expect opposition, arrest, floggings, and slander. Jesus says, "I have not come to bring peace, but a sword," and they should expect to need a sword. These are hardly advocating warmaking but are warnings of impending persecution. When one of the disciples misses the point and takes it literally, responding that they already have two swords, Jesus' response in the Greek "is impatient dismissal, indicating they have failed to grasp the point: 'Enough, already!'" When a disciple uses a sword in the Garden of Gethsemane, he tells him not to live by the sword, because that is the way of the vicious cycle of killing and retaliation.[9] Hays points out how consistent this is throughout the New Testament:

> There is not a syllable in the Pauline letters that can be cited in support of Christians employing violence. Paul's occasional uses of military imagery (e.g., 2 Cor. 10:3–6, Phil. 1:27–30) actually have the opposite effect: the warfare imagery is drafted into the service of the gospel, rather than the reverse. . . . "For though we live in the flesh, we do not wage war according to the flesh, for the weapons of our warfare are not fleshly" (2 Cor. 10:3–4). . . . The community's struggle is not against human adversaries but against "spiritual forces of darkness," and its armor and weapons are truth, righteousness, peace, faith, salvation, and the word of God. Rightly understood, these metaphors witness powerfully *against* violence as an expression of obedience to God in Christ.[10]

Tremper Longman and Daniel Reid make the same point concerning "the armor of God" in Ephesians 6:10–17 as spiritual warfare, fought with the belt of truth, the breastplate of righteousness, the gospel of peace, the shield of faith, the helmet of salvation, and the sword of the Spirit, which is the Word of God. These refer to Isaiah 11:1 and 59:17–18, and they match the characteristics of the reign of God in Isaiah and in Jesus' announcement of the kingdom.[11]

The most authoritative study of the context of Romans 13 was written by the highly respected New Testament scholar from the University of Tuebingen, Peter Stuhlmacher, and his colleagues.[12] They point out that the context is an emerging tax revolt in Rome against a new tax Nero was assessing. Paul is urging Christians in Rome not to make a rebellion but to pay to all what is due them—"taxes to whom taxes are due, revenue to whom revenue is due. . . . Owe no one anything, except to love one another" (Rom. 13:7–8 RSV). The revolt was so serious that Nero canceled the tax. When his advisors warned him of bankruptcy if he would cancel it, he then reinstated it, but for the first time published the rates publicly so that people could know if they were being overcharged by the tax collectors. About seven years prior to Paul's letter, a tax revolt had occurred by Jews following "one named Chrestus," surely meaning "one named Christ" or Messiah. The emperor expelled all Jews (including Jewish Christians like Priscilla and Aquila) from Rome. The sword (*macharia*) mentioned in Romans 13:4 is the kind that police carried who accompanied tax collectors. Paul was urging Christians not to revolt but to pay their taxes. The passage is urging peace, not war.

Now we see why the first five verses of Romans 13 are made up of common teachings in the culture of the time and say nothing specifically Christian such as Christ, grace, faith, love, mercy, or forgiveness. Paul is quoting general sayings in order to get general agreement. He begins speaking in his own specifically Christian language when he quotes Jesus' teaching about rendering taxes to Caesar (he uses the same Greek word for "render" or "pay" taxes in verse 7 as Jesus used in Mark 12:17) and loving one another. His emphasis is on paying taxes, not making war.

This passage has been misused in Christian history to persuade Christians to obey Hitler, to obey segregationist governments, to support apartheid governments. Now we see that it is not about that but about peacemaking. We see that it fits perfectly between Romans 12 and Romans 14, both of which are teaching love for the enemy and peacemaking toward enemies. What had seemed like an odd and temporary changing of the subject sandwiched between two chapters on peacemaking is in fact about rendering taxes and peacemaking toward Nero.

Jesus entered Jerusalem on a donkey at the time of the Passover, fulfilling Zechariah's prophecy of a Messiah of peace who stops war and commands peace to the nations (Zech. 9:9ff.). All four Gospels report this entry with different emphases, yet all four, in different ways, emphasize the theme of peacebringing as symbolizing Jesus' mission (Matt. 21:1–9; Mark 11:1–10; Luke 19:28–38; John 12:12–18).

Jesus' next prophetic action was to clear the temple, for a brief time, of the selling of sacrificial animals in the court of the Gentiles, citing Isaiah 56, which declares welcome to Gentiles in the temple (Matt. 21:10–17 and parallels). This was an act of inclusion of Gentiles and thus love for enemies (Isaiah 56). The Greek in John 2:15 makes clear that Jesus used the whip of cords to drive out the animals, not to do violence against people. Today's English Version, Moffatt, Goodspeed, the Zurich Bible, and commentators McGregor, Temple, Plummer, and Strachan translate it like this: "drove all the animals out of the temple, both the sheep and the cattle." "Drove out" posits no violence; elsewhere in the New Testament it means simply "sent away."[13]

Jesus' next prophetic action was the Lord's Supper, in which he made clear that his way was the way of self-sacrifice and forgiveness, not the way of domination and violent insurrection.

In the Garden of Gethsemane, he resisted the temptation to refuse the cup of death. He did not want his disciple to use his sword in defensive rebellion, nor legions of angels to come fight a war of defensive rebellion (Matt. 26:52–53).

And next came the crucifixion. This revealed the shocking sinfulness of the way of domination by violence—and other dimensions of our sin. From the cross, Jesus forgave those who crucified him, embodying the way of forgiveness rather than revenge.

The resurrection and Pentecost—and the spread of the gospel to all the nations that, prior to Jesus, had been hated and shunned by Jews as enemies—were God's vindication of Jesus' way over against sin, violence, and the separation of the different tongues.

The witness is consistent and thorough: Jesus fulfilled Isaiah's prophecy that peacemaking would be a key mark of the reign of God.

The Eight Rules of Just War Theory

The first Christian ethic for peace and war that we present—just war theory—originated with St. Ambrose and St. Augustine in the fourth century. Tested and revised through the centuries, it has made its impact in international law, in military manuals for training the armed services, and in the writings of philosophers. It makes the logical point that in order to justify the killing that occurs in war, there must be a reason so important that it overrides the truth that killing people is wrong. "The moral theory of the 'just war' . . . begins with the presumption which binds all Christians: we should do no harm to our neighbors; how we treat our enemy is the key test of whether we love our neighbor; and the possibility of taking even one human life is a prospect we should consider in fear and trembling."[14] Or as Arthur Holmes writes, "Just war theory does not try to justify war. Rather it tries to bring war under the control of justice."[15] Others emphasize the obligation to make war when it is just or is for the love of neighbor. Lisa Cahill argues that Augustine bases the obligation to make a just war on the love of neighbor, while St. Thomas Aquinas bases it on the obligation to do justice.[16] The political scientist who has written the most widely respected book on just war theory, Michael Walzer, bases just war theory on justice as the right to life, liberty, and community, and opposition to domination.[17] Just wars are obligatory to defend life, liberty, and community—of others as well as ourselves. Walzer's emphasis on the right to life is a commitment to reduce killing and violence. Scholars are debating these different grounds for just war theory.[18] I urge evangelicals, who commit themselves to following Jesus, not to marginalize Jesus' way and drop it from consideration, but—if they argue for just war theory—to argue for basing it both on the presumption against violence and on the obligation to do justice. That may help keep their advocacy honest and within its proper limits and make it responsible to Jesus' way of peacemaking and doing justice.

War may be justified by overriding reasons—but only by overriding reasons. What reasons count? The reasons come in the form of criteria for when a war is just. All Christians—and others—need to know and remember the eight criteria of just war theory. Only if we know the rules that determine when war is just or unjust can we exercise our conscientious responsibility in deciding whether to support or oppose a war the government proposes to wage on our behalf.

A. *Justice in Deciding to Go to War* (Jus ad Bellum)

1. Just *CAUSE*: The causes that can override the presumption against killing are stopping the massacre of large numbers of people or stopping the systematic and long-term violation of the human rights of life, liberty, and community.[19]

Some say that only the defense of one country from attack by another counts as just cause for war.[20] The international order that emerged after the Treaty of Westphalia in 1648 emphasized the sovereignty of each nation over what went on in that nation. But a widespread international sense is growing that when a country is massacring large numbers of its own people, there is a right of *humanitarian intervention* to stop the massacres. In East Pakistan (now Bangladesh), the Pakistani army was massacring the people. India invaded, stopped the massacres, and then got out. Similarly in Uganda, the dictator, Idi Amin, was massacring large numbers of people. Tanzania invaded, deposed Amin, stopped the massacres, and got out. By contrast, horrendous massacres of 800,000 people also occurred in Rwanda, but no country intervened until too late.

2. Just *AUTHORITY*: To commit a nation to make a war in which many will die and be maimed is an enormous responsibility. No one can do that without just authority. Constitutional processes must be followed so the people who will pay with their lives and resources will be represented in the decision. The U.S. Constitution grants the power "to declare war" to the Congress, not the president (Article I, section 8, clause 11). Presidents have sometimes sought ways to bypass Congress, notoriously in the Vietnam War, which eventually failed to maintain the support of Congress and the people. This necessitated the War Powers Act, limiting what the president can do. It is significant that in the Gulf War and the war on terrorism in Afghanistan, the two presidents Bush went to Congress to seek a congressional resolution, though not technically a declaration of war, before proceeding.

The Kellogg-Briand Pact of 1928 outlawed aggressive war as a normal tool of statecraft, and this was the basis for the Nuremberg charges against Nazi Germany for "crimes against peace." Chapter VII of the United Nations Charter introduces collective security use of military means to redress threats to international peace and stability. This is the legal basis for humanitarian intervention, and it requires collective action, not only action by one nation's decision acting alone. From a Christian perspective, all sin (Rom. 3:23), and that includes nations. Nations that decide to go to war are often wrong. Therefore, many urge that a nation needs the checks and balances provided by consulting with other nations collectively, such as the United Nations or a representative international body. Furthermore, the cost in resources, wounded, and dead will be borne by other nations as well, so they should be consulted. So both presidents Bush sought UN or international approval before the Gulf War and the attack on Afghanistan. President Clinton first got a United Nations declaration before invading Haiti in 1994, and that gave former President Carter the notice he needed to rush to Haiti before the warplanes arrived and to resolve the problem by means of conflict resolution.

For these two kinds of just authority to function in a democracy, both government truthfulness and freedom of the press are required so that people can judge accurately. Deceitful authority is unjust authority, especially when the deceit is in the service of getting people killed. This is a development since the rise of democracies and is not in the original just war theory.

John Calvin placed the responsibility to depose a dictatorial ruler on the shoulders of the "lesser magistrates"—intermediate-level rulers with just authority to act for justice. This developed into the right of revolution (by the Calvinist John Knox in Scotland), not of course by the ruling authority, but by a group representing the need for justice as shown by indications of the people's support.[21]

3. Last *RESORT*: "Christians in the just war tradition (a majority since the fourth century) have always argued that killing must be a last resort."[22] Means of negotiation, conflict resolution, and prevention that reasonably look as if they might work must be tried before resorting to war. The logic is clear: What justifies the killing in war is that it is the only way to stop the great injustice that provides the just cause. If the injustice can be stopped by a nonviolent resort, then there is no justification for the killing. There is prudential judgment and worthy debate about when the resorts have been exhausted. When an attack is already in process, as in North Korea's attack of South Korea that began the Korean War, the resorts have been exhausted.

4. Just *INTENTION* (final cause or future aim): "The only legitimate intention is to secure a just peace for all involved. Neither revenge nor conquest nor economic gain nor ideological supremacy are justified."[23] After the 9/11 attack on the World Trade Center and the Pentagon, the Pentagon initially code-named the war against terrorism "Infinite Justice." But *infinite* justice is not given to us this side of the second coming; all we can have is *better* justice. "Islamic leaders complained because only God can bestow infinite justice."[24] Faithful Christians say the same. When war is fought for grandiose ideological purposes, it usually means politicians want to whip up the fervor of people for a war, and the war turns into a crusade that kills many innocent people, justifies whatever means destroy enemies, jettisons rules against killing civilians, and flows over the boundaries of just war. So the name was changed to "Enduring Freedom." This name change functions as a nice symbol of the dimension of intentionality in just war thinking. The name might be, in Augustine's terms, "Defense of Tranquility of Order."

"Enemy states must be treated, morally as well as strategically, as future partners in some sort of international order."[25] The aim in war, "within the confines of the argument for justice," is a more secure world, "less vulnerable to territorial expansion, safer for ordinary men and women and for their domestic self-determinations." It is wrong to demand absolute conquest because of the lives that will be taken, both on one's own side and on the enemy's side, in the pursuit of absolute ends. So the aim is not to be absolutely invulnerable, but less vulnerable; not absolutely safe, but safer. "Just wars are limited wars; there are moral reasons for the statesmen and soldiers who fight them to be prudent and realistic."[26]

5. Probability of *SUCCESS*: It is wrong to enter into a war that will kill many people, depriving them of the right to life, liberty, and community, in order to achieve a more important goal, if we will quite surely lose and not achieve that goal, and all those people will die in vain. "Lives have too frequently been needlessly lost in blind and futile" wars.[27] *The Pentagon Papers* revealed that the Pentagon had calculated in advance that there was not a reasonable chance of success in the Vietnam War—and they were right. By contrast, in World War II, the Korean War, and the Gulf War, there was a reasonable hope of success.

6. *PROPORTIONALITY OF COST*: "Proportionality requires that the total good achieved by a victory will . . . outweigh the total evil and suffering that the war will cause. No one should prescribe a cure that is worse than the disease."[28] This is the rule that the U.S. Catholic bishops most emphasized when they condemned the Vietnam War as unjust: Its destructiveness far exceeded the good that was sought. Therefore, they "called for its rapid conclusion, the rebuilding of Southeast Asia, pardons and amnesties for war resisters, the rehabilitation of veterans and prisoners of war, and forgiveness and reconciliation for all Americans."[29]

7. *ANNOUNCEMENT*: The government should announce the intention to make war and of the conditions for avoiding it. Stipulating the conditions for avoiding war enables the other side to know what it would take to avoid or stop the war. George W. Bush did exactly this in preparation for the attacks on Afghanistan in October 2001. Public announcement enables the people to exercise their conscientious responsibility to weigh the justice and importance of the cause versus the killing that will be involved. It provides transparency so people may know what their government is doing in their name as it commits them to the horror of a war.

In Vietnam, the United States avoided declaring war, avoided announcing it, and sneaked into a widening war by stages. The result was a war not supported by the people. In the Gulf War, by contrast, there was a national debate and a congressional vote. The announcement was clear. That enabled Iraq to know war was surely coming, and at the last minute, they agreed to get out of Kuwait. Testing whether they really would have gotten out would have taken time that President Bush was not willing to take.

B. Justice in the Means Used in Fighting the War (Jus in Bello)

In a pragmatic culture like the United States, a frequent error is that we emphasize the justice of *the cause*, but then we overlook the requirement that *the means* of fighting must be just. To correct this error, we need to emphasize *justice in war*, or in the traditional Latin, *jus in bello*. The rule of *PROPORTIONALITY OF COST* must be applied not only to the decision to go *to war* (*ad bellum*), but also to the means used *in the war* (*in bello*). In a world with so many nuclear weapons that their full use would result in "the almost complete reciprocal slaughter of one side by the other, not to speak of the widespread devastation that would follow in the world and the deadly after-effects from the use of such weapons," using the huge arsenals of nuclear weapons would cause far worse destruction than any alleged gain, and so any large-scale nuclear war would be unjust.[30] The astonishing destructive power of many nonnuclear weapons now makes this dimension of proportionality a critical issue to consider in every war. And there is the likelihood that small-scale initiation of nuclear war will open Pandora's box by leading to rapid escalation. The opposite trend is the increasing precision of munitions: In Afghanistan, the United States literally launched precision-guided pieces of concrete (i.e., no explosive warhead) against some targets in order to reduce collateral damage.

8. And the war must be fought by *JUST MEANS*.

Just means aims at the military forces that are carrying out the attack that justifies the war. This "forbids direct, intentional attacks on nonmilitary persons."[31] "Individuals not actively contributing to the conflict (including POWs and casualties as well as civilian nonparticipants) should be immune from attack."[32] All members of an enemy nation retain the sanctity of their lives, created in the image of God. The only reason why just war overrides enemy soldiers' right to life is because there is no way of fighting without attacking soldiers. It is they who are making the war and thus opposing the just cause. Once soldiers have surrendered, they may not be killed or tortured. Noncombatants are not fighting the war, so their right to life forbids their being intentionally killed. "Any lethal force which is directed against noncombatants is therefore murder. Any terrorist violence against civilians is ruled out." Furthermore, torture is ruled out. When torture is committed, its victim is someone who has already been captured and who lacks the power to be an aggressor, "but rather is weak and helpless. Torture can constitute a greater assault on the dignity of human life even than killing. Torture is one of the surest indications of the denial of justice."[33]

Bombing a military target like a tank or a weapons factory may have the indirect effect of killing some civilians. That is a realistic and allowable consequence of war (though nonetheless horrible), so long as it truly is unintentional and indirect and its cost in lives is proportional to the gain. This is the principle of *double effect*—that is, the primary effect of the war is to kill soldiers and destroy military targets, but the secondary effect is some spillover death (to civilians) and destruction (to nonmilitary targets). Walzer adds that because civilians have the right to life, soldiers must take extra care to try to avoid killing them. He tells of French bomber pilots during World War II who flew low, at some risk to themselves, in order to bomb weapons factories more accurately and avoid hitting homes in German-occupied France. What these pilots knew about the right to life applies to all civilians because they are human.[34]

Terrorism is the practice of attacking whoever happens to be in the target location—drug stores, shopping malls, or tall office buildings, for the purpose of striking terror in civilians. It has no respect for the right to life of noncombatants and so is singularly evil. In order to guard the right to life and fundamental ethics, it is crucial not to fuzz the definition for ideological purposes. Some politicians label rebels against governmental order "terrorists." But "terrorist" is not the same as "rebel," "guerrilla," or "revolutionary." The guerrillas who shot at British troops from behind trees and stone fences during the American Revolution were not terrorists, nor are leftist guerrillas who shoot at military forces in Colombia. Only if guerrillas, regardless of what their political persuasion is, attack civilians randomly are they terrorists. Terrorism is particularly evil, and the term should be used precisely to name exactly the evil that it is. "We must condemn all reprisals against innocent people."[35] The same applies to governments that attack homes, villages, neighborhoods, civilians. This is "state terrorism," as described by Michelle Tooley in *Voices of the Voiceless*.[36]

A war that fails to meet any of these criteria is unjust, and by the logic of the just war theory we must oppose it. It is not enough to have a just cause if other possible resorts are not tried, nor is it adequate to have a just cause if the war is carried out by unjust means. Stringent application of just war theory places severe limits on warmaking, in both senses—whether or not to fight a war and how a war is fought.

How Not to Argue for Just War Theory. Lurking at the door are powerful drives of revenge, hate, nationalism, racism, economic greed, power lust, hateful stereotyping of the enemy, ideological crusades, pride, and self-righteousness (see Gen. 4:7). These seek to use just war theory not as reasonable criteria but as rationalizations for killing. They pay scant attention to its actual logic and criteria. Whenever you hear someone appealing to just war theory to argue that some wars are right, but omitting the criteria of just war theory for measuring whether the war she or he is arguing for is just, you may be in the presence of some urge to make war, using ethical words to rationalize its desires. When such toothless just war talk is used, it serves as a mask for other attitudes: Machiavellian "realism" about self-interest, crusade, Rambo attitudes, or a "war is hell" mind-set that says once war has begun no rules apply.[37] Whenever you use just war theory, examine your own loyalties and biases that may distort your perceptions.

It is also disingenuous to use just war criteria in such a way that no imaginable set of facts would get through the tests; rightly understood, the criteria are designed to distinguish just wars from unjust wars, and to be useful in limiting injustice and violence, in real decisions for and against wars and in fighting realistically. The Vietnam War failed the tests badly and partly for that reason lost support; the Korean War largely passed the tests and achieved its limited objective. One significant exception in the Korean War was the rush to the Chinese border, which lacked authorization and did not have a reasonable hope of success since it brought massive numbers of Chinese troops into the war; thus, support for the war dropped after the Chinese entry but thereafter stayed constant because the war was basically just.

I have sought to make clear that any legitimate Christian use of just war theory must be based on nonviolence, love, and justice, as taught by Jesus. A Christian who supports just war theory should see it as the most effective way to minimize violence and injustice, not merely to rationalize making war.

Just war theory should not be based on an argument that in a time of war Jesus is no longer Lord and his way is no longer relevant. *Privatism* argues that Jesus' lordship and teachings on peacemaking apply only to individual, private relationships and not to the obligation of governments to seek peace. Others argue that in our present sinful world, we must use just war theory *instead* of Jesus' teachings, as if Jesus' teachings were only for an ideal future eschatological world without sin. Jesus' ethic regularly named the vicious cycles of the real, sinful world and opposed the teachings of political parties that wanted a war of insurrection against Rome. Jesus' ethic is precisely for this sinful world. Still others focus on the claim that the government has the authority to make war (usually citing Romans 13), and then fail to deal with the criteria for judging when this authority is exercised justly and when unjustly.

These ways of marginalizing and compartmentalizing Jesus' lordship set up some other lord—the government, the need for retribution, or nationalism—as lord over the rest of life. They are therefore idolatry. And they create secularism, because they teach that in the public realm, Jesus is not relevant. Instead what is relevant are secular norms or authorities without critique from Jesus. Thus, they remove just war theory from correction by gospel ethics, so it serves some other lord and gets used dishonestly to justify wars that are not just. We argue that just war theory is not autonomous. Either it serves the purpose of reducing violence and seeking justice under Christ's lordship, or it serves some idolatrous loyalty such as rationalizing a war that we or our government wants to make. Either Jesus is Lord over just war theory, or just war theory serves some other lord over Jesus.

Once Christians define just war theory as a way to try to decrease violence and injustice, they receive a second benefit: They are affirming nonviolence and justice. Therefore, they can be more honest in affirming Jesus' teaching of peacemaking and justice. They do not need to deny that Jesus teaches peacemaking in order to defend their loyalty to just war theory. Jesus' teachings are very clear. Just war theorists are wise to accept this truth. What they need to argue is not that Jesus' teaching does not apply but that just war theory is the most effective way to implement Jesus' way of peace and justice in a sinful world.

Consistent Nonviolence

For the first three hundred years of the Christian movement, the church was almost unanimously pacifist or consistently nonviolent. Throughout church history numerous discipleship-oriented groups, such as Franciscans, Hussites, Waldensians, Anabaptists, Quakers, Brethren, and the original Pentecostals, have also been consistently nonviolent.[38] The number of pacifists within "mainstream" denominations has increased in recent decades.

A Christian committed to nonviolence is committed to making a clear witness to the way of Jesus. In this view, trying to make that witness while advocating killing enemies is wrong not only because it advocates killing people, but also because it disobeys Jesus and distorts Christian witness to his way. The clearest historical example of this distortion is the four centuries of Christian crusades against Muslims during the Middle Ages. Christian soldiers with crosses painted on their breastplates and banners, marching to kill Muslims, made a witness that turned Islam more militantly against Christian faith, with implications to this day.

This distortion of Christian faith was repeated by the Serbs at the close of the twentieth century as they rode their tanks into Kosovo, smilingly holding up three fingers as a symbol of the Trinity, on their mission to kill Muslims. It greatly intensified bitter Muslim hostility against Serbs and against their claimed Christian loyalty. An analogous danger threatens the gospel in a time of struggle against terrorism. If war is made against Muslim nations by a nation that claims to be Christian, it stiffens resistance against the gospel and threatens the lives of Christians and Christian missionaries in predominantly Muslim lands. A just war theorist will respond that the ethics of the crusade is precisely what it is opposing and seeking to correct. And the leading pacifist theologian of the last forty years of the twentieth century, John Howard Yoder, agrees that pacifists and just war theorists should be considered allies in the effort to oppose both crusades and the usual wars fought because governments decide such wars are in their interest without serious attention to the rules of just war theory.[39]

The argument for Christian nonviolence is first of all simply that it takes the way of Jesus and the witness of the New Testament as authoritative for our witness. The point is to be faithful to the way of Jesus, and Jesus clearly taught nonviolence and exemplified it in his life and in his death on the cross.

Lisa Cahill has distinguished two kinds of Christian pacifists: One is committed to nonviolence as an obligatory rule. This kind avoids any participation in war but may or may not actively work for peace. The other is committed to nonviolence as a way of life, a way of discipleship, not so much because of an obligatory rule, but because of conversion and loyalty to Jesus Christ and the presence as well as futurity of the kingdom of God. The loyalty is not to a legalistic rule but to a person: Jesus Christ is Lord. The way-of-life pacifist is committed not only to avoid doing violence, but to practice peacemaking in a positive way in all relationships. Cahill argues that it is an error to force all pacifists into a rule-based or legalistic way of reasoning, arguing too simply against pacifism as a rule, and thus missing the profound meaning of nonviolence as discipleship and a way of life.[40]

Ronald Sider defines nonviolence as "an activist confrontation with evil that respects the personhood even of the 'enemy.' [It] refers to a vast variety of methods or strategies."[41] John Howard Yoder distinguished twenty-eight varieties of pacifism.[42] He made clear that a *properly trained and disciplined* police force is logically different from an army preparing for war, so pacifists can logically support police work: (1) The threat of police violence is applied only to the offending party. (2) The police officer's violence is subject to review by higher authorities. (3) The authorized force is within a state whose laws the criminal knows apply to himself. (4) Safeguards seek to keep police violence from being applied in a wholesale way against the innocent. 5) Police power is generally great enough to overwhelm the offender so resistance is pointless.[43]

Some confuse pacifism with passivism. The two words have nothing in common. Pacifism comes from the Latin *pax facere*, to make peace. Pacifists like Martin Luther King Jr. were and are admirably active in seeking ways to make peace. In fact, Christian pacifists on the whole have taken more initiatives and witnessed more clearly to initiatives to make peace than nonpacifists have. Many distort Jesus' teachings as passivity, such as "turn the other cheek." We have corrected that above. Jesus' teachings are not mere prohibitions but are active, transforming initiatives. Therefore, it may be better to speak of "consistent nonviolence."

Yoder is known for arguing that the point of discipleship is faithfulness, not effectiveness. To try to construct an ethics based on what is most effective in achieving a particular goal is to base ethics on complex calculations about what factors are likely to influence the outcome, on what historical surprises might occur, and on our own ability to control history. Calculations like these are based on the self-interested and biased perceptions of decision-makers rather than on the suffering of those who will be impacted by the decisions. It is far wiser to act with faithfulness to what is right and let God control the outcome.[44]

Yoder argues that Tolstoy, Gandhi, and King all had faith that the cosmos is governed by some kind of discernible moral cause-effect coherence.[45] King liked to say that "the universe bends toward justice." If your rejection of violence is cosmically based, and not merely pragmatic, the impact will be greater effectiveness. Perseverance in the face of sacrifice and creativity in the face of dismay are heightened for those who believe that the grain of the universe is with them.

Furthermore, if God really is Lord, if the universe really does bend toward justice, then it makes sense to argue that faithful action is on the whole more effective. So in "Alternatives to Violence" (*The Lamb's War*), Yoder actually offers arguments for the effectiveness of nonviolent direct action.[46] He argues that nonviolence should not be judged ineffective because sometimes it does not win. Military action works less than half the time, since for every winner of a war there is also a loser, and sometimes wars are so bad that both sides are losers. Nor should nonviolence be judged ineffective because sometimes people get killed; far more get killed in military action than in nonviolent action. In what he called the "King-Che discrepancy," Yoder noted that when Martin Luther King Jr. was killed, many concluded that nonviolence had thereby been refuted. But at the same time, few concluded that the fact that Che Guevara had been gunned down in the Bolivian mountains meant that guerrilla violence had been permanently refuted.

Yoder also argues that just war theory has failed the historical test. It has been used most regularly to bless whatever war a nation wanted to make. Seldom have churches used just war theory to condemn a war their own nation was making.[47] A partial answer to that criticism is that just war theory helped a great deal to clarify what was unjust about the Vietnam War[48] and to grow the opinion of four-fifths of the American people that that war was a mistake, or wrong. It helped many see that nuclear war would be horribly wrong and must be avoided. It helped to ensure that the focus of the bombing of Iraq, Kosovo, and Afghanistan would be on military targets, not civilian targets (although we did learn after the Gulf War that military control of the news had given a false picture).

How Not to Argue for Nonviolence. Some Christians committed to nonviolence have argued that Jesus' way is only for Christians. Christians must follow Jesus and renounce violence, but we cannot expect this of non-Christians. We have nothing to say to non-Christians. The government does violence because it is not Christian; that is not our problem.

But just like the argument for just war theory that marginalized Jesus as relevant only to private relations, this way of arguing for pacifism makes Jesus something less than fully Lord. It teaches that Jesus is not relevant to public ethics for non-Christians and so produces secularism in the public realm.

Yoder and Bonhoeffer argued that Jesus really is Lord, and therefore the practices of peacemaking that Jesus taught for the church also have their normative relevance for the world. They are God's will. God is God over the whole world, not only over our private lives or only over the church.[49]

Just Peacemaking Theory

During the 1980s, major church groups issued book-length statements calling prophetically for repentance and reversal of the nuclear weapons buildup. They all said the debate between pacifism and just war theory is inadequate. It narrows the discussion to the question of whether it is ever right to fight a war. But war is so destructive that we need an ethic of prevention, an ethic of initiatives that governments are obligated to take in order to prevent war and make peace. We need a positive theology of peacemaking.

Now a *just peacemaking theory* has arisen—a third paradigm for the ethics of peace and war. In the wake of the horror of World War II and the threat of World War III during the Cold War, plus the world devastation threatened by weapons of mass destruction even today, a worldwide awareness has arisen that we must develop effective war-preventing practices. It is a gift of God that ten such practices have developed in an interdisciplinary and ecumenical peacemaking literature, and where they receive support from the people and their governments, wars are being prevented. In the wake of the threat of terrorism, thoughtful persons are sensing that it is not enough to debate whether it is right or wrong to make war; we need to focus on effective ways to prevent terrorism and war.

The practices of just peacemaking are confirmed not only by empirical studies in international relations, but also by data on what works to decrease homicides.[50]

Just peacemaking theory fills out the original intention of the other two paradigms. It encourages pacifists to be what their name, derived from the Latin *pacem-facere*, means: peace-*makers*. And it calls just war theorists to enhance the content of their underdeveloped principles of last resort and just intention. What resorts, exactly, must be tried before resorting to war? What actions must be taken to restore a just and durable peace? Furthermore, it fits Jesus' teaching of transforming initiatives of peacemaking. Jesus not only taught not to do violence; he taught *peacemaking initiatives*. Based both on Jesus' way of peacemaking and on the obligation to do what is effective in preventing war, the advocates of just peacemaking argue that these practices can and do guide us in shaping the future that is God's will and our need. They are obligations, and more. They are the way we are given to participate in the grace that God is giving in our time.

Those who developed just peacemaking theory come from different denominations and different attitudes about just war, and sought to find common ground. The majority of the authors support just war theory; some are committed to consistent nonviolence. They all agreed that it is not enough to debate whether war is justified or not; we also need guidance on what practices of peacemaking Christians are called to support, both by biblical teaching and by the proven effectiveness of these practices in preventing many wars. They reached unanimous agreement on these ten effective practices of peacemaking:

1. Support nonviolent direct action.

Nonviolent direct action as practiced effectively by Gandhi in India and Martin Luther King Jr. in the United States is spreading remarkably, ending dictatorship in the Philippines; bringing about nonviolent revolutions in Poland, East Germany, and Central Europe; and spurring democratic change in Latin America, South Africa, and many other regions.[51] It is based on the way of Jesus (Matt. 5:38ff.), and it is proving effective.

2. Take independent initiatives to reduce threat.

Independent initiatives are designed to decrease the threat and distrust that undermine support for negotiated solutions. They (1) are visible and verifiable actions, not mere promises; (2) are accompanied by an announcement that their purpose is to decrease threat and distrust and to invite reciprocation; (3) do not leave the initiator weak; (4) do not wait for the slow process of negotiations; (5) have a timing announced in advance that is carried out regardless of the other side's bluster; and (6) come in a series: If the other side fails to reciprocate, small initiatives continue in order to keep inviting reciprocation. For example, the strategy of independent initiatives freed Austria from Soviet domination in the 1950s; produced the Atmospheric Test Ban Treaty of 1963 after presidents Eisenhower and Kennedy halted atmospheric testing unilaterally; achieved dramatic reductions in nuclear weapons via the series of initiatives by President Gorbachev and the U.S. Congress, and President George H. W. Bush; and led to breakthroughs by adversaries in Northern Ireland. After years of occupying southern Lebanon, the Israeli government announced in 2000 that it would pull out all its forces and asked the Lebanese government to reciprocate by stopping insurgent groups from shooting at northern Israel. They pulled out on schedule, the shooting stopped, and the people of Israel, Lebanon, and the world applauded the rare happy result from that region.

3. Use cooperative conflict resolution.

Conflict resolution is becoming a well-known practice, seen dramatically in President Carter's achieving peace in the Camp David accords between Egypt and Israel and in his peaceful resolution of conflicts with Haiti and North Korea. A key test of the seriousness of governments' claims to be seeking peace is whether they initiate negotiations or refuse them and whether they develop imaginative solutions that show they understand their adversary's perspectives and needs. Jesus said that when there is anger between us and another, we must drop everything, go to the other, and make peace. It is a command, not an option (Matt. 5:23ff.).

4. Acknowledge responsibility for conflict and injustice; seek repentance and forgiveness.

This practice was initiated by Dietrich Bonhoeffer and then by churches in Germany, confessing the sin of support for Hitler and his unimaginable violence and injustice. Since then, not only the German government, but also the U.S. government, Japan, and the Truth and Reconciliation Commission in South Africa have lanced the boil of festering historical injustices by acknowledging responsibility and seeking change and forgiveness (Matt. 7:1ff.).

The next two practices follow from the teaching of the prophets and Jesus that injustice is the cause of war's destruction and that removing bitter injustice is essential for peacemaking:

5. Promote democracy, human rights, and religious liberty.

Spreading human rights, religious liberty, and democracy is effective in building peace. During the entire twentieth century, democracies with human rights fought *no wars* against one another. (We should be careful, however, not to use this for self-righteousness. Human rights violations happen at home, too. And many believe the power of money threatens the democracy of the elections. Human nature and sin being what they are, there will be human rights violations within democracies—witness the horrible treatment of Iraqi prisoners disclosed at the time of this writing. But in a democracy, with separation of powers, free speech, and so on, there is a much better chance that these abuses will be exposed and addressed.) Work by churches and human rights groups to press for human rights has helped convert the dictatorships of Latin America to democracies or democracies-in-process, and the trend continues in Asia, Africa, and Eastern Europe. Spreading peace is done by networks of persons willing to work together to gain public support against human rights violations. Nations with human rights and democracy, which do a better job of meeting the basic needs of their people, almost never breed terrorists. We have an opportunity in our time to move from authoritarianism to human rights, from war to justice.

6. Foster just and sustainable economic development.

A just peace requires an equitable world economy in which extreme inequalities in wealth, power, and participation are progressively overcome. East Asian economies, especially in Korea and Taiwan, have grown rapidly because their land reform distributed wealth more equitably and widely. That multiplied the number of customers for the businesses and thus stimulated the economy. By contrast, Latin America's wealth is owned by a few rich families. Local businesses lack many consumers with money. Without a market, industries cannot grow.

The final set of practices implements Jesus' command to include enemies in the community of neighbors (Matt. 5:43ff.):

7. Work with emerging cooperative forces in the international system.

Networks of international communication, international travel and migration, international church missions, and international business are stitching nations together into an international society in which enemies are brought into continuous constructive interaction. Empirical evidence shows that the more nations are involved in these webs of interaction, the less likely they are to make war.

8. Strengthen the United Nations and international efforts for cooperation and human rights.

Acting alone, states cannot solve problems of trade, debt, and interest rates; of pollution, ozone depletion, acid rain, depletion of fish stocks, and global warming; of migrations and refugees seeking asylum; of military security when weapons rapidly penetrate borders; and of international terrorism. The problems are international. Therefore, the practice of supporting cooperative action via the United Nations and regional organizations is crucial. These organizations are resolving conflicts; monitoring, nurturing, and even enforcing truces; and replacing violent conflict with the beginnings of cooperation. At the same time, there is widespread agreement that the United Nations needs to be re-formed—precisely because it is so important and useful. Empirical evidence shows that nations that are more engaged in these organizations more often avoid getting entangled in war.

9. Reduce offensive weapons and weapons trade.

Weapons have become so destructive that war is usually not worth the price. The offense cannot destroy the defense before suffering huge retaliatory dam-age. Reducing offensive weapons and shifting toward defensive force structures strengthens that equation. It makes war less likely. For example, Soviet President Gorbachev removed half the Soviet Union's tanks from Central Europe and all its river-crossing equipment, thus reducing the threat of a Soviet attack on Europe. This freed NATO to agree to get rid of all medium-range and shorter-range nuclear weapons from Western as well as Eastern Europe, in reciprocation for the Soviet Union getting rid of all its medium-range and shorter-range nuclear missiles—the first dramatic step in ending the Cold War peacefully. The wars of Serbia against Bosnia, Croatia, and Kosovo are the counterexamples that prove the rule: Serbians controlled the former Yugoslavian army and its weapons. They had the offensive weapons to make war without expecting a destructive counterattack, until world revulsion finally ended their onslaughts.

As nations turn toward democracy and human rights, their governments no longer need large militaries to keep them in power. They can reduce military spending and devote their economies to fighting inflation, paying debts, and meeting basic human needs. Arms imports by developing nations in 1995 actually dropped to one-quarter of their peak in 1988.

10. Encourage grassroots peacemaking groups and voluntary associations, especially churches.

Advocates of just peacemaking theory teach these effective practices, and their biblical grounding, in churches and other citizens' groups. And they test government actions, when governments claim to want peace, to see if they are taking these obligatory steps that do in fact lead to peace. They resist claims of politicians that we should vote for them because they claim to be Christian believers if they do not in fact do the things that make for peace, as Jesus taught.

The current struggle against terrorism demands of both Muslims and Chris-tians fidelity in concrete practices of peacemaking and justice. We need to correct the bitter injustices and heal the festering resentments that breed terrorists, as well as counter blatantly false propaganda and extremist education that fuel violence. The focus of just peacemaking on the importance of group orga-nization also suggests that counterterrorism include a focus on the dynamics and the reasoning of groups that recruit and organize terrorists.

The growing worldwide people's movement of peacemaker groups constitutes a historical force that empowers just peacemaking. A transnational network of groups, including church groups, can partially transcend captivity to narrow national or ideological perspectives. They can serve as voices for the voiceless, as they did in churches in East Germany and in women's groups in Guatemala.[52] They can help to initiate, foster, and support transforming initiatives that take risks to break out of the cycles that perpetuate violence and injustice. They can nurture the spirituality that sustains courage when just peacemaking is unpopular, that creates hope when despair and cynicism are tempting, and that fosters grace and forgiveness when just peacemaking fails.

How Not to Argue for Just Peacemaking Theory. Just peacemaking was developed by Christian ethicists, some of whom are committed to nonviolence and most of whom are just war theorists. It is supported by many from both traditions, because it asks and provides answers to questions that the usual debate between pacifism and just war theory does not answer: What steps should we be taking to prevent war? What practices make for peace? Christians need to learn these practices, advocate them, and measure governments by whether they engage in just peacemaking practices.

But just peacemaking theory does not try to answer the question that pacifism and just war theory answer: If just peacemaking fails, is it right to make war, or should we be committed to nonviolence? Everyone needs an answer to that question, because short of the second coming, just peacemaking will not prevent all wars. And when war does come, we need to be solidly either just war theorists or pacifists. Otherwise, we will be blown about by every wind of ideological interest (Eph. 4:14).

Therefore, I urge you not to say, "I support just peacemaking theory. It is better than both nonviolence and just war theory, and I support it and not them." I do urge you to support just peacemaking theory for what it actually contributes, and to teach it in your church and to demand its principles of your government. I urge you also to discuss both nonviolence and just war theory carefully, in your Christian community, and seek in prayer to discern together which is your calling. And commit yourselves in prayer and dedication to following Jesus in your ethic of peace, war, and peacemaking.

15

Human Rights

Paul Marshall

An Evangelical Commitment to Human Rights

Paralleling developments within the Roman Catholic Church, most evangelicals now believe that human rights are an essential expression of the gospel, that the language of rights is a good way to express Christian concerns,[1] and that any responsible faith-directed politics must be committed to defending and promoting human rights.[2]

This belief has now gone beyond theological and philosophical interpretation and has become the core of growing political action. This has been true for many years in the pro-life movement and in concerns about euthanasia and other aspects of modern medicine, and, for more politically liberal evangelicals, in matters of poverty and trade. But the late 1990s have also seen the rise of a broadly based evangelical movement concerned with rights overseas, especially with religious freedom. In cooperation with a broadly based coalition, it helped pass the 1998 International Religious Freedom Act and then pushed for a ceasefire and a peace agreement in Sudan, where the conflict has taken over two million lives. These efforts have often been criticized as, at bottom, only efforts to help Christians overseas and thus not a genuine universal concern for rights, but that criticism has been much more difficult to mount when the same coalition became the core, in cooperation with feminist groups, of major initiatives to stop sex trafficking and then took up the forgotten, ignored, and, to many of us, distasteful issue of prison rape.

A wide range of evangelical groups has also been in the forefront of efforts to get the U.S. government to act on AIDS, especially in Africa, and has been active in debt relief. Allen D. Hertzke maintains, "One cannot understand international relations today without comprehending the new faith-based movement aimed at shaping foreign policy—a bold assertion but one that will be born out in coming years."[3]

Despite the fact that most evangelicals believe that human rights are a good thing and flow from the gospel's influence in the West, there is no one particular approach that could appropriately be called the evangelical approach to or theory of human rights.[4] This reflects the larger fact that there is nothing that could appropriately be called the Christian approach to or theory of rights. Of course, this fragmentation of views reflects theological, philosophical, and political differences between Christians, but one other reason is that the words "right" and "rights" are used throughout the world, by Christians and non-Christians alike, in many different, and sometimes contradictory, ways. They are also applied to a bewilderingly broad range of things. Finally, since human rights are understood to be basic, fundamental, and foundational things, understanding them touches on the deepest theological, philosophical, and political questions.

The Differing Meanings of Rights

The language of human rights is now perhaps the most common contemporary way of addressing normative issues in politics worldwide.[5] Views of human rights are central to many modern theories of the nature and purpose of politics and to many laws. They occur in lectures and journals and in constitutional courts and street demonstrations. They also pervade the language of not only the academy, the courts, the legislatures, and the streets, but also the living room and the shopping mall. They have become part and parcel of our everyday language. When we believe that someone is doing something wrong, it is common no longer to say, "That is wrong," but instead to say, "You have no right to do that," or "You have no right to speak to me like that." In many cases the notion of rights and human rights has simply become the language in which people inside and outside of churches express our general concerns and hopes. Someone who claims that "everyone has a right to decent housing" might mean that this is a consequence of some specific inherent human right, or they might even mean that a proper interpretation of the law requires it. But they very often mean nothing more than that people *should have* decent housing, that it would be just and fair for the rest of us to try to make sure such housing is available. We speak of rights to decent medical treatment, to a safe environment; we say every child has a right to a stable home with two parents. In these expressions, the term "rights" has often lost any specific content and becomes a general term of approval or disapproval, commendation or criticism.

Human rights are also used to try to address issues as diverse as democracy, elections, courts, constitutions, tax policy, housing policy, war, torture, the criminal justice system, race, abortion, international trade, political freedoms, medical practice, the environment, homosexuality, marriage, and other sexual relations. Indeed, since rights can refer to so many different issues and mean so many different things, one notable feature of current political battles is that opponents usually vie with one another to appropriate the mantle of rights for their own position. As L. W. Sumner has pointed out: "It is the agility of rights, their talent for turning up on both sides of an issue, which is simultaneously their most impressive and their most troubling feature. Clearly, interest groups which agree on little else agree that rights are indispensable weapons in political debate."[6] In these debates rights are especially potent rhetorical weapons: "If one interest group has built its case on an alleged right none of its competitors can afford not to follow suit . . . they will tend to proliferate and to escalate."[7] Such proliferation and escalation is apparent throughout the world, and especially in the United States. The group that manages to get its issue defined and expressed as a call for human rights, such as a right to marry for gays, is often well on its way to political victory.

This stress on human rights is heightened by the claim that they are universal, as in the United Nation's *Universal Declaration of Human Rights*.[8] On a slightly less exalted plane, they are usually regarded as fundamental. In the 1966 United Nations *International Covenants on Human Rights*, they are described as "the foundation of freedom, justice, and peace in the world." More prosaically, they have been described as "trumps," as basic elements that, when rightfully claimed, properly override other political and legal considerations such as propriety, efficiency, and communal solidarity.[9]

As a result, despite our society's emphasis, even obsession, with rights, there is little clarity about what we mean or should mean when we talk about them. Arguments over the meaning of rights are a major part of our political disputes. People from all parts of the political spectrum have a love/hate relationship with "rights," depending on exactly what type of right they are talking about.

This means that we need to have some clarity about what we mean by rights.

Concerns about Rights

While there is a growing evangelical consensus about and action for rights, especially internationally, many Christians and others often also feel decidedly uneasy that so many domestic American issues are addressed in terms of rights. Typically, people who stress property rights reject notions of "gay rights." People who make strong demands for rights of religious freedom can be nervous about claims for free speech when obscenity and pornography come to the fore. Many things that we consider flat wrong are pushed in the name of rights.

There is also the worry that, even in cases where the issue might genuinely concern rights, then we may still overemphasize them to the exclusion of other legitimate political concerns. Many of our problems stem from good things that have been overstretched, sometimes even to the point of idolatry. As G. K. Chesterton wrote,

> When a religious scheme is shattered it is not merely the vices that are let loose. The vices are, indeed, let loose, and they wander and do damage. But the virtues are let loose also, and the virtues wander more wildly, and the virtues do more terrible damage. The modern world is full of the old Christian virtues gone mad. The virtues have gone mad because they are isolated from each other and are wandering alone. Thus some scientists care for truth; and their truth is pitiless. Thus some humanitarians only care for pity; and their pity (I am sorry to say) is often untruthful. . . .[10]

Although rights may be good, they are not the only good things, and they might squeeze out other good things. Rights emphasize what a person should have, not what they should do. If rights become the defining feature of our politics, then questions of what it is good for someone to do will tend to be subsumed under questions of what someone has a right to do, regardless of the consequences for others. The question of what others owe to us often takes priority over the question of what we might owe another. For these reasons, Kierkegaard regarded a concern for rights, even rights for all, as evocative of self-love. Simone Weil worried that rights had "a commercial flavor; essentially evocative of legal claims and arguments. Rights are always asserted in a tone of contention. . . ."[11] That was one reason that, when commissioned by the Free French Forces to produce a study on the promotion of human rights in post–Second World War France, she instead wrote a book entitled *The Need for Roots: Prelude to a Declaration of Duties towards Mankind*.[12]

Mary Ann Glendon argues that not so much rights themselves but a near exclusive fixation on them has hobbled American politics and poisoned its social relations. She describes current American rights talk as conspicuous in "its starkness and simplicity, its prodigality in bestowing the rights label, its legalistic character, its exaggerated absoluteness, its hyperindividualism, its insularity, and its silence with respect to personal, civic, and collective responsibilities."[13] It produces a "near-aphasia concerning responsibilities . . . without assuming . . . corresponding personal and civic obligations." It gives "excessive homage to individual independence and self sufficiency" and concentrates on the "individual and the state at the expense of the intermediate groups of civil society."[14] This, in turn, makes it "extremely difficult for us to develop an adequate conceptual apparatus for taking into account the sorts of groups within which human character, competence, and capacity for citizenship are formed. . . . For individual freedom and the general welfare alike, depend on the condition of the fine texture of civil society—on a fragile ecology for which we have no name."[15] Michael Ignatieff cautions that human rights can become idolatry.[16]

Similar concerns arise in evangelical circles. While most American evangelicals have a positive view of human rights, for some the whole idea is troubling. It smacks of an assertion of human pride and self-will rather than the humility that should mark our lives. A clamor for rights seems to violate any belief in sacrifice and servanthood, that we are called not to assert our own interests but first of all to serve others. The demand for rights seems to neglect the fact that, for example, the Bible pictures human beings as the clay and God as the potter who shapes our lives as he wills. In this sense, rights seem to run counter to the example of Jesus' life and to violate Paul's admonition to the Philippians: "Let each of you look not only to his own interests, but also to the interests of others. Have this mind among yourselves, which is yours in Christ Jesus, who, though he was in the form of God, did not count equality with God a thing to be grasped, but emptied himself, taking the form of a servant" (Phil. 2:4–7 RSV). It is difficult to read the story of Jesus' passion (or to see the movie *The Passion of the Christ*) and be quickly drawn to a notion of rights. However, rights need not be tied to an assertion of autonomy or self-will; they can be seen as a gift of God, as one expression of God's abundant grace.

A Basis for Rights and Rights Defenders

It is certainly true that the notion of rights can be exaggerated, overstretched, and misused—nowhere more so than in individualist North America, where every call for restraint sometimes seems to be met by the claim that "I have a right." But the misuse of something need not invalidate its proper use. Instead, we need to understand rights and their limits properly.

Furthermore, human will or self-assertion are not the only possible bases of rights. Rights can be understood as gifts, endowments. Indeed, this is an understanding reflected in the American Declaration of Independence, in which rights are described as "endowed" by God, something given to human beings that is appropriate for their nature. In thinking of rights, we should focus on the fact that all people are created by God and that every human being is made in his image. This too finds its place in America's founding documents, which speak of human beings not merely as equal, but as "*created* equal."[17] We should base our view of rights on who we are—we are created by God; what we are like—we are made in the image of God; and what has been given to us—God's free grace in Jesus Christ that justifies us before him.[18]

We are not autonomous creatures. The Scriptures know of no human beings who consist only in themselves: The core of being human is always being related to God.[19] Only by God's will are we created and do we exist (cf. Pss. 24:1, 139; Col. 1:15–20; Rev. 4:11). The great commandment is to love the Lord (Matt. 22:34–40). All sin is rooted in and manifested by a rejection of God and God's law (cf. Leviticus 19; Hosea 4). Human life is life properly lived in responsibility to God; to be human is to image God. In looking for the rights of humans, we should not look for a self-contained, inherent dignity or for the presence of a supposed defining human characteristic such as will, reason, or conscience. Instead, we should look first to our status as God's creatures.[20]

Similarly, if we are to speak of someone's rights, we cannot speak of their inherent goodness, nobility, or desert: We all have sinned and come short of the glory of God. Instead, we should understand rights in relation to the root of all right, righteousness, authority, and justice—the righteousness and justice of God manifested in the grace of God (cf. the Song of Moses, esp. Deut. 32:4–14; Ps. 89:5–19: Ps. 97; Isa. 5:16).[21]

This idea of our rights being rooted in God himself is manifest in the beginning of the Bible when the first killing occurred. When Cain murdered his brother Abel, the Lord appeared to him and said, "The voice of your brother's blood is crying to me from the ground" (Gen. 4:10 RSV). The word translated here as "crying" or "crying out" is *ze'aqah*. This word is used frequently throughout the Old Testament to mean the cry, complaint, or appeal of one who is suffering injustice. It is the word used to describe the lament of the poor and needy that led to the destruction of Sodom and Gomorrah (Gen. 18:20; Ezek. 16:49). It is the plea of Israel during their years of slavery in Egypt (Exod. 2:23–24). "Outcry" was also a technical legal term. It is similar to the current legal term "appeal," when a higher court is called to rectify injustice. If a human court does not fulfill its duty to defend the wronged, then the outcry will come to God, who is the final court, judge, and guardian of all justice. Hence, the use of the term "outcry" shows that God's appearance in response to Abel's death is being described in judicial terms. This continues throughout the Bible. God is always the one who hears the cry of the wronged (Exod. 22:22, 27). God punishes Sodom and Gomorrah as a result of the cry of the poor and needy (Gen. 18:20ff.; Ezek. 16:49). G. von Rad writes, "The word outcry (*ze'aqah*) . . . is a technical legal term and designates the cry for help which one who suffers a great injustice screams. . . . With this cry for help . . . he appeals for the protection of the legal community. What it does not hear or grant, however, comes directly before Yahweh as the guardian of all right."[22]

God decided to punish Cain for the murder of his brother but did not simply make him an outcast, an outlaw, since God in mercy also placed a mark on Cain to protect him too from wrongful killing (Gen. 4:8–17). Cain had complained that he would be hidden from God's face, and he was terrified that he would be denied God's judicial protection ("Whoever finds me will kill me," v. 14 NIV). When the Scriptures speak of God "hiding his face," they mean that God is hidden, is not responding to the cry of the people, that God is silent and does not come to his people's defense. This occurs in Psalm 27:

When evildoers assail me . . .
  [I will] inquire in his temple . . .
Hear, O LORD, when I cry aloud . . .
Thou hast said, "Seek ye my face."
  My heart says to thee,
"Thy face, LORD, do I seek."
  Hide not thy face from me.

Turn not thy servant away in anger,
  thou who hast been my help.
Cast me not off, forsake me not . . .

Verses 2, 4, 7–9

The imagery is that, when God's face is revealed, righteousness and justice prevail. When God's face is hidden, evil seems to prosper and the wicked triumph. The "mark of Cain," a mark signifying that God's face was not turned away, and hence also a mark of protection, was not merely particular to Cain as an individual: It was also a sign that God had appointed an order to maintain justice. This order embraced *every* human being and demanded that they treat each other as God intended.

Much of this interchange can be expressed in terms of rights. When Cain was murdered, his very blood is described as making a judicial appeal for justice, an appeal to which God responds. Whenever there is genuine injustice, a genuine violation of human rights, it comes to the ears of God, who demands justice.

Hence, God covenants with Abraham and promises to save his descendants when they are enslaved (Gen. 15:13–14). God then hears the outcry (*ze'aqah*) of Israel in Egypt. Israel has a claim on God, not because they are especially righteous but because of God's gracious promise (Deut. 7:7; 9:4–6). Moses relies on this claim in order to rescue Israel after the golden calf (Exod. 32:11–13; 33:12–16). Israel is continually saved through claims upon God's promises (1 Kings 8:46–53; Nehemiah 9; Dan. 9:1–19).

It is not only God who must respond to injustice: It becomes a responsibility given to the human race itself. After the story of Cain, the next figure to whom Genesis devotes major attention is Noah. Noah is not only the person entrusted with saving the animals; he is also the bearer of new human political responsibilities. As he had with Abel, God said to Noah, "I shall demand account of your life-blood" (Gen. 9:5 NJB). However, unlike the situation with Cain and Abel, when God appeared directly as a judge, this accounting was no longer solely God's responsibility: now it was shared with human beings. In Genesis 9:6, after the ark had landed, as part of the renewal of the cultural mandate, God stressed to Noah and his family the human responsibility for dealing with injustice, saying, "Who sheds the blood of man, *by man* shall his blood be shed, for in the image of God was man created" (NJB; italics added).

Many of the discussions of this text focus only on the issue of capital punishment. But here I want to emphasize not what the *penalty* was, but *who* was supposed to ensure that the penalty was applied. In the case of Cain, it was God who appeared directly. But now, God said "by man" shall blood be shed. Human beings are being charged with the responsibility for dealing with injustice directly. They were no longer simply to wait for God's appearing in justice and mercy but were themselves to be active. Eventually this would be applied not only to extreme injustice like murder, but also to other problems of human life.

A new vocation, a new ministry, had now been given. Human beings were to be not only planters and herders and artists—they were to be *judges* as well. As Noah and his offspring spread throughout the world, they would take with them the task of maintaining a just order in human relations. A responsibility for upholding justice and rights had been delegated to humankind.

These claims for a situation to be "righted," and the continuing human responsibility to right them, rest not on human merit but upon the promised justice, righteousness, and grace of God. This is why the authors of the Psalms frequently claim to be in the right—not because they are personally righteous but because God has put them in the right. This is why the Lord always defends the right of the poor and needy, not because they are themselves righteous but because God upholds righteousness and defends those who suffer unrighteousness (cf. Amos 2:4, 7; 3:10–11; 4:12–13; 5:6–7, 10–15, 24).

In the New Testament, the claims of humanity based on the grace of God achieve their focus in John's remarkable statement, "To all who received him, to those who believed in his name, he gave the right [*exousia*, authority] to become children of God" (John 1:12 NIV). Because of this claim, Paul is under an *obligation* to the Greeks and barbarians (Rom. 1:14). The root of all claims to be righted, of all human rights, is the authority to be children of God given in and by the grace of God through Jesus Christ (cf. Titus 3:4–7).

Human beings have rights because God cares for us, protects us, and demands justice for us, and in that sense gives us rights. Hence, a Christian understanding of rights should flow from the recognition that, through God's continuing justice, mercy, and provision for us, we have a claim to be in a right relation with one another and we can claim what God says is right for us. We are given a place in the world in which we can make decisions, accept responsibility, and live our lives. Whether we are aware of it or not, and whether we acknowledge it or not, we are given the responsibility, and therefore the right, to fulfill the tasks that have been given to us. In short, we have the right to do what we are properly called to do. Our rights relate to and stem from our duties and responsibilities. This is why the political order should be understood as one in which men and women can express themselves as people made in the image of God.

Rights should be unfolded in terms of our human duties and responsibilities in the world. We find the authority and responsibility of the person by understanding our place in God's creation. God has made us, male and female, and placed us within the world to love our Creator and Redeemer, to love our neighbors as ourselves, and to steward the earth. This is what we are made for; this is what we are fitted for. We all are called, both Christian and non-Christian, to live out every dimension of our lives in joyful obedience to God.

We, along with all creatures, are God's servants. We may say that each of us has a right to be a servant of God, to fulfill our particular office and calling for God's glory. Human beings have a claim to be able to do what God calls them to do. Our rights relate to our God-given human duties and responsibilities. Human beings have a right to the institutions and the resources they need to carry out their responsibilities. Hence, the political order must be one in which men and women can express themselves as God's imagers, or to put it another way, there must be social space for human personality.

This necessarily implies, first of all, the right to be, the right to life itself, the right to be unharmed.[23] This right belongs to each human life. Such human life always exists in bodies of flesh and blood and bones; hence, humans have a right to remain whole, not to be harmed, aborted, maimed, tortured, molested, placed in hostage, or terrorized. The basic needs of individuals for food, nurture, shelter, and care are implicit in the right to life itself. The biblical message pointedly indicates that the fulfillment of such needs is a matter of God's requirement of justice. This justice therefore requires an allocation of material and cultural goods such that human life is made possible, protected, and enhanced so that humans can realize their God-given tasks within human history. These tasks entail the use of "nature" and its resources. This use is not only a right of the human species or of the human "community," for each of us is also called. The earth is the Lord's, and persons have the right to a stewardly possession and use of it. In a differentiated society, this implies some right to privacy and, its concomitant, private property.

Similarly, we may speak of the rights of humans as parents to raise and educate their children, for so God has commanded us. We may also speak of the right to be allowed to marry and have family life. As God holds us responsible for the politics of this world, we may also speak of the rights of citizens to exercise responsibility and authority for the direction of the state. In each area of God's calling and callings to humankind, individually and together, we can speak of the human right to what is needed to fulfill those callings.

The Relations of and Misuse of Rights

This description of rights so far has only addressed rights as rightful claims, the things that justice requires be secured for people. It has not addressed a multitude of further complexities. One of these is the problem of sin: Do rights still pertain when humankind is fallen? Are rights forfeited, or can they be ignored, when people do not use their freedom in order to act in responsible ways? Other questions concern how rights should be related to each other, how rights relate to law and politics, and who is responsible for meeting these rights.

I have tried to suggest that our rights are not rooted in our own righteousness or independent dignity; they are rooted in God's graceful dealing with us. God's ordering of creation, the calling given to us all, does not cease because of human sin, although, because of such sin, God's provisions for us are misused and turned to evil. Hence, sin does not eradicate rights, nor does the misuse of the freedom of rights lead to their forfeiture. Their use and misuse are the responsibility of those who have such rights. The wheat and the tares will coexist until God's final day of judgment. Therefore, even though rights are granted as freedoms, as room, as social space, to act according to God's calling, one cannot be *forced* to follow that calling within one's sphere of right. If we deny this, then we must deny human rights. All of us fail in our callings, all of us misuse freedom, none of us perfectly reflects the *imago Dei*.

There is also the problem that legitimate claims and rights can conflict. There are many persons with rights, and their exercise of those rights will affect the lives and rights of others. The claim of one to free speech will affect the claim of another to be dealt with truthfully and with integrity. The claim of one to property will affect the claim of another to food and shelter. The claim of one to resources will reduce what is available to meet other claims. In this situation we cannot pretend that human rights are invariant. Rather, they are specific, varied, legitimate claims that must all be addressed simultaneously. There are claims for access to food and shelter by some, with claims for the means of education by others, with claims not to be interfered with by others. None of these claims is illegitimate, so none can be dismissed. None of these claims is invariant and contextless, for each claim always affects the treatment of other such legitimate claims. In addition, the very limits of resources mean that all possible claims cannot be met simultaneously. In this situation, *justice* points to the manner and means of weighing and simultaneously meeting different rights. Rights, in turn, as God-given arenas of authority, point to *what it is that must be related in a just fashion.*[24]

Rights, Government, and Law

So far, we have not addressed the question of how rights should find political expression. The fact that we have some understanding of what is owed to human beings, what they may rightfully claim, does not itself tell us how such an owing should find expression in laws, constitutions, or bills of rights. What should be is not the same thing as what should be required by law, backed by the possibility of state coercion.

For example, in the Scriptures, we find the right of field-workers to eat while harvesting (Deut. 23:25), limitations on slavery (Exod. 21:2; Lev. 25:10, 39ff.), protections of female slaves (Exod. 21:7–11), provisions for the equitable distribution of land (Num. 33:54; Lev. 25:14–18, 25–34), and the general theme of the subordination of rulers to law (1 Sam. 22:17; 2 Samuel 11–12). But it is not always clear that these requirements were backed by sanctions, that is, that an Israelite would be punished for violating them. Also, these rights were not universal human rights. They were held generally by the Israelites themselves but were not equally applicable to women or to aliens. (Though, since the eventual goal was to universalize God's law so that it would become clearly applicable to all humans—a theme developed in the New Testament—it may be argued that they were akin to legal human rights.)

Within a legal system, rights, or at least some rights, need to be far more than rightful moral claims. They must be strong and enforceable political and legal guarantees. With important political rights, we want more than for someone to sympathize that we did not receive what we rightfully should; instead, we want a judge or some other authority to announce that legally guaranteed human rights have been violated and that some enforceable remedy will be forthcoming. This is especially the case with fundamental human rights, where we are dealing not with just any of the myriad injustices and responsibilities that affect our lives, but expressly with the fundamental conditions of free human life. This means that we need to ascertain those rights that should be guaranteed by governments and also those rights that are fundamental, lest the whole idea of political rights be squandered or diluted by reducing them to every human claim or desire, even if legitimate. They should be reserved for those things without which free human life is not possible. And, of course, these are the areas that are most subject to political conflict and governmental intrusion.

Those rights that should be politically guaranteed require human rights laws that can direct and constrain governments in such a way that rights cannot easily be disregarded. This is a major reason why it is often desirable to place guarantees of such rights within a constitution. Constitutional laws are usually not simply rules made by the legislature for the population at large and which, hence, can be changed by the legislature, but they are meant to restrict, control, and direct the government, even if it has popular support. They are laws binding on the government itself, which cannot be changed except through a laborious process usually following a major change in public opinion. Hence, the protection of rights often and properly finds its expression in constitutional bills of rights, such as that in the Bill of Rights in the U.S. Constitution.

However, while bills of rights are vitally important, they are not the only form of human rights protection. Another important way of safeguarding human rights is democracy, since if a government is genuinely answerable to the population, then it will be far more reluctant to threaten or abuse them. Other political structures such as federalism, or the separation of political power into judicial, legislative, and executive branches, are means to prevent the overconcentration of political power and therefore can be at the same time protections against violations of human rights. This is one reason why the protections in the Bill of Rights were only added as amendments to the U.S. Constitution and were not part of the original document. Several authors of the Constitution believed that the restrictions that they had already put on the power of government through democratic elections, federalism, and the division of powers would be sufficient to protect rights: It was only subsequent pressure in order to get the Constitution ratified that led to the additional guarantees of a bill of rights in order to satisfy those more demanding.

As Johan van der Vyver notes:

> The primary function of a bill of rights is . . . on a par with other constitutional strategies for the limitation of state authority. Such strategies include the principle of representative government in a democratic dispensation; decentralization of the instruments of government in a federal structure with autonomous regional and local bureaucracies; distribution of state authority through the separation of powers; . . . surveillance of administrative acts by an ombudsman; subjection of the powers of government to the rule of law; and shielding a defined category of fundamental freedoms against legislative and executive encroachment in a bill of rights regime.[25]

Another form of protection developed in recent decades has been international human rights law. In such law, states make treaties with one another to protect rights. The rights protected by international law usually include "civil and political" rights. These typically involve freedom from discrimination; rights to life, liberty, and security of the person; freedom from torture or cruel punishment; the right to legal personality and a fair trial; freedom of movement and residence; the right to asylum, to a nationality, to marry and found a family, to property; freedom of religion, thought, conscience, opinion, and expression; and the right to take part in the government of one's country and to equal access to public services. Most human rights advocates support the rights on this list. Many charters now often include another group of rights usually referred to as "economic, social, and cultural" rights. These include the right to social security, the right to work, the right to a standard of living adequate for well-being, and the right to education. These will be discussed below.

The earliest European examples of such arrangements are probably the post-Reformation treaties that guaranteed religious freedom to minority religious groups.[26] Hugo Grotius and Emerich de Vattel, the principal theorists of international law, both made provision for the international protection of rights. This in turn helped shape the nineteenth-century conventions on slavery, the turn of the century Hague and Geneva Conventions on conduct during warfare, the labor standards formulated by the International Labor Organization (1919), and the largely impotent charter of the post–World War I League of Nations.[27]

In World War II, the protection of human rights became a rallying point for the Allied powers and hence became a key feature in the formation of the United Nations. This produced the 1948 "Universal Declaration of Human Rights and Fundamental Freedoms," which in turn acquired legal status in the form of the "International Covenant on Economic, Social and Cultural Rights" (1966) and the "International Covenant on Civil and Political Rights" (1966). Subsequently, there have been regional treaties along similar lines. These are the European "Convention for the Protection of Human Rights and Fundamental Freedoms" (1950), the "American Convention on Human Rights" (1969), and the "African Convention on Human and Peoples' Rights" (1981). At present the European system is the most developed and active.

Because these treaties exist *between* states, governments can be held accountable by others when they abuse their own populations. They cannot claim that such abuse is simply an internal matter, since it is already part of a treaty, an agreement that they have made with other countries and to which they are bound. If human rights are understood in this way, and if it is the task of governments to work for justice even beyond their own boundaries, then the protection of human rights not only is important internally in the United States, but also should be a part of foreign policy.

Different Types of Rights

While we should defend genuine rights, there is the problem that, as we have seen, the expression "human rights" means many things. How do we decide which of these are genuine, and which of these genuine ones are of the type that should be enforced by the state? One of the major examples of this debate occurs in the question of whether what are called "economic rights," such as a right to welfare or housing or education, should really be regarded as fundamental human rights. This matter is debated ferociously throughout the world, is the cause of major arguments in international relations, and has become intertwined with debates about whether a stress on rights of individual freedom is truly universal or only reflects Western individualism.[28]

Countries such as China, Iran, and Malaysia have maintained heatedly that human rights should come to very different expressions in different countries. In fact, there are increasing claims, by several Asian and Muslim countries, that many currently recognized international civil and political rights do not have a universal character at all, but are simply Western inventions and impositions. They claim that these "rights" simply reflect Western values and should properly be subordinated to their own Confucian or Islamic traditions.

Meanwhile, United Nations gatherings such as the Cairo Population Conference or the Beijing Women's Conference have continued to advocate new and wider, and wilder, rights, such as to abortion or to a clean and sustainable environment, with promiscuous abandon. Many seem never to have met any claim to a right they didn't like.

In this setting, the need to clarify the meaning of and justification for human rights is not some sterile academic exercise. It is, rather, a vital condition for clarifying some of the major cultural, social, and political problems we face, both domestically and internationally. This comes to the fore in the debates over "social" or "economic" rights.

The question of "economic rights" is also tied intimately to the vexed question of the universality of rights. Critics of such rights say that the problem with treating economic provisions as if they were rights is that there are often legitimate reasons why a particular government would not be able to fulfill such rights at a given historical juncture. Even a well-meaning government may not be able to guarantee income, or housing, or health care, or even food. Many African countries simply do not have the resources to do so. Consequently, if we were to treat economic guarantees as rights, then we would be forced to accept that rights cannot and need not be met immediately. They would be things to be *aimed for* rather than *guaranteed*. The result is that we will end up diluting rights to mere goals and denying their immediacy.

In addition, several Asian countries have attempted to use the nonimmediate character of "economic rights" to reduce all rights simply to long-term goals that governments should pursue, rather than stringent limits to which governments should adhere. China says it stresses "economic rights" as its long-term aspiration, then slides into treating the eradication of torture and press freedom also as long-term goals rather than as immediate demands. The issue of jailing and beating peaceful opponents is then put off into the long-term future on the grounds that rights are only goals.

Defenders of economic rights counter that often they can be more important than political rights. This argument usually takes some form of saying that "a hungry man or woman wants food more than elections." The common response to this is that if someone is actually starving to death in a famine, this is doubtless true, but as a general argument, it is spurious. Even when people are poor and needy, with generally not enough to eat, they may and do care very much about political freedom. People throughout the world cry out for relief from repressive governments, and just because people are hungry is no reason to repress them as well: This would be sadism of a high order.

To this response is added the argument that there need not be any real competition between political freedom and economic well-being, as though countries should put off freedom until they are wealthy. A half-century of international experience indicates that politically free societies are precisely the ones whose citizens have become the most comfortably housed and fed and have the best medical care.[29] Rather, it is the countries with authoritarian governments where people languish in poverty, sometimes to the point of starvation. While some Asian countries have managed for a while to combine economic success with authoritarian government, they are a distinct minority. They also face increasing pressure for democratization. Similarly, as Nobel Prize winner Amartya Sen has shown, countries with a free press no longer have famines, since the publicity given to people's suffering ignites action for relief, and there is no shortage of relief supplies if agencies are allowed to deliver them.[30] It is only in authoritarian settings where the government has the power to repress reports of what is happening that people can be hidden, ignored, and forgotten as they starve. Modern famines are the result of political action by corrupt governments such as in Sudan and North Korea. Consequently, there are no grounds for rejecting political rights, such as freedom of the press, in pursuit of supposed economic security. The opposite is true: Where there are political rights, economic rights are also likely to be met.

Defenders of economic rights often counter that these arguments are true but do not undercut economic rights per se. They only show that trying to pursue economic rights while denying political rights is a contradiction. They demonstrate instead that one should not downgrade or reject the importance of political and individual freedom while pursuing economic and social guarantees. Hence, they imply that the proper strategy is to pursue both kinds of rights simultaneously.

Another argument advanced by critics of the notion of economic rights is that genuine universal human rights must actually be capable of being fulfilled universally, and that economic rights often cannot make such a claim, since poverty-stricken countries can legitimately assert that they have no near-term possibility of honestly furnishing such guarantees.

Defenders of economic rights counter that some political rights, such as regular elections or the provision of legal counsel, can also suffer from the same defect of lack of resources. For example, Rwanda simply does not have enough lawyers to defend those accused in its genocide. Even a well-meaning government may lack the resources to actually make such guarantees real. This is much more so in the case of defending citizens from external attack, which may require extremely expensive armed forces, forces that many states simply cannot afford. Hence, if universal human rights are only those that all governments can actually meet at all times, then there are several political rights that cannot be universal either.

These arguments will no doubt continue. My own view is that, in suggesting what proper, *politically enforceable*, universal human rights are, we should focus not on what governments *should* do but on what they *should not* do.[31]

If a government is actually capable of exercising authority over its territory—that is, as long as it actually is a functioning government—then it can refrain from torturing, killing, or arbitrarily imprisoning its citizens. These restrictions do not require an especially powerful or wealthy government, but only a functioning government. They do not require wealth, for they do not ask a government to do something, but ask it *not* to do something. Therefore, they can be universal in the sense that any functioning government can meet them.

Hence, if rights are universal in this sense, they will usually lie in those areas of human life where governments should *refrain* from acting. This is not as peculiar as it at first might sound. It is in fact the structure of most American constitutional rights. The very first words of the Bill of Rights are: "Congress shall make *no law* . . ." In fact, the basic structure of the First, Second, Third, Fourth, Fifth, Seventh, Eighth, Ninth, and Tenth Amendments is to say what the government *cannot* do: "no law . . . not be infringed . . . no soldier . . . no person . . . no fact . . . not required . . . not be construed . . . not delegated . . ." The Third, Fifth, Eighth, and Tenth amendments do not even use the term "rights"; they simply tell the government what not to do, which has the same effect. In America, at least, most constitutional rights are focused on what governments should not do.

Conclusions

Human rights properly understood are compatible with and, indeed, flow from a Christian view of the person and of the authority of the state. The basis of human rights need not be human will or autonomy but can be understood as an expression of the grace of God extended to all. Human beings, as *imago Dei*, may rightfully claim that which they need to fulfill their God-given responsibilities. Hence, rights should not be multiplied endlessly according to the assertion of human will but must reflect a normative understanding of genuine human responsibility and authority.

Governments need to recognize human rights and guarantee those that are compatible with their own responsibility, authority, and ability. This implies that we should be careful about distinguishing human rights understood as universal moral claims from those human rights that should also be enforced by government and, perhaps, put in a constitutional bill of rights. Those who advocate for legally imposed economic and social rights should be aware that this implies that we are using the word "rights" to refer to, on the one hand, those things that governments should always or never do, and, on the other hand, those things that governments should always try to achieve. If we use the term "rights" for both of these, we should be aware that we are using it in two different senses.

Finally, we live in an age when evangelical awareness of and practical commitment to human rights are rapidly expanding. This will continue to present questions and problems such as those described here and also far beyond them. This is to be expected in a world both complex and suffused with evil and suffering. Our ongoing challenge is to continue and deepen our work, knowing that it is part of our response to the grace and rights God has bestowed on us.

Part IV

Implementation

16

In the Arena

Practical Issues in Concrete Political Engagement

Stephen Monsma and Mark Rodgers

POLITICAL ENGAGEMENT IS hundreds of miles removed from polite, theoretical discussions of lofty principles. It involves applying theoretical principles to very concrete, specific issues and situations where opinions differ, interests clash, and information is missing. Translating a framework of basic evangelical principles for political engagement—such as justice and freedom—into concrete political action is no easy task. Doing so requires wisdom and patience, combined with both a realistic understanding of the political world and much prayer. History is littered with attempts of sincere, Bible-believing Christians to bend the political world in ways Christians now agree could not have been the will of a just God. One thinks of the crusades of Medieval Europe, the religious persecutions of the Reformation era, American slave owners using biblical references with which to justify slavery, and—more recently—the opposition of many white evangelicals to Martin Luther King Jr. and his efforts to bring about greater racial justice.

These past errors stand as witnesses to the need for us to proceed with caution and careful thought when we take on the awesome task of applying basic biblical principles to today's swirling, confusing political world. But we also believe the lesson to be drawn from past errors is not to withdraw from the political world and do nothing. Our Lord calls us to be salt and light in a darkening world. We dare not disobey out of timidity and fear. In fact, a great cloud of witnesses testifies to the importance of political engagement. There is William Wilburforce, who played a key role in ending the English slave trade and initiating other reforms. There is William Lloyd Garrison, who played a key role in the abolitionist movement, and Susan B. Anthony, who did much for women's rights. In our own day there are individuals such as Mark Hatfield, Jimmy Carter, C. Everett Koop, Dan Coates, and Chuck Colson, all of whom have cited their evangelical faith as their motivating force. The world and the United States are better, more just places because of the efforts of evangelical Christians such as these. Evangelical organizations such as Prison Fellowship, Evangelicals for Social Action, Focus on the Family, the Center for Public Justice, World Vision, World Relief, the Christian Legal Society's Center for Law and Religious Freedom, and many, many more are making a difference in our nation and world. All these stand as witnesses that, by God's grace, persons and organizations can be used by him to bring greater justice and peace to this broken world.

But history also teaches Christians to move into active political engagement only after careful reflection and much prayer. This is not an area to rush into with a maximum of enthusiasm and good intentions and a minimum of thought and planning.

In this chapter we seek to aid in this thought and planning, first by suggesting some basic perspectives on taking God's truths into the political arena. Next we consider various types of political involvement that are open to Christians. We then go on to consider compromise in the political arena and what types of compromise are and are not appropriate as Christians engage the political world. This is followed by a section dealing with the ethical implication of Christians forming alliances with others who do not share our basic Christian perspectives.

Living God's Truth in a Broken World: Basic Perspectives

Three basic facts set the context within which Christians who seek to engage the political world of necessity operate. One basic fact is the sinful, broken nature of the political world. Something terrible has gone wrong in the political world. Christians acknowledge that this is true in all aspects of human society, but the political world appears from the outside to be especially prone to human greed, attempts at self-serving aggrandizement, and unethical means to achieve goals. One can debate whether it is more or less "dirty" than other human endeavors, but that is really beside the point. Anyone entering the political arena must realize one is entering a very imperfect world deeply broken by human sinfulness.

A second basic fact is that Christians entering the political world—even when they do so prayerfully and with a passion for following their risen Lord and his Word—bring with them a burden of biased perspectives, incomplete knowledge, and their own sinfulness. Good intentions and a sincere passion for a more just world are no guarantee that we will not err. We come with our own biases shaped by our backgrounds and life experiences. Also, the political world and public policy issues are typically very complex issues, with crucial facts unknown or in dispute and consequences of contemplated actions far from certain. Add to this that redeemed sinners are still sinners; we may all too easily confuse God's will with our self-centered desires, and biblical commands with what will feed our egos. It should be no surprise, therefore, that well-informed and well-meaning Christians engaged in policy development and advocacy often differ on specific proposals.

A third basic fact setting the context for Christian political engagement is that political activity is "downstream" of culture, and to truly shape the direction of the nation, Christians must be strategically "upstream" of politics. The options available to elected officials, whether legislation or executive order, are limited by public opinion, and public opinion is shaped by much more than political rhetoric. The elites in higher education, the news media, and the entertainment industry shape our worldviews—our hearts and our minds—and are as much a determinant of political outcome as the men and women we elect to represent us in the political arena.

Take the issue of gay marriage, for example. Less than a decade ago, it would have been unthinkable that states would legalize gay marriage, and public opinion was overwhelmingly on the side of traditionalists. Few believed it was necessary to pass legislation, much less a constitutional amendment, to define marriage as an institution preserved uniquely for the union of a man and a woman. It would have been easy, but who would have thought it was needed? However, in a very short time, public acceptance of homosexuality increased. The relativistic "who am I to say" ethos has created an environment such that very few elected members are willing to stand up to the cultural elite and risk being viewed as judgmental because they oppose gay marriage. Accusations such as "homophobia" and "intolerance" have defined the parameters of the possible.

And what has shaped public opinion? Not political rhetoric. In the past ten years, Congress passed the Defense of Marriage Act, and the voters of some states have passed through referenda resolutions protecting heterosexual marriage. Institutions upstream of politics have largely shaped public opinion, and in the case of homosexuality, the institutions of influence have largely been academia and entertainment. There is hardly a college that has not integrated "sensitivity" training in its freshman orientation. Many sitcoms and movies have a gay character who is presented as well adjusted and, well, more normal than the rest of us.

As elite attitudes and public opinions shift, the "moral majority" becomes a minority, and political and legislative options become limited. It is critical, therefore, for those in the church concerned about the direction of the country to look not just to politics for redemption, or worse, to withdraw once again and look just to spiritual conversion as the answer to cultural crisis. Christians must understand that to shape the direction of a country, we must shape its dominant worldview, and this means approaching the concern in a holistic manner. The church has to equip the saints for works of service, and to transform the culture, Christians must be trained as teachers, reporters, and actors.

Before we discuss political engagement more fully, we want to stress that we believe that although some success can be realized by Christians creating parallel or alternative structures (such as contemporary Christian music) to compete with mainstream, secular ones, such efforts largely aim to keep Christians from being "conformed to the world." If transformation is the goal, Christians must work within mainstream structures and institutions. Christian colleges are a vital component of the church's effort to "renew the minds" of its people. However, Christians should also seek to serve in secular colleges and universities. In politics, third-party efforts usually fail. They may help shape the debate, but they rarely elect the winner. In fact, such efforts often unfortunately end up being counterproductive. We urge the church to train men and women to be salt and light in such vocations as journalists, musicians, scriptwriters, and professors. And we urge the church to validate and support their calling when they go into the world—into New York and Hollywood, as well as Washington. Too often the church has created a hierarchy of calling and discouraged its best and brightest members from entering fields other than explicit Christian "ministry."

These three basic facts that shape the context of evangelical political engagement—the sinful nature of the political world, the limitations of Christians engaged in the political world, and the political world being downstream from culture—are not an argument for avoiding political engagement. Far from it. We are firmly convinced that God calls Christians to be active in the political world *as Christians*, that is, as persons whose stances and actions are shaped by their faith in Jesus Christ as the Lord of their lives and their Savior from sin.

We believe Christians today should take their cue from such Old Testament saints as Daniel, Esther, Mordecai, and Nehemiah. All four lived and worked in a culture even more thoroughly pagan than our own. All gained high political positions by working, so to speak, within the system, proving themselves valuable to the secular rulers by way of their abilities, dedication, and honesty. Yet they also held firmly to certain principles and were willing to risk even death rather than give up their principles or abandon their most basic goals. Think of Mordecai who coached Esther before she entered the competition to become queen. He reported a conspiracy to assassinate the king, persuaded Esther to risk death to save her people, refused to bow before Haman, the king's high official, and finally rose to be second in rank after the king, where he used his influence to work "for the good of his people and spoke up for the welfare of all the Jews" (Esther 10:3 NIV).

God has indeed used godly persons to make a difference in the midst of cultures that do not recognize him, and he continues to do so today. Our point in emphasizing the sinful nature of the political world, the limitations of Christians engaged in the political world, and the political world being downstream from culture is, first, that the Christian ought to approach political involvement with *a realistic understanding of the modest gains one is likely to achieve by political involvement.* Political change, when it comes at all, almost always comes slowly. The forces that are opposed to what one is seeking to accomplish are typically strong and their tactics often unfair. The culture sets the political agenda and limits what can be accomplished. One should never expect that God's kingdom on earth is going to be quickly and easily ushered in by political means. By God's grace and his leading, some change for the good may be brought about by political means. In recent years, new pressures have been brought to bear on foreign regimes that are engaging in religious persecution, some limited restrictions have been placed on the accessibility of abortion, limited school voucher programs have been enacted and at least one has been upheld by the Supreme Court, and some faith-based social services programs receiving government funds have been granted new religious-freedom protections. Evangelical Christians have actively helped to achieve all four of these public policy changes. There are other positive policy changes that we could cite as well. But all of these successes—as constructive and as encouraging as they are—are of a limited, partial nature and came only after monumental, lengthy struggles. Political engagement is no quick-fix shortcut to ushering in God's kingdom on earth.

A second quality with which Christians ought to approach the political world is *a strong sense of humility.* We can be certain about basic principles clearly revealed and firmly rooted in God's inspired Word; we need to be much less certain about our sincere yet often fumbling attempts to apply those basic principles to the concrete political world. As the late evangelical Congressman Paul Henry once said in a lecture, "Of course, the issue is not whether there are moral absolutes, but the degree to which we can confidently apply them absolutely without falling into moral pretense" (Koopman 262). We can be certain from the witness of Scripture, for example, that God has established the family and intends for a man and a woman to live in a lifelong bond of love and commitment, caring for each other's and their children's welfare. All Scripture witnesses to this principle, from the opening chapters of Genesis to Paul's epistles. But does this mean we as evangelical Christians should favor and work to pass family leave legislation that guarantees the right of parents to take time off from work to care for a newborn child or a family member experiencing severe illness—when this would mean a new mandate on employers? Or should Christians support a "flextime" approach that gives employees flexibility regarding time off without placing as great a burden on employers? One immediately recognizes there is a big difference between a basic principle and its application in a concrete time and place.

In applying basic principles to concrete situations, Christians inevitably face challenges such as unrealistic expectations, inadequate information, tactical questions, and the complexity of many issues that end up in the public policy arena for resolution. To compound matters, often the Word of God does not speak directly to these issues in the context of legislative remedies. The Bible clearly does not give specific direction to social security reform, international trade agreements, or State Department reauthorization. Scripture shapes our hearts and minds; it does not give answers to specific twenty-first-century public policy debates.

The results of taking a certain course of action will often be uncertain, and the exact extent or cause of a certain problem will more often than not be in dispute. Also, questions of tactics and timing frequently emerge. In regard to the persecution of Christians in China, is relief more likely to come by isolating China and imposing sanctions on the current regime, or is it more likely to come by a policy of engagement, in which commercial and cultural ties are established with China in the hope of gradually encouraging greater religious freedom through dialogue and gentle but constant pressure? No one can say with certainty. The situation becomes even more complex when one thinks in terms of concrete legislative proposals. Early in the Bush administration, there was a dispute over whether the goals of its faith-based initiative would be more fully achieved if a gradual, consensus-building approach was taken or if a strong, cut-to-the-heart-of-the-matter approach was taken by way of legislation. Questions of timing and tactics arise in the real political world. And too often Christians equate tactics with principles.

All this counsels the Christian who is actively engaged with the political world to approach that world with a deep sense of humility. One must act on the basis of the best information one has, combined with a thoughtful understanding of basic biblical principles and with prayerful consideration. But one should also act with a humble realization that one's perspective on an issue may be narrow, incorrect, or based on erroneous assumptions, and that with more and better information and further reflection and prayer, one may conclude a different approach is warranted. Christians should not be known for wagging fingers or impugning motivations. We should be known for our conviction and our civility.

These words of warning do not mean that we as evangelicals should be so overwhelmed by caution that we are immobilized, afraid to take any action out of fear that we may be wrong and out of a realization that we can make only limited gains in any case. They do not argue for a passivity that ignores the cries of the oppressed and needy. We as evangelicals have much to offer those "in authority over us," and to fail to act is to fail to shine the light of the gospel in the halls of government that are part of God's ordering of this world. They do argue, however, for a humility that should always mark the Christian and for an avoidance of a triumphalism that arrogantly believes we can bring in God's kingdom by our own efforts.

Different Forms of Involvement

As we stated earlier, we believe that it is the duty of every Christian, just as it is the duty of every citizen, to exercise his or her right in this free democracy to participate in the political process. We are blessed with a political system that, although not perfect and inhabited by fallen men and women, is open to everyone who desires to participate, whether they try to affect government policy from without or direct it deeply from within.

There are two ways to affect politics without running for office or working in government yourself—you can either go it alone or you can join with other like-minded men and women. But either way, you can't make a difference in politics unless you get involved.

Individually, the most minimal level of involvement—but a remarkable right unavailable to millions of people in other countries—is to vote. Too many people complain about their elected leaders but fail to vote when Election Day comes around. Voting starts with being registered, continues by knowing the candidates, and ends in the election booth.

The question should be not whether to vote but for whom to vote. It is critical for every Christian to be an informed voter. Politics can be complicated, and life can be more so. In the real world we all live in, with competition for our time and attention coming from work, family, church, service, and leisure, it can be difficult to find time to study up on issues and candidates. To simplify this process, we suggest that there are two basic indicators to help voters determine whom to support. First, although we do not advocate single-issue voting, there will often be an issue, such as the death penalty or abortion, that will be an "indicator issue" to help guide one's vote. There are times that both candidates may have the same position, and then other "indicator issues" will take priority. But faced with a choice of a dozen or more candidates on Election Day, knowing where they stand on an issue or issue set about which you are deeply concerned is critical.

The second indicator is party affiliation. We do not want to suggest that Christians should always support the Democratic or the Republican Party. Both have strengths and weaknesses. The Democratic Party has been strong on social justice but weak on issues of sexual morality. The Republican Party has promoted personal responsibility but has often been insensitive to environmental stewardship. However, in most legislative bodies, whichever party is the majority—whether the individual member is in support of the party's platform or not—will control the agenda. This is truer in statewide and national legislative offices than in local ones. For example, although individual candidates are not bound by their party's platform, it is nevertheless an indication as to the direction their party will take the country if their party is in the majority. Thus, it is useful and important to weigh the two parties' positions on issues as one casts one's vote.

Once Election Day is over, one's responsibility does not end. Whether it is writing letters to elected officials, visiting with them, actively campaigning for their reelection (or defeat), or working within a party structure, Christians should stay involved in the process as much as they are able. But it is a challenge, as we said before, to find the time to stay involved, especially if you try to go it alone. This is why it is important to work in association with others.

Associations are a tremendous resource to Christians who desire to be responsible, educated citizens but have limited time to devote to political involvement. We are thinking here of associations such as labor unions, business trade associations, environmental organizations, right-to-life groups, and grassroots political organizations. Specifically Christian associations such as the Center for Public Justice, the Family Research Council, and Bread for the World can be especially helpful. They offer professional, expert analysis of legislation and other information. They develop policy proposals and advocate for a specific agenda, usually from within an articulated Christian worldview. They increase a voter's influence by speaking for thousands of people in one voice. They are able to be more vigilant than those of us who do not work full-time in the field.

As we will discuss shortly, however, Christian associations can fall into the same traps that other associations do. They can use hyperbole and alarmist language to increase contributions. They can use misleading fund-raising tactics, such as "petitions" that are never sent on to members of Congress. They can demonize their opponents and other persons, including other Christians, who do not go along with their agenda. However, on balance, Christians working together, in formal association with one another, is far better than each working independently and in isolation.

Some Christians are called not just to work to influence the process from the outside, but to work to affect the process from the inside. Whether it is as an elected leader in public office, as an appointed official, or as a staff member working in the office of an official, serving the public in a full-time capacity is an important calling that many Christians have chosen to follow.

Although one can argue whether or not working in politics has ever been held in high esteem, it is the case now that the politician's reputation is only slightly better than that of the used car salesman. Many Christians view politics as dirty, full of corruption, scandal, and greed. The need to compromise to get work done is often considered untenable. God, however, views "the magistrate" in high esteem. In fact, he establishes every one of them and calls on us to be subject to and pray for them.

Christians who enter public life do so with various motivations and agendas but often with deep conviction and a sense of calling. The naïveté, however, with which many come is shed quickly in the rumble-tumble reality of the political process. There are several challenges that Christians uniquely face when they engage in public life as a full-time vocation.

First, Christians quickly realize that they must advocate in the public square for their positions using "natural law" arguments that are accessible and persuasive to all. It does little good to argue for the sanctity of life using Psalm 139:13 when your opponent, or the public you are trying to convince, does not hold the Bible as authoritative. One must craft arguments that appeal to everyone, Christian or not. Although Scripture must always be our guide, we must be able to defend our positions with arguments that resonate with those who do not share our reliance on the Bible. We can appeal to human beings' God-given reason, the evidence God has placed in his creation, and the precepts he has written on all persons' hearts (Rom. 1:19–20).

Second, as we discuss more fully later, it does not take Christians long, whether they work in the legislative, judicial, or executive branch, to realize that to compromise on tactic or policy is not always the same as compromising on principle. It is very difficult to find a majority who agrees with you all of the time; and therefore, to get things accomplished for the overall good, compromise is inevitable. As an elected member of a legislature, should you vote against every appropriations bill, for example, if you aren't in accord with how every penny is being spent? When we realize that we are not right 100 percent of the time, we can approach issues from a more realistic, humble perspective. However, many Christians enter the fray with a very stark either-or, us-versus-them view, making compromise almost impossible to achieve. They must remind themselves of the adage "Do not let the good be the victim of the perfect."

This leads to a third challenge that we believe plagues many Christians who engage in politics inside or outside of the system—discouragement and cynicism. Many tire of the need to compromise. Those who have an unrealistically high expectation of what politics can achieve, especially with a very short time frame, will only be disappointed. It has taken decades for the country to slide into modern relativism, and it will take decades to dig us out of it and its social consequences. As we develop more fully in the next section, compromise leading to incremental good is still good. If we are going in the wrong direction, standing still is better than moving forward, even as we try to turn things around. And as we argued earlier, politics has its limits. Much of the cultural transformation that Christians long to see will come not as a result of political action but from "upstream" engagement.

The combination of frustration and an "us-versus-them" mentality can lead to a fourth challenge for Christians—loving your enemy. It is very easy to vilify your opponent when you believe that everyone who is not with you is against you. Rather than loving and praying for our opponents, Christians can fall prey to disparaging and dehumanizing them. The corrective is to realize, first, that we are not always right and they are not always wrong. We also need to realize that they too are made in God's image and that they may have equally sincere intentions even while being sincerely misled. We must always be a witness in our political engagement, and there is no better way to show Christ's love than to love and pray for our opposition.

Finally, the greatest challenge we believe Christians who work within the political system face is to approach their vocation in an integrated way, rather than in a compartmentalized, dualistic manner. It is not sufficient to view the political and governmental workplace simply as a mission field for evangelism. It is also not adequate to do one's work with integrity while not giving the work process and product over to the Lord completely. The effort to integrate fully the heart and mind is a difficult one and requires an investment of time and energy. Too many Christians come to the public square and never challenge their presuppositions. The effort to read the Word and read the world at the same time has to be a conscious one; otherwise, we allow the world to conform us instead of us transforming it. We are Christians first and Democrats or Republicans, liberals or conservatives second.

Compromise and the Christian

For evangelical Christians, who have been taught to struggle for the clear, absolute truth of the Bible, the very word "compromise" has a somewhat unsavory ring to it. In a struggle to apply biblical principles to the contemporary world, is not any compromise an unacceptable accommodation to evil? We argue here that it all depends.

There are at least two types of compromise that Christians engaged in politics may face. One can be labeled half-a-loaf compromise. Here someone who is working for a certain goal is willing to compromise and accept the partial achievement of that goal on the basis that half a loaf is better than none, as it is often put. One may be working to protect fully the religious autonomy rights of faith-based organizations receiving government funding for the public services they are providing. All that one can achieve at this time is to protect the right of those organizations to use religious criteria in hiring staff, but protecting their right to include privately funded religious elements in the services they are providing is facing overwhelming opposition. Under half-a-loaf compromise, the persons working for full protection for religious autonomy rights accept the hiring protections in exchange for eliminating the protection of privately funded religious elements.

A different sort of compromise is involved when one compromises one's independence by the alliances one makes. A basic characteristic of political involvement is coalition building. No one person or group achieves its goals by working alone. Any political effort involves building a coalition among individuals and groups with common political objectives. This basic fact raises the possibility that if not careful, certain individuals and groups may incur debts that will compromise their basic independence and integrity.

The first type of compromise—half-a-loaf compromise—is not only acceptable, but in many circumstances even desirable. One must not picture the political arena as involving the struggle of absolute good versus absolute evil, of total justice versus total injustice. The real world is never that simple. Practical policy making is a craft, and it is more often the art of the possible. Trade-offs are common. Should the minimum wage be increased to $10/hour, thereby providing a "living wage" for low-income workers, or will a more modest increase ensure that fewer employees are laid off because they are no longer affordable to business? Should a majority of our federal government's $15 billion of international AIDS funds go into the UN Global AIDS Fund, or should a smaller percentage be contributed to the fund and the rest unilaterally disbursed so that we can ensure it is well spent and accountable to the American taxpayer? Should the welfare work requirement for recipients be expanded to 40 hours a week, or should it be 35 hours? And if work requirements are expanded, how much additional child care funding, if any, should be allocated to address the increased demand that this will cause?

Typically, even the Christian fully committed to applying biblical principles in a sinful world feels caught in a dense fog. He or she may recognize some landmarks and have a good sense of the general direction in which to go, but at any given point cannot be completely certain what the next step should be. As noted earlier in this chapter, in seeking to apply biblical principles to the concrete world of public policies, Christians face situations where crucial information is missing and they may very well be mistaken in their conclusions.

Sometimes Christians who have entered the real-world political arena have had a very rigid, explicit vision of what they believe needs to be accomplished and how it should be accomplished. And they have pursued that vision with a self-confidence that has degenerated into arrogance. This is wrong. One mark of Christians in politics should be a sensitivity to their own limitations and fallibility. God's Word is truth. Biblical principles are absolute. But our applications of God's truth are often fumbling and shrouded in the fog produced by extremely complex situations, missing facts, and the pressures of limited time.

All this means that when one is asked to compromise by accepting only some of what one is seeking to achieve, one is not being asked to compromise absolute principles of right and wrong, or even to compromise applications of those principles one can know with certainty are the correct applications for that time and place. Instead, one is being asked to compromise groping, uncertain applications of basic biblical principles.

Under such circumstances we believe half-a-loaf compromise is justifiable on two bases. One is rooted in very practical realities. In the political realm, one must often decide whether to achieve some of what one wants, or to insist on all of what one wants and as a result achieve nothing at all. One pushes constantly, insistently for more just policies, but progress usually comes step-by-step or not at all. Given this choice, we would opt for the step-by-step progress. By settling for half a loaf, one is not denying or acting against one's deepest convictions. One is merely accepting as much progress as can be made today and then coming back seeking more progress tomorrow.

There is also a more theoretical, even principled basis on which to insist on the morality of half-a-loaf compromise. It is that step-by-step evolution of public policies is less likely to lead to unanticipated, negative consequences.

That quantum leap into the future that one may be convinced will usher in
the ultimate in justice may, if fully attained, prove to be a disaster—or at least
much less than the vision of true justice one had in mind. It is usually better
to take some small, incremental steps, see how they work out in practice, make
needed adjustments, and then push for additional change. Thus, the more
cautious, incremental approach that the realities of the political world usually
forces one to take has some positive advantages.

We believe the second type of compromise—that of compromising away one's
basic independence—should be avoided at all costs. This type of compromise is
sometimes referred to by the extreme, but not inappropriate, phrase of "selling
one's soul." It means persons have become so indebted to others that they can
no longer follow their vision of the public good that biblical principles have
led them to embrace. This can happen to public officials or group movements
that have become heavily indebted to a small group of very large funders. Or
it can happen to a person or group that has looked so often and for so long to
some other group for support and cooperation that it no longer is free to go
its own way if it becomes convinced the other group is wrong. To do so would
be to end one's own group since it has grown overly dependent on the other
group. This concern will be discussed more fully in the next section.

Forming Alliances with Others

Working in alliance with others is an inherent part of political engagement and
does not necessarily pose moral problems. However, there is the danger that in
extreme situations one can lose one's ability to act on the basis of what one judges
is right and in keeping with God's will. Since forming alliances and working in
coalitions is an inherent part of political involvement, issues and questions that
arise in conjunction with this feature of politics are worth a closer examination.

First, it is important to note the extent to which working with others—including working with others with whom one disagrees on many issues—is
inherent in the very nature of politics. Especially in the American system with its
constitutional system of separation of powers, it is virtually impossible for any
one organization or popular movement to have such a preponderance of political
power that it can get its way on public policy issues without having to work with
other groups or organizations. Often this involves groups that—while having
different origins or being rooted in different political constituencies—share
a similar political outlook and often find themselves working together. One
thinks here, for example, of the Christian Legal Society's Center for Law and
Religious Freedom, rooted in the evangelical tradition, and the Becket Fund,
rooted in the Catholic tradition. Both are concerned with religious liberty questions and share a similar perspective on the nature and meaning of religious
freedom in the United States today. It is no wonder that they often cooperate
on court cases and legislative issues pending before Congress.

Sometimes coalitions are formed in support of a particular policy initiative that includes groups that disagree on almost all other issues. This is where the old saying that politics makes strange bedfellows originates. For example, in 1993, a coalition came together to pass the Religious Freedom Restoration Act (an act later found to be unconstitutional by the Supreme Court). That coalition included such widely differing groups as the American Civil Liberties Union, Americans United for Separation of Church and State, the Christian Legal Society's Center for Law and Religious Freedom, the Southern Baptist Convention, and the American Center for Law and Justice. Similar coalitions have been built around issues such as international human rights, sex trafficking, and cloning.

For evangelical Christians—whether as individuals or as members of organizations they have formed—to work in alliances such as these in order to gain acceptance of specific policy proposals poses no moral problems or dangers. In fact, as one works with groups whose basic philosophy or perspectives one does not share, one can not only move important policy initiatives ahead, but can also witness to the deeper perspectives and concerns that evangelicals bring to the policy process. This position may appear self-evident and not even in need of discussion. But even while being fully supportive of it, we think it important to take note of some of the consequences of such alliances. As evangelicals join such alliances, they cannot fairly expect that as a policy initiative is shaped and modified, what they see as the most appropriate tactics or the best policy alternatives will be the tactics and alternatives that will always be adopted by the larger coalition. Just as the old adage speaks of marriage being a matter of give and take, forming political alliances with others is also a matter of give and take. Evangelicals in such alliances cannot expect always to take and never to give. Here it is important to recall some of the points we have made earlier: Politics is generally not a matter of absolute good against absolute evil, with the pathway to good and just policies neatly laid out in the context of full and accurate information. Usually the disagreements that arise among coalition partners who are working toward a common policy goal arise because of tactical situations marked by many unknowns. In such a situation, a humility that does not insist on always getting one's way is more appropriate than an attitude that insists any deviation from one's position is a cause for leaving the coalition and weakening its efforts.

But there are limits to what we have just written. One is that even in coalitions working for a specific policy initiative, individual Christians or Christian organizations must be ready at some point to leave that coalition if they become convinced it has adopted tactics they cannot accept or has so modified the original policy goals that very little is to be gained by staying. Christians ought not to stick with a political alliance no matter what. They ought not to act as prima donnas who insist it is their way or "no way"; neither should they act as doormats and agree to any compromise or tactic. This is where careful, prayerful consideration of what are and are not morally proper tactics enters in, as well as of how far one ought to be willing to go in giving way on aspects of a policy initiative in order to gain a measure of success. Here it is easy for individual Christians and the leaders of Christian organizations who day and night are living a certain policy struggle to lose perspective. The danger is that they and their own egos can get so wrapped up in the struggle that they end up giving way when they should hold firm and holding firm when they should compromise. To avoid this danger, it is very useful for Christians who are deeply involved in a political struggle to intentionally create contacts with fellow Christians who understand the political arena but are not directly involved in the immediate political struggle. Such brothers and sisters, who have a certain measure of detachment, can be an invaluable means by which those in the struggle can maintain a perspective that otherwise may be lost.

In contrast to alliances composed of persons and groups that have come together to move a certain policy initiative, there are more-or-less permanent, ongoing alliances among persons and groups that regularly work together on a wide variety of policy issues. Such alliances may not pose any moral or effectiveness problems for evangelical Christians and their organizations, but they carry with them two dangers. One is that an overly dependent relationship may develop, leading to a loss of independence. At times persons or organizations that are politically engaged do not develop their own policy expertise, contacts in government and the news media, fund-raising abilities, and other ingredients of active political involvement, but instead depend on organizations with which they are allied to supply such needs. When this happens, these persons and organizations are in danger of losing their independence. They no longer have an independent base of support but are dependent on others for whatever political influence they have. Suddenly they are in a position where if they disagree with the persons or organizations with which they are allied, they may feel there is little they can do. To break with those persons or organizations would mean the loss of their political influence—they would suddenly be on the outside looking in. The pressures in such a situation to capitulate and go along with decisions one believes wrong could be overwhelming.

There is a second danger. Persons and organizations too closely allied with another organization over a long period of time will come to be identified with that organization by the news media, public officeholders, and the general public. This means that if that organization should experience a scandal or follow some foolish, embarrassing course of action, the loss of influence and approbation it suffers will inevitably rub off onto persons and organizations allied with it.

These dangers take on special significance in one particular setting—that of persons and especially organizations that ally themselves too closely with one or the other of the two major political parties. This in practice is far from a remote danger. Earlier we argued that we consider it very appropriate and clearly within biblical standards for Christians to work in either one of the two major political parties. Nevertheless, there are very clear dangers when a

Christian organization becomes overly identified and allied with one political party.

In recent decades the advocacy groups spawned by the liberal, mainline Protestant denominations have allied themselves overly closely with the Democratic Party, to the point that it has sometimes been hard to determine where the policy positions advocated by these groups differ from those of the Democratic Party. Some have suggested that this can be said of the African-American church as well. But some evangelicals and evangelical advocacy groups have made the same error by overly allying themselves with the Republican Party. It has sometimes been hard to determine where the policy positions advocated by these groups differ from those of the Republican Party.

When evangelicals and their politically active organizations align themselves too closely with either political party, three dangers emerge. One is that they will be co-opted by that political party and be used for its gain. Parties and partisan leaders are constantly struggling to advance the cause of their party against highly competitive opposition. Parties, by their very nature, are often led by individuals focused almost exclusively on advancing the fortunes of their party. Winning is the name of the game in which they are engaged. Political parties are constantly looking out to advance their cause, to add to their likelihood of success at the next election. Thus, they will tend to see Christian groups and their constituencies as potential gold mines of votes if only they can pull them into their orbit. But from their point of view, the challenge is to do this without paying too high a cost in commitments to policy positions that might alienate some of their other supporters.

It is important to note that both of the major political parties are composed of various factions. Within the Democratic Party there are strong social justice advocates, some of whom come out of a background of Christian social justice concerns. They emphasize a communal responsibility for all of us to lend assistance to those who are poor and living on the margins of mainstream society. Others in the Democratic Party are strongly committed to a secularist, libertarian approach to individual freedom issues. They take a pro-choice position on abortion, support same-sex marriages, and see limitations on pornography as illegitimate governmental censorship. Similarly, some in the Republican Party are business oriented and are primarily motivated by a desire to reduce taxes and regulatory burdens on business. Others in the Republican Party are much more motivated by a Christian-rooted respect for human life. Their priorities are to protect the unborn and to deal with other bioethical issues in a manner that gives due importance to human life. The examples of different emphases and clashing groups within both political parties could be multiplied almost endlessly.

Given the strong drive of both parties to win elections and given the parties' own internal factions, the danger is that the parties will seek to co-opt evangelical groups. They may seek to do this by means of symbolic acts such as invitations to the White House, planks included in the party's platform, and support for key pieces of legislation that does not move much beyond lip service. But "the evangelical groups" may lose out when it really matters: when justices are being appointed to the Supreme Court and when the president and congressional leaders are deciding what legislation will be near the top of their priority lists. If a party and its leaders can gain the support of evangelical leaders and their constituencies without having to modify their priorities or risk alienating other factions in the party, they will do so. Cal Thomas and Ed Dobson have written about a 1998 story in the *New York Times* that reported on a meeting of twenty-five leaders of the religious Right who fumed "that they had been used and abused, like some cheap date." Thomas and Dobson go on to comment: "What did they expect? They have been dealing with politicians, who take as much as they can get from every interest group and give back just enough to keep them on a string so that they might stay in power. Such behavior makes 'cheap date' a perfect metaphor." (Thomas and Dobson 1999, 143–44). Whenever any group and its leaders align themselves firmly with one political party, they are set up for being used in this manner. The church can lose its prophetic voice. This is the first danger in evangelicals and their advocacy groups aligning themselves overly much with either one of the two major parties.

A second danger is that they run the risk of inadvertently assisting factions of the party that are at odds with Christian principles in achieving their goals. Certain evangelical leaders or groups may support the Democratic Party because of its support for increasing the minimum wage, but if that support is unqualified, they may end up also advancing the cause of abortion-on-demand. Other evangelical leaders or groups may support the Republican Party out of their desire that inner-city children and their parents have the educational choice that vouchers would bring, but if that support is overly generalized, they may end up also advancing a foreign policy that many believe puts business interests ahead of concerns over the persecution of Christians in certain overseas countries.

A third danger in evangelicals and their leaders overly identifying with only one of the political parties is that in the public's mind, Christian political involvement will come to be identified with the political stances and inevitably with the political fortunes of that party. Alexis de Tocqueville, in his early nineteenth-century masterful analysis of American democracy, made the point that when the clergy identify too closely with the existing government, the opponents of that government then also become the opponents of religion (Tocqueville 1:308–14). If certain religious groups and the government are in league with each other, to be against the government means one must also be against those religious groups. This insight also applies to Christian groups that align themselves too solidly with one of the political parties. They may obtain recognition and some success in the short run, but the political pendulum inevitably swings. When the party with which they have bound themselves goes out of favor, the Christian groups will also go out of favor. Those who are opposed to the political programs of that political party will feel they must oppose those evangelical groups, since to support evangelical Christianity comes to be seen as supporting that party's political agenda.

Conclusion

We have come to the end of our consideration of practical issues in concrete political engagement. At times we have had to move far afield from lofty ideals and firm principles. Instead, we have dealt with the realities of a political world that—along with the rest of creation—is in the "in-between times." Christ has come, he has conquered the Evil One, and the Evil One's doom is sealed. But Christ's final triumphant coming, when every knee shall bow before him, still lies in the future. Thus, the political world is a fallen, broken world, marked by selfish ambition and uncertain objectives. Truly, we see through a glass darkly. To pursue a more just order in a broken, sinful world—that is the challenging, glorious task to which God calls his faithful servants. May those he calls respond with the humble words, "Here am I, Lord, send me."

Bibliography

Adams, Lawrence E. *Going Public: Christian Responsibility in a Divided America.* Grand Rapids: Brazos Press, 2002.

Koopman, Douglas L. *Serving the Claims of Justice: The Thoughts of Paul B. Henry.* Grand Rapids: Paul B. Henry Institute, Calvin College, 2001.

Monsma, Stephen V. *Pursuing Justice in a Sinful World.* Grand Rapids: Eerdmans, 1984.

Mouw, Richard J. *Uncommon Decency: Christian Civility in an Uncivil World.* Downers Grove, IL: InterVarsity, 1992.

Smidt, Corwin E., ed. *In God We Trust? Religion and American Political Life.* Grand Rapids: Baker, 2001.

Thomas, Cal, and Ed Dobson. *Blinded by Might: Why the Religious Right Can't Save America.* Grand Rapids: Zondervan, 1999.

Tocqueville, Alexis de. *Democracy in America.* Vols. 1 and 2. New York: Vintage Classics, Random House, 1990.

Notes

Introduction

1. See Paul Freston, *Evangelicals and Politics in Asia, Africa and Latin America* (Cambridge: Cambridge University Press, 2001).

2. Richard Cizik, Diane Knippers, JoAnne Lyon, Paul Marshall, David Neff, Ron Sider, James Skillen, and Eldin Villafane.

Chapter 1 Seeking a Place

1. Four beliefs are generally regarded as central to evangelical Protestantism: (1) an imperative for public witness and missions to spread the good news about salvation; (2) emphasis on individual acceptance of salvation; (3) belief that Jesus Christ is central to salvation; and (4) a high view of the authority of Scripture on salvation as well as other matters. Within these basic beliefs, there are many variations (see Green et al., *Religion and the Culture Wars* [Lanham, MD: Rowman & Littlefield, 1996], 13).

2. These data come from the Third National Survey of Religion and Politics, University of Akron, 2000. The item was a five-point Likert scale: "Evolution is the best explanation of life on earth." Opposition was defined as disagreeing or strongly disagreeing with the statement. For these data and others mentioned in the text, contact author for further details.

3. These data are estimated using a 1944 Gallup Poll (AIPO-335, 11/17–22/1944).

4. An example occurred in Akron, Ohio, beginning in the 1940s. A watchword of local elected officials was "Have you checked with Dallas?"—a reference to Dallas Billington, a nationally known pastor of the Bible Baptist Temple. Though a separatist fundamentalist, Billington was a force to be reckoned with in local affairs, especially when he touched on moral questions.

5. In 1938, just 6 percent of evangelicals approved of Father Coughlin, a reactionary Catholic priest allied with Gerald L. K. Smith. The data come from the Gallup Poll (USAIP044, 12/16/1938).

6. These data come from a recall question of the 1936 vote in a 1938 Gallup Poll (USAIP044, 12/16/1938).

7. These data come from the 1964 National Election Study.

8. These data were estimated using the 1976 National Election Study.

9. The 1944 vote choice data come from a 1944 Gallup Poll (AIOP-335, 11/17–22/1944). The 1964 vote choice data come from the 1964 National Election Study.

10. These data are estimated from the Third National Survey of Religion and Politics, University of Akron, 2000.

11. These data come from the 1984 and 2000 National Election Studies, respectively.

12. The following draws heavily on the websites of the ESA (www.esa-online.org), the Center for Public Justice (www.cpjustice.org), and Call to Renewal (www.calltorenewal.org).

13. These data come from the 1976 National Election Study and the Third National Survey of Religion and Politics, respectively.

Chapter 2 A History of the Public Policy Resolutions of the National Association of Evangelicals

1. Quoted in Arthur R. Matthews, *Standing Up, Standing Together* (Carol Stream, IL: National Association of Evangelicals, 1992), 28.

2. Quoted in ibid.

3. A. James Reichley, *Faith in Politics* (Washington, DC: Brookings Institution Press, 2002), 290.

4. Luke Eugene Ebersole, *Church Lobbying in the Nation's Capital* (New York: Macmillan, 1951), 46.

5. Reichley, *Faith in Politics*, 234.

6. James DeForest Murch, *Co-operation without Compromise* (Grand Rapids: Eerdmans, 1956), 45.

7. Ibid., 44.

8. Quoted in Matthews, *Standing Up, Standing Together*, 20.

9. Quoted in ibid., 44.

10. D. G. Hart, "The Mid-Life Crisis of American Evangelicalism," *Christian Century*, November 11, 1992.

11. Murch, *Co-operation without Compromise*, 70.

12. Quoted in ibid., 160.

13. Quoted in ibid.

14. Ibid.

15. Ibid., 141.

16. Quoted in ibid., 142.

17. Ibid.

18. Ibid., 137.

19. Ebersole, *Church Lobbying*, 174.

20. Quoted in ibid., 178

21. Dean M. Kelley, ed., *Government Intervention in Religious Affairs* (New York: Pilgrim, 1982), 3.

22. Murch, *Co-operation without Compromise*, 161.

23. NAE convention minutes, 1951. (Note: All minutes and resolutions quoted here and subsequently come from NAE records and files.)

24. NAE convention minutes, 1951.

25. Diane Eck, *A New Religious America: How a "Christian Country" Has Become the World's Most Religiously Diverse Nation* (San Francisco: HarperSanFrancisco, 2001), 159.

26. Murch, *Co-operation without Compromise*, 151.

27. *Life*, 1958.

28. Reichley, *Faith in Politics*, 291.

29. Ibid.

30. Quoted in ibid., 293.

31. Ibid., 292.

32. Ibid., 293.

33. Ibid., 295.

34. Ibid., 301.

35. Reichley, *Faith in Politics*, 292.

36. Francis A. Schaeffer, *A Christian Manifesto* (Westchester, IL: Crossway Books, 1981), 54.

37. Frank Rothenberg and Stuart Newport, *The Evangelical Voter* (Washington, DC: Institute for Government and Politics, 1984), 113.

38. Peter Robinson, *How Ronald Reagan Changed My Life* (New York: Regan Books, 2003), 193.

39. Robert P. Dugan Jr., *Winning the New Civil War* (Portland: Multnomah, 1991), 137–44.

40. PBS's program *Frontline*, April 29, 2004.

41. Quoted in Adelle M. Banks, "Evangelicals Encourage Morals, Shun Politics," *Orlando Sentinel*, March 9, 1993.

42. Quoted in Reichley, *Faith in Politics*, 156.

43. Ibid., 340.

44. Linda Feldman, "Wielding a New Moral Yardstick," *Christian Science Monitor*, December 23, 1998.

45. Hanna Rosin, "Prayer Breakfast Sways Ministers," *Washington Post*, September 12, 1998.

46. Nicholas D. Kristof, "The New Internationalists," *New York Times*, May 22, 2002.

47. *World Affairs* 147, no. 4 (Spring 1985): 309.

48. Quoted in ibid., 297.

49. Michael Horowitz, "New Intolerance between Crescent and Cross," *Wall Street Journal*, July 5, 1995.

50. Stephen A. Holmes, "GOP Leaders Back Bill on Religious Persecution," *New York Times*, September 11, 1997.

51. Allen D. Hertzke, "On This They Do Agree," *Wall Street Journal*, October 10, 2003.

52. Nicholas D. Kristof, "Bush vs. Women," *New York Times*, August 16, 2002.

53. Edith Bumiller, "Evangelicals Sway White House on Human Rights Issues Abroad," *New York Times*, October 26, 2003.

54. Jonathan Aitken, "The Politics of the Holy Spirit," *American Spectator*, December 2002/January 2004, 57.

55. E. J. Dionne, "A Shift Looms," *Washington Post*, October 3, 1999.

56. Quoted in John Donnelly, "Some Voice Concern over the President's Religious Rhetoric," *Boston Globe*, February 16, 2003.

57. Alan F. H. Wisdom, *Faith & Freedom*, Summer 2002, 8.

58. Alan Cooperman, "Evangelical Christians Reach Out to Muslims," *Washington Post*, April 10, 2004.

59. Quoted in "Bush Tells Evangelicals He Shares Their Values," *New York Times*, March 12, 2004.

60. Quoted in Jay Tolson, "The New Evangelicals," *U.S. News & World Report*, December 8, 2003.

Chapter 3 Evangelical Denominations at the Foundations of Modern American and British Social-Political Structures and Policies

1. Dirk Jellema, "Ethics," in *Contemporary Evangelical Thought* (Great Neck, NY: Channel Press, 1957).

2. Ernst Troeltsch, *The Social Teachings of the Christian Churches* (New York: Harper Torchbooks, 1931), 576–78.

3. J. M. Porter, ed., *Luther: Selected Political Writings* (Philadelphia: Fortress Press, 1957), 25–35.

4. Troeltsch, *Social Teachings*, 576–78.

5. Nicholas Wolterstorff, *Until Justice and Peace Embrace* (Grand Rapids: Eerdmans, 1983), 6–11.

6. Ibid., 21–22.

7. Ibid., 15–16.

8. Troeltsch, *Social Teachings*, 652–55.

9. Genesis 1:28.

10. Leviticus 25.

11. Leviticus 25:10.

12. Troeltsch, *Social Teachings*, 697.

13. Ronald Sider, "An Anabaptist Perspective," a chapter in a forthcoming book to be published by InterVarsity. See also Troeltsch, *Social Teachings*, 695–705.

14. Henry Mayer, *All on Fire: William Lloyd Garrison and the Abolition of Slavery* (New York: St. Martin's Press, 1998), 631.

15. Troeltsch, *Social Teachings*, 721–24.

16. Reinhold Niebuhr, *Children of Light and Children of Darkness* (New York: Charles Scribner's Sons, 1944), chap. 3.

17. Sydney Ahlstrom, *A Religious History of the American People* (New Haven: Yale University Press, 1972), 701–4; C. Eric Lincoln, ed., *The Black Experience in Religion* (Garden City, NY: Anchor/Doubleday, 1974), 52–54; Harry S. Stout, *The Divine Dramatist: George Whitefield and the Rise of Modern Evangelicalism* (Grand Rapids: Eerdmans, 1991), 50.

18. Coker's *Dialogue* is reproduced in Dorothy Porter, ed., *Negro Protest Pamphlets* (New York: Arno Press and *New York Times*, 1969), 33.

19. See Kevin Belmonte, *Hero for Humanity: A Biography of William Wilberforce* (Colorado Springs: NavPress, 2002).

20. See Psalm 119:105. The application of the Word in our own contexts is a necessary step in effectual Bible study. If the Word is not obeyed, it is foolishly abused. See also Matthew 7:21–29.

Chapter 4 The Mainline Protestant Tradition in the Twentieth Century

1. See Mark Noll, *A History of Christianity in the United States and Canada* (Grand Rapids: Eerdmans, 1992); Sydney F. Ahlstrom, *A Religious History of the American People* (New Haven: Yale University Press, 1972); and Timothy L. Smith, *Revivalism and Social Reform: American Protestantism on the Eve of the Civil War* (Baltimore: Johns Hopkins University Press, 1980).

2. See W. D. P. Bliss, *Encyclopedia of Social Reform* (New York: Macmillan, 1903).

3. The term "mainline Protestant" has been the subject of considerable debate. See William R. Hutchinson, ed., *Between the Times: The Travail of the Protestant Establishment in America, 1900–1960* (Cambridge: Cambridge University Press, 1989). Wade Clark Roof and William McKinney define "mainline" as "the dominant, culturally established faiths held by the majority of Americans" that occupy the religious and cultural center of American life. See Roof and McKinney, *American Mainline Religion: Its Changing Shape and Future* (New Brunswick, NJ: Rutgers University Press, 1987).

4. See Charles H. Hopkins, *The Rise of the Social Gospel in American Protestantism* (New Haven: Yale University Press, 1940); and Henry F. May, *Protestant Churches and Industrial America* (New York: Harper & Row, 1967).

5. Glen Bucher and Gordon Tait, "Social Reform Since the Great Depression," in *Encyclopedia of American Religious Experience*, vol. 3, ed. Charles H. Lippy and Peter W. Williams (New York: Charles Scribner's Sons, 1983), 1464.

6. H. Shelton Smith, Robert Handy, and Lefferts A. Loetscher, *American Christianity: An Historical Interpretation with Representative Documents* (New York: Charles Scribner's Sons, 1963).

7. Max Weber, *The Protestant Ethic and the Spirit of Capitalism* (Los Angeles: Roxbury, 1998 [Ger. 1902–4]). See also Digby Balzell, *Puritan Boston and Quaker Philadelphia* (New York: Macmillan, 1979).

8. See Max L. Stackhouse, "Jesus and Economics: A Century of Reflection," in *The Bible in American Law, Politics, and Political Rhetoric*, ed. J. T. Johnson (Philadelphia: Fortress Press, 1985), 107–51.

9. See, e.g., J. Philip Wogaman, *The Great Economic Debate* (Philadelphia: Westminster Press, 1977); Gustavo Gutierrez, *The Power of the Poor in History* (Maryknoll, NY: Orbis Books, 1983); John de Gruchy, *Liberating Reformed Theology: A South African Contribution to an Ecumenical Debate* (Grand Rapids: Eerdmans, 1991).

10. See, e.g., Robert Benne, *The Ethic of Democratic Capitalism* (Philadelphia: Fortress Press, 1981); Michael Novak, *Will It Liberate:? Questions about Liberation Theology* (New York: Paulist Press, 1986); and Max L. Stackhouse et al., eds., *Moral Business: Classical and Contemporary Resources on Ethics and Economic Life* (Grand Rapids: Eerdmans, 1995), esp. 283–489 and 861–960, which contain extensive documents from debates on these matters.

11. See Donald Meyer, *The Protestant Search for Political Realism, 1919–1941* (Middletown, CT: Wesleyan University Press, 1988).

12. See Reinhold Niebuhr, *An Interpretation of Christian Ethics* (San Francisco: Harper & Row, 1935); and John C. Bennett, *Christian Realism* (New York: Charles Scribner's Sons, 1941).

13. See George F. Kennan, *Around the Cragged Hill: A Personal and Political Philosophy* (New York: W. W. Norton, 1993). Other major treatments of Christian realism are Ronald Stone, *Reinhold Niebuhr:*

Prophet to Politicians (Nashville: Abingdon, 1972); and Robin Lovin, *Reinhold Niebuhr and Christian Realism* (New York: Cambridge University Press, 1995).

14. "The 'Ecumenical Movement' Churches, 'Global Order,' and Human Rights: 1938–48," *Human Rights Quarterly* 25, no. 4 (2003): 841–81.

15. Paul Ramsey, *War and the Christian Conscience* (Durham, NC: Duke University Press, 1961).

16. R. Bainton, *Christian Attitudes toward War and Peace* (Nashville: Abingdon, 1960); J. H. Yoder, *The Politics of Jesus* (Grand Rapids: Eerdmans, 1972); and Stanley Hauerwas, *Against the Nations: War and Survival in a Liberal Society* (Notre Dame, IN: University of Notre Dame Press, 1992).

17. See James Turner Johnson and George Weigel, *Just War and the Gulf War* (Washington, DC: Ethics and Public Policy Center, 1991).

18. See William Buckley, *Kosovo: Contending Voices in the Balkans Intervention* (Grand Rapids: Eerdmans, 2000).

19. That is the intention of James Skillen and R. M. McCarthy, eds., *Political Order and the Plural Structure of Society* (Atlanta: Scholars Press, 1991); John Witte Jr., *Christianity and Democracy in Global Context* (San Francisco: Westview Press, 1993); Luis Lugo, ed., *Religion, Pluralism, and Public Life* (Grand Rapids: Eerdmans, 1999); and Max L. Stackhouse, ed., *God and Globalization: Theological Ethics and the Spheres of Life*, 4 vols., ed. and written with sixteen others (Harrisburg, PA: Trinity Press International, 2000, 2001, 2002, forthcoming).

20. Don S. Browning, *Marriage and Modernization* (Grand Rapids: Eerdmans, 2003).

21. See John Witte, *From Sacrament to Contract: Marriage, Religion, and Law in the Western Tradition* (Louisville: Westminster John Knox Press, 1997); and Max Stackhouse, *Covenant and Commitments: Faith, Family and Economic Life* (Louisville: Westminster John Knox Press, 1997).

22. See Don Browning, *From Culture Wars to Common Ground* (Louisville: Westminster John Knox Press, 2000).

23. For example, Dr. Robert Edgar, general secretary of the National Council of Churches, withdrew his name three days after he signed "A Christian Declaration of Marriage," also signed by the chair of the National Conference of Catholic Bishops, the president of the Southern Baptist Convention, and the president of the National Association of Evangelicals. He explained that he was concerned that the statement would become "an oblique statement on same-sex unions."

24. For the most complete, if controversial, treatment of these debates, see Robert A. J. Gagnon, *The Bible and Homosexual Practice* (Nashville: Abingdon, 2001).

25. See Mark Ellingsen, *The Cutting Edge: How Churches Speak on Social Issues* (Geneva: World Council of Churches Publications, 1993), chaps. 4 and 5.

26. See Dennis N. Voskuil, "Reaching Out: Mainline Protestantism and the Media," in *Between the Times: The Travail of the Protestant Establishment in America 1900–1960*, ed. William R. Hutchison (New York: Cambridge University Press, 1989), 72ff.

27. See Henry Herx, "Religion and Film," *Encyclopedia of the American Religious Experience*, vol. 3, ed. Charles Lippy and Peter W. Williams (New York: Charles Scribner's Sons, 1988), 1341ff.

28. See George M. Marsden, *The Soul of the American University: From Protestant Establishment to Established Nonbelief* (New York: Oxford University Press, 1994).

29. See Lonnie D. Kliever, *The Shattered Spectrum: A Survey of Contemporary Theology* (Atlanta: John Knox Press, 1981).

30. For an account of the midcentury attempt by mainline Protestants to engage higher education, see Douglas Sloan, *Faith and Knowledge: Mainline Protestantism and American Higher Education* (Louisville: Westminster John Knox Press, 1994).

31. W. S. Gunter et al., *Wesley and the Quadrilateral: Renewing the Conversation* (Nashville: Abingdon, 1997).

32. For example, see Arthur J. Vidich and Stanford M. Lyman, *American Sociology: Worldly Rejections of Religion and Their Directions* (New Haven: Yale University Press, 1985).

33. See Gary Dorrien, *The Making of American Liberal Theology: Idealism, Realism, and Modernity* (Louisville: Westminster John Knox Press, 2003).

Chapter 5 Insights from Catholic Social Ethics and Political Participation

1. See United States Catholic Conference Administrative Board, "Faithful Citizenship: Civic Responsibility for a New Millennium," *Origins* 29, no. 20 (October 28, 1999): 309–18.

2. Cf. Charles E. Curran, *Catholic Social Teaching 1891–Present: A Historical, Theological and Ethical Analysis* (Washington, DC: Georgetown University Press, 2002), 23.

3. Pope Paul VI, *Octogesima adveniens*, in David O'Brien and Thomas A. Shannon, eds., *Catholic Social Thought: The Documentary Heritage* (Maryknoll, NY: Orbis Books, 1998), 265–86 at 266 (no. 4).

4. Second Vatican Council, *Gaudium et spes: Pastoral Constitution on the Church in the Modern World*, in O'Brien and Shannon, *Catholic Social Thought*, 164–237 at 167 (no. 3).

5. Richard McBrien, "Catholic Social Action," *National Catholic Reporter* 14 (March 3, 1978): 7–8, as cited in Timothy G. McCarthy, *The Catholic Tra-*

dition: *The Church in the Twentieth Century*, 2nd ed. (Chicago: Loyola Press, 1998), 260.

6. As J. Bryan Hehir puts it, the document connects "an affirmation of the church's transcendence with an equally strong assertion that the eschatological ministry of the church includes work in history to protect human dignity, promote human rights, foster the unity of society, and provide a sense of meaning to all areas of societal life." Hehir, "The Right and Competence of the Church," in John Coleman, ed., *One Hundred Years of Catholic Social Thought: Celebration and Challenge* (Maryknoll, NY: Orbis, 1991), 66–70 at 59–60.

7. While the text of *Gaudium et spes* does warn about particular temptations of a worldly focus, it does so within a framework that emphasizes the link between religious and earthly duties. For example, in reference to Romans 12:2, "Be not conformed to this world" (KJV), the council states: "By the world here is meant that spirit of vanity and malice which transforms into an instrument of sin those energies intended for the service of God and man" (no. 37). It follows up this distinction with a warning about abandoning concern for building up this earth in this life: "Therefore, while we are warned that it profits a man nothing if he gain the whole world and lose himself, the expectation of a new earth must not weaken but rather stimulate our concern for cultivating this one . . . [Earthly progress] can contribute to the better offering of human society, it is of vital concern to the Kingdom of God" (no. 39).

8. In one respect, the impact of *Dignitatis humanae* has been the depoliticization of church-state relations and that of *Gaudium et spes* has been the legitimation of social ministry. Second Vatican Council, *Dignitatis humanae*, in Walter M. Abbott, S.J., and Very Rev. Msgr. Joseph Gallagher, *The Documents of Vatican II* (New York: Guild Press, 1966), no. 4, 683.

9. The council's ecclesiological grounding of social ministry has been solidified in the 1971 and 1974 synodal documents, *Justitia in mundo* and *Evangelii nuntiandi*. For example, *Justitia in mundo*, resulting from the 1971 Synod of Bishops, famously states that "action on behalf of justice and participation in the transformation of the world fully appear to us as a constitutive dimension of preaching the gospel, or, in other words, of the church's mission for the redemption of the human race and its liberation from every oppressive structure." See 1971 Synod of Bishops, *Justitia in mundo*, in O'Brien and Shannon, *Catholic Social Thought*, 288–300 at 289 (introduction). For a detailed analysis of the legacy of *Justitia in mundo* and *Evangelii nuntiandi* and the relationship of the church's religious mission of redemption and programs of human liberation or work for justice, see Charles M. Murphy, "Action for Justice as Constitutive of the Preaching of the Gospel: What Did the 1971 Synod Mean?" *Theological Studies* 44, no. 2 (2001): 298–311.

10. A recent Congregation for the Doctrine of Faith note affirms the institutional church's role in raising the moral dimensions of public issues and the obligations of all Catholics to participate in social, economic, and political life based on Christian values. See Congregation for the Doctrine of Faith, "Doctrinal Note on Some Questions Regarding the Participation of Catholics in Public Life," *Origins* vol. 32, no. 33 (January 30, 2003): 537–43 at 539.

11. In Aquinas's view, Christians may be at home in the political order, and the sanctification by the Spirit in Christ takes place *within* that order, not over and against it. In contrast to Augustine and the reformers' stance, Aquinas holds that political authority and law do not exist due to original sin alone, but rather correspond to needs and purposes inherent in human nature itself (e.g., our social nature). Finally, government's task is to establish and maintain conditions (principally matters of justice) that allow citizens to lead the good life (rather than serving simply as "dikes against sin"). See Lisa Sowle Cahill on the Thomistic synthesis of Aristotle and Augustine in her *Love Your Enemies: Discipleship, Pacifism and Just War Theory* (Minneapolis: Fortress Press, 1994), 82–85. For Aquinas's treatment of law as it relates to our argument above, see Aquinas, *Summa Theologica*, trans. Fathers of the English Dominican Province (New York: Benziger Bros. 1948), I–II, Q 90–94.

12. Hehir, "Implications of a Structured Pluralism: A Public Church," *Origins* 14, no. 3 (31 May 1984): 40–43 at 42.

13. Pope Pius XI, *Quadragesimo anno*, in O'Brien and Shannon, *Catholic Social Thought*, no. 79, 60.

14. Pope Pius XI, *Quadragesimo anno*, in O'Brien and Shannon, *Catholic Social Thought*, 42–80 at 60 (no. 79). Subsidiarity should be understood in relation to solidarity, socialization, and justice in considerations of Catholic policy analysis, not as an independent value on its own. For "subsidiarity does not mean that the government that governs least governs best. It calls for as much government intervention as necessary to enable the other parts of civil society to contribute to the common good." See David Hollenbach, "The Common Good," in Judith Dwyer, ed., *A New Dictionary of Catholic Social Thought* (Collegeville, MN: Liturgical Press, 1994), 195.

15. See United States Catholic Conference (USCC) Administrative Board, "Political Responsibility: Proclaiming the Gospel of Life, Protecting the Least among Us, and Pursuing the Common Good," *Origins*, vol. 25, no. 22 (November 16, 1995): 369–83.

16. Ibid., 374.

17. Ibid., 376. The "Faithful Citizenship" version in 1999 adds environmental stewardship to these principles.

18. For a historical overview of how the National Catholic Welfare Conference grew out of the

National Catholic War Council (initiated during World War I to coordinate the Catholic war effort) and transitioned from an organization that defended the church's interests into a vehicle for the bishops to jointly exercise their pastoral office for the common good, see Thomas J. Reese, S.J., *A Flock of Bishops: The National Conference of Catholic Bishops* (Kansas City, MO: Sheed & Ward, 1992). See also Mary Hanna, "Bishops as Political Leaders," in Charles W. Dunn, ed., *Religion in American Politics* (Washington, DC: Congressional Quarterly Press, 1989), 75–86.

19. Those who tend to collaborate with more progressive secular groups include Catholic Charities USA, Jesuit Social Ministries, NETWORK Social Justice Lobby, and the Campaign for Human Development. The more conservative Catholic League for Religious and Civil Rights works to fight anti-Catholic bias in the media and is generally opposed by groups like the ACLU and Americans United for the Separation of Church and State. The Catholic Family and Human Rights Institute is another more conservative advocacy group that focuses on international issues. While National Right to Life, the nation's oldest anti-abortion group, is not a Catholic organization per se, it is sustained by a sizable Catholic membership. In addition, the Family Research Council and Focus on the Family count a number of conservative Catholics among their members and staff.

20. Robert Booth Fowler, Allen D. Hertzke, and Laura R. Olson, *Religion and Politics in America: Faith, Culture and Strategic Choices*, 2nd ed. (1995; repr., Boulder, CO: Westview Press, 1999), 69–71.

21. Ibid., 71.

22. Ernst Troeltsch, *The Social Teaching of the Christian Churches*, 2 vols. (New York: Harper Torchbooks, 1960). Troeltsch describes the "church type" as universal in its calling, responsible for collaborating with institutions of wider society, and able in some part to adjust itself to the world due to its endowment with objective grace and redemption. His "sect type," on the other hand, constitutes a more stringent voluntary society that lives apart from the world and is less interested in collaboration with social institutions than in witnessing to a way of life by contrast to the wider society.

23. Such Catholics are frequently engaged in lay groups such as Catholic Worker communities, Pax Christi, and some in the pro-life movement.

24. J. Bryan Hehir, "Responsibilities and Temptations of Power: A Catholic View," *Journal of Law and Religion* 8, nos. 1–2 (1990): 71–83 at 77.

25. In the early 1950s, John Courtney Murray, S.J., framed these differences that persist in contemporary Catholicism in terms of the relationship of grace to nature in ways that remain relevant. He delineated two different orientations American Catholics adopted in response to the question of Christian humanism. The first is an "eschatological humanism"

that is scripturally based and emphasizes the permanence of sin and the discontinuities between grace and human effort. This stance focuses upon the cross's inversion of human values as Christianity's central truth, thereby prescribing spiritual withdrawal. Murray called the second orientation an "incarnational humanism." This stance emphasizes the catholicity of the church's redemptive scope, the fact that (while transcendent), grace *perfects* nature, and that human nature, while sinful, is not corrupt. Murray noted that the two models were not mutually exclusive and that both were integral to the gospel, complementary, and each ran inherent risks (either of surrendering this world to the unregenerate or leading to inner self-despoilment); This distinction grew out of Murray's debates with Paul Hanley Furfey over intercredal cooperation in the 1940s. See Murray, "Christian Humanism in America: Lines of Inquiry," *Social Order* 3 (May–June 1953): 233–44; reprinted with only slight changes as chap. 8, "Is It Basket Weaving? The Question of Christianity and Human Values," in Murray, *We Hold These Truths: Catholic Reflections on the American Proposition* (New York: Sheed & Ward, 1960, 1988), 175–96. Murray's orientations reveal some ways in which proponents of different models of engagement inevitably draw upon different strands of the tradition to justify their particular approaches, and thus individuals and groups necessarily choose a canon within the canon amidst the fullness of what the tradition as a whole imparts.

26. See Michael J. Himes and Kenneth R. Himes, O.F.M., *Fullness of Faith: The Public Significance of Theology* (New York/Mahwah, NJ: Paulist Press, 1993); David Hollenbach, S.J., *The Common Good and Christian Ethics* (Cambridge: Cambridge University Press, 2002). J. Bryan Hehir's published articles as well as the influence he exerted while working with the U.S. bishops for decades constitute another important example.

27. Internal pluralism persists both in specific moral judgments and in the different roles the church plays.

28. Hehir, "A Catholic Troeltsch? Curran on the Social Ministry of the Church," in James J. Walker, Timothy E. O'Connell, and Thomas A. Shannon, eds. *A Call to Fidelity: On the Moral Theology of Charles E. Curran* (Washington, D.C.: Georgetown University Press, 2002) 191–207 at 201.

29. Hehir, "The Prophetic Voice of the Church," lecture given at Boston College sponsored by the Boisi Center for Religion and American Public Life (April 1, 2002). Transcript available at http://www.bc.edu/bc_org/research/rapl/index.htm.

30. Ibid.

31. Hehir particularly credits a more rigorist, "evangelical," "sect" type approach such as that represented by Michael Baxter, C.S.C., as serving this "purifying" purpose.

32. For an overview of an intra-Catholic interchange on the scope and authority of Episcopal documents and freedom of conscience, see Avery Dulles, "Gospel, Church and Politics," in Richard John Neuhaus, ed., *American Apostasy: The Triumph of "Other" Gospels* (Grand Rapids: Eerdmans, 1989), 29–55; and J. Bryan Hehir, "Responsibilities and Temptations of Power: A Catholic View," 71–83.

33. Glen Stassen and David Gushee, *Kingdom Ethics: Following Jesus in Contemporary Context* (Downers Grove, IL: InterVarsity, 2003), 480–81.

34. Ibid., 481. See Murray, *We Hold These Truths*.

35. Catholic theologians and historians have outlined various classifications of different American Catholic stances in recent decades. See David O'Brien's *Options* ("subcultural restoration," "evangelical radicalism," "comfortable denominationalism," and "public church") in his "Choosing Our Future: American Catholicism's Precarious Prospects," in *Annual Proceedings of the College Theology Society* (Chico, CA: Scholars Press, 1986). See also Richard McBrien, *Caesar's Coin: Religion and Politics in America* (New York: Macmillan, 1987), 46–47. O'Brien outlines more broad historical *styles* ("republican," "immigrant," and "evangelical") in his *Public Catholicism* (New York: Macmillan, 1989). Avery Dulles casts different strategies as "traditionalist," "neo-conservative," "liberal," and "radical" in "Catholicism and American Culture: The Uneasy Dialogue," *America* 162, no. 3 (January 27, 1990): 54–59. Finally, Hehir describes basic models of "educational-cultural," "legislative-policy," and "prophetic witness" in "The Right and Competence of the Church," in *One Hundred Years of Catholic Social Thought: Celebration and Challenge*, ed. John Coleman (Maryknoll, NY: Orbis, 1991), 66–70.

36. For an analysis of the foundations of justice in Catholic social teaching, see David Hollenbach, "Modern Catholic Teachings Concerning Justice," in John C. Haughey, S.J., *The Faith That Does Justice: Examining the Christian Sources for Social Change* (New York: Paulist Press, 1977), 207–31.

37. For an evangelical reflection on the preferential option for the poor, see Richard J. Mouw, "Thinking about the Poor: What Evangelicals Can Learn from the Bishops," in Charles R. Strain, ed., *Prophetic Visions and Economic Realities: Protestants, Jews and Catholics Confront the Bishops' Letter on the Economy* (Grand Rapids: Eerdmans, 1989), 20–34.

38. Thomas Aquinas describes natural law in terms of the distinctively human inclinations to "know the truth about God and to live in society," including human instincts to seek the good and act according to reason. Aquinas notes that the general principles of the natural law are inscribed on humans' hearts but that "the more we descend to matters of detail, the more frequently we encounter deviations." Thomas Aquinas, *Summa Theologica*, I–II, Question 94 ("On the Natural Law"), articles 1–6.

39. To be certain, incorporating more accessible argumentation and integrating it consistently with a thick theological vision entails some trade-offs. In the words of Hehir, however, "To choose to speak to *both* the church and the world is to lose some of the 'prophetic edge' of the scriptures, and further, in attempting to shape public policy, ecclesial bodies may in some instances be led to consensus positions which fall short of clear witness in absolute terms. Yet these tensions inherent in speaking to ecclesial and civil communities at once most closely approach the church's sense of pastoral responsibility." See Hehir, "From the Pastoral Constitution of Vatican II to *The Challenge of Peace*," in Philip J. Murnion, ed., *Catholics and Nuclear War: A Commentary on* The Challenge of Peace*, The U.S. Catholic Bishops' Pastoral Letter on War and Peace* (New York: Crossroad, 1983), 71–87 at 80–81.

40. Hehir, for example, is of this mind and describes his own approach to Catholic social ethics in this way: "First of all to understand the world in all its complexity; second, to respect it in its secularity; third to be restless about its infirmities and limitations; and fourth, to feel driven to lay hands on it, which is what Catholic social ethics calls the world to do—to lay hands on a world you respect but are not ready to accept in its present form" (see Hehir, "Catholic Theology at Its Best," *Harvard Divinity Bulletin* 27, nos. 2–3 [1998]: 13–14 at 13).

41. For a useful example of a Catholic public theology of this variety, see Michael Himes and Kenneth Himes, *Fullness of Faith*.

42. David Tracy, "Catholic Classics in American Liberal Culture," in R. Bruce Douglass and David Hollenbach, *Catholicism and Liberalism: Contributions to an American Public Philosophy* (Cambridge: Cambridge University Press, 1994), 196–216 at 196–97.

43. David Hollenbach, "The Common Good in the Postmodern Epoch: What Role for Theology?" in James Donahue and M. Theresa Moser, eds., *Religion, Ethics and the Common Good: Annual Publication of the College Theology Society*, vol. 41 (Mystic, CT: Twenty-third Publications, 1996), 3–22 at 16.

44. Pope John Paul II, *Veritatis splendor* (Washington, DC: United States Catholic Conference 1993).

45. Ibid., no. 1, 15.

46. By cultural inadequacies we simply mean the lack of community, identity, purpose; eviscerated public discourse; and prevalent individualism lamented in recent years by American social scientists like Robert Bellah and Robert Putnam.

47. This is one way Hehir describes his own approach to Catholic social engagement. See William J. Gould, "Father J. Bryan Hehir: Priest, Policy Analyst,

and Theologian of Dialogue," in Jo Renee Formicola and Hubert Morken, eds., *Religious Leaders and Faith-Based Politics: Ten Profiles* (Lanham, MD: Rowman & Littlefield, 2001), 197–223 at 201.

48. Hehir notes that this is in part how a teaching church becomes a learning church. See ibid., 202.

49. Official Catholic teaching on particular moral issues (such as abortion) entails more of an absolute quality (which does not leave such room for disagreement in concrete applications); similarly, certain policy issues have more of an uncompromising, stark nature than most.

50. Hehir, "Church-State and Church-World: The Ecclesiological Implications," *Catholic Theological Society of America Proceedings*, vol. 41 (1986): 54–74 at 69.

51. *Veritatis splendor*, no. 8, 19.

52. Ibid., no. 10, 11.

53. Ibid., no. 11, 15.

54. Ibid., no. 98.

55. Robert Booth Fowler, Allen D. Hertzke, and Laura R. Olson, *Religion and Politics in America: Faith, Culture and Strategic Choices*, 2nd ed. (Boulder, CO: Westview Press, 1999), 84–85, 133. For example, Catholics influencing public life in this regard include George Weigel, senior fellow and director of the Catholic Studies Project at the Ethics and Public Policy Center; Richard John Neuhaus, editor of *First Things*, published by the Institute on Religion and Public Life, where he serves as president; and Michael Novak, George Frederick Jewett Scholar in Religion, Philosophy and Public Policy at the American Enterprise Institute for Public Policy Research and director of Social and Political Studies. Each of these figures publishes and speaks on how Catholic resources might renew American democracy as well as the potential for democratic capitalism enriching Catholic teaching on political economy. The Faith and Reason Institute and the Catholic scholars active out of the Heritage Foundation in Washington, DC, also exert influence in a similar manner.

56. Personal interview with Anne Curtis, R.S.M., Washington, DC, July 25, 2003.

57. United States Conference of Catholic Bishops, *A Place at the Table: A Catholic Recommitment to Overcome Poverty and to Respect the Dignity of All God's Children* (Washington, DC: USCC, 2002); also available online at http://www.usccb.org/bishops/table .htm. John Carr, secretary of the USCCB's Office of Social Development and World Peace, notes that in contrast to this Catholic outlook, "the problem with Washington is that everyone is in love with one leg of the table!" Telephone interview with John Carr, April 15, 2003.

58. Joseph Cardinal Bernardin, "A Consistent Ethic of Life: An American-Catholic Dialogue," in Thomas G. Fuechtmann, ed., *Consistent Ethic of Life* (Kansas City, MO: Sheed & Ward, 1988), 1–11 at 10.

Bernardin summarizes well the style with which Christians should engage in public and political life: "The style should be persuasive, not preachy. We should use the model of the Second Vatican Council's *Pastoral Constitution on the Church in the Modern World*. We should be convinced that we have much to learn from the world and much to teach it. We should be confident but collegial with others who seek similar goals but may differ on means and methods. A confident church will speak its mind, seek as a community to live its convictions, but leave space for others to speak to us, help us to grow from their perspective, and to collaborate with them."

See Bernardin, "The Consistent Ethic after 'Webster': Opportunities and Dangers," *Commonweal* 117 (April 20, 1990): 248.

59. John Carr, plenary address, Annual Catholic Social Ministry Gathering, "Catholic Social Mission: Seeking Justice, Overcoming Poverty, Building Peace" (Washington, DC: 9–12 February, 2003), February 10, 2003.

60. Single-issue approaches have strategic advantages in some cases, such as gun control or civil rights legislation. Smaller or more focused groups will always exist, and not everyone can pursue every issue evenly. As Bernardin admits, "A consistent ethic does not say that everyone in the Church must do all things, but it does say that as individuals and groups pursue one issue . . . the *way* we oppose one threat should be related to support for a systemic vision of life. . . . And we can strive not to stand against each other when the protection *and* the promotion of life are at stake" (Bernardin, "A Consistent Ethic of Life: Continuing the Dialogue," in Fuechtmann, *Consistent Ethic of Life*, 12–19 at 15).

61. Many credit Hehir's efforts at the U.S. Catholic Conference with broadening the bishops' pro-life agenda, from what was perceived as a narrow antiabortion focus to a wider-ranging consistent ethic of life agenda that situated abortion concerns within a broader framework. Hehir was able to exercise so much influence at the USCC on a wide range of policy issues in part because he "provided the intellectual framework within which [the bishops] came to understand and evaluate major policy questions," and these efforts helped enhance the church's credibility in public policy debates. See Gould, "Father J. Bryan Hehir," 198, 207.

62. Hehir, "The Consistent Ethic: Public Policy Implications," in Fuechtmann, ed., *Consistent Ethic of Life*, 218–36 at 233.

63. This dual reality serves as the basis for Bernardin's seamless garment approach. Compare John T. Pawlikowski, O.S.M., "The American Catholic Church as a Public Church," *New Theology Review* (1988): 8–29 at 14. A recent profile of Richard Mouw and other contemporary evangelical Christians captures a related balance, that of holding together more

"conservative" theological positions with an emphasis on "some of Jesus' most daring and progressive views on peacemaking, economic justice, forgiveness and engaging the culture." Alan Rifkin, "Jesus with a Genius Grant," *Los Angeles Times Magazine*, November 23, 2003, part 9, 122. In a similar vein, recent calls have reemerged from more liberal Protestant quarters to expand American political conceptions of "religious issues" from the life and cultural issues typically associated with the Republican Party to poverty, the use of force, and the environment. See, e.g., Jim Wallis, "Putting God Back in Politics," *New York Times*, op-ed (December 28, 2003), section 4, 9.

64. USCC, "Faithful Citizenship," 312.

65. USCC, "Political Responsibility," 373–74. This said, the bishops' record on *de facto* partisan endorsements by way of a single-issue focus in twentieth-century electoral politics has been widely debated.

66. For example, *Justitia in mundo* underscores the need to safeguard rights within the church (women's participation, a living wage for church employees, the freedom of expression and thought) and admonishes believers that their use of material goods should bear witness to the gospel. Synod of Bishops, *Justitia in mundo* (1971), especially chap. 3, in O'Brien and Shannon, eds., *Catholic Social Thought: The Documentary Heritage*, 288–300, esp. 294–95.

67. *Justitia in mundo*, no. 40.

68. Hehir, "Church-State and Church-World," 59.

69. Richard Mouw, "Evangelical Protestants in the Public Square: Drawbacks and Opportunities," Annual Lecture on Prophetic Voices of the Church, Boisi Center for Religion and American Public Life, Boston College (April 10, 2003). Transcript available at http://www.bc.edu/bc_org/research/rapl/index.htm. In his address Mouw suggested evangelical Protestants could learn from the Catholic theology of the common good and spirituality of empathy, in particular.

70. Mouw credits Martin Marty's call for "convicted civility," or the need to find a way of combining a civil spirit with a "passionate intensity" about what we believe, with influencing his own approach in *Uncommon Decency: Christian Civility in an Uncivil World* (Downers Grove, IL: InterVarsity, 1992). See Mouw, "Public Religion: Through Thick and Thin," *The Christian Century*, June 7–14, 2000, 648–51 at 648.

Chapter 6 Toward an Evangelical Ethical Methodology

1. Carl F. H. Henry, *The Uneasy Conscience of Modern Fundamentalism* (Grand Rapids: Eerdmans, 1947), 65.

2. See, e.g., Dennis P. Hollinger, *Individualism and Social Ethics: An Evangelical Syncretism* (Lanham, MD:

University Press of America, 1983). The conservative political proclivities are demonstrated by Richard Pierard in *The Unequal Yoke: Evangelical Christianity and Political Conservatism* (Philadelphia: J. B. Lippincott, 1970); and Robert Booth Fowler, *A New Engagement: Evangelical Political Thought, 1966–1976* (Grand Rapids: Eerdmans, 1982).

3. George M. Mardsen, *Understanding Fundamentalism and Evangelicalism* (Grand Rapids: Eerdmans, 1991), 81.

4. Here we are deeply influenced by Thomas Oden, *The Rebirth of Orthodoxy* (New York: HarperCollins, 2003).

5. Stephen Webb, "Danger! Christian Ethics," *Books and Culture* (September/October 2001): 21.

6. Edward L. Long, *Academic Bonding and Social Concern* (Notre Dame, IN: Religious Ethics, 1984), 160.

7. Half the Fall 1989 issue of the *Journal of Religious Ethics* was devoted to "Evangelical Voices." The authors of articles included Allen Verhey, Oliver O'Donovan, Gilbert Meilaender, Richard Mouw, John Howard Yoder, Esther Byle Bruland, and Dennis Hollinger.

8. Carl F. H. Henry, *Christian Personal Ethics* (Grand Rapids: Eerdmans, 1957), 196.

9. Ibid., 209, 212.

10. For a detailed analysis of his views and the role of divine revelation, see Carl F. H. Henry, *God, Revelation and Authority*, 6 vols. (Waco: Word, 1976–1983). And for his analysis of contemporary culture, see *The Christian Mindset in a Secular Society* (Portland, OR: Multnomah Press, 1984).

11. Henry, *Christian Personal Ethics*, 192.

12. Ibid., 255.

13. Ibid., 398.

14. Ibid., 437.

15. Ibid., 219.

16. Carl F. H. Henry, *Aspects of Christian Social Ethics* (Grand Rapids: Eerdmans, 1964), 17.

17. Ibid.

18. Ibid.

19. Ibid., 19.

20. Ibid., 17.

21. For a further explication of this individualism, see Dennis Hollinger's *Individualism and Social Ethics* (see note 2), a work that does content analysis of *Christianity Today*, including a significant portion of time when Henry was its editor.

22. Richard Mouw, *Consulting the Faithful: What Christian Intellectuals Can Learn from Popular Religion* (Grand Rapids: Eerdmans, 1994).

23. Richard Mouw, *The God Who Commands: A Study in Divine Command Ethics* (Notre Dame, IN: University of Notre Dame Press, 1990), 2.

24. Ibid., 10.

25. Ibid., 22.

26. Richard Mouw, *Politics and the Biblical Drama* (Grand Rapids: Eerdmans, 1976), 12.

27. Ibid., 28.

28. Ibid., 49.

29. Mouw, *The God Who Commands*, 127.

30. Mouw, *Politics and the Biblical Drama*, 79.

31. Richard Mouw and Sander Griffioen, *Pluralisms and Horizons: An Essay in Christian Public Philosophy* (Grand Rapids: Eerdmans, 1993), 175. See also Mouw's *Uncommon Decency: Christian Civility in an Uncivil World* (Downers Grove, IL: InterVarsity, 1992).

32. See, e.g., Walter Klaassen, *Anabaptism: Neither Catholic nor Protestant* (Waterloo, ON: Conrad Press, 1973).

33. John Howard Yoder, *The Politics of Jesus* (Grand Rapids: Eerdmans, 1972), 15.

34. Ibid., 23.

35. Ibid., 63.

36. Ibid., 157.

37. John Howard Yoder, *The Christian Witness to the State* (Newton, KS: Faith and Life Press, 1964), 17.

38. Ibid., 32–33.

39. John Howard Yoder, *Body Politics: Five Practices of the Christian Community before the Watching World* (Nashville: Discipleship Resources, 1992), chap. 2.

40. John Howard Yoder, *The Priestly Kingdom: Social Ethics as Gospel* (Notre Dame, IN: University of Notre Dame, 1984), 83.

41. Ibid., 110.

42. Richard Mouw and John H. Yoder, "Evangelical Ethics and the Anabaptist-Reformed Dialogue," *Journal of Religious Ethics* 17, no. 2 (Fall 1989): 130, 133.

43. Quoted in Leon O. Hynson, *To Reform the Nation: Theological Foundations of Wesley's Ethics* (Grand Rapids: Zondervan, 1984), 9.

44. Stephen Charles Mott, *Biblical Ethics and Social Change* (New York: Oxford Press, 1982), xii.

45. Ibid., ix.

46. Stephen Mott, *Jesus and Social Ethics* (Bramcotte, Notts, UK: Grove Books, 1984), 18.

47. Ibid., 19.

48. Mott, *Biblical Ethics*, 208.

49. Oliver O'Donovan, *Resurrection and Moral Order: An Outline for Evangelical Ethics* (Grand Rapids: Eerdmans, 1986), 11.

50. See, for example, O'Donovan's "How Can Theology Be Moral?" *Journal of Religious Ethics* 17, no. 2 (Fall 1989): 81–94, in which he argues for a partnership of theology and ethics.

51. O'Donovan, *Resurrection and Moral Order*, 13.

52. Ibid., 15.

53. Ibid., 16.

54. Ibid., 76.

55. Ibid., 102, 106.

56. Ibid., 25.

57. Ibid., 257.

58. James W. McClendon Jr., *Systematic Theology: Ethics* (Nashville: Abingdon, 1986), 35.

Chapter 8 Justice, Human Rights, and Government

1. For my methodology, see my "Toward an Evangelical Political Philosophy," in *Christians and Politics beyond the Culture Wars: An Agenda for Engagement*, ed. David P. Gushee (Grand Rapids: Baker, 2000), 79–96.

2. Nicholas Wolterstorff, "Justice and Peace," in *New Dictionary of Christian Ethics and Pastoral Theology*, ed. David J. Atkinson et. al. (Downers Grove, IL: InterVarsity, 1995), 17. Justice, of course, refers not only to rights but also to responsibilities.

3. Emil Brunner, *Justice and the Social Order*, trans. Mary Hottinger (New York: Harper and Brothers, 1945), 7.

4. Ibid., 89.

5. Karen Lebacqz, *Six Theories of Justice: Perspectives from Philosophical and Theological Ethics* (Minneapolis: Augsburg, 1986), 73.

6. Ibid., 28.

7. Quoted in ibid., 55.

8. For example, Ronald H. Nash, *Freedom, Justice and the State* (Lanham, MD: University Press of America, 1980), 43–75; Doug Bandow, *Beyond Good Intentions: A Biblical View of Politics* (Westchester, IL: Crossway, 1988), 87; E. Calvin Beisner, *Prosperity and Poverty: The Compassionate Use of Resources in a World of Scarcity* (Westchester, IL: Crossway Books, 1988), 54. It is important to note that these evangelicals all agree that Christians must help the poor. The debate is over the role of government.

9. David Hollenbach, *Claims in Conflict: Retrieving and Renewing the Catholic Human Rights Tradition* (New York: Paulist, 1979), 13.

10. Quoted in ibid., 14.

11. For a longer discussion see Sider, "Toward an Evangelical Political Philosophy," 79–96, and Stephen Mott and Ronald J. Sider, "Economic Justice: A Biblical Paradigm," in *Toward a Just and Caring Society: Christian Responses to Poverty in America*, ed. David P. Gushee (Grand Rapids: Baker, 1999), 15–24. This jointly authored article (from which I draw a great deal in this chapter) used earlier pieces by both of us. See especially Mott's *A Christian Perspective on Political Thought* (New York: Oxford, 1993) and Mott's *Biblical Ethics and Social Change* (New York: Oxford, 1982).

12. See Joan O'Donovan for a sharp contrast with the modern, secular view of human rights: "Rights, Law and Political Community: A Theological and

Historical Perspective," *Transformation*, January 2003, 30–38.

13. Mott and Sider, "Economic Justice," 20.

14. The following few paragraphs are taken from Mott and Sider, "Economic Justice," 22–24.

15. For more, see Mott and Sider, "Economic Justice," 15–24.

16. *Theological Dictionary of the Old Testament* [hereafter *TDOT*] (Grand Rapids: Eerdmans, 1974–1999), 9:87.

17. *TDOT*, 12:250, 253.

18. The following lengthy section comes from Ronald J. Sider, *Just Generosity: A New Vision for Overcoming Poverty in America* (Grand Rapids: Baker, 1999), 56ff., and Mott and Sider, "Economic Justice," 26ff.

19. Mott's translation.

20. Cf. Isa. 30:18; Jer. 9:24; Hosea 2:19; 12:6; Micah 6:8.

21. Our translation. Cf. Ps. 40:10; 43:1–2; 65:6; 71:1–2, 24; 72:1–4; 116:5–6; 119:123; Isa. 45:8; 46:12–13; 59:11, 17; 61:10; 62:1–2; 63:7–8 (LXX); and frequently with *pillet* for "deliver": Ps. 31:1; 37:28, 40.

22. Cf. Job 29:12, 14; Prov. 24:11.

23. "Triumphs" in the NRSV translates the word for "justice" (*tsedaqah*) in the plural—i.e., "acts of justice" (compare the NIV, "righteous acts").

24. Cf. Ps. 107; 113:7–9.

25. Literally! See the collection (about two hundred pages of biblical texts) in Ronald J. Sider, *For They Shall Be Fed* (Dallas: Word, 1997).

26. Cf. Norman H. Snaith, *The Distinctive Ideas of the Old Testament* (London: Epworth, 1944), 68, 71–72; James H. Cone, *God of the Oppressed* (New York: Seabury, 1975), 70–71.

27. This is not to ignore the fact that there are many causes of poverty—including laziness and other sinful choices (see Ronald J. Sider, *Rich Christians in an Age of Hunger*, chap. 6). God wants people who are poor because of their own sinful choices to repent and be changed by the power of the Holy Spirit.

28. Ps. 72:1–4; Prov. 31:8–9; Isa. 1:10, 17, 23, 26; Jer. 22:2–3, 14–15; Dan. 4:27.

29. The following section is adapted from Ronald J. Sider, *Genuine Christianity* (Grand Rapids: Zondervan, 1996), 137–41.

30. See further Stephen Charles Mott, "The Partiality of Biblical Justice," *Transformation*, January–March 1993, 24.

31. Mott and Sider, "Economic Justice," 31–33.

32. Mott's translation.

33. Rights are the privileges of membership in the communities to which we belong; cf. Max L. Stackhouse, *Creeds, Society, and Human Rights: A Study in Three Cultures* (Grand Rapids: Eerdmans, 1984), 5, 44, 104–5.

34. C. Spicq, *Les Épîtres Pastorales* (Paris: Gabalda, 1969), 190 (on 1 Tim. 6:8).

35. Cf. Job 22 where injustice includes sins of omission—i.e., failure to provide drink for the weary and bread for the hungry (v. 7; cf. 31:17), as well as the exploitative use of economic power (22:6a). In 31:19 the omission is failure to provide clothing. Compare the important modern statement of benefit rights by Pope John Paul XXIII in his encyclical *Pacem in Terris*, where he says that each person has the right "to the means necessary for the proper development of life, particularly food, clothing, shelter, medical care, rest, and finally, the necessary social services." Pope John XXIII, *Pacem in Terris*, 11, in *Papal Encyclicals, Vol. 5: 1958–1981*, ed. C. Carlen (n.p., Consortium, 1981), 108.

36. Cf. Mott, "The Contribution of the Bible to Economic Thought," *Transformation*, June–September/October–December 1987, 31.

37. Eryl W. Davies, *Prophesy and Ethics: Isaiah and the Ethical Traditions of Israel* (Sheffield, *Journal for the Study of the Old Testament, Supplement Series 16*, Sheffield, UK: University of Sheffield, 1981), 69, 116.

38. Leslie Poles Hartley, *Facial Justice* (London: H. Hamilton, 1960).

39. See Roland de Vaux, *Ancient Israel: Its Life and Institutions*, trans. John McHugh (London: Darton, Longman and Todd, 1961), 1:164.

40. H. Eberhard von Waldow, "Social Responsibility and Social Structure in Early Israel," *Catholic Biblical Quarterly* 32 (1970): 195.

41. See the discussion and the literature cited in Mott, *Biblical Ethics and Social Change* (see note 11), 65–66; and Stephen Charles Mott, "Egalitarian Aspects of the Biblical Theory of Justice," in the *American Society of Christian Ethics, Selected Papers 1978*, ed. Max Stackhouse (Newton, MA: American Society of Christian Ethics, 1978), 8–26.

42. In his study of early Israel, Norman Gottwald concluded that Israel was "an egalitarian, extended-family, segmentary tribal society with an agricultural-pastoral economic base . . . characterized by profound resistance and opposition to the forms of political domination and social stratification that had become normative in the chief cultural and political centers of the ancient Near East." *The Tribes of Yahweh: A Sociology of the Religion of Liberated Israel 1250–1050 BCE* (London: SCM Press, 1979), 10.

43. For a survey of the literature on Leviticus 25, see R. Gnuse, "Jubilee Legislation in Leviticus: Israel's Vision of Social Reform," *Biblical Theological Bulletin* 15 (1983): 43–48.

44. See in this connection the fine article by Paul G. Schrotenboer, "The Return of Jubilee," *International Reformed Bulletin*, Fall 1973, 19ff. (esp. 23–24).

45. On the centrality of the land in Israel's self-understanding, see further Christopher J. H. Wright,

An Eye for an Eye: The Place of Old Testament Ethics Today (Downers Grove, IL: InterVarsity, 1983), esp. chaps. 3 and 4. Walter Brueggermann's *The Land* (Philadelphia: Fortress Press, 1977) is also a particularly important work on this topic.

46. See Jeremiah 34 for a fascinating account of God's anger at Israel for their failure to obey this command.

47. Some modern commentators think that Deuteronomy 15:1–11 provides for a one-year suspension of repayment of loans rather than an outright remission of them. See, e.g., C. J. H. Wright, *God's People in God's Land* (Grand Rapids: Eerdmans, 1990), 148, and S. R. Driver, *Deuteronomy*, International Critical Commentary, 3rd ed. (Edinburgh: T. and T. Clark, 1895), 179–80. But Driver's argument is basically that remission would have been *impractical*. He admits that v. 9 seems to point toward remission of loans. So too Gerhard von Rad, *Deuteronomy* (Philadelphia: Westminster, 1966), 106.

48. See de Vaux, *Ancient Israel*, 1:174–75, for discussion of the law's implementation. In the Hellenistic period, there is clear evidence that it was put into effect.

49. See esp. John Mason's excellent article, "Assisting the Poor: Assistance Programmes in the Bible," *Transformation*, April–June 1987, 1–14.

50. Ibid., 7.

51. See ibid., 8, for some examples; cf. also the earlier discussion of Beisner and Henry.

52. Ibid., 9.

53. Mason (p. 14, n. 39) comments: "Two Hebrew words are used for 'rights' or 'cause': the predominant word is *mishpat*, which is used elsewhere to refer to the laws and judgments of God; at Ps. 140:12 (with *mishpat*), Prov. 29:7, 31:9, and Jer. 22:16 the word is *din* and means most likely 'righteous judgment' or 'legal claim' (TDOT 3:190–91; TWOT *Theological Wordbook of the Old Testament*, ed. R. Laird Harris (Chicago, Moody Press, 1981) 2:752–55, 947–49)."

54. Ibid., 9.

55. For a much longer discussion of both the passages in Acts and Paul's collection, see Sider, *Rich Christians in an Age of Hunger*, 79–89.

56. So too the U.S. Catholic Bishops (see the discussion in Hollenbach, *Claims in Conflict*, 66–67; and Lebacqz, *Six Theories of Justice*, 74–75) and the Reformed Ecumenical Synod, *RES Testimony on Human Rights* (1983), esp. 151–52.

57. Hollenbach, *Claims in Conflict*, 204.

58. William Temple, *Christianity and the State* (London: Macmillan, 1929), 66. For purposes of this essay, I use "state" and "government" interchangeably although I recognize that for some purposes it is crucial to distinguish the two—e.g., the state institutions of Congress and the courts etc. are different from the

Republican (or Democratic) government that currently occupies the White House etc.

59. Paul Marshall, *Thine Is the Kingdom* (Grand Rapids: Eerdmans, 1984), 43–45.

60. Temple, *Christianity and the State*, 108.

61. J. Philip Wogaman, *Christian Perspectives on Politics* (Philadelphia: Fortress, 1988), 13. Pacifist and nonpacifist Christians disagree over whether God *wants* the state to use *lethal* violence as it compels compliance, but it is a matter of historical fact that most states over the course of human history have done so.

62. Temple, *Christianity and the State*, 88.

63. Marshall, *Thine Is the Kingdom*, 42.

64. John Calvin, *Institutes of the Christian Religion*, ed. J. McNeill (Philadelphia: Westminster, Library of Christian Classics 20–21, 1960), 4.20.3, 4, 22 (1488, 1490, 1510); cf. Harro Höpfl, *The Christian Polity of John Calvin* (Cambridge; New York: Cambridge University Press, 1982), 44–46. Similarly for Luther, government is an inestimable blessing of God and one of God's best gifts; compare W. D. J. Cargill Thompson, *The Political Thought of Martin Luther*, ed. P. Broadhead (Sussex: Harvester, 1984), 66.

65. Cf. 1 Peter 2:14: Government officials are sent by God "to punish those who do wrong and to praise those who do right."

66. Marshall, *Thine Is the Kingdom*, 42.

67. Ibid.

68. Ibid., 48–49.

69. See, e.g., Helmut Thielicke, *Theological Ethics: Politics* (Grand Rapids: Eerdmans, 1979), 250.

70. The following paragraphs are adapted from Mott and Sider, "Economic Justice," 42ff.

71. The state molds the process of mutual support among the groups (Reinhold Niebuhr, *The Nature and Destiny of Man, Vol 2: Human Destiny* [New York: Scribner's, 1964], 266).

72. Meredith G. Kline, *Kingdom Prologue* (Hamilton, MA: Meredith G. Kline, 1983), 34, citing Daniel 4:27 in support.

73. Brunner, *Justice and the Social Order*, 139–40, 205.

74. The position presented here has parallels to that developed in the Catholic social tradition's principle of subsidiarity. See, e.g., David Hollenbach, *Justice, Peace and Human Rights: America Catholic Social Ethics in a Pluralistic Context* (New York: Crossroad, 1988), 81.

Chapter 9 Citizenship, Civil Society, and the Church

1. "A Call to Civil Society: Why Democracy Needs Moral Truths," A Report to the Nation from the Council on Civil Society, Institute for American Values, 1998.

2. Andrew Sullivan, "This Is a Religious War," *New York Times Magazine*, October 7, 2001.

3. Jean Bethke Elshtain, "Faith of Our Fathers and Mothers: Religion and the American Democracy," *American Experiment Quarterly*, Fall 2003.

4. Remarks by James H. Billington, Librarian of Congress, at Awarding of Templeton Prize for Progress in Religion, May 16, 2000.

5. Gary Wills, *James Madison* (New York: Henry Holt and Co., 2002), 18.

6. Don Eberly, *America's Promise: Civil Society and the Renewal of American Culture* (Lanham, MD: Rowman & Littlefield, 1998), 194.

7. Paul Johnson, *A History of the American People* (New York: HarperCollins, 1997), 208–9.

8. Carl F. Kaestle, ed., *Pillars of the Republic: Common Schools and American Society, 1780–1860* (New York: Hill and Wang, 1983), 44–47.

9. James Davison Hunter, *Culture Wars* (New York: Basic Books, 1991), 134.

10. Warren A. Nord, *Religion and American Education: Rethinking a National Dilemma* (Chapel Hill, NC: University of North Carolina Press, 1995), 71.

11. Quoted in Nord, *Religion and American Education*, 76.

12. "Church, State and Education," *New York Times*, editorial, December 1, 2003.

13. "The Wrong Ruling on Vouchers," *New York Times*, editorial, June 28, 2002.

14. Cited in "Breaking Up a Monopoly," *Christianity Today*, editorial, August 2, 2002.

15. David Sikkink, "The Loyal Opposition: Evangelicals and Public Schools," in *Evangelicals and Civic Engagement: A Public Faith*, ed. Michael Cromartie (Lanham, MD: Rowman & Littlefield, 2003). See also Christian Smith, *Christian America? What Evangelicals Really Want* (Los Angeles: University of California Press, 2000), 129–59.

16. Charles Glenn, "Public Education Changes Partners," in *Religion Returns to the Public Square*, ed. Hugh Heclo and Wilfred M. McClay (Washington, DC: Woodrow Wilson Center Press, 2003), 299–325.

17. Warren A. Nord and Charles C. Haynes, *Taking Religion Seriously across the Curriculum* (Alexandria, VA: ASCD, 1998), 38–39.

18. Interview with Virgil Gulker, February 2, 2004. See also "Churches, Charity and Children: How Religious Organizations Are Reaching America's At-Risk Kids," by Joseph Loconte and Lia Fantuzzo, Center for Research on Religion and Urban Civil Society, the University of Pennsylvania, 2002.

19. Ted Olsen, "Supreme Court Apparently Offers 'Good News' for Bible Club," *Christianity Today*, February 26, 2002.

20. Richard Landes, "Faith-Based Good Works Have a Place," *Los Angeles Times*, October 23, 2000.

21. Isaac Kramnick and R. Laurence Moore, "Can Churches Save the Cities?" *American Prospect*, November–December 1997, 47–53.

22. Ram Cnaan and Gaynor I. Yancey, "Our Hidden Safety Net," in *What's God Got to Do with the American Experiment?* ed. E. J. Dionne Jr. and John J. DiIulio Jr. (Washington, DC: Brookings Institution, 2000), 154–55.

23. Ram A. Cnaan, "Keeping Faith in the City: How 401 Urban Religious Congregations Serve Their Neediest Neighbors," University of Pennsylvania and Public/Private Ventures, CRRUCS Report 2000–2001.

24. John G. West Jr., *The Politics of Revelation and Reason* (Lawrence, KS: University Press of Kansas, 1996), 83.

25. George M. Marsden, *Religion and American Culture* (New York: Harcourt Brace Jovanovich, 1990), 48.

26. Alexis de Tocqueville, *Democracy in America*, vol. 2 (Vintage Books Edition, July 1990), 110.

27. A. James Reichley, *Religion in American Public Life* (Washington, DC: Brookings Institution, 1985), 176.

28. Quoted in Anson Phelps Stokes, *Church and State in the United States*, vol. 1 (New York: Harper, 1950), 653, 662.

29. Joel Schwartz, *Fighting Poverty with Virtue: Moral Reform and America's Urban Poor, 1825–2000* (Bloomington, IN: Indiana University Press, 2000), 240.

30. Marvin Olasky, *The Tragedy of American Compassion* (Washington, DC: Regnery Publishing, 1992), 130.

31. Sydney Ahlstrom, *A Religious History of the American People*, vol. 2 (Garden City, NY: Doubleday, 1975), 200.

32. Olasky, *Tragedy of American Compassion*, 131.

33. Mark A. Noll, *A History of Christianity in the United States and Canada* (Grand Rapids: Eerdmans, 1992), 304.

34. Olasky, *Tragedy of American Compassion*, 113.

35. Loconte and Fantuzzo, "Churches, Charity and Children."

36. Byron Johnson and David Larson, "Religion: The Forgotten Factor in Delinquency Research and New Research Findings Concerning Faith-Factor Efficacy in Urban Settings." Prepared for the Manhattan Institute, November 13, 1998.

37. Don S. Browning, "Altruism, Civic Virtue, and Religion," in *Seedbeds of Virtue: Sources of Competence, Character and Citizenship in American Society*, ed. Mary Ann Glendon and David Blankenhorn (New York: Madison Books, 1995), 120.

38. James Q. Wilson, "Religion and Public Life," in *What's God Got to Do with the American Experiment?* 160–70.

39. Sidney Blumenthal, "The Religious Right and Republicans," in *Piety and Politics: Evangelicals and Fundamentalists Confront the World* (Washington, DC: Ethics and Public Policy Center, 1987), 273.

40. Kimberly Blaker, ed. *The Fundamentals of Extremism: The Christian Right in America* (Plymouth, MI: New Boston Books, 2003).

41. Stephen L. Carter, *The Culture of Disbelief* (New York: Basic Books, 1993), 9.

42. John G. West Jr., *The Politics of Revelation and Reason* (Lawrence, KS: University Press of Kansas, 1996), 177.

43. Albert J. Raboteau, *African-American Religion* (Oxford: Oxford University Press, 1999), 29–45.

44. A. James Reichley, *Religion in American Public Life* (Washington, DC: Brookings Institution, 1985), 191.

45. George M. Marsden, *Religion and American Culture* (Orlando, FL: Harcourt Brace Jovanovich, 1990), 63.

46. Noll, *History of Christianity*, 314.

47. Richard J. Carwardine, *Evangelicals and Politics in Antebellum America* (Knoxville: University of Tennessee Press, 1997), 239.

48. Reichley, *Religion in American Public Life*, 193.

49. Carwardine, *Evangelicals and Politics in Antebellum America*, 36.

50. Walter Rauschenbusch, *Christianizing the Social Order* (New York: Macmillan, 1912), 458.

51. Martin E. Marty, *Pilgrims in Their Own Land: 500 Years of Religion in America* (New York: Penguin Books, 1984), 352.

52. Stephen L. Carter, *God's Name in Vain* (New York: Basic Books, 2000), 27.

53. Martin Luther King Jr., "Letter from Birmingham Jail," April, 16, 1963.

54. Carter, *God's Name in Vain*, 35.

55. Robert W. Fogel, *The Fourth Great Awakening and the Future of Egalitarianism* (Chicago: University of Chicago Press, 2000), 7.

56. Allen D. Hertzke, "Evangelicals and International Engagement," in *A Public Faith: Evangelicals and Civic Engagement*, ed. Michael Cromartie (Lanham, MD: Rowman & Littlefield, 2003), 215–33.

57. Holly Burkhalter, "The Politics of AIDS," *Foreign Affairs*, January/February 2004, 8.

58. Edward C. Green, "Faith-Based Organizations: Contributions to HIV Prevention," Harvard Center for Population and Development Studies, September 2003.

59. Eberly, *America's Promise*, 191.

60. Quoted in *The Great Experiment: Faith and Freedom in the American Republic* (Burke, VA: Trinity Forum, 1999), x.

61. Cal Thomas and Ed Dobson, *Blinded by Might* (Grand Rapids: Zondervan, 1999), 181, 187.

62. Theda Skocpol, "Religion, Civil Society, and Social Provision in the U.S.," in *Who Will Provide? The Changing Role of Religion in American Social Welfare*, ed. Mary Jo Bane, Brent Coffin, and Ronald Thiemann (Boulder, CO: Westview Press, 2000), 24.

63. Christopher Lasch, *The Revolt of the Elites and the Betrayal of Democracy* (New York: W.W. Norton & Co., 1995), 85.

64. Glendon and Blankenhorn, *Seedbeds of Virtue*, 17.

65. Clinton Rossiter, ed. *The Federalist Papers* (New York: Mentor, 1999), 310.

66. Alexis de Tocqueville, *Democracy in America*, vol. 1 (New York: Vintage Books, 1990), 307.

67. Glenn Tinder, "Can We Be Good without God?" in *The New Religious Humanists*, ed. Gregory Wolfe (New York: Free Press, 1997), 169.

Chapter 10 The Sanctity of Life in the Twenty-first Century

1. Nigel M. de S. Cameron, "Evangelicals and Bioethics: An Extraordinary Failure," in *A Public Faith: Evangelicals and Civil Engagement*, ed. Michael Cromartie (Lanham, MD: Rowan & Littlefield, 2003), 117–24.

2. Ian Kennedy, *The Unmasking of Medicine* (London: Allan & Unwin, 1981).

3. Nigel M. de S. Cameron, "Evangelicals and Bioethics"; see also Cameron, "Christianity in Bioethics," in *Encyclopedia of Bioethics*, 3rd ed., forthcoming.

4. For an original report, see R. A. Vonderlehr, T. Clark, O. C. Wenger, J. R. Heller, Jr., "Untreated Syphilis in the Male Negro: A Comparative Study of Treated and Untreated Cases," *Ven. Dis. Inform.* 17 (1936): 260–65.

5. For a recent statement from a Christian perspective on research ethics, see www.thecbc.org.

6. Judith Jarvis Thomson, "A Defense of Abortion," *Philosophy and Public Affairs*, vol. 1, no. 1 (Princeton, NJ: Princeton University Press, 1971).

7. Helga Kuhse, *The Sanctity of Life Doctrine: A Critique* (Oxford: Clarendon Press, 1996).

8. See Nigel M. de S. Cameron, *The New Medicine: Life and Death after Hippocrates* (London: Hodder & Stoughton, 1991), 92–128.

9. Euthanasia is a complex topic, though one of the basic weaknesses of the position of those who argue for it as a matter of individual choice is that they are in fact offering an argument for the approval of suicide, as well as for the participation of others (typically, physicians) in killing; both are entailed in the general case for euthanasia-as-choice. Yet the same advocates then typically pull back from advocacy of suicide, since they are aware that the suicidal are widely agreed to need discouragement and counsel, not the offer of a lethal drug! If the desire for euthanasia, which is cer-

tainly seen in a minority of patients, is understood as a suicidal intent, it is clear that the socially responsible intervention will not be to call Dr. Kevorkian.

10. This collaboration is now focused, here in the United States, in the Institute on Biotechnology and the Human Future, at the Illinois Institute of Technology (www.thehumanfuture.org).

11. This is powerfully illustrated by "The Sanctity of Life in a Brave New World: A Manifesto on Biotechnology and Human Dignity" issued by a group of representative evangelical (and some Catholic) leaders in February 2002. Initial signatories, in addition to the present writer, included Charles W. Colson, Joni Eareckson Tada, and James Dobson. Its text carefully locates the issues of Bioethics 2 in the context of the sanctity of life. (See appendix at the end of chapter 10.)

12. These useful terms are from Spielberg's movie *AI: Artificial Intelligence*, generally memorable only for its special effects.

13. *Wired* magazine, April 2000; available at www .wired.com.

14. C. S. Lewis, *The Abolition of Man* (New York: Macmillan, 1943).

15. This is a fast-developing field, summarized by Christopher Hook, M.D., in *Human Dignity for the Biotech Century: A Christian Vision for Public Policy*, ed. Charles W. Colson and Nigel M. de S. Cameron, (Downers Grove, IL: InterVarsity, 2004).

16. A unique process bringing together Christians, "progressive" critics of technology, and leading advocates of nanotechnology and other innovations was initiated by the Center for Bioethics and Culture in Oakland, California, in 2003 and Washington, DC, in 2004 (details at www.thecbc.org).

17. Charles Hodge, *Systematic Theology*, vol. 2 (Grand Rapids: Eerdmans, 1952), 637.

18. Appendix was written by Nigel M. de S. Cameron.

Chapter 11 Caring for the Vulnerable

1. See, for example, David Martin's *Tongues of Fire: The Explosion of Protestantism in Latin America* (Oxford: Blackwell Publishing, 1993).

2. Encarta, http://Encarta.msn.com.

3. This is 29 percent of the total population in the low- and middle-income countries. The Millennium Development Goals (MDGs), which all 189 United Nations member countries, including the United States, have endorsed, call for a 50 percent reduction in the number of people living on less than one dollar per day by the year 2015. However, at the current level of investment, this goal will not be met. See www.undp.org for an extensive discussion of the MDGs. See www.micahchallenge.org for an evangelical perspective on the MDGs.

4. See www.unhcr.ch. World Relief is the leading evangelical organization involved in refugee resettlement. See www.worldrelief.org. The U.S. Committee for Refugees also has a substantial collection of documents and articles on refugees throughout the world. See www.irsa-uscr.org.

5. The Religious Liberty Commission of the World Evangelical Alliance does an excellent job of monitoring persecution based on religion (www .worldevangelical.org/rlc.html). Other good sources include the U.S. Commission for International Religious Freedom (www.uscirf.gov) and the State Department annual reports on religious liberty and on human rights (www.state.gov).

6. www.salvationarmy.org.

7. Milton Rokeach, quoted in David A. Moberg, *The Great Reversal* (London: Scripture Union, 1973), 53–57.

8. In many cases, better translated "brothers and sisters"—it is clear that women and girls are included.

9. Relocation of rich Christians to poor communities is one of the "three Rs" of Christian community development, as promoted by John Perkins and the Christian Community Development Association. See www.ccda.org.

10. Raymond Fung, *The Isaiah Vision* (Geneva: WCC, 1992).

11. See the other chapters in this book that discuss these issues in greater detail.

12. Richard J. Mouw, *Political Evangelism* (Grand Rapids: Eerdmans, 1973), 55.

13. See the numerous studies published by the Cato Institute, www.cato.org.

14. Bread for the World Institute, *Agriculture in the Global Economy* (Washington: BFW Institute, 2003), 3.

15. Haddon Wilmer, "Toward a Theology of the State," in *Essays in Evangelical Social Ethics* (Wilton, CT: Morehouse-Barlow, 1979), 95.

16. Immigrants add at least $10 billion to the U.S. economy. See www.immigrationforum.org for links to numerous studies documenting the economic contributions of immigrants.

17. The Millennium Development Goals were endorsed by all 189 United Nations members in 2000. The eight goals, to be achieved by 2015, are:

1. *Eradicate extreme poverty and hunger.* Target: Halve the proportion of people living on less than a dollar a day and those who suffer from hunger.

2. *Achieve universal primary education.* Target: Ensure that all boys and girls complete primary school.

3. *Promote gender equality and empower women.* Targets: Eliminate gender disparities in primary and secondary education preferably by 2005, and at all levels by 2015.

4. *Reduce child mortality.* Target: Reduce by two-thirds the mortality rate among children under five

5. *Improve maternal health.* Target: Reduce by three-quarters the ratio of women dying in childbirth.

6. *Combat HIV/AIDS, malaria, and other diseases.* Target: Halt and begin to reverse the spread of HIV/AIDS and the incidence of malaria and other major diseases.

7. *Ensure environmental sustainability.* Targets:
   - Integrate the principles of sustainable development into country policies and programs and reverse the loss of environmental resources.
   - By 2015, reduce by half the proportion of people without access to safe drinking water.
   - By 2020, achieve significant improvement in the lives of at least 100 million slum dwellers.

8. *Develop a global partnership for development.* Targets:
   - Develop further an open trading and financial system that includes a commitment to good governance, development, and poverty reduction—nationally and internationally.
   - Address the least developed countries' special needs, and the special needs of landlocked and small island developing states.
   - Deal comprehensively with developing countries' debt problems.
   - Develop decent and productive work for youth.
   - In cooperation with pharmaceutical companies, provide access to affordable essential drugs in developing countries.
   - In cooperation with the private sector, make available the benefits of new technologies—especially information and communications technologies.

For more details see www.undp.org.

Chapter 12 Family Integrity

1. "Married-Couple and Unmarried-Partner Households: 2000," U.S. Census Bureau, February 2003.

2. Here is a partial list of the major organizations: Dennis Rainey's Family Life Today, The Family Research Council, David Popenoe and Barbara Whitehead's The National Marriage Project, Don Browing's The Religion, Culture and Family Project, John Rosemond's The Center for Affirmative Parenting, Ken Canfield's The Center on Fathering, The National Fatherhood Initiative, Diane Sollee's The Coalition for Marriage, Family and Couples Education, Gary Smalley's Today's Family, Drs. Les and Leslie Parrott's The Center for Relationship Development, Dr. James Dobson's Focus on the Family, The Cana Institute: Caring for the Soul of Marriage and Family, Engaged and Marriage Encounter, Mike and Harriet McManus's Marriage Savers, Michele Weiner-Davis's Divorce Buster Center, Promise Keepers, David Blankenhorn's Institute for American Values and its Marriage and Motherhood Projects as well as the Council on Families in America, Mothers of Preschoolers, Parenting Today's Teen, Dr. Neil Clark Warren's eharmony, Dr. John Gottman's Institute for The Art and Science of Love, David and Claudia Arp's Marriage Alive International, Dr. Willard Harley's Marriage Builders, Inc., John Gray's The Mars Venus Institute, Drs. Howard Markman and Scott Stanley's PREP Program, Retrouvaille (a highly successful program for recovering seriously troubled marriages), Dr. David Olson's PREPARE & ENRICH, the vibrant network of state Family Policy Councils initiated by Focus on the Family, The Art of Loving Well Project, RQ: Relationship Intelligence, etc. The list goes on seemingly without end.

3. Sara McLanahan and Gary Sandefur, *Growing Up with a Single Parent: What Hurts, What Helps* (Cambridge: Harvard University Press, 1994); Ronald Angel and Jacqueline Angel, *Painful Inheritance: Health and the New Generation of Fatherless Families* (Madison: University of Wisconsin Press, 1993); Judith Wallerstein et al., *The Unexpected Legacy of Divorce* (New York: Hyperion, 2000); Paul R. Amato and Alan Booth, *A Generation at Risk: Growing Up in an Era of Family Upheaval* (Cambridge, MA: Harvard University Press, 1997); Linda J. Waite and Maggie Gallagher, *The Case for Marriage: Why Married People Are Happier, Healthier, and Better Off Financially* (New York: Doubleday, 2000); Steven L. Nock, *Marriage in Men's Lives* (New York: Oxford University Press, 1998); Robert Coombs, "Marital Status and Personal Well-Being: A Literature Review," *Family Relations* 40 (1991): 97–102; Jan E. Stets, "The Link between Past and Present Intimate Relationships," *Journal of Family Issues* 14 (1993), 236–60; David Popenoe, *Life without Father: Compelling New Evidence That Fatherhood and Marriage Are Indispensable for the Good of Children and Society* (New York: Free Press, 1996); Barbara Dafoe Whitehead, *The Divorce Culture* (New York: Alfred A. Knopf, 1997).

4. Kyle D. Pruett, *Fatherneed: Why Father Care Is as Essential as Mother Care for Your Child* (New York: Free Press, 2000); Brenda Hunter, *The Power*

of Mother Love: Transforming Both Mother and Child (Colorado Springs, CO: Waterbrook Press, 1999); McLanahan and Sandefur, Growing Up with a Single Parent; Popenoe, Life without Father.

5. Suzanne G. Frayser, Varieties of Sexual Experience: An Anthropological Perspective on Human Sexuality (New Haven: Human Relations Area Files Press, 1985); Edward Westermarck, The History of Human Marriage, vols. 1–3 (New York: Allerton Book Company, 1922); Helen E. Fischer, Anatomy of Love: The Natural History of Monogamy, Adultery and Divorce (New York: W. W. Norton, 1992); George P. Murdock, Social Structure (New York: Macmillan, 1949); Bronislaw Malinowski, Sex, Culture and Myth (New York: Harcourt, Brace & World, 1962), 62–63.

Chapter 13 Stewardship

1. Jurgen Moltmann, God in Creation (London: SCM Press, 1985), 258–59.

2. Ibid., 49.

3. Ronald J. Sider, Good News and Good Works (Grand Rapids: Baker, 1993), 173–74.

4. Bryant Myers, Walking with the Poor (Maryknoll, NY: Orbis Books, 1999), 26.

5. Karl Barth, Church Dogmatics IV/1, ed. G. W. Bromiley and T. F. Torrance (Edinburgh: T & T Clark, 1956), 436.

6. Matthew 6:24 (NIV).

7. Jacques Ellul, Money and Power (Downers Grove, IL: InterVarsity, 1985), 76.

8. Richard Foster, The Challenge of the Disciplined Life (San Francisco: HarperCollins, 1989), 24–25.

9. My treatment of a two-kingdom lifestyle is not to be confused with Luther's two-kingdom ethic. I am talking here about a personal division we make between our spiritual and secular worlds, and my aim is to show that such a division is in direct opposition to God's will and our calling to submit all of our lives to the one lordship of Jesus Christ. Luther believed God ordained and God calls us to allegiance to two kingdoms; the spiritual government that governs the lives of Christians and the temporal government that is necessary to constrain the ungodly. He writes, "For this reason God has ordained two governments: the spiritual, by which the Holy Spirit produces Christians and righteous people under Christ; and the temporal, which restrains the un-Christian and wicked so that—no thanks to them—they are obliged to keep still and to maintain an outward peace." Luther's Works, vol. 45, trans. Charles M. Jacobs and Rev. Walther I. Brandt (Philadelphia: Fortress Press, 1966), 89–90.

10. Tim Dearborn, "God, Grace and Salvation," in Christ in our Place, ed. Trevor A. Hart and Daniel P. Thimell (Exeter: Paternoster Press, 1989), 287.

11. Ray Anderson, "Christopraxis: Christ's Ministry for the World," in Christ in Our Place (Exeter: Paternoster Press, 1989), 14.

12. Ibid.

13. Sider, Good News and Good Works, 92.

14. See also Michael Novak, The Spirit of Democratic Capitalism (New York: Simon & Schuster, 1982).

15. Fred Van Dyke, David Mahan, Joseph Sheldon, and Raymond Brand, Redeeming Creation: The Biblical Basis for Environmental Stewardship (Downers Grove, IL: InterVarsity, 1996), 98–99.

16. See, e.g., "The Cornwall Declaration on Environmental Stewardship," in Environmental Stewardship in the Judeo-Christian Tradition (Grand Rapids: Acton Institute, 2000)

17. "An Evangelical Declaration on the Care of Creation," published by the Evangelical Environmental Network, a ministry of Evangelicals for Social Action.

18. Myers, Walking with the Poor, 58.

Chapter 14 The Ethics of War and Peacemaking

1. I want to express thanks to New Testament scholars Craig Blomberg of Denver Theological Seminary and Donald Hagner of Fuller Theological Seminary for their helpful suggestions that are incorporated in the section on New Testament teachings. And thanks to Martin Cook, professor of philosophy at the U.S. Air Force Academy and widely recognized expert on just war theory, for suggestions that have been incorporated in the presentation of just war theory. Special gratitude to Dean Curry of Messiah College and to Ted Koontz of Associated Mennonite Biblical Seminary for carefully reading the whole chapter from their different perspectives (just war and pacifism), and for their helpful suggestions.

2. N. T. Wright, Jesus and the Victory of God (Philadelphia: Fortress, 1996), 151–60, 250–53, 268–71, 296, 385.

3. Richard Bauckham, The Climax of Prophecy: Studies on the Book of Revelation (Edinburgh: T & T Clark: 1993), 233ff.

4. G. K. Beale, The Book of Revelation: A Commentary on the Greek Text (Grand Rapids: Eerdmans: 1999), 580.

5. John Goldingay, Theological Diversity and the Authority of the Old Testament (Grand Rapids: Eerdmans, 1987); Goldingay, Models for Interpretation of Scripture (Grand Rapids: Eerdmans, 1995).

6. John H. Yoder, The Lamb's War, ed. Glen Stassen and Mark Thiessen Nation (forthcoming); Millard Lind, Yahweh Is a Warrior (Scottdale, PA: Herald, 1986).

7. Richard B. Hays, The Moral Vision of the New Testament (San Francisco: HarperSanFrancisco, 1996), 319–29; Walter Wink, Engaging the Powers: Discernment and Resistance in a World of Domination (Min-

neapolis: Augsburg Fortress, 1992), 175ff.; Stassen and Gushee, *Kingdom Ethics*, chap. 6.

8. Glen Stassen, "The Fourteen Triads of the Sermon on the Mount: Matthew 5:21–7:12," *Journal of Biblical Literature* 122, no. 2 (Summer 2003): 267–308; Stassen and Gushee, *Kingdom Ethics*, chap. 6 et passim.

9. Hays, *Moral Vision*, 332ff.

10. Ibid., 331.

11. Tremper Longman and Daniel Reid, *God Is a Warrior* (Grand Rapids: Zondervan, 1995), 167–71.

12. Johannes Friedrich, Wolfgang Pöhlmann, and Peter Stuhlmacher, "Zur historischen Situation und Intention von Rm 13:1–10," *Zeitschrift für Theologie und Kirche* (1976).

13. Ched Myers, *Binding the Strong Man* (Maryknoll, NY: Orbis, 1997), 299.

14. U.S. National Conference of Catholic Bishops, *The Challenge of Peace* (Washington, DC: U.S. Catholic Conference, 1983), #80.

15. Arthur Holmes, "The Just War," in *War: Four Christian Views*, ed. Robert G. Clouse (Downers Grove, IL: InterVarsity: 1991), 119; cf. Cahill, *Love Your Enemy* (see note 16), 237ff.

16. Lisa Sowle Cahill, *Love Your Enemy: Discipleship, Pacifism, and Just War Theory* (Minneapolis: Augsburg Fortress, 1994), chaps. 4 and 5.

17. Michael Walzer, *Just and Unjust Wars* (New York: Basic Books: 1977), xv–xvi, 53–54, 59, 61ff., 72, 108, 134–37, 254; and 29, 70–71.

18. David Gushee, "Just War Divide: One Tradition, Two Views," *Christian Century*, 119, no. 17 (August 14–27, 2002): 26–28.

19. Walzer, *Just and Unjust Wars*, xvi, 53, 101, 106, 108.

20. Richard B. Miller, "Just-War Criteria and Theocentric Ethics," in *Christian Ethics: Problems and Prospects*, ed. Lisa Sowle Cahill and James F. Childress (New York: Pilgrim, 1996), 342ff.

21. Calvin, *Institutes*, bk. 4, chap. 20, sections 31–32; Stephen Mott, *Biblical Ethics and Social Change* (New York: Oxford University Press, 1982), 187–91.

22. Ronald Sider, *Non-Violence: The Invincible Weapon?* (Dallas: Word, 1999), 2.

23. Holmes, "The Just War," 120.

24. *Los Angeles Times*, September 21, 2001, A6.

25. Walzer, *Just and Unjust Wars*, 116.

26. Ibid., 120–22.

27. Mott, *Biblical Ethics*, 188; Walzer, *Just and Unjust Wars*, 110.

28. David K. Clark and Robert V. Rakestraw, *Readings in Christian Ethics*, vol. 2 (Grand Rapids: Baker: 1996), 490.

29. Ronald G. Musto, *The Catholic Peace Tradition* (Maryknoll, NY: Orbis: 1986), 257.

30. *Challenge of Peace*, #101.

31. Clark and Rakestraw, *Readings in Christian Ethics*, 490.

32. Holmes, "The Just War," 121.

33. Mott, *Biblical Ethics*, 190; cf. Walzer, *Just and Unjust Wars*, 36, 47.

34. Walzer, *Just and Unjust Wars*, 151–59; Cahill Childress, *Christian Ethics* (see note 20), 45.

35. Walzer, *Just and Unjust Wars*, 197ff., 215.

36. Michelle Tooley, *Voices of the Voiceless: Women, Justice, and Human Rights in Guatemala* (Scottdale, PA: Herald, 1997).

37. John H. Yoder, *Nevertheless: Varieties and Shortcomings of Religious Pacifism* (Scottdale, PA: Herald, 1992), 151–54.

38. For Pentecostals, see Jay Beaman, *Pentecostal Pacifism: The Origin, Development, and Rejection of Pacific Belief among Pentecostals* (Hillsboro, OR: Center for Mennonite Brethren Studies, 1989); and Murray Dempster, "Reassessing the Moral Rhetoric of Early American Pentecostal Pacifism," *Crux* 26, no. 1 (March 1990): 23–36; see also the dialogue between Dempster and Beaman in the journal *Proclaim Peace* (1997), 31–57 and 82–93.

39. Yoder, *The Lamb's War*.

40. Cahill, *Love Your Enemies*, 210ff.

41. Sider, *Non-Violence*, 3.

42. Yoder, *Nevertheless*.

43. John H. Yoder, *Politics of Jesus* (1972; Grand Rapids: Eerdmans, 1994), 204; Tobias Winwright, "From Police Officers to Peace Officers," in *The Wisdom of the Cross: Essays in Honor of John Howard Yoder*, ed. Stanley Hauerwas et al. (Grand Rapids: Eerdmans, 1999), 84–114.

44. Yoder, *Politics of Jesus*, chap. 12.

45. "The Political Meaning of Hope," in Yoder, *The Lamb's War*.

46. Gene Sharp, *The Politics of Nonviolent Action* (Boston: Porter Sargent, 1974), documents hundreds of cases of effective nonviolent action.

47. John H. Yoder, *When War Is Unjust* (Minneapolis: Augsburg, 1984); and *The Lamb's War*.

48. Ralph Potter, *War and Moral Discourse* (Richmond: John Knox Press, 1969); Walzer, *Just and Unjust Wars*.

49. See Yoder, *The Lamb's War*, "Theological Point of Reference."

50. Glen Stassen, ed., *Just Peacemaking: Ten Practices for Abolishing War* (1998; New York: Pilgrim, 2004), "Kingdom Ethics," chap. 8.

51. Daniel Buttry, *Christian Peacemaking* (Valley Forge, PA: Judson, 1994), chap. 4.

52. Tooley, *Voices of the Voiceless*.

Chapter 15 Human Rights

1. On the development of a right to religious freedom, see David Little, "The Development in the West of the Right to Freedom of Religion and

Conscience: A Basis for Comparison with Islam," in *Human Rights and the Conflict of Cultures: Western and Islamic Perspectives on Religious Liberty*, ed. D. Little, J. Kelsay, and A. Sachedina (Columbia, SC: University of North Carolina Press, 1988), 13–32. A classic statement of a Catholic approach to rights, one that applies far beyond the Catholic Church, is Jacques Maritain, *Man and the State* (Chicago: University of Chicago Press, 1951).

2. The best survey of religion and human rights is found in *Religious Human Rights in Global Perspective: Legal Perspectives,* and *Religious Human Rights in Global Perspective: Religious Perspectives*, ed. John Witte and Johan van der Vyver (Leiden: Martinus Nijhoff, 1996). See also Kieran Cronin, *Rights and Christian Ethics* (Cambridge: Cambridge University Press, 1992).

3. Allen D. Hertzke, *Freeing God's Children: The Unlikely Alliance for Human Rights* (Lanham, MD: Rowman & Littlefield, forthcoming). See also Paul Marshall, *Their Blood Cries Out: The Untold Story of Modern Christians Who Are Dying for Their Faith* (Nashville: W Publishing, 1997); Nina Shea, *In the Lion's Den* (Nashville: Broadman and Holman, 1997); and Holly Burkhalter, "The Politics of AIDS: Engaging Conservative Activists," *Foreign Affairs*, January/February 2004.

4. Michael Perry argues that human rights necessarily have something sacred about them; see his *The Idea of Human Rights: Four Inquiries* (New York: Oxford University Press, 2000).

5. See Paul Marshall, "Two Types of Rights," *Canadian Journal of Political Science* 25, no. 4 (December 1992): 661–76.

6. L. W. Sumner, *The Moral Foundation of Rights* (Oxford: Clarendon Press, 1987), 8.

7. Ibid.

8. On the development and meaning of the Universal Declaration of Human Rights, see Mary Ann Glendon, *A World Made New: Eleanor Roosevelt and the Universal Declaration of Human Rights* (New York: Random House, 2002).

9. While a view of rights as "trumps" was articulated most clearly by Ronald Dworkin, it points more widely to a feature common in modern jurisprudence. See the survey provided in H. Gillman, "The Evolution of the Rights Trump in the American Constitutional Tradition," paper presented at the Annual Meeting of the American Political Science Association, Washington, DC, September 1991.

10. G. K. Chesterton, *Orthodoxy* (New York: Doubleday, 1924), 30–31.

11. See Meirlys Owens, "The Notion of Human Rights: A Reconsideration," *American Philosophical Quarterly* 6 (1969): 244.

12. Simone Weil, *The Need for Roots: Prelude to a Declaration of Duties Towards Mankind*, 2nd ed. (New York: Routledge, 2001).

13. Mary Ann Glendon, *Rights Talk: The Impoverishment of Political Discourse* (New York: Basic Books, 1991).

14. Ibid., x–xi, 14.

15. Ibid., 109–10. Similar themes occur in attempts to import the notion of rights into ecological discussions; see Paul Marshall, "Do Animals Have Rights?" *Studies in Christian Ethics* 6, no. 2 (Summer 1993): 31–49.

16. Michael Ignatieff et al., *Human Rights as Politics and Idolatry* (Princeton, NJ: Princeton University Press, 2003).

17. Thomas A. West, "Religious Liberty: The View from the Founding," in *On Faith and Free Government*, ed. Daniel C. Palm (Lanham, MD: Rowman & Littlefield, 1997). My point here is not that leaders such as Washington, Madison, Jefferson, or later Lincoln were all orthodox in their theology. It is that their thinking was shaped in fundamental ways by Christian beliefs. In the case of Lincoln, a man "visibly influenced" by a faith he did not share, see Allen Guelzo, *Abraham Lincoln: Redeemer President* (Grand Rapids: Eerdmans, 1999). See also James H. Hutson, ed., *Religion and the New Republic: Faith in the Founding of America* (Lanham, MD: Rowman & Littlefield, 2000); Michael Novak, *God's Country: Taking the Declaration Seriously* (Washington, DC: American Enterprise Institute, 2000).

18. Paul Marshall, *Human Rights Theories in Christian Perspective* (Toronto: ICS, 1983).

19. The following discussion relies heavily on Christopher J. H. Wright's *Human Rights: A Study in Biblical Themes* (Bramcote: Grove Books, 1979). See also James Limburg, "Human Rights in the Old Testament," in Alois Muller and Norbert Greinacher, *The Church and the Rights of Man* (New York: Seabury, 1979), 25–26; and Josef Blank, "The Justice of God as the Humanization of Man—The Problem of Human Rights in the New Testament," in Muller and Greinacher, *The Church and the Right of Man*, 27–58.

20. See also Paul Marshall, "Dooyeweerd's Empirical Theory of Rights," in *The Legacy of Herman Dooyeweerd*, ed. C. T. McIntire (Lanham, MD: University Press of America, 1985), 119–42.

21. On the notion of rights as endowments by God, in this case dealing with the rights of animals, see Andrew Linzey, *Animal Rights: A Christian Assessment of Man's Treatment of Animals* (London: SCM, 1976).

22. G. von Rad, *Genesis: A Commentary*, rev. ed. (London: SCM, 1961), 211. See also Meredith Kline, "Oracular Origin of the State," in G. Tuttle, *Biblical and Near Eastern Studies* (Grand Rapids: Eerdmans, 1978), 132–41; Paul Marshall, *God and the Constitution: Christianity and American Politics* (Lanham, MD: Rowman & Littlefield, 2002), chap. 3.

23. This paragraph relies heavily on B. Zylstra, "Using the Constitution to Defend Religious Rights,"

in *Freedom and Faith: The Impact of Law on Religious Liberty*, ed. Lynn R. Buzzard (Westchester, IL: Crossway Books, 1982), 96.

24. On the importance of stressing justice rather than equality in addressing rights claims, see Julius Stone, "Justice Not Equality," *Hastings Law Journal* 29 (1978): 995–1024.

25. Johan van der Vyver, "Constitutional Options for Post-Apartheid South Africa," *Emory Law Journal* 40 (1991): 771.

26. On the history of rights, see Richard Tuck's excellent *Natural Rights Theories: Their Origin and Development* (Cambridge: Cambridge University Press, 1979). Tuck points out that in Greek and Roman discussions we do not find the concept of a right; "*Ius*" is not, in the continental sense, a "subjective right" but more of a legal claim, an entitlement due under law. One does not get the sense that it is an entitlement that precedes the positive law or justice. See also A. S. McGrade, "Ockham and the Birth of Individual Rights," in *Authority and Power: Studies in Medieval Law and Government*, ed. B. Tierney and P. Linehan (Cambridge: Cambridge University Press, 1980), 149–65; M. Villey, "La genèse du droit subjectif chez Guillaume d'Occam," *Archives de philosophie du droit* 9 (1964): 97–127; B. Tierney "Villey, Ockham and the Origins of Individual Rights," in *The Weightier Matters of the Law: Essays on Law and Religion*, ed. J. Witte and F. S. Alexander (Atlanta: Scholars Press, 1988), 1–32; L.Vereecke, "Individu et communauté selon Guillaume d'Ockham," *Studia Moralia* 3 (1965): 150–77.

27. In this respect it is important to note the influence of Christian Democratic views on the development of the charters. John Humphrey, who produced the first draft of the Universal Declaration of Human Rights, noted, "It seemed at times that the chief protagonists in the conference room were the Roman Catholics and the Communists, with the latter a poor second." John P. Humphrey, *Human Rights and the United Nations: A Great Adventure* (Dobbs Ferry, NY: Transnational Publishers, 1984), 32, summarized in Sally Morphet, "Economic, Social and Cultural Rights: The Development of Governments' Views,"

in *Economic, Social and Cultural Rights: Progress and Achievement*, Ralph Beddard and Dilys M. Hill (London: Macmillan, 1992), 77. On the European developments, see Joan Lockwood O'Donovan's excellent "Subsidiarity and Political Authority in Theological Perspective," *Studies in Christian Ethics*, 6, no.1 (1993): 17–34.

28. One of the striking features of many treatments of economic and welfare rights (see, e.g., Ellen Frankel Paul, Fred D. Miller Jr., and Jeffrey Paul, eds., *Economic Rights* [New York: Cambridge University Press, 1992]) is that, despite their precision over aspects of social policy, the authors never really ask what they mean by a right. The "Introduction" says, "It is difficult to think of any moral or political theory which does not implicitly or explicitly incorporate some theory of economic rights" (vii). A useful survey is given in Morphet, "Economic, Social and Cultural Rights," 74–92. See also Maurice Cranston, *What Are Human Rights?* (New York: Basic Books, 1962), chap. 3 and p. 54; "Human Rights: Real and Supposed," in D. D. Raphael, *Political Theory and the Rights of Man* (London: Macmillan, 1967), 52. For a summary of these discussions, see Jack Donnelly, *Universal Human Rights in Theory and Practice* (Ithaca: Cornell University Press, 1989), 31ff.

29. See the results in the annual Freedom House surveys *Freedom in the World* and *Press Freedom in the World*.

30. Amartya Sen, *Development as Freedom* (New York: Knopf, 1999).

31. See my "On the Universality of Human Rights," in *International Morality in the Post Cold War Era*, ed. Luis Lugo (Lanham, MD: Rowman & Littlefield). This touches on themes well explored in Isaiah Berlin's famous distinction of "positive" and "negative" liberties in his "Two Concepts of Liberty," 118–72 of his *Four Essays on Liberty* (New York: Oxford University Press, 1969). Alan Wolfe has some worthwhile comments to make on the distinction between, and the advantages and disadvantages of, absolute and conditional welfare rights in his "The Rights to Welfare and the Obligation to Society," *The Responsive Community* 2 (Spring, 1991): 12–22.

For the Health of the Nation

An Evangelical Call to Civic Responsibility

Preamble

Evangelical Christians in America face a historic opportunity. We make up fully one quarter of all voters in the most powerful nation in history. Never before has God given American evangelicals such an awesome opportunity to shape public policy in ways that could contribute to the well-being of the entire world. Disengagement is not an option. We must seek God's face for biblical faithfulness and abundant wisdom to rise to this unique challenge.

The special circumstances of this historic moment underline both the opportunity and the challenge.

- Although we have the privilege to help shape the actions of the world's lone superpower, only half of all evangelical Christians bother to vote.
- The presence and role of religion in public life is attacked more fiercely now than ever, making the bias of aggressive secularism the last acceptable prejudice in America.
- Since the atrocities of September 11, 2001, the spiritual and religious dimensions of global conflict have been sharpened.
- Secular media outlets have long acknowledged evangelical involvement in pro- life and family issues, but are taking belated notice of evangelicals' global involvement in activities such as disaster relief, refugee resettlement, and the fights against AIDS/HIV, human rights abuses, slavery, sexual trafficking, and prison rape.
- Some key American political leaders now conceive of their roles in moral terms. And they see themselves as stewards of the blessings of representative democracy, religious freedom, and human rights in a world where many nations are endangered by the forces of authoritarianism or radical secularism.

Evangelicals may not always agree about policy, but we realize that we have many callings and commitments in common: commitments to the protection and well-being of families and children, of the poor, the sick, the disabled, and the unborn, of the persecuted and oppressed, and of the rest of the created order. While these issues do not exhaust the concerns of good government, they provide the platform for evangelicals to engage in common action.

Despite our common commitments and this moment of opportunity, American evangelicals continue to be ambivalent about civic engagement.

In 1947, Carl F. H. Henry pricked our uneasy consciences and spurred us toward responsible social and political engagement. In the years since, the National Association of Evangelicals has routinely engaged our political leaders through its Office of Governmental Affairs and worked to educate member churches on current issues. In recent decades, a variety of evangelical political voices have emerged. Yet evangelicals have failed to engage with the breadth, depth, and consistency to which we are called.

Scholars and leaders have inspired us by drawing attention to historical exemplars of evangelical public responsibility from Wilberforce and the Booths in England to Edwards, Backus, Garnet, Finney, and Palmer in America. Our spiritual ancestors did not always agree on the specifics of governance and the best roads to social reform. Yet their passion and sacrifice inspire us to creative engagement, even when we cannot fully agree on policy prescriptions.

Against this historical background and in view of these common commitments, we offer the following principled framework for evangelical public engagement.

The Basis for Christian Civic Engagement

We engage in public life because God created our first parents in his image and gave them dominion over the earth (Gen. 1:27–28). The responsibilities that emerge from that mandate are many, and in a modern society those responsibilities rightly flow to many different institutions, including governments, families, churches, schools, businesses, and labor unions. Just governance is part of our calling in creation.

We also engage in public life because Jesus is Lord over every area of life. Through him all things were created (Col. 1:16–17), and by him all things will be brought to fullness (Rom. 8:19–21). To restrict our stewardship to the private sphere would be to deny an important part of his dominion and to functionally abandon it to the Evil One. To restrict our political concerns to matters that touch only on the private and the domestic spheres is to deny the all-encompassing Lordship of Jesus (Rev. 19:16).

Following in the tradition of the Hebrew prophets, Jesus announced the arrival of God's kingdom (God's "reign" or "rule") (Matt. 4:17; Mark 1:15). This kingdom would be marked by justice, peace, forgiveness, restoration, and healing for all. Jesus' followers have come to understand the time between his first and second comings as a period of "already, but not yet," in which we experience many of the blessings of God's reign and see initial signs of restoration, while we continue to suffer many of the results of the Fall. We know that we must wait for God to bring about the fullness of the kingdom at Christ's return. But in this interim, the Lord calls the church to speak prophetically to society and work for the renewal and reform of its structures. The Lord also calls the church to practice the righteous deeds of the kingdom and point to the kingdom by the wholeness and integrity of the church's common life. This example will require us to demonstrate God's love for all, by crossing racial, ethnic, economic, and national boundaries. It will also often involve following Jesus' example by suffering and living sacrificially for others.

As Christian citizens, we believe it is our calling to help government live up to its divine mandate to render justice (Rom. 13:1–7; 1 Pet. 2:13–17). From the teachings of the Bible and our experience of salvation, we Christians bring a unique vision to our participation in the political order and a conviction that changed people and transformed communities are possible. In the power of the Holy Spirit, we are compelled outward in service to God and neighbor.

Jesus calls us as his followers to love our neighbors as ourselves. Our goal in civic engagement is to bless our neighbors by making good laws. Because we have been called to do justice to our neighbors, we foster a free press, participate in open debate, vote, and hold public office. When Christians do justice, it speaks loudly about God. And it can show those who are not believers how the Christian vision can contribute to the common good and help alleviate the ills of society.

The Method of Christian Civic Engagement

Every political judgment requires both a normative vision and factual analysis. The more carefully and precisely we Christians think about the complex details of both, the more clearly we will be able to explain our views to others and understand—and perhaps overcome—disagreements with others.

Every normative vision has some understanding of persons, creation, history, justice, life, family, and peace. As Christians committed to the full authority of Scripture, our normative vision must flow from the Bible and from the moral order that God has embedded in his creation.

Evangelical Christians seek in every area of life to submit to the authority of Scripture (2 Tim. 3:16–17; Rom. 15:4; 1 Cor. 10:11). Nevertheless, many contemporary political decisions—whether about environmental science, HIV/AIDS, or international trade—deal with complex sociological or technological issues not discussed explicitly in the Bible. As Christians engaged in public policy, we must do detailed social, economic, historical, jurisprudential, and political analysis if we are to understand our society and wisely apply our normative vision to political questions. Only if we deepen our Christian vision and also study our contemporary world can we engage in politics faithfully and wisely.

From the Bible, experience, and social analysis, we learn that social problems arise and can be substantially corrected by both personal decisions and structural changes. On the one hand, personal sinful choices contribute significantly to destructive social problems (Prov. 6:9–11), and personal conversion through faith in Christ can transform broken persons into wholesome, productive citizens. On the other hand, unjust systems also help create social problems (Amos 5:10–15; Isa. 10:1–2) and wise structural change (for example legislation to strengthen marriage or increase economic opportunity for all) can improve society. Thus Christian civic engagement must seek to transform both individuals and institutions. While individuals transformed by the gospel change surrounding society, social institutions also shape individuals. While good laws encourage good behavior, bad laws and systems foster destructive action. Lasting social change requires both personal conversion and institutional renewal and reform.

The Bible makes it clear that God cares a great deal about the well-being of marriage, the family, the sanctity of human life, justice for the poor, care for creation, peace, freedom, and racial justice. While individual persons and organizations are at times called by God to concentrate on one or two issues, faithful evangelical civic engagement must champion a biblically balanced agenda.

Humility and Civility

As sinners who are thankful for God's grace, we know that we do not always live up to our civic responsibility. Christians must approach political engagement with humility and with earnest prayer for divine guidance and wisdom. Because power structures are often entrenched, perfect solutions are unobtainable. Because cultural changes produce problems that are often not amenable to legislative solutions, we must not expect political activity to achieve more than it can. Because social systems are complex and our knowledge is incomplete, we cannot predict all the effects of laws, policies, and regulations. As a result, we must match our high ideals with careful social analysis and critical reflection on our experience in order to avoid supporting policies that produce unintended and unfortunate consequences.

We will differ with other Christians and with non-Christians over the best policies. Thus we must practice humility and cooperation to achieve modest and attainable goals for the good of society. We must take care to employ the language of civility and to avoid denigrating those with whom we disagree. Because political work requires persuasion and cooperation with those who do not share our Christian commitment, we must offer a reasoned and easy-to-grasp defense of our goals.

When we as Christians engage in political activity, we must maintain our integrity and keep our biblical values intact. While we may frequently settle for "half-a-loaf," we must never compromise principle by engaging in unethical behavior or endorsing or fostering sin. As we rightly engage in supporting legislation, candidates, and political parties, we must be clear that biblical faith is vastly larger and richer than every limited, inevitably imperfect political agenda and that commitment to the Lordship of Christ and his one body far transcends all political commitments.

The Structures of Public Life

In the beginning, God called human beings to govern and to care for the creation. Faithfulness to this call has taken different forms as human beings have lived in family groups, in tribes and clans, in kingdoms and empires, and now in modern nation-states in an increasingly interconnected global community. Today we live in a complex society in which few people are directly involved in governing and in which complicated problems do not readily yield straightforward solutions.

God has ordered human society with various institutions and set in place forms of government to maintain public order, to restrain human evil, and to promote the common good. God has called all people to share responsibility for creating a healthy society. Human beings work out their different ways of obeying God's call as spouses, parents, workers, and participants in the wide variety of human networks. Some, however, are called to particular roles of governance. We must support and pray for all those who shoulder the burdens of government (1 Tim. 2:1–2).

Representative Democracy

We thank God for the blessings of representative democracy, which allow all citizens to participate in government by electing their representatives, helping to set the priorities for government, and sharing publicly the insights derived from their experience. We are grateful that we live in a society in which citizens can hold government responsible for fulfilling its responsibilities to God and abiding by the norms of justice.

We support the democratic process in part because people continue to be sufficiently blessed by God's common grace that they can seek not only their own betterment, but also the welfare of others. We also support democracy because we know that since the Fall, people often abuse power for selfish purposes. As Lord Acton noted, power tends to corrupt and absolute power corrupts absolutely. Thus we thank God for a constitutional system that decentralizes power through the separation of powers, fair elections, limited terms of office, and division among national, state, and local authorities.

As Christians we confess that our primary allegiance is to Christ, his kingdom, and Christ's worldwide body of believers, not to any nation. God has blessed America with bounty and with strength, but unless these blessings are used for the good of all, they will turn to our destruction. As Christian citizens of the United States, we must keep our eyes open to the potentially self-destructive tendencies of our society and our government. We must also balance our natural affection for our country with a love for people of all nations and an active desire to see them prosper. We invite Christians outside the United States to aid us in broadening our perspectives on American life and action.

Just Government and Fundamental Liberty

God is the source of all true law and genuine liberty. He both legitimates and limits the state's authority. Thus, while we owe Caesar his due (Matt. 22:15–22; Mark 12:13–17; Luke 20:20–26), we regard only Jesus as Lord. As King of Kings, Jesus' authority extends over Caesar. As followers of Jesus, we obey government authorities when they act in accord with God's justice and his laws (Titus 3:1). But we also resist government when it exercises its power in an unjust manner (Acts 5:27–32) or tries to dominate other institutions in society. A good government preserves the God-ordained responsibilities of society's other institutions, such as churches, other faith-centered organizations, schools, families, labor unions, and businesses.

Principles of Christian Political Engagement

We Work to Protect Religious Freedom and Liberty of Conscience

God has ordained the two coexisting institutions of church and state as distinct and independent of each other with each having its own areas of responsibility (Rom. 13:1–7; Mark 12:13–17; Eph. 4:15–16; 5:23–32). We affirm the principles of religious freedom and liberty of conscience, which are both historically and logically at the foundation of the American experiment. They are properly called the First Freedom and are now vested in the First Amendment. The First Amendment's guarantees of freedom of speech, association, and religion provide the political space in which we can carry out our differing responsibilities. Because human beings are responsible to God, these guarantees are crucial to the exercise of their God-given freedom. As God allows the wheat and tares to grow together until the harvest, and as God sends the rain on the just and on the unjust, so those who obey and those who disobey God coexist in society and share in its blessings (Matt. 5:45; 13:24–30). This "gospel pluralism" is foundational to the religious liberty of all.

Participating in the public square does not require people to put aside their beliefs or suspend the practice of their religion. All persons should have equal access to public forums, regardless of the religious content or viewpoint of their speech. Likewise, judicial standards should protect and respect not only religiously compelled practices, but also religiously motivated behavior.

The First Amendment's Establishment Clause is directed only at government and restrains its power. Thus, for example, the clause was never intended to shield individuals from exposure to the religious views of nongovernmental speakers. Exemptions from regulations of tax burdens do not violate the Establishment Clause, for government does not establish religion by leaving it alone. When government assists nongovernmental organizations as part of an evenhanded educational, social service, or health care program, religious organizations receiving such aid do not become "state actors" with constitutional duties. Courts should respect church autonomy in matters relating to doctrine, polity, the application of its governing documents, church discipline, clergy and staff employment practices, and other matters within the province of the church (Acts 18:12–17).

Religion is not just an individual matter, but also refers to rich communal traditions of ultimate belief and practice. We resist the definition of religion becoming either radically individualized or flattened out to mean anything that passes for a serious conviction. Thus, while the First Amendment protects religiously informed conscience, it does not protect all matters of sincere concern.

We Work to Nurture Family Life and Protect Children

From Genesis onward, the Bible tells us that the family is central to God's vision for human society. God has revealed himself to us in the language of family, adopting us as his children (Rom. 8:23; Gal. 4:5) and teaching us by the Holy Spirit to call him *Abba Father* (Rom. 8:15; Gal. 4:6). Marriage, which is a lifetime relationship between one man and one woman, is the predominant biblical icon of God's relationship with his people (Isa. 54:5; Jer. 3:20; 31:32; Ezek. 16:32; Eph. 5:23, 31–32). In turn, family life reveals something to us about God, as human families mirror, however faintly, the inner life of the Trinity.

The mutuality and service of family life contrast strongly with the hypermodern emphasis on individual freedom and rights. Marriage, sexuality, and family life are fundamental to society. Whether we are married or single, it is in the family that we learn mutual responsibility, we learn to live in an ordered society with complementary and distinct roles, we learn to submit and to obey, we learn to love and to trust, we learn both justice and mercy, and we learn to deny ourselves for the well-being of others. Thus the family is at the heart of the organic functioning of society.

Government does not have the primary responsibility for guaranteeing wholesome family life. That is the job of families themselves and of other institutions, especially churches. But governments should understand that people are more than autonomous individuals; they live in families and many are married. While providing individuals with ways to remedy or escape abusive relationships, governments should promote laws and policies that strengthen the well-being of families.

Many social evils—such as alcohol, drug, gambling, or credit-card abuse, pornography, sexual libertinism, spousal or child sexual abuse, easy divorce, abortion on demand—represent the abandonment of responsibility or the violation of trust by family members, and they seriously impair the ability of family members to function in society. These evils must be viewed not only as matters of individual sin and dysfunction, but also as violations of family integrity. Because the family is so important to society, violations of its integrity threaten public order. Similarly, employment, labor, housing, health care, and educational policies concern not only individuals but seriously affect families. In order to strengthen the family, we must promote biblical moral principles, responsible personal choices, and good public policies on marriage and divorce law, shelter, food, health care, education, and a family wage (James 5:1–6).

Good family life is so important to healthy human functioning that we oppose government efforts to trespass on its territory: whether by encroaching on parental responsibilities to educate their children, by treating other kinds of households as the family's social and legal equivalent, or by creating economic disincentives to marriage.

We commit ourselves to work for laws that protect and foster family life, and against government attempts to interfere with the integrity of the family. We also oppose innovations such as same-sex "marriage." We will work for measures that strengthen the economic viability of marriages and families, especially among the poor. We likewise commit ourselves to work within the church and society to strengthen marriages, to reduce the rate of divorce, and to prepare young adults for healthy family life.

We Work to Protect the Sanctity of Human Life and to Safeguard Its Nature

Because God created human beings in his image, all people share in the divine dignity. And because the Bible reveals God's calling and care of persons before they are born, the preborn share in this dignity (Ps. 139:13).

We believe that abortion, euthanasia, and unethical human experimentation violate the God-given dignity of human beings. As these practices gain social approval and become legitimized in law, they undermine the legal and cultural protections that our society has provided for vulnerable persons. Human dignity is indivisible. A threat to the aged, to the very young, to the unborn, to those with disabilities, or to those with genetic disease is a threat to all.

The book of Genesis portrays human attempts to transcend creaturely humility before God as rebellion against God. Christians must witness in the political sphere to the limits of our creatureliness and warn against the dangers of dissatisfaction with human limits.

As many others in the West, we have had such faith in science and its doctrine of progress that we are unprepared for the choices biotechnology now brings us. We urge evangelicals with specialized scientific knowledge to help Christians and policymakers to think through these issues. As technologies related to cloning and creating inheritable genetic modifications are being refined, society is less able to create a consensus on what is good and what limits we should place on human modification. The uniqueness of human nature is at stake.

Where the negative implications of biotechnology are unknown, government ought to err on the side of caution. Christians must welcome and support medical research that uses stem cells from adult donors and other ethical avenues of research. But we must work toward complete bans on human cloning and embryonic stem-cell research, as well as for laws against discrimination based on genetic information.

We Seek Justice and Compassion for the Poor and Vulnerable

Jesus summed up God's law by commanding us to love God with all that we are and to love our neighbors as ourselves (Matt. 22:35–40). By deed and parable, he taught us that anyone in need is our neighbor (Luke 10:29–37). Because all people are created in the image of God, we owe each other help in time of need.

God identifies with the poor (Ps. 146:5–9) and says that those who "are kind to the poor lend to the Lord" (Prov. 19:17), while those who oppress the poor "show contempt for their Maker" (Prov. 14:31). Jesus said that those who do not care for the needy and the imprisoned will depart eternally from the living God (Matt. 25:31–46). The vulnerable may include not only the poor, but women, children, the aged, persons with disabilities, immigrants, refugees, minorities, the persecuted, and prisoners. God measures societies by how they treat the people at the bottom.

God's prophets call his people to create just and righteous societies (Isa. 10:1–4; 58:3–12; Jer. 5:26–29; 22:13–19; Amos 2:6–7; 4:1–3; 5:10–15). The prophetic teaching insists on both a fair legal system (which does not favor either the rich or the poor) and a fair economic system (which does not tolerate perpetual poverty). Though the Bible does not call for economic equality, it condemns gross disparities in opportunity and outcome that cause suffering and perpetuate poverty, and it calls us to work toward equality of opportunity. God wants every person and family to have access to productive resources so that if they act responsibly they can care for their economic needs and be dignified members of their community. Christians reach out to help others in various ways: through personal charity, effective faith-based ministries, and other nongovernmental associations, and by advocating for effective government programs and structural changes.

Economic justice includes both the mitigation of suffering and also the restoration of wholeness. Wholeness includes full participation in the life of the community. Health care, nutrition, and education are important ingredients in helping people transcend the stigma and agony of poverty and re-enter community. Since healthy family systems are important for nurturing healthy individuals and overcoming poverty, public policy should encourage marriage and sexual abstinence outside marriage, while discouraging early onset of sexual activity, out-of-wedlock births, and easy divorce. Government should also hold fathers and mothers responsible for the maintenance of their families, enforcing where necessary the collection of child-support payments.

Restoring people to wholeness means that governmental social welfare must aim to provide opportunity and restore people to self-sufficiency. While basic standards of support must be put in place to provide for those who cannot care for their families and themselves, incentives and training in marketable skills must be part of any well-rounded program. We urge Christians who work in the political realm to shape wise laws pertaining to the creation of wealth, wages, education, taxation, immigration, health care, and social welfare that will protect those trapped in poverty and empower the poor to improve their circumstances.

We further believe that care for the vulnerable should extend beyond our national borders. American foreign policy and trade policies often have an impact on the poor. We should try to persuade our leaders to change patterns of trade that harm the poor and to make the reduction of global poverty a central concern of American foreign policy. We must support policies that encourage honesty in government, correct unfair socioeconomic structures, generously support effective programs that empower the poor, and foster economic development and prosperity. Christians should also encourage continued government support of international aid agencies, including those that are faith based.

Especially in the developing world, extreme poverty, lack of health care, the spread of HIV/AIDS, inadequate nutrition, unjust and unstable economies, slavery and sexual trafficking, the use of rape as a tool of terror and oppression, civil war, and government cronyism and graft create the conditions in which large populations become vulnerable. We support Christian agencies and American foreign policy that effectively correct these political problems and promote just, democratic structures.

We Work to Protect Human Rights

Because God created human beings in his image, we are endowed with rights and responsibilities. In order to carry out these responsibilities, human beings need the freedom to form associations, formulate and express beliefs, and act on conscientiously held commitments.

As recipients of God's gift of embodied life, people need food, nurture, shelter, and care. In order to fulfill their God-given tasks, all people have a right to private property. God's design for human existence also implies a right to marry, enjoy family life, and raise and educate children. While it is not the primary role of government to provide everything that humans need for their well-being, governments are obligated to ensure that people are not unjustly deprived of them and to strengthen families, schools, businesses, hospitals, social-service organizations, and other institutions so they can contribute to human welfare. At the same time, government must fulfill its responsibilities to provide for the general welfare and promote the common good.

Governments should be constitutionally obligated to protect basic human rights. Documents like the UN's Universal Declaration of Human Rights are attempts to articulate the kind of treatment that every person deserves from the government under which they live. Insofar as a person has a human right, that person should be able to appeal to an executive, legislative, or judicial authority to enforce or adjudicate that right. We believe that American foreign policy should reward those countries that respect human rights and should not reward (and prudently employ certain sanctions against) those countries that abuse or deny such rights. We urge the United States to increase its commitments to developing democracy and civil society in former colonial lands, Muslim nations, and countries emerging from Communism.

Because the Creator gave human beings liberty, we believe that religious liberty, including the right to change one's religion, is a foundational right that must be respected by governments (Article 18, Universal Declaration of Human Rights). Freedom of expression and freedom of assembly are closely related to religious liberty, and people must be free to express their vision for a just social order without fear of torture or other reprisal.

We also oppose the expansion of "rights talk" to encompass so-called rights such as "same-sex marriage" or "the right to die." Inappropriately expanded rights language has begun to function as a trump card in American discourse that unfairly shuts down needed discussion.

America has a tragic history of mistreating Native Americans, the cruel practice of slavery, and the subsequent segregation and exploitation of the descendants of slaves. While the United States has achieved legal and social equality in principle, the legacy of racism still makes many African Americans, Hispanics, and other ethnic minorities particularly vulnerable to a variety of social ills. Our churches have a special responsibility to model good race relations (Rom. 10:12). To correct the lingering effects of our racist history, Christians should support well-conceived efforts that foster dignity and responsibility.

We Seek Peace and Work to Restrain Violence

Jesus and the prophets looked forward to the time when God's reign would bring about just and peaceful societies in which people would enjoy the fruits of their labor without interference from foreign oppressors or unjust rulers. But from the beginning, Christians have recognized that God did not call them to bring in God's kingdom by force. While all Christians have agreed that governments should protect and restore just and peaceful social orders, we have long differed on when governments may use force and whether we may participate in government-authorized force to defend our homelands, rescue others from attack, or liberate other people from oppression.

The peaceful settling of disputes is a gift of common grace. We urge governments to pursue thoroughly nonviolent paths to peace before resorting to military force. We believe that if governments are going to use military force, they must use it in the service of peace and not merely in their national interest. Military force must be guided by the classical just-war principles, which are designed to restrain violence by establishing the right conditions for and right conduct in fighting a war. In an age of nuclear and biological terrorism, such principles are more important than ever.

We urge followers of Jesus to engage in practical peacemaking locally, nationally, and internationally. As followers of Jesus, we should, in our civic capacity, work to reduce conflict by promoting international understanding and engaging in nonviolent conflict resolution.

We Labor to Protect God's Creation

As we embrace our responsibility to care for God's earth, we reaffirm the important truth that we worship only the Creator and not the creation. God gave the care of his earth and its species to our first parents. That responsibility has passed into our hands. We affirm that God-given dominion is a sacred responsibility to steward the earth and not a license to abuse the creation of which we are a part. We are not the owners of creation, but its stewards, summoned by God to "watch over and care for it" (Gen. 2:15). This implies the principle of sustainability: our uses of the earth must be designed to conserve and renew the earth rather than to deplete or destroy it.

The Bible teaches us that God is not only redeeming his people, but is also restoring the whole creation (Rom. 8:18–23). Just as we show our love for the Savior by reaching out to the lost, we believe that we show our love for the Creator by caring for his creation.

Because clean air, pure water, and adequate resources are crucial to public health and civic order, government has an obligation to protect its citizens from the effects of environmental degradation. This involves both the urgent need to relieve human suffering caused by bad environmental practice. Because natural systems are extremely complex, human actions can have unexpected side effects. We must therefore approach our stewardship of creation with humility and caution.

Human beings have responsibility for creation in a variety of ways. We urge Christians to shape their personal lives in creation-friendly ways: practicing effective recycling, conserving resources, and experiencing the joy of contact with nature. We urge government to encourage fuel efficiency, reduce pollution, encourage sustainable use of natural resources, and provide for the proper care of wildlife and their natural habitats.

Our Commitment

We commit ourselves to support Christians who engage in political and social action in a manner consistent with biblical teachings. We call on Christian leaders in public office or with expertise in public policy and political life to help us deepen our perspective on public policy and political life so that we might better fulfill our civic responsibility.

We call on all Christians to become informed and then to vote, as well as to regularly communicate biblical values to their government representatives. We urge all Christians to take their civic responsibility seriously even when they are not full-time political activists so that they might more adequately call those in government to their task. We also encourage our children to consider vocations in public service.

We call churches and transdenominational agencies to cultivate an understanding of civic responsibility and public justice among their members. Seminaries and Christian colleges have a special responsibility to imbue future leaders with a sense of civic responsibility. We call all Christians to a renewed political engagement that aims to protect the vulnerable and poor, to guard the sanctity of human life, to further racial reconciliation and justice, to renew the family, to care for creation, and to promote justice, freedom, and peace for all.

Above all, we commit ourselves to regular prayer for those who govern, that God may prosper their efforts to nurture life, justice, freedom, and peace.

Contributors

Clive Calver is president of World Relief, an organization committed to relieve human suffering, poverty, and hunger worldwide in the name of Jesus Christ. He has led the Evangelical Alliance of the United Kingdom for fourteen years, served as program director for Billy Graham's Mission England, was national director of Britain's Youth for Christ, and was cofounder of Spring Harvest Festival, the largest annual evangelical gathering in Europe. His media work includes ABC's *Nightline*, CNN, National Public Radio, *New York Times*, *Time*, *The 700 Club*, *Christian World News*, *Christianity Today*, and *Charisma*. As an author and coauthor of more than seventeen books, Calver's observations have reached millions by radio, TV, and newsprint.

Nigel M. de S. Cameron, research professor of bioethics at Chicago-Kent College of Law (Illinois Institute of Technology) and president of the Institute on Biotechnology and the Human Future, is former dean of the Wilberforce Forum. Former provost and distinguished professor of theology and culture at Trinity International University and Trinity Evangelical Divinity School in Deerfield, Illinois, Cameron is a recognized spokesman for Judeo-Christian and Hippocratic perspectives on medicine and bioethics. He has authored and edited several volumes in the fields of theology and bioethics, including his seminal *The New Medicine*. In addition, he has been a frequent guest on network television, appearing on ABC's *Nightline*, PBS's *Frontline*, CNN, and the BBC.

Galen Carey is the director of Advocacy and Policy for World Relief. Prior to his current position, he served as World Relief's Africa regional director, helping churches develop programs in the areas of maternal and child health, HIV/AIDS, microfinance, food security, disaster response, and refugee assistance. A son of missionaries to the Philippines, Carey has lived with and among the poor most of his life. In his twenty-one years with World Relief, he has served in Croatia, Mozambique, and Kenya, as well as the inner city of Chicago.

Richard Cizik is vice president for governmental affairs of the National Association of Evangelicals (NAE), which is the most distinguished evangelical organization of its kind in the United States, with a membership of 51 denominations, 43,000 churches, and 27 million adherents. His primary responsibilities, as the most senior NAE staff member with twenty-four years of service, include providing direction over the association's public-policy stands and advocacy before the Congress of the United States, the White House, and the Supreme Court. Cizik is frequently quoted in the *New York Times*, the *Washington Post*, and the *Washington Times* and regularly appears on *CNN Headline News*, C-SPAN, PBS's *Ethics & Religion News Weekly*, WORLD NET, Voice of America, and many other media outlets.

Paul de Vries is founder and president of New York Evangelical Seminary Fund—developing New York Divinity School for Christ-centered, Bible-based, Spirit-led ministry training of the city. De Vries has served twenty-five years in higher education administration, designing and leading innovative programs to incarnate biblical truth into people's living and learning. He founded the Center for Applied Christian Ethics at Wheaton College where he was also associate dean. He has also been the lead author of several books, including *The Taming of the Shrewd*, *Ethics Applied*, and *Business Ethics Applied*.

John C. Green is distinguished professor of political science and director of the Ray C. Bliss Institute of Applied Politics at the University of Akron. He has published extensively on religion and American politics in the scholarly and popular press, with a special emphasis on evangelical Protestants. He is coauthor of *The Diminishing Divide: Religion's Changing Role in American Politics*, *The Bully Pulpit: The Politics of Protestant Clergy*, and *Religion and The Culture Wars: Dispatches from the Front*.

David P. Gushee is Graves Professor of Moral Philosophy and senior fellow of the Carl F. H. Henry Center for Moral Leadership at Union University. Prior to his eight years of service at Union, he taught Christian ethics at Southern Baptist Theological Seminary and worked on the staff of Evangelicals for Social Action. Gushee is the author, coauthor, or editor of eight books, including the award-winning *Kingdom Ethics* and *Getting Marriage Right*. He writes regular syndicated columns for Religion News Service. His work often appears as book chapters and in magazines and journals such as *Christianity Today*, *Books & Culture*, *PRISM*, *Christian Century*, and the *Journal of Church and State*. He has lectured at dozens of colleges, seminaries, and churches around the nation and abroad.

Kristin E. Heyer is assistant professor of Christian ethics in the department of theological studies at Loyola Marymount University. She received her doctorate in theological ethics at Boston College. She has published several articles in *Political Theology* on public theology and discipleship and citizenship. Her current research involves Roman Catholic social ethics and political advocacy.

Dennis P. Hollinger is president and professor of Christian ethics at Evangelical School of Theology in Myerstown, Pennsylvania. Prior to assuming his present role, he served as vice provost, college pastor, and professor of Christian ethics at Messiah College. A frequent speaker at churches, pastors' conferences, and academic forums, he is the author of three books, including *Choosing the Good: Christian Ethics in a Complex World*. He is a board member for the C. S. Lewis Institute in Washington, DC, sits on the Health Care Ethics Committee at Holy Spirit Hospital in Camp Hill, Pennsylvania, and is a fellow with the Center for Bioethics and Human Dignity in Bannockburn, Illinois.

Joseph Loconte is the William E. Simon Fellow in Religion and a Free Society at the Heritage Foundation and a regular commentator for National Public Radio. He is the author of *God, Government and the Good Samaritan* and editor of *The End of Illusions: America's Churches and Hitler's Gathering Storm, 1938–41*.

Paul Marshall is senior fellow at the Center for Religious Freedom, Freedom House, Washington, DC. He has lectured throughout the world and has testified many times before Congress. He is the author or editor of many books and booklets, including *God and the Constitution: Christianity and American Politics* and *Heaven Is Not My Home*. His book *Their Blood Cries Out* won an Evangelical Christian Publishers Association Gold Medallion Award. He is in frequent demand for lectures and media appearances including interviews on ABC; CNN; Fox News; PBS; the BBC; and the Australian, Canadian, South African, and Japanese Broadcasting Corporations. His work has been published in or the subject of articles in the *New York Times*, the *Washington Post*, the *Wall Street Journal*, the *Weekly Standard*, *First Things*, and several hundred other newspapers and magazines.

Tom Minnery has been vice president of public policy for Focus on the Family since 1988. His staff produces *Citizen*, a monthly issues magazine; *Family News in Focus*, a daily information and analysis radio program; and *CitizenLink*, a daily email alert on hot issues and legislation. Prior to coming to Focus on the Family, Minnery was senior editor at *Christianity Today*, and before that he was a Capitol Hill correspondent and a manager in the Washington Bureau of Gannett Newspapers. He is the author of the book entitled *Why You Can't Stay Silent*. He also serves as chairman of the board of the Alliance Defense Fund, a national organization devoted to the legal strategy and funding of court cases involving pro-life, religious freedom, and family values issues.

Stephen Monsma is a fellow at the Center for Public Justice and a research fellow at the Henry Institute for the Study of Christianity and Politics, Calvin College. A professor emeritus of political science at Pepperdine University, he served on the faculty from 1987 to 2004 and held the Blanche E. Seaver chair in social science. He also taught at Calvin College (1967–72) and served in the Michigan House of Representatives (1972–78) and the Michigan Senate (1978–82). Monsma has published widely in the fields of church-state relations and faith-based nonprofit organizations. Among his best-known works are *Putting Faith in Partnerships: Welfare-to-Work in Four Cities*, *The Challenge of Pluralism: Church and State in Five Democracies* (with J. Christopher Soper), and *Positive Neutrality*.

Raymond R. Roberts has authored *Whose Kids Are They Anyway? Religion and Morality in America's Public Schools* as well as numerous magazine articles. He has worked as a pastor for twenty years and currently serves Grace Presbyterian Church in Jenkintown, Pennsylvania.

Mark Rodgers is the staff director of the Senate Republican Conference, which is the third-ranking Republican leadership office in the U.S. Senate. He formerly served as the chief of staff for ten years to Senator Rick Santorum (R-PA), four of which when the senator was a House member. Rodgers was the president of the National Institute for Lay Education, which he founded to develop adult education curriculum to encourage reflective Christian involvement in politics. He then worked as director of resource development at the Pittsburgh Leadership Foundation, a faith-based organization committed to addressing the social needs of Pittsburgh from a Christian perspective.

R. Scott Rodin has been in Christian not-for-profit leadership for twenty years. He is currently the president of his own consulting firm in Spokane, Washington, and serves as vice president of the John R. Frank Consulting Group in Seattle, Washington. He consults with Christian colleges, seminaries, schools, churches, and parachurch ministries in the areas of leadership, fund-raising, strategic planning, and organizational development. Prior to starting his firm, Rodin held development posts with firms including World Concern, University Preparatory Academy, the University of Aberdeen, and Eastern Baptist Theological Seminary—where from 1997–2002 he served as president and also taught theology and ethics. His books include *Stewards in the Kingdom* and *Evil and Theodicy in the Theology of Karl Barth*.

Max L. Stackhouse is the Rimmer and Ruth de Vries Professor of Reformed Theology and Public Life at Princeton Theological Seminary and director of the Kuyper Center for Public Theology. He is presently at work on the fourth and final volume of *God and Globalization*. His specialty is analysis of the relation of religious and ethical influences on material forces in society to see how Christian and other faiths shape cultures and the lives of persons. Using a covenantal view of social morality, together with doctrinal and socio-political resources, he invites a "public theological" discussion—one intended for those outside as well as inside the church, to shape the common life. He is the author or editor of numerous articles and books, including *Covenant and Commitments: Faith, Family, and Economic Life* and *Public Theology and Political Economy*.

Glenn T. Stanton is director of social research and cultural affairs and senior research analyst for marriage and sexuality at Focus on the Family. He is the author of *Why Marriage Matters: Reasons to Believe in Marriage in Postmodern Society*, which examines the rich and diverse benefits marriage brings to adults, children, and society. He is a contributor to two books, *The Fatherhood Movement: A Call to Action* and *The Little Big Book for Dads*. He is also the author of *My Crazy, Imperfect Christian Family* and coauthor (with Bill Maier) of *Marriage on Trial*, which deals with why same-sex marriage and same-sex parenting are not good ideas. He is currently serving the Bush administration as a consultant on increasing fatherhood involvement in the Head Start program.

Glen H. Stassen has been since 1997 the Lewis B. Smedes Professor of Christian Ethics at Fuller Theological Seminary. Formerly professor of Christian ethics at Southern Baptist Theological Seminary, he is the author of several books, including *Kingdom Ethics: Following Jesus in Contemporary Context* (with David Gushee) and *Just Peacemaking: Transforming Initiatives for Justice and Peace*. He currently serves as the chairperson of religion and the social sciences section of the American Academy of Religion. In addition, he is active on the board of editorial advisors for *Sojourners* and *Creation Care* magazines.

Nicholas Wolterstorff is Noah Porter Professor Emeritus of Philosophical Theology and fellow of Berkeley College at Yale University. After teaching for thirty years at Calvin College, he joined the Yale Divinity School, where he was also adjunct professor in the philosophy and religious studies departments. He has been president of the American Philosophical Association (Central Division) and of the Society of Christian Philosophers. He has given the Wilde Lectures at Oxford University, the Gifford Lectures at St. Andrews University, and the Stone Lectures at Princeton Seminary. He has taught at a number of other schools, including the University of Notre Dame, Princeton University, and the Free University of Amsterdam. Among his recent publications are *Divine Discourse, John Locke and the Ethics of Belief, Thomas Reid and the Story of Epistemology*, and *Educating for Life*.

Ronald J. Sider is professor of theology, holistic ministry, and public policy, and director of the Sider Center on Ministry and Public Policy at Eastern Baptist Theological Seminary and president of Evangelicals for Social Action. A widely known evangelical speaker and writer, Sider has spoken on six continents and published twenty-seven books and scores of articles. His *Rich Christians in an Age of Hunger* was recognized by *Christianity Today* as one of the one hundred most influential religious books of the twentieth century. Sider is the publisher of *PRISM* magazine and a contributing editor of *Christianity Today* and *Sojourners*. He serves on many advisory boards including Pew Forum on Religion and Public Life and Faith and Service Technical Education Network of the National Crime Prevention Council.

Diane Knippers is the president of the Washington, DC–based Institute on Religion and Democracy, an interdenominational organization that works for the reform of the U.S. churches' social and political witness. She is an advisory editor for *Christianity Today*, vice chair of the Association for Church Renewal, and secretary of the National Association of Evangelicals. She also serves on the Religious Liberty Commission of the World Evangelical Fellowship. Knippers has written for publications such as *The Wall Street Journal, The Weekly Standard*, and *Christianity Today* and has appeared on CBS's *60 Minutes* and PBS's *Religion and Ethics Newsweekly*.